LETTERS FROM A STOIC

Seneca
Translated by Richard Mott Gummere

VIGEO PRESS
Est. 2016

Sourced from: *Ad Lucilium Epistulae Morales: Moral letters to Lucilius.* Vol. 1-3
William Heinemann, London: 1917-1925.

Vigeo Press Reprint, 2016

Paperback ISBN 978-1-941129-47-0

CONTENTS

INTRODUCTION

Among the personalities of the early Roman Empire there are few who offer to the readers of to-day such dramatic interest as does Lucius Annaeus Seneca, the author of the Epistles which are translated in this volume. Born in a province, educated at Rome, prominent at the bar, a distinguished exile, a trusted minister of State, and a doomed victim of a capricious emperor, Seneca is so linked with the age in which he lived that in reading his works we read those of a true representative of the most thrilling period of Roman history.

Seneca was born in the year 4 B.C., a time of great opportunity, at Corduba, in Spain, son of the talented rhetorician, Annaeus Seneca. We gather that the family moved to Rome during the boyhood of Lucius, that he was educated for the bar, and that he was soon attracted by the Stoic philosophy, the stern nurse of heroes during the first century of the Empire. That his social connexions were distinguished we infer from the prominence and refinement of his brother Gallio,–the Gallio of the New Testament,–from the fact that he himself was noticed and almost condemned to death by the Emperor Caligula soon after he began to speak in public, and especially because his aunt, whom he visited in Egypt, was the wife of the governor of that country.

Up to the year 41 he prospered. He makes mention of his children, of his mother who, like the mother of Goethe, seems to have imbued him with idealism and a certain amount of mysticism, and of many valued friends. But during that year, as a result of court intrigue, he was banished to the island of Corsica. The charge against him was a too great intimacy with Iulia Livilla, unfortunate sister of the late emperor, and the arch-foe of Messalina, whose husband, Claudius, had recalled the princess from exile. We may discount any crime on Seneca's part because even the gossip-laden Suetonius says: "The charge was vague and the accused was given no opportunity to defend himself."

The eight years of exile were productive of much literary work. The tragedies, which have had such influence on later drama, are the fruit of this period, besides certain essays on philosophic subjects, and a rather cringing letter to Polybius, a rich freedman at the court of Claudius. In 49, however, Fortune, whom Seneca as a Stoic so often ridicules, came to his rescue. Agrippina had him recalled and appointed tutor to her young son, later to become the Emperor Nero. Holding the usual offices of state, and growing in prominence, Seneca administered the affairs of the prince, in partnership with Burrus, the praetorian. Together they maintained the balance of power between throne and Senate until the death of Burrus in the year 62. After that time, a philosopher without the support of military power was unable to cope with the vices and whims of the monster on the throne.

The last two years of Seneca's life were spent in travelling about southern Italy, composing essays on natural history and relieving his burdened soul by correspondence with his friend Lucilius. In the year 65 came his suicide, anticipating an act of violence on the Emperor's part; in this deed of heroism he was nobly supported by his young wife Paulina. The best account of these dark days is given in Tacitus.

These letters are all addressed to Lucilius. From internal evidence we gather that the native country of this Lucilius was Campania, and his native city Pompeii or Naples. He was a Roman knight, having gained that position, as Seneca tells us, by sheer industry. Prominent in the civil service, he had filled many important positions and was, at the time when the *Letters* were written, procurator in Sicily. He seems to have had Epicurean tendencies, like so many men from this part of Italy; the author argues and tries to win him over to Stoicism, in the kindliest manner. Lucilius wrote books, was interested in philosophy and geography, knew intimately many persons in high places, and is thought by some to be the author of the extant poem *Aetna*.

When their friendship began we cannot say. The *Naturales Quaestiones* and the *Letters* are the work of Seneca's closing years. Both are addressed to Lucilius. The essay *De Providentia*, which was also dedicated to him, is of doubtful date, and may be fixed at any time between the beginning of the exile in Corsica and the period when the *Letters* were written.

In spite of the many problems which confront us, it may be safely said that the years 63-65 constitute the period of the *Letters*. We find possible allusions to the Campanian earthquake of 63, a reference to the conflagration at Lyons, which took place either in 64 or in 65, and various hints that the philosopher was travelling about Italy in order to forget politics. The form of this work, as Bacon says, is a collection of essays rather than of letters. The recipient is often mentioned by name; but his identity is secondary to the main purpose. The language at the beginning of the seventy-fifth letter, for example, might lead one to suppose that they were dashed off in close succession: "You complain that you receive from me letters which are rather carelessly written;" but the ingenious juxtaposition of effective words, the balance in style and thought, and the continual striving after point, indicate that the language of the diatribe had affected the informality of the epistle.[1]

The structure of each letter is interesting. A concrete fact, such as the mention of an illness, a voyage by sea or land, an incident like the adventure in the Naples tunnel, a picnic party, or an assemblage of friends who discuss questions from Plato, or Aristotle, or Epicurus,–these are the elements which serve to justify the reflections which follow. After such an introduction, the writer takes up his theme; he deals with abstract subjects, such as the contempt of death, the stout-heartedness of the sage, or the quality of the Supreme Good. We shall not mention the sources of all these topics in footnotes, but shall aim only to explain that which is obscure in meaning or unusual in its import. Plato's Theory of Ideas, Aristotle's Categories, Theophrastus on Friendship, Epicurus on Pleasure, and all the countless doctrinal shades of difference which we find in the Stoic leaders, are at least sketched in outline.

But we must give full credit to the philosopher's own originality. In these letters, it is impossible to ignore the advance from a somewhat stiff and Ciceronian point of view into the attractive and debatable land of what one may fairly call modern ideas. The style of the Epistles is bold, and so is the thought.

Considered en masse, the letters form a fruitful and helpful handbook, of the very widest scope and interest. The value of intelligent reading and the studies which make for culture is presented to Lucilius with frequency, notably in Nos. II. and LXXXVIII. Seneca agrees with the definition of higher studies as "those which have no reference to mere utility." The dignity of the orator's profession (XL. and CXIV.) is brought to the attention of a young self-made merchant who seems inclined towards platform display. The modern note is struck when the author protests against the swinish and debasing effects of slavery or gladiatorial combats (XLVII. and LXX.); preaches against the degeneracy of drunkenness (LXXXIII.); portrays the charms of plain living and love of nature (LVII., LXVII., LXXIX., LXXXVI., LXXXVII., XC., XCIV.); recommends retirement (XVIII., LI., LVI., LXXX., CXXII.); or manifests a Baconian interest in scientific inventions (LVII., LXXIX.). Most striking of all is the plea (XCIV.) for the equality of the sexes and for conjugal fidelity in the husband, to be interpreted no less strictly than honour on the part of the wife. The craze for athletics is also analyzed and rebuked (XV.).

The Epistles contain also, of course, the usual literary types which every Roman epistolographer would feel bound to introduce. There is the *consolatio*; there is the theme of friendship; there are second-hand lectures on philosophy taken from Plato and Aristotle and Theophrastus, as we have indicated above; and several characteristically Roman laudations of certain old men (including the author himself) who wrestle with physical infirmities. But the Stoic doctrine is interpreted better, from the Roman point of view, by no other Latin writer. The facts of Seneca's life prove the sincerity of his utterances, and blunt the edge of many of the sneers which we find in Dio Cassius, regarding the fabulous sums which he had out at interest and the costly tables purchased for the palace of a millionaire.

Finally, in no pagan author, save perhaps Vergil, is the beauty of holiness (XLI.) so sincerely presented from a Roman standpoint. Although his connexion with the early Church has been disproved, Seneca shows the modern, the Christian, spirit. Three of the ideals mentioned above, the hatred of combats in the arena, the humane treatment of slaves, and the sanctity of marriage, draw us towards Seneca as towards a teacher like Jeremy Taylor.

There is no pretence of originality in the Latin text; the translator has adopted, with very few deviations, that of O. Hense's second edition. This text he has found to be excellent, and he has also derived assistance from the notes accompanying the Selected Letters of W. C. Summers.

Richard M. Gummere.
Haverford College, May, 1916.

Footnotes

1. How Seneca came by this "pointed" style will be evident to one who reads the sample speeches given in the handbook of the Elder Seneca.

I. ON SAVING TIME

Greetings from Seneca to his friend Lucilius.

[1]Continue to act thus, my dear Lucilius—set yourself free for your own sake; gather and save your time, which till lately has been forced from you, or filched away, or has merely slipped from your hands. Make yourself believe the truth of my words,—that certain moments are torn from us, that some are gently removed, and that others glide beyond our reach. The most disgraceful kind of loss, however, is that due to carelessness. Furthermore, if you will pay close heed to the problem, you will find that the largest portion of our life passes while we are doing ill, a goodly share while we are doing nothing, and the whole while we are doing that which is not to the purpose. [2]What man can you show me who places any value on his time, who reckons the worth of each day, who understands that he is dying daily? For we are mistaken when we look forward to death; the major portion of death has already passed. Whatever years be behind us are in death's hands.

Therefore, Lucilius, do as you write me that you are doing: hold every hour in your grasp. Lay hold of to-day's task, and you will not need to depend so much upon to-morrow's. While we are postponing, life speeds by. [3]Nothing, Lucilius, is ours, except time. We were entrusted by nature with the ownership of this single thing, so fleeting and slippery that anyone who will can oust us from possession. What fools these mortals be! They allow the cheapest and most useless things, which can easily be replaced, to be charged in the reckoning, after they have acquired them; but they never regard themselves as in debt when they have received some of that precious commodity,—time! And yet time is the one loan which even a grateful recipient cannot repay.

[4]You may desire to know how I, who preach to you so freely, am practising. I confess frankly: my expense account balances, as you would expect from one who is free-handed but careful. I cannot boast that I waste nothing, but I can at least tell you what I am wasting, and the cause and manner of the loss; I can give you the reasons why I am a poor man. My situation, however, is the same as that of many who are reduced to slender means through no fault of their own: every one forgives them, but no one comes to their rescue.

[5]What is the state of things, then? It is this: I do not regard a man as poor, if the little which remains is enough for him. I advise you, however, to keep what is really yours; and you cannot begin too early. For, as our ancestors believed, it is too late to spare when you reach the dregs of the cask.[1] Of that which remains at the bottom, the amount is slight, and the quality is vile. Farewell.

Footnotes

1. Hesiod, *Works and Days*, 369.

II. ON DISCURSIVENESS IN READING

[1]Judging by what you write me, and by what I hear, I am forming a good opinion regarding your future. You do not run hither and thither and distract yourself by changing your abode; for such restlessness is the sign of a disordered spirit. The primary indication, to my thinking, of a well-ordered mind is a man's ability to remain in one

place and linger in his own company. [2]Be careful, however, lest this reading of many authors and books of every sort may tend to make you discursive and unsteady. You must linger among a limited number of master thinkers, and digest their works, if you would derive ideas which shall win firm hold in your mind. Everywhere means nowhere. When a person spends all his time in foreign travel, he ends by having many acquaintances, but no friends. And the same thing must hold true of men who seek intimate acquaintance with no single author, but visit them all in a hasty and hurried manner. [3]Food does no good and is not assimilated into the body if it leaves the stomach as soon as it is eaten; nothing hinders a cure so much as frequent change of medicine; no wound will heal when one salve is tried after another; a plant which is often moved can never grow strong. There is nothing so efficacious that it can be helpful while it is being shifted about. And in reading of many books is distraction.

Accordingly, since you cannot read all the books which you may possess, it is enough to possess only as many books as you can read. [4]"But," you reply, "I wish to dip first into one book and then into another." I tell you that it is the sign of an overnice appetite to toy with many dishes; for when they are manifold and varied, they cloy but do not nourish. So you should always read standard authors; and when you crave a change, fall back upon those whom you read before. Each day acquire something that will fortify you against poverty, against death, indeed against other misfortunes as well; and after you have run over many thoughts, select one to be thoroughly digested that day. [5]This is my own custom; from the many things which I have read, I claim some one part for myself.

The thought for today is one which I discovered in Epicurus;[1] for I am wont to cross over even into the enemy's camp,—not as a deserter, but as a scout. [6]He says: "Contented poverty is an honourable estate." Indeed, if it be contented, it is not poverty at all. It is not the man who has too little, but the man who craves more, that is poor. What does it matter how much a man has laid up in his safe, or in his warehouse, how large are his flocks and how fat his dividends, if he covets his neighbour's property, and reckons, not his past gains, but his hopes of gains to come? Do you ask what is the proper limit to wealth? It is, first, to have what is necessary, and, second, to have what is enough. Farewell.

Footnotes

1. Frag. 475 Usener

III. ON TRUE AND FALSE FRIENDSHIP

[1]You have sent a letter to me through the hand of a "friend" of yours, as you call him. And in your very next sentence you warn me not to discuss with him all the matters that concern you, saying that even you yourself are not accustomed to do this; in other words, you have in the same letter affirmed and denied that he is your friend. [2]Now if you used this word of ours[1] in the popular sense, and called him "friend" in the same way in which we speak of all candidates for election as "honourable gentlemen," and as we greet all men whom we meet casually, if their names slip us for the moment, with the salutation "my dear sir,"—so be it. But if you consider any man a friend whom you do not trust as you trust yourself, you are mightily mistaken and you do not sufficiently understand what true friendship means. Indeed, I would have you discuss everything with a friend; but first of all discuss the man himself. When friendship is settled, you must trust; before friendship is formed, you must pass judgment. Those persons indeed put last first and confound their duties, who, violating the rules of Theophrastus,[2] judge a man after they have made him their friend, instead of making him their friend after they have judged him. Ponder for a long time whether you shall admit a given person to your friendship; but when you have decided to admit him, welcome him with all your heart and soul. Speak as boldly with him as with yourself. [3]As to yourself, although you should live in such a way that you trust your own self with

from the customs of our fellow-men? Inwardly, we ought to be different in all respects, but our exterior should conform to society. [3]Do not wear too fine, nor yet too frowzy, a toga. One needs no silver plate, encrusted and embossed in solid gold; but we should not believe the lack of silver and gold to be proof of the simple life. Let us try to maintain a higher standard of life than that of the multitude, but not a contrary standard; otherwise, we shall frighten away and repel the very persons whom we are trying to improve. We also bring it about that they are unwilling to imitate us in anything, because they are afraid lest they might be compelled to imitate us in everything.

[4]The first thing which philosophy undertakes to give is fellow-feeling with all men; in other words, sympathy and sociability. We part company with our promise if we are unlike other men. We must see to it that the means by which we wish to draw admiration be not absurd and odious. Our motto,[1] as you know, is "Live according to Nature"; but it is quite contrary to nature to torture the body, to hate unlaboured elegance, to be dirty on purpose, to eat food that is not only plain, but disgusting and forbidding. [5]Just as it is a sign of luxury to seek out dainties, so it is madness to avoid that which is customary and can be purchased at no great price. Philosophy calls for plain living, but not for penance; and we may perfectly well be plain and neat at the same time. This is the mean of which I approve; our life should observe a happy medium between the ways of a sage and the ways of the world at large; all men should admire it, but they should understand it also.

[6]"Well then, shall we act like other men? Shall there be no distinction between ourselves and the world?" Yes, a very great one; let men find that we are unlike the common herd, if they look closely. If they visit us at home, they should admire us, rather than our household appointments. He is a great man who uses earthenware dishes as if they were silver; but he is equally great who uses silver as if it were earthenware. It is the sign of an unstable mind not to be able to endure riches.

[7]But I wish to share with you to-day's profit also. I find in the writings of our[2] Hecato that the limiting of desires helps also to cure fears: "Cease to hope," he says, "and you will cease to fear." "But how," you will reply, "can things so different go side by side?" In this way, my dear Lucilius: though they do seem at variance, yet they are really united. Just as the same chain fastens the prisoner and the soldier who guards him, so hope and fear, dissimilar as they are, keep step together; fear follows hope. [8]I am not surprised that they proceed in this way; each alike belongs to a mind that is in suspense, a mind that is fretted by looking forward to the future. But the chief cause of both these ills is that we do not adapt ourselves to the present, but send our thoughts a long way ahead. And so foresight, the noblest blessing of the human race, becomes perverted. [9]Beasts avoid the dangers which they see, and when they have escaped them are free from care; but we men torment ourselves over that which is to come as well as over that which is past. Many of our blessings bring bane to us; for memory recalls the tortures of fear, while foresight anticipates them. The present alone can make no man wretched. Farewell.

Footnotes

1. i.e., of the Stoic school.
2. Frag. 25 Fowler.

VI. ON SHARING KNOWLEDGE

[1]I feel, my dear Lucilius, that I am being not only reformed, but transformed. I do not yet, however, assure myself, or indulge the hope, that there are no elements left in me which need to be changed. Of course there are many that should be made more compact, or made thinner, or be brought into greater prominence. And indeed this very fact is proof that my spirit is altered into something better,—that it can see its own faults, of which it was previously ignorant. In certain cases sick men are congratulated because they themselves have perceived that they are sick.

[2]I therefore wish to impart to you this sudden change in myself; I should then begin to place a surer trust in our friendship,—the true friendship which hope and fear and self-interest cannot sever, the friendship in which and for the sake of which men meet death.

[3]I can show you many who have lacked, not a friend, but a friendship; this, however, cannot possibly happen when souls are drawn together by identical inclinations into an alliance of honourable desires. And why can it not happen? Because in such cases men know that they have all things in common, especially their troubles.

You cannot conceive what distinct progress I notice that each day brings to me. [4]And when you say: "Give me also a share in these gifts which you have found so helpful," I reply that I am anxious to heap all these privileges upon you, and that I am glad to learn in order that I may teach. Nothing will ever please me, no matter how excellent or beneficial, if I must retain the knowledge of it to myself. And if wisdom were given me under the express condition that it must be kept hidden and not uttered, I should refuse it. No good thing is pleasant to possess, without friends to share it.

[5]I shall therefore send to you the actual books; and in order that you may not waste time in searching here and there for profitable topics, I shall mark certain passages, so that you can turn at once to those which I approve and admire. Of course, however, the living voice and the intimacy of a common life will help you more than the written word. You must go to the scene of action, first, because men put more faith in their eyes than in their ears,[1] and second, because the way is long if one follows precepts, but short and helpful, if one follows patterns.

[6]Cleanthes could not have been the express image of Zeno, if he had merely heard his lectures; he shared in his life, saw into his hidden purposes, and watched him to see whether he lived according to his own rules. Plato, Aristotle, and the whole throng of sages who were destined to go each his different way, derived more benefit from the character than from the words of Socrates. It was not the class-room of Epicurus, but living together under the same roof, that made great men of Metrodorus, Hermarchus, and Polyaenus. Therefore I summon you, not merely that you may derive benefit, but that you may confer benefit; for we can assist each other greatly.

[7]Meanwhile, I owe you my little daily contribution; you shall be told what pleased me to-day in the writings of Hecato;[2] it is these words: "What progress, you ask, have I made? I have begun to be a friend to myself." That was indeed a great benefit; such a person can never be alone. You may be sure that such a man is a friend to all mankind. Farewell.

Footnotes

1. Cf. Herodotus, i. 8 ὦτα τυγχάνει ἀνθρώποισι ἐόντα ἀπιστότερα ὀφθαλμῶν.

2. Frag. 26 Fowler.

VII. ON CROWDS

[1]Do you ask me what you should regard as especially to be avoided? I say, crowds; for as yet you cannot trust yourself to them with safety. I shall admit my own weakness, at any rate; for I never bring back home the same character that I took abroad with me. Something of that which I have forced to be calm within me is disturbed; some of the foes that I have routed return again. Just as the sick man, who has been weak for a long time, is in such a condition that he cannot be taken out of the house without suffering a relapse, so we ourselves are affected when our souls are recovering from a lingering disease. [2]To consort with the crowd is harmful; there is no person who does not make some vice attractive to us, or stamp it upon us, or taint us unconsciously therewith. Certainly, the greater the mob with which we mingle, the greater the danger.

But nothing is so damaging to good character as the habit of lounging at the games; for then it is that vice steals subtly upon one through the avenue of pleasure. [3]What do you think I mean? I mean that I come home more greedy, more ambitious,

⁷But I must stop, and pay my customary contribution, to balance this letter. The payment shall not be made from my own property; for I am still conning Epicurus.⁵ I read to-day, in his works, the following sentence: "If you would enjoy real freedom, you must be the slave of Philosophy." The man who submits and surrenders himself to her is not kept waiting; he is emancipated⁶ on the spot. For the very service of Philosophy is freedom.

⁸It is likely that you will ask me why I quote so many of Epicurus's noble words instead of words taken from our own school. But is there any reason why you should regard them as sayings of Epicurus and not common property? How many poets give forth ideas that have been uttered, or may be uttered, by philosophers! I need not touch upon the tragedians and our writers of national drama;⁷ for these last are also somewhat serious, and stand half-way between comedy and tragedy. What a quantity of sagacious verses lie buried in the mime! How many of Publilius's lines are worthy of being spoken by buskin-clad actors, as well as by wearers of the slipper!⁸ ⁹I shall quote one verse of his, which concerns philosophy, and particularly that phase of it which we were discussing a moment ago, wherein he says that the gifts of Chance are not to be regarded as part of our possessions:

> Still alien is whatever you have gained
> By coveting.⁹

¹⁰I recall that you yourself expressed this idea much more happily and concisely:

> What Chance has made yours is not really yours.¹⁰

And a third, spoken by you still more happily, shall not be omitted:

> The good that could be given, can be removed.¹¹

I shall not charge this up to the expense account, because I have given it to you from your own stock. Farewell.

Footnotes

1. As contrasted with the general Stoic doctrine of taking part in the world's work.

2. See Ep. lxxxv. 33 for the famous saying of the Rhodian pilot.

3. *cernulat*, equivalent to Greek ἀναχαιτίζω, of a horse which throws a rider over its head.

4. Cf. the Stoic precept *nil admirandum*.

5. Frag. 199 Usener.

6. Literally "spun around" by the master and dismissed to freedom. Cf. Persius, v. 75f.

7. *Fabulae togatae* were plays which dealt with Roman subject matter, as contrasted with adaptations from the Greek, called *palliatae*. The term, in the widest sense includes both comedy and tragedy.

8. i.e., comedians or mimes.

9. *Syri Sententiae*, p. 309 Ribbeck².

10. *Com. Rom. Frag.* p. 394 Ribbeck².

11. *ibidem*.

IX. ON PHILOSOPHY AND FRIENDSHIP

¹You desire to know whether Epicurus is right when, in one of his letters,¹ he rebukes those who hold that the wise man is self-sufficient and for that reason does not stand in need of friendships. This is the objection raised by Epicurus against Stilbo and those who believe² that the Supreme Good is a soul which is insensible to feeling.

²We are bound to meet with a double meaning if we try to express the Greek term "lack of feeling" summarily, in a single word, rendering it by the Latin word *impatientia*. For it may be understood in the meaning the opposite to that which we wish it to have. What we mean to express is, a soul which rejects any sensation of evil; but

people will interpret the idea as that of a soul which can endure no evil. Consider, therefore, whether it is not better to say "a soul that cannot be harmed," or "a soul entirely beyond the realm of suffering." [3]There is this difference between ourselves and the other school:[3] our ideal wise man feels his troubles, but overcomes them; their wise man does not even feel them. But we and they alike hold this idea,–that the wise man is self-sufficient. Nevertheless, he desires friends, neighbours, and associates, no matter how much he is sufficient unto himself. [4]And mark how self-sufficient he is; for on occasion he can be content with a part of himself. If he lose a hand through disease or war, or if some accident puts out one or both of his eyes, he will be satisfied with what is left, taking as much pleasure in his impaired and maimed body as he took when it was sound. But while he does not pine for these parts if they are missing, he prefers not to lose them. [5]In this sense the wise man is self-sufficient, that he can do without friends, not that he desires to do without them. When I say "can," I mean this: he endures the loss of a friend with equanimity.

But he need never lack friends, for it lies in his own control how soon he shall make good a loss. Just as Phidias, if he lose a statue, can straightway carve another, even so our master in the art of making friendships can fill the place of a friend he has lost. [6]If you ask how one can make oneself a friend quickly, I will tell you, provided we are agreed that I may pay my debt[4] at once and square the account, so far as this letter is concerned. Hecato,[5] says: "I can show you a philtre, compounded without drugs, herbs, or any witch's incantation: 'If you would be loved, love.'" Now there is great pleasure, not only in maintaining old and established friendships, but also in beginning and acquiring new ones. [7]There is the same difference between winning a new friend and having already won him, as there is between the farmer who sows and the farmer who reaps. The philosopher Attalus used to say: "It is more pleasant to make than to keep a friend, as it is more pleasant to the artist to paint than to have finished painting." When one is busy and absorbed in one's work, the very absorption affords great delight; but when one has withdrawn one's hand from the completed master-piece, the pleasure is not so keen. Henceforth it is the fruits of his art that he enjoys; it was the art itself that he enjoyed while he was painting. In the case of our children, their young manhood yields the more abundant fruits, but their infancy was sweeter.

[8]Let us now return to the question. The wise man, I say, self-sufficient though he be, nevertheless desires friends if only for the purpose of practising friendship, in order that his noble qualities may not lie dormant. Not, however, for the purpose mentioned by Epicurus[6] in the letter quoted above: "That there may be someone to sit by him when he is ill, to help him when he is in prison or in want;" but that he may have someone by whose sick-bed he himself may sit, someone a prisoner in hostile hands whom he himself may set free. He who regards himself only, and enters upon friendships for this reason, reckons wrongly. The end will be like the beginning: he has made friends with one who might assist him out of bondage; at the first rattle of the chain such a friend will desert him. [9]These are the so-called "fair-weather" friend-ships; one who is chosen for the sake of utility will be satisfactory only so long as he is useful. Hence prosperous men are blockaded by troops of friends; but those who have failed stand amid vast loneliness their friends fleeing from the very crisis which is to test their worth. Hence, also, we notice those many shameful cases of persons who, through fear, desert or betray. The beginning and the end cannot but harmonize. He who begins to be your friend because it pays will also cease because it pays. A man will be attracted by some reward offered in exchange for his friendship, if he be attracted by aught in friendship other than friendship itself.

[10]For what purpose, then, do I make a man my friend? In order to have someone for whom I may die, whom I may follow into exile, against whose death I may stake my own life, and pay the pledge, too. The friendship which you portray is a bargain and not a friendship; it regards convenience only, and looks to the results. [11]Beyond question the feeling of a lover has in it something akin to friendship; one might call it friendship run mad. But, though this is true, does anyone love for the sake of gain, or promotion, or renown? Pure[7] love, careless of all other things, kindles the soul with

⁶Do me the favour, when men surround you and try to talk you into believing that you are unhappy, to consider not what you hear but what you yourself feel, and to take counsel with your feelings and question yourself independently, because you know your own affairs better than anyone else does. Ask: "Is there any reason why these persons should condole with me? Why should they be worried or even fear some infection from me, as if troubles could be transmitted? Is there any evil involved, or is it a matter merely of ill report, rather than an evil?" Put the question voluntarily to yourself: "Am I tormented without sufficient reason, am I morose, and do I convert what is not an evil into what is an evil?" ⁷You may retort with the question: "How am I to know whether my sufferings are real or imaginary?" Here is the rule for such matters: we are tormented either by things present, or by things to come, or by both. As to things present, the decision is easy. Suppose that your person enjoys freedom and health, and that you do not suffer from any external injury. As to what may happen to it in the future, we shall see later on. To-day there is nothing wrong with it. ⁸"But," you say, "something will happen to it." First of all, consider whether your proofs of future trouble are sure. For it is more often the case that we are troubled by our apprehensions, and that we are mocked by that mocker, rumour, which is wont to settle wars, but much more often settles individuals. Yes, my dear Lucilius; we agree too quickly with what people say. We do not put to the test those things which cause our fear; we do not examine into them; we blench and retreat just like soldiers who are forced to abandon their camp because of a dust-cloud raised by stampeding cattle, or are thrown into a panic by the spreading of some unauthenticated rumour. ⁹And somehow or other it is the idle report that disturbs us most. For truth has its own definite boundaries, but that which arises from uncertainty is delivered over to guesswork and the irresponsible license of a frightened mind. That is why no fear is so ruinous and so uncontrollable as panic fear. For other fears are groundless, but this fear is witless.

¹⁰Let us, then, look carefully into the matter. It is likely that some troubles will befall us; but it is not a present fact. How often has the unexpected happened! How often has the expected never come to pass! And even though it is ordained to be, what does it avail to run out to meet your suffering? You will suffer soon enough, when it arrives; so look forward meanwhile to better things. ¹¹What shall you gain by doing this? Time. There will be many happenings meanwhile which will serve to postpone, or end, or pass on to another person, the trials which are near or even in your very presence. A fire has opened the way to flight. Men have been let down softly by a catastrophe. Sometimes the sword has been checked even at the victim's throat. Men have survived their own executioners. Even bad fortune is fickle. Perhaps it will come, perhaps not; in the meantime it is not. So look forward to better things.

¹²The mind at times fashions for itself false shapes of evil when there are no signs that point to any evil; it twists into the worst construction some word of doubtful meaning; or it fancies some personal grudge to be more serious than it really is, considering not how angry the enemy is, but to what lengths he may go if he is angry. But life is not worth living, and there is no limit to our sorrows, if we indulge our fears to the greatest possible extent; in this matter, let prudence help you, and contemn with a resolute spirit even when it is in plain sight. If you cannot do this, counter one weakness with another, and temper your fear with hope. There is nothing so certain among these objects of fear that it is not more certain still that things we dread sink into nothing and that things we hope for mock us.

¹³Accordingly, weigh carefully your hopes as well as your fears, and whenever all the elements are in doubt, decide in your own favour; believe what you prefer. And if fear wins a majority of the votes, incline in the other direction anyhow, and cease to harass your soul, reflecting continually that most mortals, even when no troubles are actually at hand or are certainly to be expected in the future, become excited and disquieted. No one calls a halt on himself, when he begins to be urged ahead; nor does he regulate his alarm according to the truth. No one says; "The author of the story is a fool, and he who has believed it is a fool, as well as he who fabricated it." We let ourselves drift with every breeze; we are frightened at uncertainties, just as if they were

certain. We observe no moderation. The slightest thing turns the scales and throws us forthwith into a panic.

[14]But I am ashamed either to admonish you sternly or to try to beguile you with such mild remedies.[2] Let another say. "Perhaps the worst will not happen." You yourself must say. "Well, what if it does happen? Let us see who wins! Perhaps it happens for my best interests; it may be that such a death will shed credit upon my life." Socrates was ennobled by the hemlock draught. Wrench from Cato's hand his sword, the vindicator of liberty, and you deprive him of the greatest share of his glory. [15]I am exhorting you far too long, since you need reminding rather than exhortation. The path on which I am leading you is not different from that on which your nature leads you; you were born to such conduct as I describe. Hence there is all the more reason why you should increase and beautify the good that is in you.

[16]But now, to close my letter, I have only to stamp the usual seal upon it, in other words, to commit thereto some noble message to be delivered to you: "The fool, with all his other faults, has this also, he is always getting ready to live."[3] Reflect, my esteemed Lucilius, what this saying means, and you will see how revolting is the fickleness of men who lay down every day new foundations of life, and begin to build up fresh hopes even at the brink of the grave. [17]Look within your own mind for individual instances; you will think of old men who are preparing themselves at that very hour for a political career, or for travel, or for business. And what is baser than getting ready to live when you are already old? I should not name the author of this motto, except that it is somewhat unknown to fame and is not one of those popular sayings of Epicurus which I have allowed myself to praise and to appropriate. Farewell.

Footnotes

1. Seneca dismisses the topic of "exaggerated ills," because judgements will differ concerning present troubles; the Stoics, for example, would not admit that torture was an evil at all. He then passes on to the topic of "imaginary ills," §§ 6-7, and afterwards to "anticipated ills," §§ 8-11. From § 12 on, he deals with both imaginary and anticipated ills.

2. Cf. Solon's καί με κωτίλλοντα λείως τραχὺν ἐκφανεῖ νόον.

3. Epicurus, Frag. 494 Usener.

XIV. ON THE REASONS FOR WITHDRAWING FROM THE WORLD

[1]I confess that we all have an inborn affection for our body; I confess that we are entrusted with its guardianship. I do not maintain that the body is not to be indulged at all; but I maintain that we must not be slaves to it. He will have many masters who makes his body his master, who is over-fearful in its behalf, who judges everything according to the body. [2]We should conduct ourselves not as if we ought to live for the body, but as if we could not live without it. Our too great love for it makes us restless with fears, burdens us with cares, and exposes us to insults. Virtue is held too cheap by the man who counts his body too dear. We should cherish the body with the greatest care; but we should also be prepared, when reason, self-respect, and duty demand the sacrifice, to deliver it even to the flames.

[3]Let us, however, in so far as we can, avoid discomforts as well as dangers, and withdraw to safe ground, by thinking continually how we may repel all objects of fear. If I am not mistaken, there are three main classes of these: we fear want, we fear sickness, and we fear the troubles which result from the violence of the stronger. [4]And of all these, that which shakes us most is the dread which hangs over us from our neighbour's ascendancy; for it is accompanied by great outcry and uproar. But the natural evils which I have mentioned,—want and sickness, steal upon us silently with no shock of terror to the eye or to the ear. The other kind of evil comes, so to speak, in the form of a huge parade. Surrounding it is a retinue of swords and fire and chains

a tedium that irks us. It moulds and constructs the soul; it orders our life, guides our conduct, shows us what we should do and what we should leave undone; it sits at the helm and directs our course as we waver amid uncertainties. Without it, no one can live fearlessly or in peace of mind. Countless things that happen every hour call for advice; and such advice is to be sought in philosophy.

⁴Perhaps someone will say: "How can philosophy help me, if Fate exists? Of what avail is philosophy, if God rules the universe? Of what avail is it, if Chance governs everything? For not only is it impossible to change things that are determined, but it is also impossible to plan beforehand against what is undetermined; either God has forestalled my plans, and decided what I am to do, or else Fortune gives no free play to my plans." ⁵Whether the truth, Lucilius, lies in one or in all of these views, we must be philosophers; whether Fate binds us down by an inexorable law, or whether God as arbiter of the universe has arranged everything, or whether Chance drives and tosses human affairs without method, philosophy ought to be our defence. She will encourage us to obey God cheerfully, but Fortune defiantly; she will teach us to follow God and endure Chance. ⁶But it is not my purpose now to be led into a discussion as to what is within our own control,–if foreknowledge is supreme, or if a chain of fated events drags us along in its clutches, or if the sudden and the unexpected play the tyrant over us; I return now to my warning and my exhortation, that you should not allow the impulse of your spirit to weaken and grow cold. Hold fast to it and establish it firmly, in order that what is now impulse may become a habit of the mind.

⁷If I know you well, you have already been trying to find out, from the very beginning of my letter, what little contribution it brings to you. Sift the letter, and you will find it. You need not wonder at any genius of mine; for as yet I am lavish only with other men's property.–But why did I say "other men"? Whatever is well said by anyone is mine. This also is a saying of Epicurus:² "If you live according to nature, you will never be poor; if you live according to opinion, you will never be rich." ⁸Nature's wants are slight; the demands of opinion are boundless. Suppose that the property of many millionaires is heaped up in your possession. Assume that fortune carries you far beyond the limits of a private income, decks you with gold, clothes you in purple, and brings you to such a degree of luxury and wealth that you can bury the earth under your marble floors; that you may not only possess, but tread upon, riches. Add statues, paintings, and whatever any art has devised for the luxury; you will only learn from such things to crave still greater.

⁹Natural desires are limited; but those which spring from false opinion can have no stopping-point. The false has no limits. When you are travelling on a road, there must be an end; but when astray, your wanderings are limitless. Recall your steps, therefore, from idle things, and when you would know whether that which you seek is based upon a natural or upon a misleading desire, consider whether it can stop at any definite point. If you find, after having travelled far, that there is a more distant goal always in view, you may be sure that this condition is contrary to nature. Farewell.

Footnotes

1. i.e., have merely advanced in years.
2. Frag. 201 Usener.

XVII. ON PHILOSOPHY AND RICHES

¹Cast away everything of that sort, if you are wise; nay, rather that you may be wise; strive toward a sound mind at top speed and with your whole strength. If any bond holds you back, untie it, or sever it. "But," you say, "my estate delays me; I wish to make such disposition of it that it may suffice for me when I have nothing to do, lest either poverty be a burden to me, or I myself a burden to others." ²You do not seem, when you say this, to know the strength and power of that good which you are considering. You do indeed grasp the all important thing, the great benefit which philosophy

confers, but you do not yet discern accurately its various functions, nor do you yet know how great is the help we receive from philosophy in everything, everywhere,—how, (to use Cicero's language,[1]) it not only succours us in the greatest matters but also descends to the smallest. Take my advice; call wisdom into consultation; she will advise you not to sit for ever at your ledger. [3]Doubtless, your object, what you wish to attain by such postponement of your studies, is that poverty may not have to be feared by you. But what if it is something to be desired? Riches have shut off many a man from the attainment of wisdom; poverty is unburdened and free from care. When the trumpet sounds, the poor man knows that he is not being attacked; when there is a cry of "Fire,"[2] he only seeks a way of escape, and does not ask what he can save; if the poor man must go to sea, the harbour does not resound, nor do the wharves bustle with the retinue of one individual. No throng of slaves surrounds the poor man,—slaves for whose mouths the master must covet the fertile crops of regions beyond the sea. [4]It is easy to fill a few stomachs, when they are well trained and crave nothing else but to be filled. Hunger costs but little; squeamishness costs much. Poverty is contented with fulfilling pressing needs.

Why, then, should you reject Philosophy as a comrade? [5]Even the rich man copies her ways when he is in his senses. If you wish to have leisure for your mind, either be a poor man, or resemble a poor man. Study cannot be helpful unless you take pains to live simply; and living simply is voluntary poverty. Away, then, with all excuses like: "I have not yet enough; when I have gained the desired amount, then I shall devote myself wholly to philosophy." And yet this ideal, which you are putting off and placing second to other interests, should be secured first of all; you should begin with it. You retort: "I wish to acquire something to live on." Yes, but learn while you are acquiring it; for if anything forbids you to live nobly, nothing forbids you to die nobly. [6]There is no reason why poverty should call us away from philosophy,—no, nor even actual want. For when hastening after wisdom, we must endure even hunger. Men have endured hunger when their towns were besieged, and what other reward for their endurance did they obtain than that they did not fall under the conqueror's power? How much greater is the promise of the prize of everlasting liberty, and the assurance that we need fear neither God nor man! Even though we starve, we must reach that goal. [7]Armies have endured all manner of want, have lived on roots, and have resisted hunger by means of food too revolting to mention. All this they have suffered to gain a kingdom, and,—what is more marvellous,—to gain a kingdom that will be another's. Will any man hesitate to endure poverty, in order that he may free his mind from madness?

Therefore one should not seek to lay up riches first; one may attain to philosophy, however, even without money for the journey. [8]It is indeed so. After you have come to possess all other things, shall you then wish to possess wisdom also? Is philosophy to be the last requisite in life,—a sort of supplement? Nay, your plan should be this: be a philosopher now, whether you have anything or not,—for if you have anything, how do you know that you have not too much already?—but if you have nothing, seek understanding first, before anything else. [9]"But," you say, "I shall lack the necessities of life." In the first place, you cannot lack them; because nature demands but little, and the wise man suits his needs to nature. But if the utmost pinch of need arrives, he will quickly take leave of life and cease being a trouble to himself. If, however, his means of existence are meagre and scanty, he will make the best of them, without being anxious or worried about anything more than the bare necessities; he will do justice to his belly and his shoulders; with free and happy spirit he will laugh at the bustling of rich men, and the flurried ways of those who are hastening after wealth, [10]and say: "Why of your own accord postpone your real life to the distant future? Shall you wait for some interest to fall due, or for some income on your merchandise, or for a place in the will of some wealthy old man, when you can be rich here and now. Wisdom offers wealth in ready money, and pays it over to those in whose eyes she has made wealth superfluous." These remarks refer to other men; you are nearer the rich class. Change the age in which you live, and you have too much. But in every age, what is enough remains the same.

[11]I might close my letter at this point, if I had not got you into bad habits. One cannot greet Parthian royalty without bringing a gift; and in your case I cannot say farewell without paying a price. But what of it? I shall borrow from Epicurus:[3] "The acquisition of riches has been for many men, not an end, but a change, of troubles." [12]I do not wonder. For the fault is not in the wealth, but in the mind itself. That which had made poverty a burden to us, has made riches also a burden. Just as it matters little whether you lay a sick man on a wooden or on a golden bed, for whithersoever he be moved he will carry his malady with him; so one need not care whether the diseased mind is bestowed upon riches or upon poverty. His malady goes with the man. Farewell,

Footnotes

1. Perhaps from the *Hortensius*; see Müller, Frag. 98, p. 326.

2. Literally, "Water!"

3. Frag. 479 Usener.

XVIII. ON FESTIVALS AND FASTING

[1]It is the month of December, and yet the city is at this very moment in a sweat. License is given to the general merrymaking. Everything resounds with mighty preparations,– as if the Saturnalia differed at all from the usual business day! So true it is that the difference is nil, that I regard as correct the remark of the man who said: "Once December was a month; now it is a year."[1]

[2]If I had you with me, I should be glad to consult you and find out what you think should be done,–whether we ought to make no change in our daily routine, or whether, in order not to be out of sympathy with the ways of the public, we should dine in gayer fashion and doff the toga.[2] As it is now, we Romans have changed our dress for the sake of pleasure and holiday-making, though in former times that was only customary when the State was disturbed and had fallen on evil days. [3]I am sure that, if I know you aright, playing the part of an umpire you would have wished that we should be neither like the liberty-capped[3] throng in all ways, nor in all ways unlike them; unless, perhaps, this is just the season when we ought to lay down the law to the soul, and bid it be alone in refraining from pleasures just when the whole mob has let itself go in pleasures; for this is the surest proof which a man can get of his own constancy, if he neither seeks the things which are seductive and allure him to luxury, nor is led into them. [4]It shows much more courage to remain dry and sober when the mob is drunk and vomiting; but it shows greater self-control to refuse to withdraw oneself and to do what the crowd does, but in a different way,–thus neither making oneself conspicuous nor becoming one of the crowd. For one may keep holiday without extravagance.

[5]I am so firmly determined, however, to test the constancy of your mind that, drawing from the teachings of great men, I shall give you also a lesson: Set aside a certain number of days, during which you shall be content with the scantiest and cheapest fare, with coarse and rough dress, saying to yourself the while: "Is this the condition that I feared?" [6]It is precisely in times of immunity from care that the soul should toughen itself beforehand for occasions of greater stress, and it is while Fortune is kind that it should fortify itself against her violence. In days of peace the soldier performs manoeuvres, throws up earthworks with no enemy in sight, and wearies himself by gratuitous toil, in order that he may be equal to unavoidable toil. If you would not have a man flinch when the crisis comes, train him before it comes. Such is the course which those men[4] have followed who, in their imitation of poverty, have every month come almost to want, that they might never recoil from what they had so often rehearsed.

[7]You need not suppose that I mean meals like Timon's, or "paupers' huts,"[5] or any other device which luxurious millionaires use to beguile the tedium of their lives. Let

the pallet be a real one, and the coarse cloak; let the bread be hard and grimy. Endure all this for three or four days at a time, sometimes for more, so that it may be a test of yourself instead of a mere hobby. Then, I assure you, my dear Lucilius, you will leap for joy when filled with a pennyworth of food, and you will understand that a man's peace of mind does not depend upon Fortune; for, even when angry she grants enough for our needs.

[8]There is no reason, however, why you should think that you are doing anything great; for you will merely be doing what many thousands of slaves and many thousands of poor men are doing every day. But you may credit yourself with this item,– that you will not be doing it under compulsion, and that it will be as easy for you to endure it permanently as to make the experiment from time to time. Let us practise our strokes on the "dummy";[6] let us become intimate with poverty, so that Fortune may not catch us off our guard. We shall be rich with all the more comfort, if we once learn how far poverty is from being a burden.

[9]Even Epicurus, the teacher of pleasure, used to observe stated intervals, during which he satisfied his hunger in niggardly fashion; he wished to see whether he thereby fell short of full and complete happiness, and, if so, by what amount he fell short, and whether this amount was worth purchasing at the price of great effort. At any rate, he makes such a statement in the well known letter written to Polyaenus in the archonship of Charinus.[7] Indeed, he boasts that he himself lived on less than a penny, but that Metrodorus, whose progress was not yet so great, needed a whole penny. [10]Do you think that there can be fullness on such fare? Yes, and there is pleasure also,–not that shifty and fleeting Pleasure which needs a fillip now and then, but a pleasure that is steadfast and sure. For though water, barley-meal, and crusts of barley-bread, are not a cheerful diet, yet it is the highest kind of Pleasure to be able to derive pleasure from this sort of food, and to have reduced one's needs to that modicum which no unfairness of Fortune can snatch away. [11]Even prison fare is more generous; and those who have been set apart for capital punishment are not so meanly fed by the man who is to execute them. Therefore, what a noble soul must one have, to descend of one's own free will to a diet which even those who have been sentenced to death have not to fear! This is indeed forestalling the spearthrusts of Fortune.

[12]So begin, my dear Lucilius, to follow the custom of these men, and set apart certain days on which you shall withdraw from your business and make yourself at home with the scantiest fare. Establish business relations with poverty.

> Dare, O my friend, to scorn the sight of wealth,
> And mould thyself to kinship with thy God.[8]

[13]For he alone is in kinship with God who has scorned wealth. Of course I do not forbid you to possess it, but I would have you reach the point at which you possess it dauntlessly; this can be accomplished only by persuading yourself that you can live happily without it as well as with it, and by regarding riches always as likely to elude you.

[14]But now I must begin to fold up my letter. "Settle your debts first," you cry. Here is a draft on Epicurus; he will pay down the sum: "Ungoverned anger begets madness."[9] You cannot help knowing the truth of these words, since you have had not only slaves, but also enemies. [15]But indeed this emotion blazes out against all sorts of persons; it springs from love as much as from hate, and shows itself not less in serious matters than in jest and sport. And it makes no difference how important the provocation may be, but into what kind of soul it penetrates. Similarly with fire; it does not matter how great is the flame, but what it falls upon. For solid timbers have repelled a very great fire; conversely, dry and easily inflammable stuff nourishes the slightest spark into a conflagration. So it is with anger, my dear Lucilius; the outcome of a mighty anger is madness, and hence anger should be avoided, not merely that we may escape excess, but that we may have a healthy mind. Farewell.

Footnotes

1. i.e., the whole year is a Saturnalia.

dependants.

XX. ON PRACTISING WHAT YOU PREACH

[1]If you are in good health and if you think yourself worthy of becoming at last your own master, I am glad. For the credit will be mine, if I can drag you from the floods in which you are being buffeted without hope of emerging. This, however, my dear Lucilius, I ask and beg of you, on your part, that you let wisdom sink into your soul, and test your progress, not by mere speech or writings, but by stoutness of heart and decrease of desire. Prove your words by your deeds.

[2]Far different is the purpose of those who are speech-making and trying to win the approbation of a throng of hearers, far different that of those who allure the ears of young men and idlers by many-sided or fluent argumentation; philosophy teaches us to act, not to speak; it exacts of every man that he should live according to his own standards, that his life should not be out of harmony with his words, and that, further, his inner life should be of one hue and not out of harmony with all his activities. This, I say, is the highest duty and the highest proof of wisdom,–that deed and word should be in accord, that a man should be equal to himself under all conditions, and always the same.

"But," you reply, "who can maintain this standard?" Very few, to be sure; but there are some. It is indeed a hard undertaking, and I do not say that the philosopher can always keep the same pace. But he can always travel the same path. [3]Observe yourself, then, and see whether your dress and your house are inconsistent, whether you treat yourself lavishly and your family meanly, whether you eat frugal dinners and yet build luxurious houses. You should lay hold, once for all, upon a single norm to live by, and should regulate your whole life according to this norm. Some men restrict themselves at home, but strut with swelling port before the public; such discordance is a fault, and it indicates a wavering mind which cannot yet keep its balance. [4]And I can tell you, further, whence arise this unsteadiness and disagreement of action and purpose; it is because no man resolves upon what he wishes, and, even if he has done so, he does not persist in it, but jumps the track; not only does he change, but he returns and slips back to the conduct which he has abandoned and abjured. [5]Therefore, to omit the ancient definitions of wisdom and to include the whole manner of human life, I can be satisfied with the following: "What is wisdom? Always desiring the same things, and always refusing the same things."[1] You may be excused from adding the little proviso,–that what you wish, should be right; since no man can always be satisfied with the same thing, unless it is right.

[6]For this reason men do not know what they wish, except at the actual moment of wishing; no man ever decided once and for all to desire or to refuse. Judgment varies from day to day, and changes to the opposite, making many a man pass his life in a kind of game. Press on, therefore, as you have begun; perhaps you will be led to perfection, or to a point which you alone understand is still short of perfection.

[7]"But what," you say, "will become of my crowded household without a household income?" If you stop supporting that crowd, it will support itself; or perhaps you will learn by the bounty of poverty what you cannot learn by your own bounty. Poverty will keep for you your true and tried friends; you will be rid of the men who were not seeking you for yourself, but for something which you have. Is it not true, however, that you should love poverty, if only for this single reason,–that it will show you those by whom you are loved? O when will that time come, when no one shall tell lies to compliment you! [8]Accordingly, let your thoughts, your efforts, your desires, help to make you content with your own self and with the goods that spring from yourself; and commit all your other prayers to God's keeping! What happiness could come closer home to you? Bring yourself down to humble conditions, from which you cannot be ejected and in order that you may do so with greater alacrity, the contribution contained in this letter shall refer to that subject; I shall bestow it upon you forthwith.

⁹Although you may look askance, Epicurus² will once again be glad to settle my indebtedness: "Believe me, your words will be more imposing if you sleep on a cot and wear rags. For in that case you will not be merely saying them; you will be demonstrating their truth." I, at any rate, listen in a different spirit to the utterances of our friend Demetrius, after I have seen him reclining without even a cloak to cover him, and, more than this, without rugs to lie upon. He is not only a teacher of the truth, but a witness to the truth. ¹⁰"May not a man, however, despise wealth when it lies in his very pocket?" Of course; he also is great-souled, who sees riches heaped up round him and, after wondering long and deeply because they have come into his possession, smiles, and hears rather than feels that they are his. It means much not to be spoiled by intimacy with riches; and he is truly great who is poor amidst riches. ¹¹"Yes, but I do not know," you say, "how the man you speak of will endure poverty, if he falls into it suddenly." Nor do I, Epicurus, know whether the poor man you speak of will despise riches, should he suddenly fall into them; accordingly, in the case of both, it is the mind that must be appraised, and we must investigate whether your man is pleased with his poverty, and whether my man is displeased with his riches. Otherwise, the cot-bed and the rags are slight proof of his good intentions, if it has not been made clear that the person concerned endures these trials not from necessity but from preference.

¹²It is the mark, however, of a noble spirit not to precipitate oneself into such things³ on the ground that they are better, but to practise for them on the ground that they are thus easy to endure. And they are easy to endure, Lucilius; when, however, you come to them after long rehearsal, they are even pleasant; for they contain a sense of freedom from care,–and without this nothing is pleasant. ¹³I hold it essential, therefore, to do as I have told you in a letter that great men have often done: to reserve a few days in which we may prepare ourselves for real poverty by means of fancied poverty. There is all the more reason for doing this, because we have been steeped in luxury and regard all duties as hard and onerous. Rather let the soul be roused from its sleep and be prodded, and let it be reminded that nature has prescribed very little for us. No man is born rich. Every man, when he first sees light, is commanded to be content with milk and rags. Such is our beginning, and yet kingdoms are all too small for us!⁴ Farewell.

Footnotes

1. Seneca applies to wisdom the definition of friendship, Salust, *Catiline*, 20. 4 *idem velle atque idem nolle, ea demum firma amicitia est*.

2. Frag. 206 Usener.

3. i.e., the life of voluntary poverty.

4. Adapted from the epigram on Alexander the Great, *"hic est quem non capit orbis."* See Plutarch, *Alexander*, § 6 ὦ παῖ ζήτει σεαυτῷ βασιλείαν ἴσην. Μακεδονια γάρ σε οὐ χωρεῖ, and Seneca, Ep. cxix. 8.

XXI. ON THE RENOWN WHICH MY WRITINGS WILL BRING YOU

¹Do you conclude that you are having difficulties with those men about whom you wrote to me? Your greatest difficulty is with yourself; for you are your own stumbling-block. You do not know what you want. You are better at approving the right course than at following it out. You see where the true happiness lies, but you have not the courage to attain it. Let me tell you what it is that hinders you, inasmuch as you do not of yourself discern it.

²You think that this condition, which you are to abandon, is one of importance, and after resolving upon that ideal state of calm into which you hope to pass, you are held back by the lustre of your present life, from which it is your intention to depart, just as if you were about to fall into a state of filth and darkness. This is a mistake, Lucilius; to go from your present life into the other is a promotion. There is the same difference between these two lives as there is between mere brightness and real light;

the latter has a definite source within itself, the other borrows its radiance; the one is called forth by an illumination coming from the outside, and anyone who stands between the source and the object immediately turns the latter into a dense shadow; but the other has a glow that comes from within.

It is your own studies that will make you shine and will render you eminent, Allow me to mention the case of Epicurus. [3]He was writing[1] to Idomeneus and trying to recall him from a showy existence to sure and steadfast renown. Idomeneus was at that time a minister of state who exercised a rigorous authority and had important affairs in hand. "If," said Epicurus, "you are attracted by fame, my letters will make you more renowned than all the things which you cherish and which make you cherished." [4]Did Epicurus speak falsely? Who would have known of Idomeneus, had not the philosopher thus engraved his name in those letters of his? All the grandees and satraps, even the king himself, who was petitioned for the title which Idomeneus sought, are sunk in deep oblivion. Cicero's letters keep the name of Atticus from perishing. It would have profited Atticus nothing to have an Agrippa for a son-in-law, a Tiberius for the husband of his grand-daughter, and a Drusus Caesar for a great-grandson; amid these mighty names his name would never be spoken, had not Cicero bound him to himself.[2] [5]The deep flood of time will roll over us; some few great men will raise their heads above it, and, though destined at the last to depart into the same realms of silence, will battle against oblivion and maintain their ground for long.

That which Epicurus could promise his friend, this I promise you, Lucilius. I shall find favour among later generations; I can take with me names that will endure as long as mine. Our poet Vergil promised an eternal name to two heroes, and is keeping his promise:[3]

> Blest heroes twain! If power my song possess,
> The record of your names shall never be
> Erased from out the book of Time, while yet
> Aeneas' tribe shall keep the Capitol,
> That rock immovable, and Roman sire
> Shall empire hold.

[6]Whenever men have been thrust forward by fortune, whenever they have become part and parcel of another's influence, they have found abundant favour, their houses have been thronged, only so long as they themselves have kept their position; when they themselves have left it, they have slipped at once from the memory of men. But in the case of innate ability, the respect in which it is held increases, and not only does honour accrue to the man himself, but whatever has attached itself to his memory is passed on from one to another.[4]

[7]In order that Idomeneus may not be introduced free of charge into my letter, he shall make up the indebtedness from his own account. It was to him that Epicurus addressed the well-known saying[5] urging him to make Pythocles rich, but not rich in the vulgar and equivocal way. "If you wish," said he, "to make Pythocles rich, do not add to his store of money, but subtract from his desires." [8]This idea is too clear to need explanation, and too clever to need reinforcement. There is, however, one point on which I would warn you,–not to consider that this statement applies only to riches; its value will be the same, no matter how you apply it. "If you wish to make Pythocles honourable, do not add to his honours, but subtract from his desires"; "if you wish Pythocles to have pleasure for ever, do not add to his pleasures, but subtract from his desires"; "if you wish to make Pythocles an old man, filling his life to the full, do not add to his years, but subtract from his desires." [9]There is no reason why you should hold that these words belong to Epicurus alone; they are public property. I think we ought to do in philosophy as they are wont to do in the Senate: when someone has made a motion, of which I approve to a certain extent, I ask him to make his motion in two parts, and I vote for the part which I approve. So I am all the more glad to repeat the distinguished words of Epicurus, in order that I may prove to those who have recourse to him through a bad motive, thinking that they will have in him a screen for their own vices, that they must live honourably, no matter what school they follow.

[10]Go to his Garden and read the motto carved there:

"Stranger, here you will do well to tarry; here our highest good is pleasure."

The care-taker of that abode, a kindly host, will be ready for you; he will welcome you with barley-meal and serve you water also in abundance, with these words: "Have you not been well entertained?" "This garden," he says, "does not whet your appetite; it quenches it. Nor does it make you more thirsty with every drink; it slakes the thirst by a natural cure, a cure that demands no fee. This is the 'pleasure' in which I have grown old."

[11]In speaking with you, however, I refer to those desires which refuse alleviation, which must be bribed to cease. For in regard to the exceptional desires, which may be postponed, which may be chastened and checked, I have this one thought to share with you: a pleasure of that sort is according to our nature, but it is not according to our needs; one owes nothing to it; whatever is expended upon it is a free gift. The belly will not listen to advice; it makes demands, it importunes. And yet it is not a troublesome creditor; you can send it away at small cost, provided only that you give it what you owe, not merely all you are able to give. Farewell.

Footnotes

1. Epicurus, Frag. 132 Usener.

2. i.e., Cicero's letters did more to preserve the name of Atticus than such a connexion with the imperial house would have done.

3. *Aeneid*, ix. 446 ff.

4. As in the case of Epicurus and Idomeneus, Cicero and Atticus, Vergil and Euryalus and Nisus, and Seneca and Lucilius!

5. Frag. 135 Usener.

XXII. ON THE FUTILITY OF HALF-WAY MEASURES

[1]You understand by this time that you must withdraw yourself from those showy and depraved pursuits; but you still wish to know how this may be accomplished. There are certain things which can be pointed out only by someone who is present. The physician cannot prescribe by letter the proper time for eating or bathing; he must feel the pulse. There is an old adage about gladiators,—that they plan their fight in the ring; as they intently watch, something in the adversary's glance, some movement of his hand, even some slight bending of his body, gives a warning. [2]We can formulate general rules and commit them to writing, as to what is usually done, or ought to be done; such advice may be given, not only to our absent friends, but also to succeeding generations. In regard, however, to that second[1] question,—when or how your plan is to be carried out,—no one will advise at long range; we must take counsel in the presence of the actual situation. [3]You must be not only present in the body, but watchful in mind, if you would avail yourself of the fleeting opportunity. Accordingly, look about you for the opportunity; if you see it, grasp it, and with all your energy and with all your strength devote yourself to this task—to rid yourself of those business duties.

Now listen carefully to the opinion which I shall offer; it is my opinion that you should withdraw either from that kind of existence, or else from existence altogether. But I likewise maintain that you should take a gentle path, that you may loosen rather than cut the knot which you have bungled so badly in tying,—provided that if there shall be no other way of loosening it, you may actually cut it. No man is so faint-hearted that he would rather hang in suspense for ever than drop once for all. [4]Meanwhile,—and this is of first importance,—do not hamper yourself; be content with the business into which you have lowered yourself, or, as you prefer to have people think, have tumbled. There is no reason why you should be struggling on to something further; if you do, you will lose all grounds of excuse, and men will see that it was not a tumble.

a care-free countenance, or with a "blithe and gay" expression, as our young dandies are accustomed to say? Or can one thus open his door to poverty, or hold the curb on his pleasures, or contemplate the endurance of pain? He who ponders these things[1] in his heart is indeed full of joy; but it is not a cheerful joy. It is just this joy, however, of which I would have you become the owner; for it will never fail you when once you have found its source. [5]The yield of poor mines is on the surface; those are really rich whose veins lurk deep, and they will make more bountiful returns to him who delves unceasingly. So too those baubles which delight the common crowd afford but a thin pleasure, laid on as a coating, and even joy that is only plated lacks a real basis. But the joy of which I speak, that to which I am endeavouring to lead you, is something solid, disclosing itself the more fully as you penetrate into it. [6]Therefore I pray you, my dearest Lucilius, do the one thing that can render you really happy: cast aside and trample under foot all the things that glitter outwardly and are held out to you[2] by another or as obtainable from another; look toward the true good, and rejoice only in that which comes from your own store. And what do I mean by "from your own store"? I mean from your very self, that which is the best part of you. The frail body, also, even though we can accomplish nothing without it, is to be regarded as necessary rather than as important; it involves us in vain pleasures, short-lived, and soon to be regretted, which, unless they are reined in by extreme self-control, will be transformed into the opposite. This is what I mean: pleasure, unless it has been kept within bounds, tends to rush headlong into the abyss of sorrow.

But it is hard to keep within bounds in that which you believe to be good. The real good may be coveted with safety. [7]Do you ask me what this real good is, and whence it derives? I will tell you: it comes from a good conscience, from honourable purposes, from right actions, from contempt of the gifts of chance, from an even and calm way of living which treads but one path. For men who leap from one purpose to another, or do not even leap but are carried over by a sort of hazard,–how can such wavering and unstable persons possess any good that is fixed and lasting? [8]There are only a few who control themselves and their affairs by a guiding purpose; the rest do not proceed; they are merely swept along, like objects afloat in a river. And of these objects, some are held back by sluggish waters and are transported gently; others are torn along by a more violent current; some, which are nearest the bank, are left there as the current slackens; and others are carried out to sea by the onrush of the stream. Therefore, we should decide what we wish, and abide by the decision.

[9]Now is the time for me to pay my debt. I can give you a saying of your friend Epicurus[3] and thus clear this letter of its obligation. "It is bothersome always to be beginning life." Or another, which will perhaps express the meaning better: "They live ill who are always beginning to live." [10]You are right in asking why; the saying certainly stands in need of a commentary. It is because the life of such persons is always incomplete. But a man cannot stand prepared for the approach of death if he has just begun to live. We must make it our aim already to have lived long enough. No one deems that he has done so, if he is just on the point of planning his life. [11]You need not think that there are few of this kind; practically everyone is of such a stamp. Some men, indeed, only begin to live when it is time for them to leave off living. And if this seems surprising to you, I shall add that which will surprise you still more: Some men have left off living before they have begun. Farewell.

Footnotes

1. Death, poverty, temptation, and suffering.
2. By the various sects which professed to teach how happiness is to be obtained.
3. Frag. 493 Usener.

XXIV. ON DESPISING DEATH[1]

[1]You write me that you are anxious about the result of a lawsuit, with which an angry

opponent is threatening you; and you expect me to advise you to picture to yourself a happier issue, and to rest in the allurements of hope. Why, indeed, is it necessary to summon trouble,–which must be endured soon enough when it has once arrived, or to anticipate trouble and ruin the present through fear of the future? It is indeed foolish to be unhappy now because you may be unhappy at some future time. ²But I shall conduct you to peace of mind by another route: if you would put off all worry, assume that what you fear may happen will certainly happen in any event; whatever the trouble may be, measure it in your own mind, and estimate the amount of your fear. You will thus understand that what you fear is either insignificant or short-lived. ³And you need not spend a long time in gathering illustrations which will strengthen you; every epoch has produced them. Let your thoughts travel into any era of Roman or foreign history, and there will throng before you notable examples of high achievement or of high endeavour.

If you lose this case, can anything more severe happen to you than being sent into exile or led to prison? Is there a worse fate that any man may fear than being burned or being killed? Name such penalties one by one, and mention the men who have scorned them; one does not need to hunt for them,–it is simply a matter of selection. ⁴Sentence of conviction was borne by Rutilius as if the injustice of the decision were the only thing which annoyed him. Exile was endured by Metellus with courage, by Rutilius even with gladness; for the former consented to come back only because his country called him; the latter refused to return when Sulla summoned him,–and nobody in those days said "No" to Sulla! Socrates in prison discoursed, and declined to flee when certain persons gave him the opportunity; he remained there, in order to free mankind from the fear of two most grievous things, death and imprisonment. ⁵Mucius put his hand into the fire. It is painful to be burned; but how much more painful to inflict such suffering upon oneself! Here was a man of no learning, not primed to face death and pain by any words of wisdom, and equipped only with the courage of a soldier, who punished himself for his fruitless daring; he stood and watched his own right hand falling away piecemeal on the enemy's brazier,² nor did he withdraw the dissolving limb, with its uncovered bones, until his foe removed the fire. He might have accomplished something more successful in that camp, but never anything more brave. See how much keener a brave man is to lay hold of danger than a cruel man is to inflict it: Porsenna was more ready to pardon Mucius for wishing to slay him than Mucius to pardon himself for failing to slay Porsenna!

⁶"Oh," say you, "those stories have been droned to death in all the schools; pretty soon, when you reach the topic 'On Despising Death,' you will be telling me about Cato." But why should I not tell you about Cato, how he read Plato's³ book on that last glorious night, with a sword laid at his pillow? He had provided these two requisites for his last moments,–the first, that he might have the will to die, and the second, that he might have the means. So he put his affairs in order,–as well as one could put in order that which was ruined and near its end,–and thought that he ought to see to it that no one should have the power to slay or the good fortune to save⁴ Cato. ⁷Drawing the sword,–which he had kept unstained from all bloodshed against the final day, he cried: "Fortune, you have accomplished nothing by resisting all my endeavours. I have fought, till now, for my country's freedom, and not for my own, I did not strive so doggedly to be free, but only to live among the free. Now, since the affairs of mankind are beyond hope, let Cato be withdrawn to safety." ⁸So saying, he inflicted a mortal wound upon his body. After the physicians had bound it up, Cato had less blood and less strength, but no less courage; angered now not only at Caesar but also at himself, he rallied his unarmed hands against his wound, and expelled, rather than dismissed, that noble soul which had been so defiant of all worldly power.

⁹I am not now heaping up these illustrations for the purpose of exercising my wit, but for the purpose of encouraging you to face that which is thought to be most terrible. And I shall encourage you all the more easily by showing that not only resolute men have despised that moment when the soul breathes its last, but that certain persons, who were craven in other respects, have equalled in this regard the courage of the

bravest. Take, for example, Scipio, the father-in-law of Gnaeus Pompeius: he was driven back upon the African coast by a head-wind and saw his ship in the power of the enemy. He therefore pierced his body with a sword; and when they asked where the commander was, he replied: "All is well with the commander." [10]These words brought him up to the level of his ancestors and suffered not the glory which fate gave to the Scipios in Africa[5] to lose its continuity. It was a great deed to conquer Carthage, but a greater deed to conquer death. "All is well with the commander!" Ought a general to die otherwise, especially one of Cato's generals? [11]I shall not refer you to history, or collect examples of those men who throughout the ages have despised death; for they are very many. Consider these times of ours, whose enervation and over-refinement call forth our complaints; they nevertheless will include men of every rank, of every lot in life, and of every age, who have cut short their misfortunes by death.

Believe me, Lucilius; death is so little to be feared that through its good offices nothing is to be feared. [12]Therefore, when your enemy threatens, listen unconcernedly. Although your conscience makes you confident, yet, since many things have weight which are outside your case,[6] both hope for that which is utterly just, and prepare yourself against that which is utterly unjust. Remember, however, before all else, to strip things of all that disturbs and confuses, and to see what each is at bottom; you will then comprehend that they contain nothing fearful except the actual fear. [13]That you see happening to boys happens also to ourselves, who are only slightly bigger boys: when those whom they love, with whom they daily associate, with whom they play, appear with masks on, the boys are frightened out of their wits. We should strip the mask, not only from men, but from things, and restore to each object its own aspect.

[14]"Why dost thou[7] hold up before my eyes swords, fires, and a throng of executioners raging about thee? Take away all that vain show, behind which thou lurkest and scarest fools! Ah! thou art naught but Death, whom only yesterday a manservant of mine and a maid-servant did despise! Why dost thou again unfold and spread before me, with all that great display, the whip and the rack? Why are those engines of torture made ready, one for each several member of the body, and all the other innumerable machines for tearing a man apart piecemeal? Away with all such stuff, which makes us numb with terror! And thou, silence the groans the cries, and the bitter shrieks ground out of the victim as he is torn on the rack! Forsooth thou are naught but Pain, scorned by yonder gout-ridden wretch, endured by yonder dyspeptic in the midst of his dainties, borne bravely by the girl in travail. Slight thou art, if I can bear thee; short thou art if I cannot bear thee!"

[15]Ponder these words which you have often heard and often uttered. Moreover, prove by the result whether that which you have heard and uttered is true. For there is a very disgraceful charge often brought against our school,–that we deal with the words, and not with the deeds, of philosophy.

What, have you only at this moment learned that death is hanging over your head, at this moment exile, at this moment grief? You were born to these perils. Let us think of everything that can happen as something which will happen. [16]I know that you have really done what I advise you to do; I now warn you not to drown your soul in these petty anxieties of yours; if you do, the soul will be dulled and will have too little vigour left when the time comes for it to arise. Remove the mind from this case of yours to the case of men in general. Say to yourself that our petty bodies are mortal and frail; pain can reach them from other sources than from wrong or the might of the stronger. Our pleasures themselves become torments; banquets bring indigestion, carousals paralysis of the muscles and palsy, sensual habits affect the feet, the hands, and every joint of the body.

[17]I may become a poor man; I shall then be one among many. I may be exiled; I shall then regard myself as born in the place to which I shall be sent. They may put me in chains. What then? Am I free from bonds now? Behold this clogging burden of a body, to which nature has fettered me! "I shall die," you say; you mean to say "I shall cease to run the risk of sickness; I shall cease to run the risk of imprisonment; I shall cease to run the risk of death." [18]I am not so foolish as to go through at this juncture the

arguments which Epicurus harps upon, and say that the terrors of the world below are idle,–that Ixion does not whirl round on his wheel, that Sisyphus does not shoulder his stone uphill, that a man's entrails cannot be restored and devoured every day;[8] no one is so childish as to fear Cerberus, or the shadows, or the spectral garb of those who are held together by naught but their unfleshed bones. Death either annihilates us or strips us bare. If we are then released, there remains the better part, after the burden has been withdrawn; if we are annihilated, nothing remains; good and bad are alike removed.

[19] Allow me at this point to quote a verse of yours, first suggesting that, when you wrote it, you meant it for yourself no less than for others. It is ignoble to say one thing and mean another; and how much more ignoble to write one thing and mean another! I remember one day you were handling the well-known commonplace,–that we do not suddenly fall on death, but advance towards it by slight degrees; we die every day. [20] For every day a little of our life is taken from us; even when we are growing, our life is on the wane. We lose our childhood, then our boyhood, and then our youth. Counting even yesterday, all past time is lost time; the very day which we are now spending is shared between ourselves and death. It is not the last drop that empties the water-clock, but all that which previously has flowed out; similarly, the final hour when we cease to exist does not of itself bring death; it merely of itself completes the death-process. We reach death at that moment, but we have been a long time on the way. [21] In describing this situation, you said in your customary, style (for you are always impressive, but never more pungent than when you are putting the truth in appropriate words):

> Not single is the death which comes; the death
> Which takes us off is but the last of all.

I prefer that you should read your own words rather than my letter; for then it will be clear to you that this death, of which we are afraid, is the last but not the only death. [22] I see what you are looking for; you are asking what I have packed into my letter, what inspiriting saying from some master-mind, what useful precept. So I shall send you something dealing with this very subject which has been under discussion. Epicurus[9] upbraids those who crave, as much as those who shrink from, death: "It is absurd," he says, "to run towards death because you are tired of life, when it is your manner of life that has made you run towards death." [23] And in another passage:[10] "What is so absurd as to seek death, when it is through fear of death that you have robbed your life of peace?" And you may add a third statement, of the same stamp:[11] "Men are so thoughtless, nay, so mad, that some, through fear of death, force themselves to die."

[24] Whichever of these ideas you ponder, you will strengthen your mind for the endurance alike of death and of life. For we need to be warned and strengthened in both directions,–not to love or to hate life overmuch; even when reason advises us to make an end of it, the impulse is not to be adopted without reflection or at headlong speed. [25] The grave and wise man should not beat a hasty retreat from life; he should make a becoming exit. And above all, he should avoid the weakness which has taken possession of so many,–the lust for death. For just as there is an unreflecting tendency of the mind towards other things, so, my dear Lucilius, there is an unreflecting tendency towards death; this often seizes upon the noblest and most spirited men, as well as upon the craven and the abject. The former despise life; the latter find it irksome.

[26] Others also are moved by a satiety of doing and seeing the same things, and not so much by a hatred of life as because they are cloyed with it. We slip into this condition, while philosophy itself pushes us on, and we say; "How long must I endure the same things? Shall I continue to wake and sleep, be hungry and be cloyed, shiver and perspire? There is an end to nothing; all things are connected in a sort of circle; they flee and they are pursued. Night is close at the heels of day, day at the heels of night; summer ends in autumn, winter rushes after autumn, and winter softens into spring; all nature in this way passes, only to return. I do nothing new; I see nothing new; sooner or later one sickens of this, also." There are many who think that living is not painful, but superfluous. Farewell.

Death will deliver the final judgment in your case. This is what I mean: your debates and learned talks, your maxims gathered from the teachings of the wise, your cultured conversation,–all these afford no proof of the real strength of your soul. Even the most timid man can deliver a bold speech. What you have done in the past will be manifest only at the time when you draw your last breath. I accept the terms; I do not shrink from the decision." [7]This is what I say to myself, but I would have you think that I have said it to you also. You are younger; but what does that matter? There is no fixed count of our years. You do not know where death awaits you; so be ready for it everywhere.

[8]I was just intending to stop, and my hand was making ready for the closing sentence; but the rites are still to be performed and the travelling money for the letter disbursed. And just assume that I am not telling where I intend to borrow the necessary sum; you know upon whose coffers I depend. Wait for me but a moment, and I will pay you from my own account;[3] meanwhile, Epicurus will oblige me with these words:[4] "Think on death," or rather, if you prefer the phrase, on "migration to heaven." [9]The meaning is clear,–that it is a wonderful thing to learn thoroughly how to die. You may deem it superfluous to learn a text that can be used only once; but that is just the reason why we ought to think on a thing. When we can never prove whether we really know a thing, we must always be learning it. [10]"Think on death." In saying this, he bids us think on freedom. He who has learned to die has unlearned slavery; he is above any external power, or, at any rate, he is beyond it. What terrors have prisons and bonds and bars for him? His way out is clear. There is only one chain which binds us to life, and that is the love of life. The chain may not be cast off, but it may be rubbed away, so that, when necessity shall demand, nothing may retard or hinder us from being ready to do at once that which at some time we are bound to do. Farewell.

Footnotes

1. See the twelfth letter. Seneca was by this time at least sixty-five years old, and probably older.

2. This passage is hopelessly corrupt. The course of the argument requires something like this: For it is just as much to my advantage not to be able to do what I do not want to do, as it is to be able to do whatever gives me pleasure.

3. i.e., the money will be brought from home,–the saying will be one of Seneca's own.

4. Epicurus, Frag. 205 Usener.

XXVII. ON THE GOOD WHICH ABIDES

[1]"What," say you, "are you giving me advice? Indeed, have you already advised yourself, already corrected your own faults? Is this the reason why you have leisure to reform other men?" No, I am not so shameless as to undertake to cure my fellow-men when I am ill myself. I am, however, discussing with you troubles which concern us both, and sharing the remedy with you, just as if we were lying ill in the same hospital. Listen to me, therefore, as you would if I were talking to myself. I am admitting you to my inmost thoughts, and am having it out with myself, merely making use of you as my pretext. [2]I keep crying out to myself: "Count your years, and you will be ashamed to desire and pursue the same things you desired in your boyhood days. Of this one thing make sure against your dying day,–let your faults die before you die. Away with those disordered pleasures, which must be dearly paid for; it is not only those which are to come that harm me, but also those which have come and gone. Just as crimes, even if they have not been detected when they were committed, do not allow anxiety to end with them; so with guilty pleasures, regret remains even after the pleasures are over. They are not substantial, they are not trustworthy; even if they do not harm us, they are fleeting. [3]Cast about rather for some good which will abide. But there can be no such good except as the soul discovers it for itself within itself. Virtue alone affords everlasting and peace-giving joy; even if some obstacle arise, it is but like an intervening cloud, which floats beneath the sun but never prevails against it."

'When will it be your lot to attain this joy? Thus far, you have indeed not been sluggish, but you must quicken your pace. Much toil remains; to confront it, you must yourself lavish all your waking hours, and all your efforts, if you wish the result to be accomplished. This matter cannot be delegated to someone else. ⁵The other kind of literary activity¹ admits of outside assistance. Within our own time there was a certain rich man named Calvisius Sabinus; he had the bank-account and the brains of a freed-man. ² I never saw a man whose good fortune was a greater offence against propriety. His memory was so faulty that he would sometimes forget the name of Ulysses, or Achilles, or Priam,–names which we know as well as we know those of our own at-tendants. No major-domo in his dotage, who cannot give men their right names, but is compelled to invent names for them,–no such man, I say, calls off the names³ of his master's tribesmen so atrociously as Sabinus used to call off the Trojan and Achaean heroes. But none the less did he desire to appear learned. ⁶So he devised this short cut to learning: he paid fabulous prices for slaves,–one to know Homer by heart and an-other to know Hesiod; he also delegated a special slave to each of the nine lyric poets. You need not wonder that he paid high prices for these slaves; if he did not find them ready to hand he had them made to order. After collecting this retinue, he began to make life miserable for his guests; he would keep these fellows at the foot of his couch, and ask them from time to time for verses which he might repeat, and then frequently break down in the middle of a word. ⁷Satellius Quadratus, a feeder, and consequent-ly a fawner, upon addle-pated millionaires, and also (for this quality goes with the other two) a flouter of them, suggested to Sabinus that he should have philologists to gather up the bits.⁴ Sabinus remarked that each slave cost him one hundred thousand sesterces; Satellius replied: "You might have bought as many book-cases for a smaller sum." But Sabinus held to the opinion that what any member of his household knew, he himself knew also. ⁸This same Satellius began to advise Sabinus to take wrestling lessons,–sickly, pale, and thin as he was, Sabinus answered: "How can I? I can scarce-ly stay alive now." "Don't say that, I implore you," replied the other, "consider how many perfectly healthy slaves you have!" No man is able to borrow or buy a sound mind; in fact, as it seems to me, even though sound minds were for sale, they would not find buyers. Depraved minds, however, are bought and sold every day.

⁹But let me pay off my debt and say farewell: "Real wealth is poverty adjusted to the law of Nature."⁵ Epicurus has this saying in various ways and contexts; but it can never be repeated too often, since it can never be learned too well. For some persons the remedy should be merely prescribed; in the case of others, it should be forced down their throats. Farewell.

Footnotes

1. i.e., ordinary studies, or literature, as contrasted with philosophy.

2. Compare with the following the vulgarities of Trimalchio in the Satire of Petronius, and the bad taste of Nasidienus in Horace (*Sat.* ii. 8).

3. At the *salutatio*, or morning call. The position of *nomenclator*, "caller-of-names," was originally devoted more strictly to political purposes. Here it is primarily social.

4. i.e., all the ideas that dropped out of the head of Sabinus. The slave who picked up the crumbs was called *analecta*.

5. Epicurus, Frag. 477 Usener.

XXVIII. ON TRAVEL AS A CURE FOR DISCONTENT

¹Do you suppose that you alone have had this experience? Are you surprised, as if it were a novelty, that after such long travel and so many changes of scene you have not been able to shake off the gloom and heaviness of your mind? You need a change of soul rather than a change of climate.¹ Though you may cross vast spaces of sea, and though, as our Vergil² remarks,

along the city streets and in foreign places will not help you; for this God of whom I speak, though the highest and most powerful of beings, carries all things on his own shoulders. Neither can beauty or strength make you blessed, for none of these qualities can withstand old age.

[11]What we have to seek for, then, is that which does not each day pass more and more under the control of some power which cannot be withstood.[8] And what is this? It is the soul,–but the soul that is upright, good, and great. What else could you call such a soul than a god dwelling as a guest in a human body? A soul like this may descend into a Roman knight just as well as into a freedman's son or a slave. For what is a Roman knight, or a freedmen's son, or a slave? They are mere titles, born of ambition or of wrong. One may leap to heaven from the very slums. Only rise

> And mould thyself to kinship with thy God.[9]

This moulding will not be done in gold or silver; an image that is to be in the likeness of God cannot be fashioned of such materials; remember that the gods, when they were kind unto men,[10] were moulded in clay. Farewell.

Footnotes

1. The argument is that work is not, in itself, a good; if it were, it would not be praiseworthy at one time and to be deprecated at another. It belongs, therefore, to the class of things which the Stoics call ἀδιάφορα, *indifferentia, res mediae*; cf. Cicero, *de Fin.* iii. 16.

2. Literally, "come to the end of his furrow."

3. i.e., philosophy.

4. The Great St. Bernard and Little St. Bernard routes over the Alps.

5. A mountain in Illyria, over which the Via Egnatia ran.

6. Dangerous quick-sands along the north coast of Africa.

7. The *toga praetexta*, badge of the official position of Lucilius.

8. For example, Time or Chance.

9. Vergil, *Aeneid,* viii. 364 f.

10. In the Golden Age, described in Ep. xc., when men were nearest to nature and "fresh from the gods."

XXXII. ON PROGRESS

[1]I have been asking about you, and inquiring of everyone who comes from your part of the country, what you are doing, and where you are spending your time, and with whom. You cannot deceive me; for I am with you. Live just as if I were sure to get news of your doings, nay, as if I were sure to behold them. And if you wonder what particularly pleases me that I hear concerning you, it is that I hear nothing, that most of those whom I ask do not know what you are doing.

[2]This is sound practice–to refrain from associating with men of different stamp and different aims. And I am indeed confident that you cannot be warped, that you will stick to your purpose, even though the crowd may surround and seek to distract you. What, then, is on my mind? I am not afraid lest they work a change in you; but I am afraid lest they may hinder your progress. And much harm is done even by one who holds you back, especially since life is so short; and we make it still shorter by our unsteadiness, by making ever fresh beginnings at life, now one and immediately another. We break up life into little bits, and fritter it away. [3]Hasten ahead, then, dearest Lucilius, and reflect how greatly you would quicken your speed if an enemy were at your back, or if you suspected the cavalry were approaching and pressing hard upon your steps as you fled. It is true; the enemy is indeed pressing upon you; you should therefore increase your speed and escape away and reach a safe position, remembering continually what a noble thing it is to round out your life before death comes, and then await in peace the remaining portion of your time, claiming[1] nothing for yourself,

since you are in possession of the happy life; for such a life is not made happier for being longer. 'O when shall you see the time when you shall know that time means nothing to you, when you shall be peaceful and calm, careless of the morrow, because you are enjoying your life to the full?

Would you know what makes men greedy for the future? It is because no one has yet found himself. Your parents, to be sure, asked other blessings for you; but I myself pray rather that you may despise all those things which your parents wished for you in abundance. Their prayers plunder many another person, simply that you may be enriched. Whatever they make over to you must be removed from someone else. 'I pray that you may get such control over yourself that your mind, now shaken by wandering thoughts, may at last come to rest and be steadfast, that it may be content with itself and, having attained an understanding of what things are truly good,–and they are in our possession as soon as we have this knowledge,–that it may have no need of added years. He has at length passed beyond all necessities–he has won his honourable discharge and is free,–who still lives after his life has been completed. Farewell.

Footnotes

1. The text seems to be corrupt. Hense thinks that *expectare* is to be supplied with *nihil sibi*–"To expect nothing for oneself"; but the use of the verb in two meanings would be harsh. The thought seems to be "asking for no added years"; and one suspects that the loss of a word like *adrogantem* before *nihil*.

XXXIII. ON THE FUTILITY OF LEARNING MAXIMS

[1]You wish me to close these letters also, as I closed my former letters, with certain utterances taken from the chiefs of our school. But they did not interest themselves in choice extracts; the whole texture of their work is full of strength. There is unevenness, you know, when some objects rise conspicuous above others. A single tree is not remarkable if the whole forest rises to the same height. [2]Poetry is crammed with utterances of this sort, and so is history. For this reason I would not have you think that these utterances belong to Epicurus. they are common property and are emphatically our own.[1] They are, however, more noteworthy in Epicurus, because they appear at infrequent intervals and when you do not expect them, and because it is surprising that brave words should be spoken at any time by a man who made a practice of being effeminate. For that is what most persons maintain. In my own opinion, however, Epicurus is really a brave man, even though he did wear long sleeves.[2] Fortitude, energy, and readiness for battle are to be found among the Persians,[3] just as much as among men who have girded themselves up high.

[3]Therefore, you need not call upon me for extracts and quotations; such thoughts as one may extract here and there in the works of other philosophers run through the whole body of our writings. Hence we have no "show-window goods," nor do we deceive the purchaser in such a way that, if he enters our shop, he will find nothing except that which is displayed in the window. We allow the purchasers themselves to get their samples from anywhere they please. [4]Suppose we should desire to sort out each separate motto from the general stock; to whom shall we credit them? To Zeno, Cleanthes, Chrysippus, Panaetius, or Posidonius? We Stoics are not subjects of a despot: each of us lays claim to his own freedom. With them,[4] on the other hand, whatever Hermarchus says or Metrodorus, is ascribed to one source. In that brotherhood, everything that any man utters is spoken under the leadership and commanding authority [5] of one alone. We cannot, I maintain, no matter how we try, pick out anything from so great a multitude of things equally good.

Only the poor man counts his flock.[6]

Wherever you direct your gaze, you will meet with something that might stand out from the rest, if the context in which you read it were not equally notable.

ever portion of my strength has yielded to age will return to me from your strength, although there is not so very much difference in our ages. [3]But yet I wish to rejoice in the accomplished fact. We feel a joy over those whom we love, even when separated from them, but such a joy is light and fleeting; the sight of a man, and his presence, and communion with him, afford something of living pleasure; this is true, at any rate, if one not only sees the man one desires, but the sort of man one desires. Give yourself to me, therefore, as a gift of great price, and, that you may strive the more, reflect that you yourself are mortal, and that I am old. [4]Hasten to find me, but hasten to find yourself first. Make progress, and, before all else, endeavour to be consistent with yourself. And when you would find out whether you have accomplished anything, consider whether you desire the same things today that you desired yesterday. A shifting of the will indicates that the mind is at sea, heading in various directions, according to the course of the wind. But that which is settled and solid does not wander from its place. This is the blessed lot of the completely wise man, and also, to a certain extent, of him who is progressing and has made some headway. Now what is the difference between these two classes of men? The one is in motion, to be sure, but does not change its position; it merely tosses up and down where it is; the other is not in motion at all. Farewell.

Footnotes

1. The question of Lucilius represents the popular view, which regards love as including friendship. But according to Seneca it is only the perfect love, from which all selfishness has been removed, that becomes identical with friendship.

XXXVI. ON THE VALUE OF RETIREMENT

[1]Encourage your friend to despise stout-heartedly those who upbraid him because he has sought the shade of retirement and has abdicated his career of honours, and, though he might have attained more, has preferred tranquillity to them all. Let him prove daily to these detractors how wisely he has looked out for his own interests. Those whom men envy will continue to march past him; some will be pushed out of the ranks, and others will fall. Prosperity is a turbulent thing; it torments itself. It stirs the brain in more ways than one, goading men on to various aims,–some to power, and others to high living. Some it puffs up; others it slackens and wholly enervates.

[2]"But," the retort comes, "so-and-so carries his prosperity well." Yes; just as he carries his liquor. So you need not let this class of men persuade you that one who is besieged by the crowd is happy; they run to him as crowds rush for a pool of water, rendering it muddy while they drain it. But you say: "Men call our friend a trifler and a sluggard." There are men, you know, whose speech is awry, who use the contrary[1] terms. They called him happy; what of it? Was he happy? [3]Even the fact that to certain persons he seems a man of a very rough and gloomy cast of mind, does not trouble me. Aristo[2] used to say that he preferred a youth of stern disposition to one who was a jolly fellow and agreeable to the crowd. "For," he added, "wine which, when new, seemed harsh and sour, becomes good wine; but that which tasted well at the vintage cannot stand age." So let them call him stern and a foe to his own advancement, it is just this sternness that will go well when it is aged, provided only that he continues to cherish virtue and to absorb thoroughly the studies which make for culture,–not those with which it is sufficient for a man to sprinkle himself, but those in which the mind should be steeped. [4]Now is the time to learn. "What? Is there any time when a man should not learn?" By no means; but just as it is creditable for every age to study, so it is not creditable for every age to be instructed. An old man learning his A B C is a disgraceful and absurd object; the young man must store up, the old man must use. You will therefore be doing a thing most helpful to yourself if you make this friend of yours as good a man as possible; those kindnesses, they tell us, are to be both sought for and bestowed, which benefit the giver no less than the receiver; and they are unquestionably the best kind.

[5]Finally, he has no longer any freedom in the matter; he has pledged his word. And

it is less disgraceful to compound with a creditor than to compound with a promising future. To pay his debt of money, the business man must have a prosperous voyage, the farmer must have fruitful fields and kindly weather; but the debt which your friend owes can be completely paid by mere goodwill. [6]Fortune has no jurisdiction over character. Let him so regulate his character that in perfect peace he may bring to perfection that spirit within him which feels neither loss nor gain, but remains in the same attitude, no matter how things fall out. A spirit like this, if it is heaped with worldly goods, rises superior to its wealth; if, on the other hand, chance has stripped him of a part of his wealth, or even all, it is not impaired.

[7]If your friend had been born in Parthia, he would have begun, when a child, to bend the bow; if in Germany, he would forthwith have been brandishing his slender spear; if he had been born in the days of our forefathers, he would have learned to ride a horse and smite his enemy hand to hand. These are the occupations which the system of each race recommends to the individual,–yes, prescribes for him. [8]To what, then, shall this friend[3] of yours devote his attention? I say, let him learn that which is helpful against all weapons, against every kind of foe,–contempt of death; because no one doubts that death has in it something that inspires terror, so that it shocks even our souls, which nature has so moulded that they love their own existence; for otherwise[4] there would be no need to prepare ourselves, and to whet our courage, to face that towards which we should move with a sort of voluntary instinct, precisely as all men tend to preserve their existence. [9]No man learns a thing in order that, if necessity arises, he may lie down with composure upon a bed of roses; but he steels his courage to this end, that he may not surrender his plighted faith to torture, and that, if need be, he may some day stay out his watch in the trenches, even though wounded, without even leaning on his spear; because sleep is likely to creep over men who support themselves by any prop whatsoever.

In death there is nothing harmful; for there must exist something to which it is harmful.[5] [10]And yet, if you are possessed by so great a craving for a longer life, reflect that none of the objects which vanish from our gaze and are re-absorbed into the world of things, from which they have come forth and are soon to come forth again, is annihilated; they merely end their course and do not perish. And death, which we fear and shrink from, merely interrupts life, but does not steal it away; the time will return when we shall be restored to the light of day; and many men would object to this, were they not brought back in forgetfulness of the past.

[11]But I mean to show you later,[6] with more care, that everything which seems to perish merely changes. Since you are destined to return, you ought to depart with a tranquil mind. Mark how the round of the universe repeats its course; you will see that no star in our firmament is extinguished, but that they all set and rise in alternation. Summer has gone, but another year will bring it again; winter lies low, but will be restored by its own proper months; night has overwhelmed the sun, but day will soon rout the night again. The wandering stars retrace their former courses; a part of the sky is rising unceasingly, and a part is sinking. [12]One word more, and then I shall stop; infants, and boys, and those who have gone mad, have no fear of death, and it is most shameful if reason cannot afford us that peace of mind to which they have been brought by their folly. Farewell.

Footnotes

1. i.e., they are no more correct now, when they called him a trifler, than they were before, when they called him happy.

2. Aristo of Chios, Frag. 388 von Armin.

3. As a Roman, living in an age when philosophy was recommended and prescribed.

4. i.e., if death inspired no terror.

5. And since after death we do not exist, death cannot be harmful to us. Seneca has in mind the argument of Epicurus (Diogenes Laertius, x. 124-5): "Therefore the most dread-inspiring of all evils, death, is nothing to us; for when we exist; death is not present in us, and when death is present, then we do not exist. Therefore it does not concern

become indispensable. And so they are the slaves of their pleasures instead of enjoying them; they even love their own ills,[4]–and that is the worst ill of all! Then it is that the height of unhappiness is reached, when men are not only attracted, but even pleased, by shameful things, and when there is no longer any room for a cure, now that those things which once were vices have become habits. Farewell.

Footnotes

1. The regular method of studying philosophy was, as we infer from this letter, a course of reading in the philosophers. Seneca deprecates the use of the "cram" which is only a memory-help, as a substitute for reading, on the ground that by its use one does not, in the first place, learn the subject, and, in the second place and chiefly, that one loses the inspiration to be derived by direct contact with great thinkers. The request of Lucilius for a cram thus suggests the main topic of the letter, which is taken up in the second paragraph.

2. i.e., the word *breviarium*, "abridgment," "abstract," has displaced the better word *summarium*, "outline of chief points."

3. i.e., to do the reading and to review it by means of the summary. The reading will enable Lucilius to identify for himself the authors of the several passages or doctrines.

4. i.e., their pleasures. These ills, by being cultivated, become vices.

XL. ON THE PROPER STYLE FOR A PHILOSOPHER'S DISCOURSE

[1]I thank you for writing to me so often; for you are revealing your real self to me in the only way you can. I never receive a letter from you without being in your company forthwith. If the pictures of our absent friends are pleasing to us, though they only re-fresh the memory and lighten our longing by a solace that is unreal and unsubstantial, how much more pleasant is a letter, which brings us real traces, real evidences, of an absent friend! For that which is sweetest when we meet face to face is afforded by the impress of a friend's hand upon his letter,–recognition.

[2]You write me that you heard a lecture by the philosopher Serapio,[1] when he land-ed at your present place of residence. "He is wont," you say, "to wrench up his words with a mighty rush, and he does not let them flow forth one by one, but makes them crowd and dash upon each other.[2] For the words come in such quantity that a single voice is inadequate to utter them." I do not approve of this in a philosopher; his speech, like his life, should be composed; and nothing that rushes headlong and is hurried is well ordered. That is why, in Homer, the rapid style, which sweeps down without a break like a snow-squall, is assigned to the younger speaker; from the old man elo-quence flows gently, sweeter than honey.[3]

[3]Therefore, mark my words; that forceful manner of speech, rapid and copious, is more suited to a mountebank than to a man who is discussing and teaching an import-ant and serious subject. But I object just as strongly that he should drip out his words as that he should go at top speed; he should neither keep the ear on the stretch, nor deafen it. For that poverty-stricken and thin-spun style also makes the audience less attentive because they are weary of its stammering slowness; nevertheless, the word which has been long awaited sinks in more easily than the word which flits past us on the wing. Finally, people speak of "handing down" precepts to their pupils; but one is not "handing down" that which eludes the grasp. [4]Besides, speech that deals with the truth should be unadorned and plain. This popular style has nothing to do with the truth; its aim is to impress the common herd, to ravish heedless ears by its speed; it does not offer itself for discussion, but snatches itself away from discussion. But how can that speech govern others which cannot itself be governed? May I not also remark that all speech which is employed for the purpose of healing our minds, ought to sink into us? Remedies do not avail unless they remain in the system.

[5]Besides, this sort of speech contains a great deal of sheer emptiness; it has more sound than power. My terrors should be quieted, my irritations soothed, my illusions

shaken off, my indulgences checked, my greed rebuked. And which of these cures can be brought about in a hurry? What physician can heal his patient on a flying visit? May I add that such a jargon of confused and ill-chosen words cannot afford pleasure, either? [6]No; but just as you are well satisfied, in the majority of cases, to have seen through tricks which you did not think could possibly be done,[4] so in the case of these word-gymnasts to have heard them once is amply sufficient. For what can a man desire to learn or to imitate in them? What is he to think of their souls, when their speech is sent into the charge in utter disorder, and cannot be kept in hand? [7]Just as, when you run down hill, you cannot stop at the point where you had decided to stop, but your steps are carried along by the momentum of your body and are borne beyond the place where you wished to halt; so this speed of speech has no control over itself, nor is it seemly for philosophy; since philosophy should carefully place her words, not fling them out, and should proceed step by step.

[8]"What then?" you say; "should not philosophy sometimes take a loftier tone?" Of course she should; but dignity of character should be preserved, and this is stripped away by such violent and excessive force. Let philosophy possess great forces, but kept well under control; let her stream flow unceasingly, but never become a torrent. And I should hardly allow even to an orator a rapidity of speech like this, which cannot be called back, which goes lawlessly ahead; for how could it be followed by jurors, who are often inexperienced and untrained? Even when the orator is carried away by his desire to show off his powers, or by uncontrollable emotion, even then he should not quicken his pace and heap up words to an extent greater than the ear can endure.

[9]You will be acting rightly, therefore, if you do not regard those men who seek how much they may say, rather than how they shall say it, and if for yourself you choose, provided a choice must be made, to speak as Publius Vinicius the stammerer does. When Asellius was asked how Vinicius spoke, he replied: "Gradually"! (It was a remark of Geminus Varius, by the way: "I don't see how you can call that man 'eloquent'; why, he can't get out three words together.") Why, then, should you not choose to speak as Vinicius does? [10]Though of course some wag may cross your path, like the person who said, when Vinicius was dragging out his words one by one, as if he were dictating and not speaking. "Say, haven't you anything to say?" And yet that were the better choice, for the rapidity of Quintus Haterius, the most famous orator of his age, is, in my opinion, to be avoided by a man of sense. Haterius never hesitated, never paused; he made only one start, and only one stop.

[11]However, I suppose that certain styles of speech are more or less suitable to nations also; in a Greek you can put up with the unrestrained style, but we Romans, even when writing, have become accustomed to separate our words.[5] And our compatriot Cicero, with whom Roman oratory sprang into prominence, was also a slow pacer.[6] The Roman language is more inclined to take stock of itself, to weigh, and to offer something worth weighing. [12]Fabianus, a man noteworthy because of his life, his knowledge, and, less important than either of these, his eloquence also, used to discuss a subject with dispatch rather than with haste; hence you might call it ease rather than speed. I approve this quality in the wise man; but I do not demand it; only let his speech proceed unhampered, though I prefer that it should be deliberately uttered rather than spouted.

[13]However, I have this further reason for frightening you away from the latter malady, namely, that you could only be successful in practising this style by losing your sense of modesty; you would have to rub all shame from your countenance,[7] and refuse to hear yourself speak. For that heedless flow will carry with it many expressions which you would wish to criticize. [14]And, I repeat, you could not attain it and at the same time preserve your sense of shame. Moreover, you would need to practise every day, and transfer your attention from subject matter to words. But words, even if they came to you readily and flowed without any exertion on your part, yet would have to be kept under control. For just as a less ostentatious gait becomes a philosopher, so does a restrained style of speech, far removed from boldness. Therefore, the ultimate kernel of my remarks is this: I bid you be slow of speech. Farewell

Footnotes

1. This person cannot be identified.

2. The explanation of Professor Summers seems sound, that the metaphor is taken from a mountain-torrent. Compare the description of Cratinus' style in Aristophanes, *Ach.* 526, or that of Pindar in Horace, *Od.* iv. 2. 5 ff.

3. *Iliad*, iii. 222 (Odysseus), and i. 249 (Nestor).

4. Seneca's phrase, *quae fieri posse non crederes*, has been interpreted as a definition of παράδοξα. It is more probable, however, that he is comparing with the juggler's tricks the verbal performances of certain lecturers, whose jargon one marvels at but does not care to hear again.

5. The Greek texts were still written without separation of the words, in contrast with the Roman.

6. *Gradarius* may be contrasted with *tolutarius*, "trotter." The word might also mean one who walks with dignified step, as in a religious procession.

7. Cf. Martial, xi. 27. 7 *aut cum perfricuit frontem posuitque pudorem*. After a violent rubbing, the face would not show blushes.

XLI. ON THE GOD WITHIN US

[1]You are doing an excellent thing, one which will be wholesome for you, if, as you write me, you are persisting in your effort to attain sound understanding; it is foolish to pray for this when you can acquire it from yourself. We do not need to uplift our hands towards heaven, or to beg the keeper of a temple to let us approach his idol's ear, as if in this way our prayers were more likely to be heard. God is near you, he is with you, he is within you. [2]This is what I mean, Lucilius: a holy spirit indwells within us, one who marks our good and bad deeds, and is our guardian. As we treat this spirit, so are we treated by it. Indeed, no man can be good without the help of God. Can one rise superior to fortune unless God helps him to rise? He it is that gives noble and upright counsel. In each good man

> A god doth dwell, but what god know we not.[1]

[3]If ever you have come upon a grove that is full of ancient trees which have grown to an unusual height, shutting out a view of the sky by a veil of pleached and intertwining branches, then the loftiness of the forest, the seclusion of the spot, and your marvel at the thick unbroken shade in the midst of the open spaces, will prove to you the presence of deity. Or if a cave, made by the deep crumbling of the rocks, holds up a mountain on its arch, a place not built with hands but hollowed out into such spaciousness by natural causes, your soul will be deeply moved by a certain intimation of the existence of God. We worship the sources of mighty rivers; we erect altars at places where great streams burst suddenly from hidden sources; we adore springs of hot water as divine, and consecrate certain pools because of their dark waters or their immeasurable depth. [4]If you see a man who is unterrified in the midst of dangers, untouched by desires, happy in adversity, peaceful amid the storm, who looks down upon men from a higher plane, and views the gods on a footing of equality, will not a feeling of reverence for him steal over you, will you not say: "This quality is too great and too lofty to be regarded as resembling this petty body in which it dwells? A divine power has descended upon that man." [5]When a soul rises superior to other souls, when it is under control, when it passes through every experience as if it were of small account, when it smiles at our fears and at our prayers, it is stirred by a force from heaven. A thing like this cannot stand upright unless it be propped by the divine. Therefore, a greater part of it abides in that place from whence it came down to earth. Just as the rays of the sun do indeed touch the earth, but still abide at the source from which they are sent; even so the great and hallowed soul, which has come down in order that we may have a nearer knowledge of divinity, does indeed associate with us, but still cleaves to its origin; on that source it depends, thither it turns its gaze and strives to go,

and it concerns itself with our doings only as a being superior to ourselves.

⁶What, then, is such a soul? One which is resplendent with no external good, but only with its own. For what is more foolish than to praise in a man the qualities which come from without? And what is more insane than to marvel at characteristics which may at the next instant be passed on to someone else? A golden bit does not make a better horse. The lion with gilded mane, in process of being trained and forced by weariness to endure the decoration, is sent into the arena in quite a different way from the wild lion whose spirit is unbroken; the latter, indeed, bold in his attack, as nature wished him to be, impressive because of his wild appearance,–and it is his glory that none can look upon him without fear,–is favoured[2] in preference to the other lion, that languid and gilded brute.

⁷No man ought to glory except in that which is his own. We praise a vine if it makes the shoots teem with increase, if by its weight it bends to the ground the very poles which hold its fruit; would any man prefer to this vine one from which golden grapes and golden leaves hang down? In a vine the virtue peculiarly its own is fertility; in man also we should praise that which is his own. Suppose that he has a retinue of comely slaves and a beautiful house, that his farm is large and large his income; none of these things is in the man himself; they are all on the outside. ⁸Praise the quality in him which cannot be given or snatched away, that which is the peculiar property of the man. Do you ask what this is? It is soul, and reason brought to perfection in the soul. For man is a reasoning animal. Therefore, man's highest good is attained, if he has fulfilled the good for which nature designed him at birth. ⁹And what is it which this reason demands of him? The easiest thing in the world,–to live in accordance with his own nature. But this is turned into a hard task by the general madness of mankind; we push one another into vice. And how can a man be recalled to salvation, when he has none to restrain him, and all mankind to urge him on? Farewell.

Footnotes

1. Vergil, *Aeneid*, viii. 352, *Hoc nemus, hune, inquit, frondoso vertice collem, Quis deus incertum est, habitat deus,* and cf. Quintillian, i. 10. 88, where he is speaking of Ennius, whom *"sicut sacros vetustate lucos adoremus, in quibus grandia et antiqua robora iam non tantum habent speciem quantem religionem."*

2. The spectators of the fight, which is to take place between the two lions, applaud the wild lion and bet on him.

XLII. ON VALUES

¹Has that friend of yours already made you believe that he is a good man? And yet it is impossible in so short a time for one either to become good or be known as such.[1] Do you know what kind of man I now mean when I speak of "a good man"? I mean one of the second grade, like your friend. For one of the first class perhaps springs into existence, like the phoenix, only once in five hundred years. And it is not surprising, either, that greatness develops only at long intervals; Fortune often brings into being commonplace powers, which are born to please the mob; but she holds up for our approval that which is extraordinary by the very fact that she makes it rare.

²This man, however, of whom you spoke, is still far from the state which he professes to have reached. And if he knew what it meant to be "a good man," he would not yet believe himself such; perhaps he would even despair of his ability to become good. "But," you say, "he thinks ill of evil men." Well, so do evil men themselves; and there is no worse penalty for vice than the fact that it is dissatisfied with itself and all its fellows. ³"But he hates those who make an ungoverned use of great power suddenly acquired." I retort that he will do the same thing as soon as he acquires the same powers. In the case of many men, their vices, being powerless, escape notice; although, as soon as the persons in question have become satisfied with their own strength, the vices will be no less daring than those which prosperity has already disclosed. ⁴These men simply lack the means whereby they may unfold their wickedness. Similarly, one

anything that can make life happy, it is good on its own merits; for it cannot degenerate into evil. [7]Where, then, lies the mistake, since all men crave the happy life? It is that they regard the means for producing happiness as happiness itself, and, while seeking happiness, they are really fleeing from it. For although the sum and substance of the happy life is unalloyed freedom from care, and though the secret of such freedom is unshaken confidence, yet men gather together that which causes worry, and, while travelling life's treacherous road, not only have burdens to bear, but even draw burdens to themselves; hence they recede farther and farther from the achievement of that which they seek, and the more effort they expend, the more they hinder themselves and are set back. This is what happens when you hurry through a maze; the faster you go, the worse you are entangled. Farewell.

Footnotes

1. Alluding to seats reserved for the knights at the theatre.

2. Plato, *Theaetetus*, p. 174 E.

3. Compare with the whole argument Menander, Frag. 533 Kock, ending: ὃς ἂν εὖ γεγονὼς ᾖ τῇ φύσει πρὸς τἀγαθά, κἂν Αἰθίοψ ᾖ, μῆτερ, ἐστὶν εὐγενής.

XLV. ON SOPHISTICAL ARGUMENTATION

[1]You complain that in your part of the world there is a scant supply of books. But it is quality, rather than quantity, that matters; a limited list of reading benefits; a varied assortment serves only for delight. He who would arrive at the appointed end must follow a single road and not wander through many ways. What you suggest is not travelling; it is mere tramping.

[2]"But," you say, "I should rather have you give me advice than books." Still, I am ready to send you all the books I have, to ransack the whole storehouse. If it were possible, I should join you there myself; and were it not for the hope that you will soon complete your term of office, I should have imposed upon myself this old man's journey; no Scylla or Charybdis or their storied straits could have frightened me away. I should not only have crossed over, but should have been willing to swim over those waters, provided that I could greet you and judge in your presence how much you had grown in spirit.

[3]Your desire, however, that I should dispatch to you my own writings does not make me think myself learned, any more than a request for my picture would flatter my beauty. I know that it is due to your charity rather than to your judgment. And even if it is the result of judgment, it was charity that forced the judgment upon you. [4]But whatever the quality of my works may be, read them as if I were still seeking, and were not aware of, the truth, and were seeking it obstinately, too. For I have sold myself to no man; I bear the name of no master. I give much credit to the judgment of great men; but I claim something also for my own. For these men, too, have left to us, not positive discoveries, but problems whose solution is still to be sought. They might perhaps have discovered the essentials, had they not sought the superfluous also. [5]They lost much time in quibbling about words and in sophistical argumentation; all that sort of thing exercises the wit to no purpose. We tie knots and bind up words in double meanings, and then try to untie them.

Have we leisure enough for this? Do we already know how to live, or die? We should rather proceed with our whole souls towards the point where it is our duty to take heed lest things, as well as words, deceive us. [6]Why, pray, do you discriminate between similar words, when nobody is ever deceived by them except during the discussion? It is things that lead us astray: it is between things that you must discriminate. We embrace evil instead of good; we pray for something opposite to that which we have prayed for in the past. Our prayers clash with our prayers, our plans with our plans. [7]How closely flattery resembles friendship! It not only apes friendship, but outdoes it, passing it in the race; with wide-open and indulgent ears it is welcomed and sinks to the depths of the heart, and it is pleasing precisely wherein it does harm. Show me how I may be able to see through this resemblance! An enemy comes to me full of compliments, in the guise of a friend. Vices creep into our hearts under the name of virtues, rashness lurks beneath the appellation of bravery, moderation is called slug-gishness, and the coward is regarded as prudent; there is great danger if we go astray in these matters. So stamp them with special labels.

[8]Then, too, the man who is asked whether he has horns on his head[1] is not such a fool as to feel for them on his forehead, nor again so silly or dense that you can per-suade him by means of argumentation, no matter how subtle, that he does not know the facts. Such quibbles are just as harmlessly deceptive as the juggler's cup and dice, in which it is the very trickery that pleases me. But show me how the trick is done, and I have lost my interest therein. And I hold the same opinion about these tricky word-plays; for by what other name can one call such sophistries? Not to know them does no harm, and mastering them does no good. [9]At any rate, if you wish to sift doubtful meanings of this kind, teach us that the happy man is not he whom the crowd deems happy, namely, he into whose coffers mighty sums have flowed, but he whose possessions are all in his soul, who is upright and exalted, who spurns inconstancy, who sees no man with whom he wishes to change places, who rates men only at their value as men, who takes Nature for his teacher, conforming to her laws and living as she commands, whom no violence can deprive of his possessions, who turns evil into good, is unerring in judgment, unshaken, unafraid, who may be moved by force but never moved to distraction, whom Fortune when she hurls at him with all her might the deadliest missile in her armoury, may graze, though rarely, but never wound. For Fortune's other missiles, with which she vanquishes mankind in general, rebound from such a one, like hail which rattles on the roof with no harm to the dweller therein, and then melts away.

[10]Why do you bore me with that which you yourself call the "liar fallacy,"[2] about which so many books have been written? Come now, suppose that my whole life is a lie; prove that to be wrong and, if you are sharp enough, bring that back to the truth. At present it holds things to be essential of which the greater part is superfluous. And even that which is not superfluous is of no significance in respect to its power of mak-ing one fortunate and blest. For if a thing be necessary, it does not follow that it is a good. Else we degrade the meaning of "good," if we apply that name to bread and bar-ley-porridge and other commodities without which we cannot live. [11]The good must in every case be necessary; but that which is necessary is not in every case a good, since certain very paltry things are indeed necessary. No one is to such an extent ignorant of the noble meaning of the word "good," as to debase it to the level of these humdrum utilities.

[12]What, then? Shall you not rather transfer your efforts to making it clear to all men that the search for the superfluous means a great outlay of time, and that many have gone through life merely accumulating the instruments of life? Consider individuals, survey men in general; there is none whose life does not look forward to the morrow. [13]"What harm is there in this," you ask? Infinite harm; for such persons do not live, but are preparing to live. They postpone everything. Even if we paid strict attention, life would soon get ahead of us; but as we are now, life finds us lingering and passes us by as if it belonged to another, and though it ends on the final day, it perishes every day.

But I must not exceed the bounds of a letter, which ought not to fill the read-er's left hand.[3] So I shall postpone to another day our case against the hair-splitters, those over-subtle fellows who make argumentation supreme instead of subordinate. Farewell.

Footnotes

1. Cf. Gellius, xviii. 2. 9 *quod non perdidisti, habes; cornua non perdidisti; habes igitur cornua;* cf. also Seneca, Ep. xlviii.

2. e.g. Gellius, xviii. 2. 10 *cum mentior et mentiri me dico, mentior an verum dico?*

3. A book was unrolled with the right hand; the reader gathered up the part already

perused with the left hand. Nearly all books at this time were papyrus rolls, as were letters of any great length.

XLVI. ON A NEW BOOK BY LUCILIUS

[1]I received the book of yours which you promised me. I opened it hastily with the idea of glancing over it at leisure; for I meant only to taste the volume. But by its own charm the book coaxed me into traversing it more at length. You may understand from this fact how eloquent it was; for it seemed to be written in the smooth style,[1] and yet did not resemble your handiwork or mine, but at first sight might have been ascribed to Titus Livius or to Epicurus. Moreover, I was so impressed and carried along by its charm that I finished it without any postponement. The sunlight called to me, hunger warned, and clouds were lowering; but I absorbed the book from beginning to end.

[2]I was not merely pleased; I rejoiced. So full of wit and spirit it was! I should have added "force," had the book contained moments of repose, or had it risen to energy only at intervals. But I found that there was no burst of force, but an even flow, a style that was vigorous and chaste. Nevertheless I noticed from time to time your sweetness, and here and there that mildness of yours. Your style is lofty and noble; I want you to keep to this manner and this direction. Your subject also contributed something; for this reason you should choose productive topics, which will lay hold of the mind and arouse it.

[3]I shall discuss the book more fully after a second perusal; meantime, my judgment is somewhat unsettled, just as if I had heard it read aloud, and had not read it myself. You must allow me to examine it also. You need not be afraid; you shall hear the truth. Lucky fellow, to offer a man no opportunity to tell you lies at such long range! Unless perhaps, even now, when excuses for lying are taken away, custom serves as an excuse for our telling each other lies! Farewell.

Footnotes

1. Possibly *levis* in the sense of *light*, referring to size.

XLVII. ON MASTER AND SLAVE

[1]I am glad to learn, through those who come from you, that you live on friendly terms with your slaves. This befits a sensible and well-educated man like yourself. "They are slaves," people declare.[1] Nay, rather they are men. "Slaves!" No, comrades. "Slaves!" No, they are unpretentious friends. "Slaves!" No, they are our fellow-slaves, if one reflects that Fortune has equal rights over slaves and free men alike.

[2]That is why I smile at those who think it degrading for a man to dine with his slave. But why should they think it degrading? It is only because purse-proud etiquette surrounds a householder at his dinner with a mob of standing slaves. The master eats more than he can hold, and with monstrous greed loads his belly until it is stretched and at length ceases to do the work of a belly; so that he is at greater pains to discharge all the food than he was to stuff it down. [3]All this time the poor slaves may not move their lips, even to speak. The slightest murmur is repressed by the rod; even a chance sound,–a cough, a sneeze, or a hiccup,–is visited with the lash. There is a grievous penalty for the slightest breach of silence. All night long they must stand about, hungry and dumb.

[4]The result of it all is that these slaves, who may not talk in their master's presence, talk about their master. But the slaves of former days, who were permitted to converse not only in their master's presence, but actually with him, whose mouths were not

stitched up tight, were ready to bare their necks for their master, to bring upon their own heads any danger that threatened him; they spoke at the feast, but kept silence during torture. ⁵Finally, the saying, in allusion to this same high-handed treatment, becomes current: "As many enemies as you have slaves." They are not enemies when we acquire them; we make them enemies.

I shall pass over other cruel and inhuman conduct towards them; for we maltreat them, not as if they were men, but as if they were beasts of burden. When we recline at a banquet, one slave mops up the disgorged food, another crouches beneath the table and gathers up the left-overs of the tipsy guests. ⁶Another carves the priceless game birds; with unerring strokes and skilled hand he cuts choice morsels along the breast or the rump. Hapless fellow, to live only for the purpose of cutting fat capons correctly–unless, indeed, the other man is still more unhappy than he, who teaches this art for pleasure's sake, rather than he who learns it because he must. ⁷Another, who serves the wine, must dress like a woman and wrestle with his advancing years; he cannot get away from his boyhood; he is dragged back to it; and though he has already acquired a soldier's figure, he is kept beardless by having his hair smoothed away or plucked out by the roots, and he must remain awake throughout the night, dividing his time between his master's drunkenness and his lust; in the chamber he must be a man, at the feast a boy.² ⁸Another, whose duty it is to put a valuation on the guests, must stick to his task, poor fellow, and watch to see whose flattery and whose immodesty, whether of appetite or of language, is to get them an invitation for to-morrow. Think also of the poor purveyors of food, who note their masters' tastes with delicate skill, who know what special flavours will sharpen their appetite, what will please their eyes, what new combinations will rouse their cloyed stomachs, what food will excite their loathing through sheer satiety, and what will stir them to hunger on that particular day. With slaves like these the master cannot bear to dine; he would think it beneath his dignity to associate with his slave at the same table! Heaven forfend!

But how many masters is he creating in these very men! ⁹I have seen standing in the line, before the door of Callistus, the former master,³ of Callistus; I have seen the master himself shut out while others were welcomed,–the master who once fastened the "For Sale" ticket on Callistus and put him in the market along with the good-for-nothing slaves. But he has been paid off by that slave who was shuffled into the first lot of those on whom the crier practises his lungs; the slave, too, in his turn has cut his name from the list and in his turn has adjudged him unfit to enter his house. The master sold Callistus, but how much has Callistus made his master pay for!

¹⁰Kindly remember that he whom you call your slave sprang from the same stock, is smiled upon by the same skies, and on equal terms with yourself breathes, lives, and dies. It is just as possible for you to see in him a free-born man as for him to see in you a slave. As a result of the massacres in Marius's⁴ day, many a man of distinguished birth, who was taking the first steps toward senatorial rank by service in the army, was humbled by fortune, one becoming a shepherd, another a caretaker of a country cottage. Despise, then, if you dare, those to whose estate you may at any time descend, even when you are despising them.

¹¹I do not wish to involve myself in too large a question, and to discuss the treatment of slaves, towards whom we Romans are excessively haughty, cruel, and insulting. But this is the kernel of my advice: Treat your inferiors as you would be treated by your betters. And as often as you reflect how much power you have over a slave, remember that your master has just as much power over you. ¹²"But I have no master," you say. You are still young; perhaps you will have one. Do you not know at what age Hecuba entered captivity, or Croesus, or the mother of Darius, or Plato, or Diogenes?⁵

¹³Associate with your slave on kindly, even on affable, terms; let him talk with you, plan with you, live with you. I know that at this point all the exquisites will cry out against me in a body; they will say: "There is nothing more debasing, more disgraceful, than this." But these are the very persons whom I sometimes surprise kissing the hands of other men's slaves. ¹⁴Do you not see even this, how our ancestors removed from masters everything invidious, and from slaves everything insulting? They called

the master "father of the household," and the slaves "members of the household," a custom which still holds in the mime. They established a holiday on which masters and slaves should eat together,—not as the only day for this custom, but as obligatory on that day in any case. They allowed the slaves to attain honours in the household and to pronounce judgment;[6] they held that a household was a miniature commonwealth.

[15] "Do you mean to say," comes the retort, "that I must seat all my slaves at my own table?" No, not any more than that you should invite all free men to it. You are mistaken if you think that I would bar from my table certain slaves whose duties are more humble, as, for example, yonder muleteer or yonder herdsman; I propose to value them according to their character, and not according to their duties. Each man acquires his character for himself, but accident assigns his duties. Invite some to your table because they deserve the honor, and others that they may come to deserve it. For if there is any slavish quality in them as the result of their low associations, it will be shaken off by intercourse with men of gentler breeding. [16] You need not, my dear Lucilius, hunt for friends only in the forum or in the Senate-house; if you are careful and attentive, you will find them at home also. Good material often stands idle for want of an artist; make the experiment, and you will find it so. As he is a fool who, when purchasing a horse, does not consider the animal's points, but merely his saddle and bridle; so he is doubly a fool who values a man from his clothes or from his rank, which indeed is only a robe that clothes us.

[17] "He is a slave." His soul, however, may be that of a freeman. "He is a slave." But shall that stand in his way? Show me a man who is not a slave; one is a slave to lust, another to greed, another to ambition, and all men are slaves to fear. I will name you an ex-consul who is slave to an old hag, a millionaire who is slave to a serving-maid; I will show you youths of the noblest birth in serfdom to pantomime players! No servitude is more disgraceful than that which is self-imposed.

You should therefore not be deterred by these finicky persons from showing yourself to your slaves as an affable person and not proudly superior to them; they ought to respect you rather than fear you. [18] Some may maintain that I am now offering the liberty-cap to slaves in general and toppling down lords from their high estate, because I bid slaves respect their masters instead of fearing them. They say: "This is what he plainly means: slaves are to pay respect as if they were clients or early-morning callers!" Anyone who holds this opinion forgets that what is enough for a god cannot be too little for a master. Respect means love, and love and fear cannot be mingled. [19] So I hold that you are entirely right in not wishing to be feared by your slaves, and in lashing them merely with the tongue; only dumb animals need the thong.

That which annoys us does not necessarily injure us; but we are driven into wild rage by our luxurious lives, so that whatever does not answer our whims arouses our anger. [20] We don the temper of kings. For they, too, forgetful alike of their own strength and of other men's weakness, grow white-hot with rage, as if they had received an injury, when they are entirely protected from danger of such injury by their exalted station. They are not unaware that this is true, but by finding fault they seize upon opportunities to do harm; they insist that they have received injuries, in order that they may inflict them.

[21] I do not wish to delay you longer; for you need no exhortation. This, among other things, is a mark of good character: it forms its own judgments and abides by them; but badness is fickle and frequently changing, not for the better, but for something different. Farewell.

Footnotes

1. Much of the following is quoted by Macrobius, *Sat.* i. 11. 7 ff., in the passage beginning *vis tu cogitare eos, quos ios tuum vocas, isdem seminibus ortos eodem frui caelo,* etc.

2. *Glabri, delicati,* or *exoleti* were favourite slaves, kept artifically youthful by Romans of the more dissolute class. Cf. Catullus, lxi. 142, and Seneca, *De Brevitate Vitae,* 12. 5 (a passage closely resembling the description given above by Seneca), where the master prides himself upon the elegant appearance and graceful gestures of these favourites.

3. The master of Callistus, before he became the favourite of Caligula, is unknown.

4. There is some doubt whether we should not read Variana, as Lipsius suggests. This method of qualifying for senator suits the Empire better than the Republic. Variana would refer to the defeat of Varus in Germany, A.D. 9.

5. Plato was about forty years old when he visited Sicily, whence he was afterwards deported by Dionysius the Elder. He was sold into slavery at Aegina and ransomed by a man from Cyrene. Diogenes, while travelling from Athens to Aegina, is said to have been captured by pirates and sold in Crete, where he was purchased by a certain Corinthian and given his freedom.

6. i.e., as the praetor himself was normally accustomed to do.

XLVIII. ON QUIBBLING AS UNWORTHY OF THE PHILOSOPHER

[1]In answer to the letter which you wrote me while travelling,–a letter as long as the journey itself,–I shall reply later. I ought to go into retirement, and consider what sort of advice I should give you. For you yourself, who consult me, also reflected for a long time whether to do so; how much more, then, should I myself reflect, since more deliberation is necessary in settling than in propounding a problem! And this is particularly true when one thing is advantageous to you and another to me. Am I speaking again in the guise of an Epicurean?[1] [2]But the fact is, the same thing is advantageous to me which is advantageous to you; for I am not your friend unless whatever is at issue concerning you is my concern also. Friendship produces between us a partnership in all our interests. There is no such thing as good or bad fortune for the individual; we live in common. And no one can live happily who has regard to himself alone and transforms everything into a question of his own utility; you must live for your neighbour, if you would live for yourself. [3]This fellowship, maintained with scrupulous care, which makes us mingle as men with our fellow-men and holds that the human race have certain rights in common, is also of great help in cherishing the more intimate fellowship which is based on friendship, concerning which I began to speak above. For he that has much in common with a fellow-man will have all things in common with a friend.

[4]And on this point, my excellent Lucilius, I should like to have those subtle dialecticians of yours advise me how I ought to help a friend, or how a fellow man, rather than tell me in how many ways the word "friend" is used, and how many meanings the word "man" possesses. Lo, Wisdom and Folly are taking opposite sides. Which shall I join? Which party would you have me follow? On that side, "man" is the equivalent of "friend"; on the other side, "friend" is not the equivalent of "man." The one wants a friend for his own advantage; the other wants to make himself an advantage to his friend.[2] What *you* have to offer me is nothing but distortion of words and splitting of syllables. [5]It is clear that unless I can devise some very tricky premises and by false deductions tack on to them a fallacy which springs from the truth, I shall not be able to distinguish between what is desirable and what is to be avoided! I am ashamed! Old men as we are, dealing with a problem so serious, we make play of it!

[6]"'Mouse' is a syllable.[3] Now a mouse eats its cheese; therefore, a syllable eats cheese." Suppose now that I cannot solve this problem; see what peril hangs over my head as a result of such ignorance! What a scrape I shall be in! Without doubt I must beware, or some day I shall be catching syllables in a mousetrap, or, if I grow careless, a book may devour my cheese! Unless, perhaps, the following syllogism is shrewder still: "'Mouse' is a syllable. Now a syllable does not eat cheese. Therefore a mouse does not eat cheese." [7]What childish nonsense! Do we knit our brows over this sort of problem? Do we let our beards grow long for this reason? Is this the matter which we teach with sour and pale faces?

Would you really know what philosophy offers to humanity? Philosophy offers counsel. Death calls away one man, and poverty chafes another; a third is worried either by his neighbour's wealth or by his own. So-and-so is afraid of bad luck; another desires to get away from his own good fortune. Some are ill-treated by men, others by the gods. [8]Why, then, do you frame for me such games as these? It is no occasion for jest; you are retained as counsel for unhappy mankind. You have promised to help those in peril by sea, those in captivity, the sick and the needy, and those whose heads are under the poised axe. Whither are you straying? What are you doing?

This friend, in whose company you are jesting, is in fear. Help him, and take the noose from about his neck. Men are stretching out imploring hands to you on all sides; lives ruined and in danger of ruin are begging for some assistance; men's hopes, men's resources, depend upon you. They ask that you deliver them from all their restlessness, that you reveal to them, scattered and wandering as they are, the clear light of truth. ⁹Tell them what nature has made necessary, and what superfluous; tell them how simple are the laws that she has laid down, how pleasant and unimpeded life is for those who follow these laws, but how bitter and perplexed it is for those who have put their trust in opinion rather than in nature.

I should deem your games of logic to be of some avail in relieving men's burdens, if you could first show me what part of these burdens they will relieve. What among these games of yours banishes lust? Or controls it? Would that I could say that they were merely of no profit! They are positively harmful. I can make it perfectly clear to you whenever you wish, that a noble spirit when involved in such subtleties is impaired and weakened. ¹⁰I am ashamed to say what weapons they supply to men who are destined to go to war with fortune, and how poorly they equip them! Is this the path to the greatest good? Is philosophy to proceed by such claptrap⁴ and by quibbles which would be a disgrace and a reproach even for expounders⁵ of the law? For what else is it that you men are doing, when you deliberately ensnare the person to whom you are putting questions, than making it appear that the man has lost his case on a technical error?⁶ But just as the judge can reinstate those who have lost a suit in this way, so philosophy has reinstated these victims of quibbling to their former condition. ¹¹Why do you men abandon your mighty promises, and, after having assured me in high-sounding language that you will permit the glitter of gold to dazzle my eyesight no more than the gleam of the sword, and that I shall, with mighty steadfastness, spurn both that which all men crave and that which all men fear, why do you descend to the ABC's of scholastic pedants? What is your answer?

Is this the path to heaven?⁷

For that is exactly what philosophy promises to me, that I shall be made equal to God. For this I have been summoned, for this purpose have I come. Philosophy, keep your promise!

¹²Therefore, my dear Lucilius, withdraw yourself as far as possible from these exceptions and objections of so-called philosophers. Frankness, and simplicity beseem true goodness. Even if there were many years left to you, you would have had to spend them frugally in order to have enough for the necessary things; but as it is, when your time is so scant, what madness it is to learn superfluous things! Farewell.

Footnotes

1. The Epicureans, who reduced all goods to "utilities," could not regard a friend's advantage as identical to one's own advantage. And yet they laid great stress upon friendship as one of the chief sources of pleasure. For an attempt to reconcile these two positions see Cicero, *De Finibus*, i. 65 ff. Seneca has inadvertently used a phrase that implies a difference between a friend's interest and one's own. This leads him to reassert the Stoic view of friendship, which adopted as its motto κοινὰ τὰ τῶν φίλων.

2. The sides are given in the reverse order in the two clauses: to the Stoic the terms "friend" and "man" are co-extensive; he is the friend of everybody, and his motive in friendship is to be of service; the Epicurean, however, narrows the definition of "friend" and regards him merely as an instrument to his own happiness.

3. In this paragraph Seneca exposes the folly of trying to prove a truth by means of logical tricks, and offers a caricature of those which were current among the philosophers whom he derides.

4. Literally, "or if or if not," words constantly employed by the logicians in legal instruments. For the latter cf. Cicero, *Pro Caecina*, 23. 65 *tum illud, quod dicitur, "sive nive" irrident, tum aucupia verborum et litterarum tendiculas in invidiam vocant.*

5. Literally, "to those who sit studying the praetor's edicts." The *album* is the bulletin-board, on which the edicts of the praetor were posted, giving the formulae and stipulations for legal processes of various kinds.

6. In certain actions the praetor appointed a judge and established a formula, indicating the plaintiff's claim and the judge's duty. If the statement was false, or the claim excessive, the plaintiff lost his case; under certain conditions (see last sentence of Seneca § 11) the defendant could claim annulment of the formula and have the case tried again. Such cases were not lost on their merits, and for that reason the lawyer who purposely took such an advantage was doing a contemptible thing.

7. Vergil, *Aeneid*, ix. 641.

XLIX. ON THE SHORTNESS OF LIFE

[1]A man is indeed lazy and careless, my dear Lucilius, if he is reminded of a friend only by seeing some landscape which stirs the memory; and yet there are times when the old familiar haunts stir up a sense of loss that has been stored away in the soul, not bringing back dead memories, but rousing them from their dormant state, just as the sight of a lost friend's favourite slave, or his cloak, or his house, renews the mourner's grief, even though it has been softened by time.

Now, lo and behold, Campania, and especially Naples and your beloved Pompeii,[1] struck me, when I viewed them, with a wonderfully fresh sense of longing for you. You stand in full view before my eyes. I am on the point of parting from you. I see you choking down your tears and resisting without success the emotions that well up at the very moment when you try to check them. I seem to have lost you but a moment ago. For what is not "but a moment ago" when one begins to use the memory? [2]It was but a moment ago that I sat, as a lad, in the school of the philosopher Sotion,[2] but a moment ago that I began to plead in the courts, but a moment ago that I lost the desire to plead, but a moment ago that I lost the ability. Infinitely swift is the flight of time, as those see more clearly who are looking backwards. For when we are intent on the present, we do not notice it, so gentle is the passage of time's headlong flight. [3]Do you ask the reason for this? All past time is in the same place; it all presents the same aspect to us, it lies together. Everything slips into the same abyss. Besides, an event which in its entirety is of brief compass cannot contain long intervals. The time which we spend in living is but a point, nay, even less than a point. But this point of time, infinitesimal as it is, nature has mocked by making it seem outwardly of longer duration; she has taken one portion thereof and made it infancy, another childhood, another youth, another the gradual slope, so to speak, from youth to old age, and old age itself is still another. How many steps for how short a climb! [4]It was but a moment ago that I saw you off on your journey; and yet this "moment ago" makes up a goodly share of our existence, which is so brief, we should reflect, that it will soon come to an end altogether. In other years time did not seem to me to go so swiftly; now, it seems fast beyond belief, perhaps, because I feel that the finish-line is moving closer to me, or it may be that I have begun to take heed and reckon up my losses.

[5]For this reason I am all the more angry that some men claim the major portion of this time for superfluous things,–time which, no matter how carefully it is guarded, cannot suffice even for necessary things. Cicero[3] declared that if the number of his days were doubled, he should not have time to read the lyric poets.[4] And you may rate the dialecticians in the same class; but they are foolish in a more melancholy way. The lyric poets are avowedly frivolous; but the dialecticians believe that they are themselves engaged upon serious business. [6]I do not deny that one must cast a glance at dialectic; but it ought to be a mere glance, a sort of greeting from the threshold, merely that one may not be deceived, or judge these pursuits to contain any hidden matters of great worth.

Why do you torment yourself and lose weight over some problem which it is more clever to have scorned than to solve? When a soldier is undisturbed and travelling at his ease, he can hunt for trifles along his way; but when the enemy is closing in on the rear, and a command is given to quicken the pace, necessity makes him throw away not bitter; for just as soon as it is curing us it begins to give pleasure. One enjoys other cures only after health is restored, but a draught of philosophy is at the same moment wholesome and pleasant. Farewell.

LI. ON BAIAE AND MORALS

¹Every man does the best he can, my dear Lucilius! You over there have Etna,¹ that lofty and most celebrated mountain of Sicily; (although I cannot make out why Messala,– or was it Valgius? for I have been reading in both,–has called it "unique," inasmuch as many regions belch forth fire, not merely the lofty ones where the phenomenon is more frequent,–presumably because fire rises to the greatest possible height,–but low-lying places also.) As for myself, I do the best I can; I have had to be satisfied with Baiae;² and I left it the day after I reached it; for Baiae is a place to be avoided, because, though it has certain natural advantages, luxury has claimed it for her own exclusive resort. ²"What then," you say, "should any place be singled out as an object of aversion?" Not at all. But just as, to the wise and upright man, one style of clothing is more suitable than another, without his having an aversion for any particular colour, but because he thinks that some colours do not befit one who has adopted the simple life; so there are places also, which the wise man or he who is on the way toward wisdom will avoid as foreign to good morals. ³Therefore, if he is contemplating withdrawal from the world, he will not select Canopus³ (although Canopus does not keep any man from living simply), nor Baiae either; for both places have begun to be resorts of vice. At Canopus luxury pampers itself to the utmost degree; at Baiae it is even more lax, as if the place itself demanded a certain amount of licence.

⁴We ought to select abodes which are wholesome not only for the body but also for the character. Just as I do not care to live in a place of torture, neither do I care to live in a cafe. To witness persons wandering drunk along the beach, the riotous revelling of sailing parties, the lakes a-din with choral⁴ song, and all the other ways in which luxury, when it is, so to speak, released from the restraints of law not merely sins, but blazons its sins abroad,–why must I witness all this? ⁵We ought to see to it that we flee to the greatest possible distance from provocations to vice. We should toughen our minds, and remove them far from the allurements of pleasure. A single winter relaxed Hannibal's fibre; his pampering in Campania took the vigour out of that hero who had triumphed over Alpine snows. He conquered with his weapons, but was conquered by his vices. ⁶We too have a war to wage, a type of warfare in which there is allowed no rest or furlough. To be conquered, in the first place, are pleasures, which, as you see, have carried off even the sternest characters. If a man has once understood how great is the task which he has entered upon, he will see that there must be no dainty or effeminate conduct. What have I to do with those hot baths or with the sweating-room where they shut in the dry steam which is to drain your strength? Perspiration should flow only after toil.

⁷Suppose we do what Hannibal did,–check the course of events, give up the war, and give over our bodies to be coddled. Every one would rightly blame us for our untimely sloth, a thing fraught with peril even for the victor, to say nothing of one who is only on the way to victory. And we have even less right to do this than those followers of the Carthaginian flag; for our danger is greater than theirs if we slacken, and our toil is greater than theirs even if we press ahead. ⁸Fortune is fighting against me, and I shall not carry out her commands. I refuse to submit to the yoke; nay rather, I shake off the yoke that is upon me,–an act which demands even greater courage. The soul is not to be pampered; surrendering to pleasure means also surrendering to pain, surrendering to toil, surrendering to poverty. Both ambition and anger will wish to have the same rights over me as pleasure, and I shall be torn asunder, or rather pulled to pieces, amid all these conflicting passions. ⁹I have set freedom before my eyes; and I am striving for that reward. And what is freedom, you ask? It means not being a slave to any circumstance, to any constraint, to any chance; it means compelling Fortune to enter the lists

on equal terms. And on the day when I know that I have the upper hand, her power will be naught. When I have death in my own control, shall I take orders from her? [10]Therefore, a man occupied with such reflections should choose an austere and pure dwelling-place. The spirit is weakened by surroundings that are too pleasant, and without a doubt one's place of residence can contribute towards impairing its vigour. Animals whose hoofs are hardened on rough ground can travel any road; but when they are fattened on soft marshy meadows their hoofs are soon worn out. The bravest soldier comes from rock-ribbed regions; but the town-bred and the home-bred are sluggish in action. The hand which turns from the plough to the sword never objects to toil; but your sleek and well-dressed dandy quails at the first cloud of dust. [11]Being trained in a rugged country strengthens the character and fits it for great undertakings. It was more honourable in Scipio to spend his exile at Liternum,[5] than at Baiae; his downfall did not need a setting so effeminate. Those also into whose hands the rising fortunes of Rome first transferred the wealth of the state, Gaius Marius, Gnaeus Pompey, and Caesar, did indeed build villas near Baiae; but they set them on the very tops of the mountains. This seemed more soldier-like, to look down from a lofty height upon lands spread far and wide below. Note the situation, position, and type of building which they chose; you will see that they were not country-places,–they were camps. [12]Do you suppose that Cato would ever have dwelt in a pleasure-palace, that he might count the lewd women as they sailed past, the many kinds of barges painted in all sorts of colours, the roses which were wafted about the lake, or that he might listen to the nocturnal brawls of serenaders? Would he not have preferred to remain in the shelter of a trench thrown up by his own hands to serve for a single night? Would not anyone who is a man have his slumbers broken by a war-trumpet rather than by a chorus of serenaders?

[13]But I have been haranguing against Baiae long enough; although I never could harangue often enough against vice. Vice, Lucilius, is what I wish you to proceed against, without limit and without end. For it has neither limit nor end. If any vice rend your heart, cast it away from you; and if you cannot be rid of it in any other way, pluck out your heart also. Above all, drive pleasures from your sight. Hate them beyond all other things, for they are like the bandits whom the Egyptians call "lovers,"[6] who embrace us only to garrotte us. Farewell.

Footnotes

1. Etna was of especial interest to Lucilius. Besides being a Govenor in Sicily, he may have written the poem Aetna. For Seneca's own curiosity regarding the mountain compare Ep. lxxix. 5 ff.

2. Not far from Naples, and across the bay from Puteoli. It was a fashionable and dissolute watering place.

3. Situated at the mouth of the westernmost branch of the Nile, and proverbial in Latin literature for the laxity of its morals.

4. There is considerable doubt whether *symphonia* was vocal or instrumental music. The passage probably refers either to glee-singers (as in Venice to-day) or to bands of flute-players playing part-music. Cicero (*Verr.* iii. 44. 105) mentions them as providing entertainment at banquets.

5. See Letter lxxxvi.

6. The Egyptians used the word φηλητής in the sense of "knave" or "foot-pad." The word is found in the Hecate of Callimachus. Hesychius defines it as equal to κλώψ "thief." It was pronounced in the same way as φιλητής "lover," and in late Greek was spelt in the same way.

LII. ON CHOOSING OUR TEACHERS

[1]What is this force, Lucilius, that drags us in one direction when we are aiming in another, urging us on to the exact place from which we long to withdraw? What is it that wrestles with our spirit, and does not allow us to desire anything once for all? We

the calm weather, which had enticed me, came to naught. The storm had not yet begun, but the ground-swell was on, and the waves kept steadily coming faster. I began
to ask the pilot to put me ashore somewhere; he replied that the coast was rough and
a bad place to land, and that in a storm he feared a lee shore more than anything else.
³But I was suffering too grievously to think of the danger, since a sluggish seasickness
which brought no relief was racking me, the sort that upsets the liver without clearing
it. Therefore I laid down the law to my pilot, forcing him to make for the shore, wil-
ly-nilly. When we drew near, I did not wait for things to be done in accordance with
Vergil's orders, until

> Prow faced seawards³

or

> Anchor plunged from bow;⁴

I remembered my profession⁵ as a veteran devotee of cold water, and, clad as I was
in my cloak, let myself down into the sea, just as a cold-water bather should. ⁴What
do you think my feelings were, scrambling over the rocks, searching out the path, or
making one for myself? I understood that sailors have good reason to fear the land. It
is hard to believe what I endured when I could not endure myself; you may be sure
that the reason why Ulysses was shipwrecked on every possible occasion was not so
much because the sea-god was angry with him from his birth; he was simply subject to
seasickness. And in the future I also, if I must go anywhere by sea, shall only reach my
destination in the twentieth year.⁶
⁵When I finally calmed my stomach (for you know that one does not escape sea-
sickness by escaping from the sea) and refreshed my body with a rubdown, I began to
reflect how completely we forget or ignore our failings, even those that affect the body,
which are continually reminding us of their existence,–not to mention those which are
more serious in proportion as they are more hidden. ⁶A slight ague deceives us; but
when it has increased and a genuine fever has begun to burn, it forces even a hardy
man, who can endure much suffering, to admit that he is ill. There is pain in the foot,
and a tingling sensation in the joints; but we still hide the complaint and announce that
we have sprained a joint, or else are tired from over-exercise. Then the ailment, uncertain at first, must be given a name; and when it begins to swell the ankles also, and has
made both our feet "right" feet,⁷ we are bound to confess that we have the gout. ⁷The
opposite holds true of diseases of the soul; the worse one is, the less one perceives it.
You need not be surprised, my beloved Lucilius. For he whose sleep is light pursues
visions during slumber, and sometimes, though asleep, is conscious that he is asleep;
but sound slumber annihilates our very dreams and sinks the spirit down so deep that
it has no perception of self. ⁸Why will no man confess his faults? Because he is still in
their grasp; only he who is awake can recount his dream, and similarly a confession of
sin is a proof of sound mind.

Let us, therefore, rouse ourselves, that we may be able to correct our mistakes.
Philosophy, however, is the only power that can stir us, the only power that can shake
off our deep slumber. Devote yourself wholly to philosophy. You are worthy of her;
she is worthy of you; greet one another with a loving embrace. Say farewell to all other
interests with courage and frankness. Do not study philosophy merely during your
spare time.⁸
⁹If you were ill, you would stop caring for your personal concerns, and forget
your business duties; you would not think highly enough of any client to take active
charge of his case during a slight abatement of your sufferings. You would try your
hardest to be rid of the illness as soon as possible. What, then? Shall you not do the
same thing now? Throw aside all hindrances and give up your time to getting a sound
mind; for no man can attain it if he is engrossed in other matters. Philosophy wields
her own authority; she appoints her own time and does not allow it to be appointed
for her. She is not a thing to be followed at odd times, but a subject for daily practice;
she is mistress, and she commands our attendance. ¹⁰Alexander, when a certain state
promised him a part of its territory and half its entire property, replied: "I invaded

Asia with the intention, not of accepting what you might give, but of allowing you to keep what I might leave." Philosophy likewise keeps saying to all occupations: "I do not intend to accept the time which you have left over, but I shall allow you to keep what I myself shall leave."

[11]Turn to her, therefore, with all your soul, sit at her feet, cherish her; a great distance will then begin to separate you from other men. You will be far ahead of all mortals, and even the gods will not be far ahead of you. Do you ask what will be the difference between yourself and the gods? They will live longer. But, by my faith, it is the sign of a great artist to have confined a full likeness to the limits of a miniature. The wise man's life spreads out to him over as large a surface as does all eternity to a god. There is one point in which the sage has an advantage over the god; for a god is freed from terrors by the bounty of nature, the wise man by his own bounty. [12]What a wonderful privilege, to have the weaknesses of a man and the serenity of a god! The power of philosophy to blunt the blows of chance is beyond belief. No missile can settle in her body; she is well-protected and impenetrable. She spoils the force of some missiles and wards them off with the loose folds of her gown, as if they had no power to harm; others she dashes aside, and hurls them back with such force that they recoil upon the sender. Farewell.

Footnotes

1. The poetical name for Naples; perhaps it was once a town near by which gave a sort of romantic second title to the larger city. Professor Summers thinks that this poetical name, together with *tua*, indicates a reference to a passage from the verse of Lucilius. Perhaps, however, *tua* means nothing more than "the place which you love so well," being in the neighbourhood of Pompeii, the birthplace of Lucilius.

2. An islet near the mouth of the bay wherein Baiae was situated. Puteoli was on the opposite side of the bay from Baiae.

3. *Aeneid*, vi. 3. This was the usual method of mooring a ship in ancient times.

4. *Aeneid*, iii. 277.

5. Compare Ep. lxxxiii. 5.

6. Ulysses took ten years on his journey, because of sea-sickness; Seneca will need twice as many.

7. That is, they are so swollen that left and right look alike.

8. Literally "on sufferance," whenever other matters permit. Cf. Pliny, *Ep.* vii. 30 *precario studeo,*–"subject to interruption from others."

LIV. ON ASTHMA AND DEATH

[1]My ill-health had allowed me a long furlough, when suddenly it resumed the attack. "What kind of ill-health?" you say. And you surely have a right to ask; for it is true that no kind is unknown to me. But I have been consigned, so to speak, to one special ailment. I do not know why I should call it by its Greek name;[1] for it is well enough described as "shortness of breath." Its attack is of very brief duration, like that of a squall at sea; it usually ends within an hour. Who indeed could breathe his last for long? [2]I have passed through all the ills and dangers of the flesh; but nothing seems to me more troublesome than this. And naturally so; for anything else may be called illness; but this is a sort of continued "last gasp."[2] Hence physicians call it "practising how to die." For some day the breath will succeed in doing what it has so often essayed. [3]Do you think I am writing this letter in a merry spirit, just because I have escaped? It would be absurd to take delight in such supposed restoration to health, as it would be for a defendant to imagine that he had won his case when he had succeeded in postponing his trial. Yet in the midst of my difficult breathing I never ceased to rest secure in cheerful and brave thoughts.

[4]"What?" I say to myself; "does death so often test me? Let it do so; I myself have for a long time tested death." "When?" you ask. Before I was born. Death is non-ex-

will read with greater pleasure than all my deadly talk about death. Farewell.

Footnotes

1. This theme was emphasized by Lucretius, i. 136 and 832, and iii. 260. Munro thinks, however, that "Lucretius had too much instead of too little technical language for a poet." Seneca knew Lucretius; cf. Epp. lviii. 12, xc. 11, etc.

2. The gad-fly.

3. *Georgics*, iii. 146 ff.

4. *Aeneid*, xii. 708 f.

5. *Aeneid*, xi. 467.

6. Cicero usually says *natura*. The word, according to Quintilian, was first used by a certain Sergius Flavus. It is also found in Apulcius, Macrobius, and Sidonius.

7. See Ep. c. Papirius Fabianus, who lived in the times of Tiberius and Caligula, was a pupil of the Sextius of Ep. lix., and was (Pliny, *N. H.* xxxvi. 15. 24) *naturae rerum peritissimus*. He is praised by the elder Seneca (*Cont.* 2. *Praef.*) who, however, says of him *deerat robur–splendor aderat*.

8. i.e., I must not use other imported words to explain *essentia*, which is not a native Latin word, but invented as a literal translation of οὐσία.

9. Cf. § 16.

10. *Categories* 2 b 11 and often.

11. i.e., the *genus* beyond "that which exists."

12. Cf. § 8. Plato's usual division was threefold,–αἰσθητά, μαθηματικά, εἴδη (*sensibilia, mathematica, ideae*),–a division which is often quoted by Aristotle.

13. Εἶναι κατ᾿ ἐξοχήν. After illustrating the poet κατ᾿ ἐξοχήν, Homer, he passes to τὸ ὂν κατ᾿ ἐξοχήν, God.

14. Ὄντως τὰ ὄντα. "Each idea is a single, independent, separate, self-existing, perfect, and eternal essence"; Adam, *The Republic of Plato*, ii. 169. See Zeller's *Plato* (p. 237) for a list of Greek words used by Plato to indicate the reality of these ideas.

15. Cf., for example, *Parmenides* 132 D. What follows is not a direct quotation, and the same thought is found elsewhere.

16. Εἶδος.

17. i.e., the "original."

18. i.e., κυρίως ὄντα. See above, § 16f

19. Frag. 49ª Diels² ποταμοῖς τοῖς αὐτοῖς ἐμβαίνομέν τε καὶ οὐκ ἐμβαίνομεν, εἶμέν τε καὶ οὐκ εἶμεν.

20. This idea Seneca has already developed in Ep. xxiv. 20.

21. Diogenes Laertius, iii. 1, who records also other explanations of the name Plato, which replaced the given name Aristocles.

22. Cf. Plato, *Phaedo*, 114 D καὶ ἄξιον κινδυνεῦσαι, οἰομένῳ οὕτως ἔχειν· καλὸς γὰρ ὁ κίνδυνος, the "chance" being immortality.

23. Since *vale* means "keep well" no less than "good bye."

LIX. ON PLEASURE AND JOY

[1]I received great pleasure from your letter; kindly allow me to use these words in their everyday meaning, without insisting upon their Stoic import. For we Stoics hold that pleasure is a vice. Very likely it is a vice; but we are accustomed to use the word when we wish to indicate a happy state of mind. [2]I am aware that if we test words by our formula,[1] even pleasure is a thing of ill repute, and joy can be attained only by the wise. For "joy" is an elation of spirit, of a spirit which trusts in the goodness and truth of its own possessions. The common usage, however, is that we derive great "joy" from a friend's position as consul, or from his marriage, or from the birth of his child; but these events, so far from being matters of joy, are more often the beginnings of sorrow

to come. No, it is a characteristic of real joy that it never ceases, and never changes into its opposite.[2]

[3]Accordingly, when our Vergil speaks of

The evil joys of the mind,[3]

his words are eloquent, but not strictly appropriate. For no "joy" can be evil. He has given the name "joy" to pleasures, and has thus expressed his meaning. For he has conveyed the idea that men take delight in their own evil. [4]Nevertheless, I was not wrong in saying that I received great "pleasure" from your letter; for although an ignorant[4] man may derive "joy" if the cause be an honourable one, yet, since his emotion is wayward, and is likely soon to take another direction, I call it "pleasure"; for it is inspired by an opinion concerning a spurious good; it exceeds control and is carried to excess.

But, to return to the subject, let me tell you what delighted me in your letter. You have your words under control. You are not carried away by your language, or borne beyond the limits which you have determined upon. [5]Many writers are tempted by the charm of some alluring phrase to some topic other than that which they had set themselves to discuss. But this has not been so in your case; all your words are compact, and suited to the subject, You say all that you wish, and you mean still more than you say. This is a proof of the importance of your subject matter, showing that your mind, as well as your words, contains nothing superfluous or bombastic.

[6]I do, however,[5] find some metaphors, not, indeed, daring ones, but the kind which have stood the test of use. I find similes also; of course, if anyone forbids us to use them, maintaining that poets alone have that privilege, he has not, apparently, read any of our ancient prose writers, who had not yet learned to affect a style that should win applause. For those writers, whose eloquence was simple and directed only towards proving their case, are full of comparisons; and I think that these are necessary, not for the same reason which makes them necessary for the poets, but in order that they may serve as props to our feebleness, to bring both speaker and listener face to face with the subject under discussion. [7]For example, I am at this very moment reading Sextius;[6] he is a keen man, and a philosopher who, though he writes in Greek, has the Roman standard of ethics. One of his similes appealed especially to me, that of an army marching in hollow square,[7] in a place where the enemy might be expected to appear from any quarter, ready for battle. "This," said he, "is just what the wise man ought to do; he should have all his fighting qualities deployed on every side, so that wherever the attack threatens, there his supports may be ready to hand and may obey the captain's command without confusion." This is what we notice in armies which serve under great leaders; we see how all the troops simultaneously understand their general's orders, since they are so arranged that a signal given by one man passes down the ranks of cavalry and infantry at the same moment. [8]This, he declares, is still more necessary for men like ourselves; for soldiers have often feared an enemy without reason, and the march which they thought most dangerous has in fact been most secure; but folly brings no repose, fear haunts it both in the van and in the rear of the column, and both flanks are in a panic. Folly is pursued, and confronted, by peril. It blenches at everything; it is unprepared; it is frightened even by auxiliary troops.[8] But the wise man is fortified against all inroads; he is alert; he will not retreat before the attack of poverty, or of sorrow, or of disgrace, or of pain. He will walk undaunted both against them and among them.

[9]We human beings are fettered and weakened by many vices; we have wallowed in them for a long time and it is hard for us to be cleansed. We are not merely defiled; we are dyed by them. But, to refrain from passing from one figure[9] to another, I will raise this question, which I often consider in my own heart: why is it that folly holds us with such an insistent grasp? It is, primarily, because we do not combat it strongly enough, because we do not struggle towards salvation with all our might; secondly, because we do not put sufficient trust in the discoveries of the wise, and do not drink in their words with open hearts; we approach this great problem in too trifling a spirit. [10]But how can a man learn, in the struggle against his vices, an amount that is enough,

greed? Not at all. How small is the amount which will satisfy nature? A very little will send her away contented. It is not the natural hunger of our bellies that costs us dear, but our solicitous cravings. [4]Therefore those who, as Sallust[1] puts it, "hearken to their bellies," should be numbered among the animals, and not among men; and certain men, indeed, should be numbered, not even among the animals, but among the dead. He really lives who is made use of by many; he really lives who makes use of himself. Those men, however, who creep into a hole and grow torpid[2] are no better off in their homes than if they were in their tombs. Right there on the marble lintel of the house of such a man you may inscribe his name,[3] for he has died before he is dead. Farewell.

Footnotes

1. Catiline, i. 1.

2. i.e., like animals.

3. i.e., you may put an epitaph upon his dwelling as if it were a tomb.

LXI. ON MEETING DEATH CHEERFULLY

[1]Let us cease to desire that which we have been desiring. I, at least, am doing this: in my old age I have ceased to desire what I desired when a boy. To this single end my days and my nights are passed; this is my task, this the object of my thoughts,–to put an end to my chronic ills. I am endeavouring to live every day as if it were a complete life. I do not indeed snatch it up as if it were my last; I do regard it, however, as if it might even be my last. [2]The present letter is written to you with this in mind as if death were about to call me away in the very act of writing. I am ready to depart, and I shall enjoy life just because I am not over-anxious as to the future date of my departure.

Before I became old I tried to live well; now that I am old, I shall try to die well; but dying well means dying gladly. See to it that you never do anything unwillingly. [3]That which is bound to be a necessity if you rebel, is not a necessity if you desire it. This is what I mean: he who takes his orders gladly, escapes the bitterest part of slavery,–doing what one does not want to do. The man who does something under orders is not unhappy; he is unhappy who does something against his will. Let us therefore so set our minds in order that we may desire whatever is demanded of us by circumstances, and above all that we may reflect upon our end without sadness. [4]We must make ready for death before we make ready for life. Life is well enough furnished, but we are too greedy with regard to its furnishings; something always seems to us lacking, and will always seem lacking. To have lived long enough depends neither upon our years nor upon our days, but upon our minds. I have lived, my dear friend Lucilius, long enough. I have had my fill;[1] I await death. Farewell.

Footnotes

1. A reminiscence of Lucretius, iii. 938 f. *Cur non ut plenus vitae conviva recedus Aequo animoque capis securam, stulte, quietem?* Cf. also Horace, *Sat.* i. 1. 118 f. *vitae Cedat uti conviva satur.*

LXII. ON GOOD COMPANY

[1]We are deceived by those who would have us believe that a multitude of affairs blocks their pursuit of liberal studies; they make a pretence of their engagements, and multiply them, when their engagements are merely with themselves. As for me, Lucilius, my time is free; it is indeed free, and wherever I am, I am master of myself. For I do not surrender myself to my affairs, but loan myself to them, and I do not hunt out excuses for wasting my time. And wherever I am situated, I carry on my own meditations and ponder in my mind some wholesome thought. [2]When I give myself to my friends, I do not withdraw from my own company, nor do I linger with those who are

associated with me through some special occasion or some case which arises from my official position. But I spend my time in the company of all the best; no matter in what lands they may have lived, or in what age, I let my thoughts fly to them. ³Demetrius,¹ for instance, the best of men, I take about with me, and, leaving the wearers of purple and fine linen, I talk with him, half-naked as he is, and hold him in high esteem. Why should I not hold him in high esteem? I have found that he lacks nothing. It is in the power of any man to despise all things, but of no man to possess all things. The shortest cut to riches is to despise riches. Our friend Demetrius, however, lives not merely as if he has learned to despise all things, but as if he has handed them over for others to possess.² Farewell.

Footnotes

1. Demetrius of Sunium, the Cynic philosopher, who taught in Rome in the reign of Caligula and was banished by Nero.

2. i.e., he has achieved the Stoic ideal of independence of all external control; he is a king and has all things to bestow upon others, but needs nothing for himself.

LXIII. ON GRIEF FOR LOST FRIENDS

¹I am grieved to hear that your friend Flaccus is dead, but I would not have you sorrow more than is fitting. That you should not mourn at all I shall hardly dare to insist; and yet I know that it is the better way. But what man will ever be so blessed with that ideal steadfastness of soul, unless he has already risen far above the reach of Fortune? Even such a man will be stung by an event like this, but it will be only a sting. We, however, may be forgiven for bursting into tears, if only our tears have not flowed to excess, and if we have checked them by our own efforts. Let not the eyes be dry when we have lost a friend, nor let them overflow. We may weep, but we must not wail.

²Do you think that the law which I lay down for you is harsh, when the greatest of Greek poets has extended the privilege of weeping to one day only, in the lines where he tells us that even Niobe took thought of food?¹ Do you wish to know the reason for lamentations and excessive weeping? It is because we seek the proofs of our bereavement in our tears, and do not give way to sorrow, but merely parade it. No man goes into mourning for his own sake. Shame on our ill-timed folly! There is an element of self-seeking even in our sorrow.

³"What," you say, "am I to forget my friend?" It is surely a short-lived memory that you vouchsafe to him, if it is to endure only as long as your grief; presently that brow of yours will be smoothed out in laughter by some circumstance, however casual. It is to a time no more distant than this that I put off the soothing of every regret, the quieting of even the bitterest grief. As soon as you cease to observe yourself, the picture of sorrow which you have contemplated will fade away; at present you are keeping watch over your own suffering. But even while you keep watch it slips away from you, and the sharper it is, the more speedily it comes to an end.

⁴Let us see to it that the recollection of those whom we have lost becomes a pleasant memory to us. No man reverts with pleasure to any subject which he will not be able to reflect upon without pain. So too it cannot but be that the names of those whom we have loved and lost come back to us with a sort of sting; but there is a pleasure even in this sting. ⁵For, as my friend Attalus² used to say: "The remembrance of lost friends is pleasant in the same way that certain fruits have an agreeably acid taste, or as in extremely old wines it is their very bitterness that pleases us. Indeed, after a certain lapse of time, every thought that gave pain is quenched, and the pleasure comes to us unalloyed." ⁶If we take the word of Attalus for it, "to think of friends who are alive and well is like enjoying a meal of cakes and honey; the recollection of friends who have passed away gives a pleasure that is not without a touch of bitterness. Yet who will deny that even these things, which are bitter and contain an element of sourness, do serve to arouse the stomach?" ⁷For my part, I do not agree with him. To me, the

relieve granulation of the eyelids, that to reduce the swelling of the lids, this to prevent sudden pain or a rush of tears, that to sharpen the vision. Then compound these several prescriptions, watch for the right time of their application, and supply the proper treatment in each case.

The cures for the spirit also have been discovered by the ancients; but it is our task to learn the method and the time of treatment. [9]Our predecessors have worked much improvement, but have not worked out the problem. They deserve respect, however, and should be worshipped with a divine ritual. Why should I not keep statues of great men to kindle my enthusiasm, and celebrate their birthdays? Why should I not continually greet them with respect and honour? The reverence which I owe to my own teachers I owe in like measure to those teachers of the human race, the source from which the beginnings of such great blessings have flowed. [10]If I meet a consul or a praetor, I shall pay him all the honour which his post of honour is wont to receive: I shall dismount, uncover, and yield the road. What, then? Shall I admit into my soul with less than the highest marks of respect Marcus Cato, the Elder and the Younger, Laelius the Wise, Socrates and Plato, Zeno and Cleanthes? I worship them in very truth, and always rise to do honour to such noble names. Farewell.

Footnotes

1. See on Ep. lix. 7. As the following sentence indicates, he seems to have considered himself an eclectic in philosophy, and to have been half-Stoic, half-Pythagorean.

2. Vergil, *Aeneid*, iv. 158 f. The boy Ascanius, at Dido's hunt, longs for wilder game than the deer and the goats.

LXV. ON THE FIRST CAUSE

[1]I shared my time yesterday with ill health;[1] it claimed for itself all the period before noon; in the afternoon, however, it yielded to me. And so I first tested my spirit by reading; then, when reading was found to be possible, I dared to make more demands upon the spirit, or perhaps I should say, to make more concessions to it. I wrote a little, and indeed with more concentration than usual, for I am struggling with a difficult subject and do not wish to be downed. In the midst of this, some friends visited me, with the purpose of employing force and of restraining me, as if I were a sick man indulging in some excess. [2]So conversation was substituted for writing; and from this conversation I shall communicate to you the topic which is still the subject of debate; for we have appointed you referee.[2] You have more of a task on your hands than you suppose, for the argument is threefold.

Our Stoic philosophers, as you know, declare that there are two things in the universe which are the source of everything,–namely, cause and matter.[3] Matter lies sluggish, a substance ready for any use, but sure to remain unemployed if no one sets it in motion. Cause, however, by which we mean reason, moulds matter and turns it in whatever direction it will, producing thereby various concrete results. Accordingly, there must be, in the case of each thing, that from which it is made, and, next, an agent by which it is made. The former is its material, the latter its cause.

[3]All art is but imitation of nature; therefore, let me apply these statements of general principles to the things which have to be made by man. A statue, for example, has afforded matter which was to undergo treatment at the hands of the artist, and has had an artist who was to give form to the matter. Hence, in the case of the statue, the material was bronze, the cause was the workman. And so it goes with all things,–they consist of that which is made and of the maker. [4]The Stoics believe in one cause only– the maker; but Aristotle thinks that the word "cause" can be used in three ways: "The first cause," he says, "is the actual matter, without which nothing can be created. The second is the workman. The third is the form, which is impressed upon every work,–a statue, for example." This last is what Aristotle calls the *idos*.[4] "There is, too," says he, "a fourth,–the purpose of the work as a whole." [5]Now I shall show you what this last

means. Bronze is the "first cause" of the statue, for it could never have been made un-less there had been something from which it could be cast and moulded. The "second cause" is the artist; for without the skilled hands of a workman that bronze could not have been shaped to the outlines of the statue. The "third cause" is the form, inasmuch as our statue could never be called The Lance-Bearer or The Boy Binding his Hair[5] had not this special shape been stamped upon it. The "fourth cause" is the purpose of the work. For if this purpose had not existed, the statue would not have been made. [6]Now what is this purpose? It is that which attracted the artist which he followed when he made the statue. It may have been money, if he has made it for sale; or renown, if he has worked for reputation; or religion, if he has wrought it as a gift for a temple. There-fore this also is a cause contributing towards the making of the statue; or do you think that we should avoid including, among the causes of a thing which has been made, that element without which the thing in question would not have been made?

[7]To these four Plato adds a fifth cause,–the pattern which he himself calls the "idea"; for it is this that the artist gazed upon[6] when he created the work which he had decided to carry out. Now it makes no difference whether he has this pattern outside himself, that he may direct his glance to it, or within himself, conceived and placed there by himself. God has within himself these patterns of all things, and his mind comprehends the harmonies and the measures of the whole totality of things which are to be carried out; he is filled with these shapes which Plato calls the "ideas,"–im-perishable, unchangeable, not subject to decay. And therefore, though men die, hu-manity itself, or the idea of man, according to which man is moulded, lasts on, and though men toil and perish, it suffers no change. [8]Accordingly, there are five causes, as Plato says:[7] the material, the agent, the make-up, the model, and the end in view. Last comes the result of all these. Just as in the case of the statue,–to go back to the figure with which we began,–the material is the bronze, the agent is the artist, the make-up is the form which is adapted to the material, the model is the pattern imitated by the agent, the end in view is the purpose in the maker's mind, and, finally, the result of all these is the statue itself. [9]The universe also, in Plato's opinion, possesses all these ele-ments. The agent is God; the source, matter; the form, the shape and the arrangement of the visible world. The pattern is doubtless the model according to which God has made this great and most beautiful creation. [10]The purpose is his object in so doing. Do you ask what God's purpose is? It is goodness. Plato, at any rate, says: "What was God's reason for creating the world? God is good, and no good person is grudging of anything that is good. Therefore, God made it the best world possible." Hand down your opinion, then, O judge; state who seems to you to say what is truest, and not who says what is absolutely true. For to do that is as far beyond our ken as truth itself.

[11]This throng of causes, defined by Aristotle and by Plato, embraces either too much or too little.[8] For if they regard as "causes" of an object that is to be made every-thing without which the object cannot be made, they have named too few. Time must be included among the causes; for nothing can be made without time. They must also include place; for if there be no place where a thing can be made, it will not be made. And motion too; nothing is either made or destroyed without motion. There is no art without motion, no change of any kind. [12]Now, however, I am searching for the first, the general cause; this must be simple, inasmuch as matter, too, is simple. Do we ask what cause is? It is surely Creative Reason,[9]–in other words, God. For those elements to which you referred are not a great series of independent causes; they all hinge on one alone, and that will be the creative cause. [13]Do you maintain that form is a cause? This is only what the artist stamps upon his work; it is part of a cause, but not the cause. Neither is the pattern a cause, but an indispensable tool of the cause. His pattern is as indispensable to the artist as the chisel or the file; without these, art can make no prog-ress. But for all that, these things are neither parts of the art, nor causes of it. [14]"Then," perhaps you will say, "the purpose of the artist, that which leads him to undertake to create something, is the cause." It may be a cause; it is not, however, the efficient cause, but only an accessory cause. But there are countless accessory causes; what we are discussing is the general cause. Now the statement of Plato and Aristotle is not in

it was because she wished to prove to us that an absolutely strong and happy mind can lie hidden under any exterior. Be that as it may, Claranus overcomes all these hindrances, and by despising his own body has arrived at a stage where he can despise other things also. [2] The poet who sang

> Worth shows more pleasing in a form that's fair,[1]

is, in my opinion, mistaken. For virtue needs nothing to set it off; it is its own great glory, and it hallows the body in which it dwells. At any rate, I have begun to regard Claranus in a different light; he seems to me handsome, and as well-setup in body as in mind. [3] A great man can spring from a hovel; so can a beautiful and great soul from an ugly and insignificant body. For this reason Nature seems to me to breed certain men of this stamp with the idea of proving that virtue springs into birth in any place whatever. Had it been possible for her to produce souls by themselves and naked, she would have done so; as it is, Nature does a still greater thing, for she produces certain men who, though hampered in their bodies, none the less break through the obstruction. [4] I think Claranus has been produced as a pattern, that we might be enabled to understand that the soul is not disfigured by the ugliness of the body, but rather the opposite, that the body is beautified by the comeliness of the soul.

Now, though Claranus and I have spent very few days together, we have nevertheless had many conversations, which I will at once pour forth and pass on to you. [5] The first day we investigated this problem: how can goods be equal if they are of three kinds?[2] For certain of them, according to our philosophical tenets, are primary, such as joy, peace, and the welfare of one's country. Others are of the second order, moulded in an unhappy material, such as the endurance of suffering, and self-control during severe illness. We shall pray outright for the goods of the first class; for the second class we shall pray only if the need shall arise. There is still a third variety, as, for example, a modest gait, a calm and honest countenance, and a bearing that suits the man of wisdom. [6] Now how can these things be equal when we compare them, if you grant that we ought to pray for the one and avoid the other? If we would make distinctions among them, we had better return to the First Good, and consider what its nature is: the soul that gazes upon truth, that is skilled in what should be sought and what should be avoided, establishing standards of value not according to opinion, but according to nature,–the soul that penetrates the whole world and directs its contemplating gaze upon all its Phenomena, paying strict attention to thoughts and actions, equally great and forceful, superior alike to hardships and blandishments, yielding itself to neither extreme of fortune, rising above all blessings and tribulations, absolutely beautiful, perfectly equipped with grace as well as with strength, healthy and sinewy,[3] unruffled, undismayed, one which no violence can shatter, one which acts of chance can neither exalt nor depress,–a soul like this is virtue itself. [7] There you have its outward appearance, if it should ever come under a single view and show itself once in all its completeness. But there are many aspects of it. They unfold themselves according as life varies and as actions differ; but virtue itself does not become less or greater.[4] For the Supreme Good cannot diminish, nor may virtue retrograde; rather is it transformed, now into one quality and now into another, shaping itself according to the part which it is to play. [8] Whatever it has touched it brings into likeness with itself, and dyes with its own colour. It adorns our actions, our friendships, and sometimes entire households which it has entered and set in order. Whatever it has handled it forthwith makes lovable, notable, admirable.

Therefore the power and the greatness of virtue cannot rise to greater heights, because increase is denied to that which is superlatively great. You will find nothing straighter than the straight, nothing truer than the truth, and nothing more temperate than that which is temperate. [9] Every virtue is limitless; for limits depend upon definite measurements. Constancy cannot advance further, any more than fidelity, or truthfulness, or loyalty. What can be added to that which is perfect? Nothing otherwise that was not perfect to which something has been added. Nor can anything be added to virtue, either, for if anything can be added thereto, it must have contained a defect. Honour, also, permits of no addition; for it is honourable because of the very qualities which I have mentioned.[5] What then? Do you think that propriety, justice, lawfulness, do not also belong to the same type, and that they are kept within fixed limits? The ability to increase is proof that a thing is still imperfect.

[10]The good, in every instance, is subject to these same laws. The advantage of the state and that of the individual are yoked together; indeed it is as impossible to separate them as to separate the commendable from the desirable. Therefore, virtues are mutually equal; and so are the works of virtue, and all men who are so fortunate as to possess these virtues. [11]But, since the virtues of plants and of animals are perishable, they are also frail and fleeting and uncertain. They spring up, and they sink down again, and for this reason they are not rated at the same value; but to human virtues only one rule applies. For right reason is single and of but one kind. Nothing is more divine than the divine, or more heavenly than the heavenly. [12]Mortal things decay, fall, are worn out, grow up, are exhausted, and replenished. Hence, in their case, in view of the uncertainty of their lot, there is inequality; but of things divine the nature is one. Reason, however, is nothing else than a portion of the divine spirit set in a human body.[6] If reason is divine, and the good in no case lacks reason, then the good in every case is divine. And furthermore, there is no distinction between things divine; hence there is none between goods, either. Therefore it follows that joy and a brave unyielding endurance of torture are equal goods; for in both there is the same greatness of soul relaxed and cheerful in the one case, in the other combative and braced for action. [13]What? Do you not think that the virtue of him who bravely storms the enemy's stronghold is equal to that of him who endures a siege with the utmost patience? Great is Scipio when he invests Numantia,[7] and constrains and compels the hands of an enemy, whom he could not conquer, to resort to their own destruction. Great also are the souls of the defenders–men who know that, as long as the path to death lies open, the blockade is not complete, men who breathe their last in the arms of liberty. In like manner, the other virtues are also equal as compared with one another: tranquillity, simplicity, generosity, constancy, equanimity, endurance. For underlying them all is a single virtue–that which renders the soul straight and unswerving.

[14]"What then," you say; "is there no difference between joy and unyielding endurance of pain?" None at all, as regards the virtues themselves; very great, however, in the circumstances in which either of these two virtues is displayed. In the one case, there is a natural relaxation and loosening of the soul; in the other there is an unnatural pain. Hence these circumstances, between which a great distinction can be drawn, belong to the category of indifferent things,[8] but the virtue shown in each case is equal. [15]Virtue is not changed by the matter with which it deals; if the matter is hard and stubborn, it does not make the virtue worse; if pleasant and joyous, it does not make it better. Therefore, virtue necessarily remains equal. For, in each case, what is done is done with equal uprightness, with equal wisdom, and with equal honour. Hence the states of goodness involved are equal, and it is impossible for a man to transcend these states of goodness by conducting himself better, either the one man in his joy, or the other amid his suffering. And two goods, neither of which can possibly be better, are equal. [16]For if things which are extrinsic to virtue can either diminish or increase virtue, then that which is honourable[9] ceases to be the only good. If you grant this, honour has wholly perished. And why? Let me tell you: it is because no act is honourable that is done by an unwilling agent, that is compulsory. Every honourable act is voluntary. Alloy it with reluctance, complaints, cowardice, or fear, and it loses its best characteristic–self-approval. That which is not free cannot be honourable; for fear means slavery. [17]The honourable is wholly free from anxiety and is calm; if it ever objects, laments, or regards anything as an evil, it becomes subject to disturbance and begins to flounder about amid great confusion. For on one side the semblance of right calls to it, on the other the suspicion of evil drags it back, therefore, when a man is about to do something honourable, he should not regard any obstacles as evils, even though he regard them as inconvenient, but he should will to do the deed, and do it willingly. For every honourable act is done without commands or compulsion; it is unalloyed and contains no admixture of evil.

only in adversity,–for example, equanimity in enduring severe illness or exile. Certain goods are indifferent; these are no more according to nature than contrary to nature, as, for example, a discreet gait and a sedate posture in a chair. For sitting is an act that is not less according to nature than standing or walking. [37]The two kinds of goods which are of a higher order are different; the primary are according to nature,–such as deriving joy from the dutiful behaviour of one's children and from the well-being of one's country. The secondary are contrary to nature,–such as fortitude in resisting torture or in enduring thirst when illness makes the vitals feverish. [38]"What then," you say; "can anything that is contrary to nature be a good?" Of course not; but that in which this good takes its rise is sometimes contrary to nature. For being wounded, wasting away over a fire, being afflicted with bad health,–such things are contrary to nature; but it is in accordance with nature for a man to preserve an indomitable soul amid such distresses. [39]To explain my thought briefly, the material with which a good is concerned is sometimes contrary to nature, but a good itself never is contrary, since no good is without reason, and reason is in accordance with nature.

"What, then," you ask, "is reason?" It is copying nature.[15] "And what," you say, "is the greatest good that man can possess?" It is to conduct oneself according to what nature wills. [40]"There is no doubt," says the objector, "that peace affords more happiness when it has not been assailed than when it has been recovered at the cost of great slaughter." "There is no doubt also," he continues, "that health which has not been impaired affords more happiness than health which has been restored to soundness by means of force, as it were, and by endurance of suffering, after serious illnesses that threaten life itself. And similarly there will be no doubt that joy is a greater good than a soul's struggle to endure to the bitter end the torments of wounds or burning at the stake." [41]By no means. For things that result from hazard admit of wide distinctions, since they are rated according to their usefulness in the eyes of those who experience them, but with regard to goods, the only point to be considered is that they are in agreement with nature; and this is equal in the case of all goods. When at a meeting of the Senate we vote in favour of someone's motion, it cannot be said, "A. is more in accord with the motion than B." All alike vote for the same motion. I make the same statement with regard to virtues,–they are all in accord with nature; and I make it with regard to goods also,–they are all in accord with nature. [42]One man dies young, another in old age, and still another in infancy, having enjoyed nothing more than a mere glimpse out into life. They have all been equally subject to death, even though death has permitted the one to proceed farther along the pathway of life, has cut off the life of the second in his flower, and has broken off the life of the third at its very beginning. [43]Some get their release at the dinner-table. Others extend their sleep into the sleep of death. Some are blotted out during dissipation.[16] Now contrast with these persons individuals who have been pierced by the sword, or bitten to death by snakes, or crushed in ruins, or tortured piecemeal out of existence by the prolonged twisting of their sinews. Some of these departures may be regarded as better, some as worse; but the act of dying is equal in all. The methods of ending life are different; but the end is one and the same. Death has no degrees of greater or less; for it has the same limit in all instances,–the finishing of life.

[44]The same thing holds true, I assure you, concerning goods; you will find one amid circumstances of pure pleasure, another amid sorrow and bitterness. The one controls the favours of fortune; the other overcomes her onslaughts. Each is equally a good, although the one travels a level and easy road, and the other a rough road. And the end of them all is the same–they are goods, they are worthy of praise, they accompany virtue and reason. Virtue makes all the things that it acknowledges equal to one another. [45]You need not wonder that this is one of our principles; we find mentioned in the works of Epicurus[17] two goods, of which his Supreme Good, or blessedness, is composed, namely, a body free from pain and a soul free from disturbance. These goods, if they are complete, do not increase; for how can that which is complete increase? The body is, let us suppose, free from pain; what increase can there be to this absence of pain? The soul is composed and calm; what increase can there be to this tranquillity?

[46]Just as fair weather, purified into the purest brilliancy, does not admit of a still greater degree of clearness; so, when a man takes care of his body and of his soul, weaving the texture of his good from both, his condition is perfect, and he has found the consummation of his prayers, if there is no commotion in his soul or pain in his body. Whatever delights fall to his lot over and above these two things do not increase his Supreme Good; they merely season it, so to speak, and add spice to it. For the absolute good of man's nature is satisfied with peace in the body and peace in the soul. [47]I can show you at this moment in the writings of Epicurus[18] a graded list of goods just like that of our own school. For there are some things, he declares, which he prefers should fall to his lot, such as bodily rest free from all inconvenience, and relaxation of the soul as it takes delight in the contemplation of its own goods. And there are other things which, though he would prefer that they did not happen, he nevertheless praises and approves, for example, the kind of resignation, in times of ill-health and serious suffering, to which I alluded a moment ago, and which Epicurus displayed on that last and most blessed day of his life. For he tells us[19] that he had to endure excruciating agony from a diseased bladder and from an ulcerated stomach, so acute that it permitted no increase of pain; "and yet," he says, "that day was none the less happy." And no man can spend such a day in happiness unless he possesses the Supreme Good.

[48]We therefore find mentioned, even by Epicurus,[20] those goods which one would prefer not to experience; which, however, because circumstances have decided thus, must be welcomed and approved and placed on a level with the highest goods. We cannot say that the good which has rounded out[21] a happy life, the good for which Epicurus rendered thanks in the last words he uttered, is not equal to the greatest. [49]Allow me, excellent Lucilius, to utter a still bolder word: if any goods could be greater than others, I should prefer those which seem harsh to those which are mild and alluring, and should pronounce them greater. For it is more of an accomplishment to break one's way through difficulties than to keep joy within bounds. [50]It requires the same use of reason, I am fully aware, for a man to endure prosperity well and also to endure misfortune bravely. What man may be just as brave who sleeps in front of the ramparts without fear of danger when no enemy attacks the camp, as the man who, when the tendons of his legs have been severed, holds himself up on his knees and does not let fall his weapons; but it is to the blood-stained soldier returning from the front that men cry: "Well done, thou hero!"[22] And therefore I should bestow greater praise upon those goods that have stood trial and show courage, and have fought it out with fortune. [51]Should I hesitate whether to give greater praise to the maimed and shrivelled hand of Mucius[23] than to the uninjured hand of the bravest man in the world? There stood Mucius, despising the enemy and despising the fire, and watched his hand as it dripped blood over the fire on his enemy's altar, until Porsenna, envying the fame of the hero whose punishment he was advocating, ordered the fire to be removed against the will of the victim.

[52]Why should I not reckon this good among the primary goods, and deem it in so far greater than those other goods which are unattended by danger and have made no trial of fortune, as it is a rarer thing to have overcome a foe with a hand lost than with a hand armed? "What then?" you say; "shall you desire this good for yourself?" Of course I shall. For this is a thing that a man cannot achieve unless he can also desire it. [53]Should I desire, instead, to be allowed to stretch out my limbs for my slaves to massage,[24] or to have a woman, or a man changed into the likeness of a woman, pull my finger-joints? I cannot help believing that Mucius was all the more lucky because he manipulated the flames as calmly as if he were holding out his hand to the manipulator. He had wiped out all his previous mistakes; he finished the war unarmed and maimed; and with that stump of a hand he conquered two kings.[25] Farewell.

Footnotes

1. Vergil, *Aeneid*, v. 344.

2. Seneca is not speaking here of the three generic virtues (physical, ethical, logical), nor of the three kinds of goods (based on bodily advantage) which were classified by

the Peripatetic school; he is only speaking of three sorts of circumstances under which the good can manifest itself. And in §§ 36 ff. he shows that he regards only the first two classes as real goods. See Zeller, *Stoics*, p. 230, n. 3.

3. *Siccus* (not in the sense of Ep. xviii. 4) here means "vigorous," "healthy," "dry"; i.e., free from dropsy, catarrh, etc.

4. Cf., from among many passages, Ep. lxxi. 20 f. and xcii. 16 ff.

5. i.e., constancy, fidelity, etc.

6. *Ratio* (λόγος) is also defined as God, as Absolute Truth, Destiny, etc. The same idea is evident in the definition of *sapientia* (the object of philosophy) as *rerum divinarum et humanarum . . . scientia* (Cic. *Off.* ii. 2. 5, etc.), and *nosse divina et humana et horum causas*, etc.

7. A Spanish city, reduced and razed to the ground in 133 B.C. by Scipio Africanus, the conqueror of Carthage.

8. Cf. Ep. xxxi. 4 and footnote (Vol. I.).

9. Cf. Cicero, De Fin. ii. 14 f. Rackham translates as "moral worth,"–a reminiscence of τὸ καλόν.

10. One of the stock bits of heroism attributed to the ideal wise man. Cf. Epicurus (Frag. 601 Usener), Cicero, *Tusc.* ii. 7. 17, etc.

11. A slight variation of the idea in Cicero, *De Orat.* i. 196 *si nos . . . nostra patria delectat, cuius rei tanta est vis ac tanta natura, ut Ithacam illam in asperrimis saxulis tamquam nidulum adfixam sapientissimus vir immortalitati anteponeret.*

12. i.e., of the soul, of the body, and of external goods.

13. Buecheler thinks that this alliterative phrase of Seneca's is an echo of some popular proverb or line taken from a play.

14. Here Seneca is reminding Lucillius, as he so often does in the earlier letters, that the evidence of the senses is only a stepping-stone to higher ideas–an Epicurean tenet.

15. Another definition, developing further the thought expressed in § 12.

16. *Transcriber's Note: The Latin, which Gummere translates politely, is: "Aliquem concubitus extinxit," i.e., "Others are extinguished during sex."*

17. Frag. 434 Usener.

18. Frag. 449 Usener.

19. Frag. 138 Usener.

20. See above, § 47.

21. *Clausula* has, among other meanings, that of "a period" (Quintil. viii. 5), and "the rhythmic close of a period" (Cic. *De Orat.* iii. 192).

22. For a full discussion of this phrase see Conington, *Excursus to Vergil's Aeneid*, ix. 641.

23. For the story see Livy, ii. 12 ff.

24. A rare word–sometimes spelled *malacisso*,–used by Plautus (*Bacch.* 73) and Laberius, but not in a technical sense.

25. Porsenna and Tarquin.

LXVII. ON ILL-HEALTH AND ENDURANCE OF SUFFERING

[1]If I may begin with a commonplace remark,[1] spring is gradually disclosing itself; but though it is rounding into summer, when you would expect hot weather, it has kept rather cool, and one cannot yet be sure of it. For it often slides back into winter weather. Do you wish to know how uncertain it still is? I do not yet trust myself to a bath which is absolutely cold; even at this time I break its chill. You may say that this is no way to show the endurance either of heat or of cold; very true, dear Lucilius, but at my time of life one is at length contented with the natural chill of the body. I can scarcely thaw out in the middle of summer. Accordingly, I spend most of the time bundled up; [2]and I thank old age for keeping me fastened to my bed.[2] Why should I not thank old

age on this account? That which I ought not to wish to do, I lack the ability to do. Most of my converse is with books. Whenever your letters arrive, I imagine that I am with you, and I have the feeling that I am about to speak my answer, instead of writing it. Therefore let us together investigate the nature of this problem of yours, just as if we were conversing with one another.[3]

[3] You ask me whether every good is desirable. You say: "If it is a good to be brave under torture, to go to the stake with a stout heart, to endure illness with resignation, it follows that these things are desirable. But I do not see that any of them is worth praying for. At any rate I have as yet known of no man who has paid a vow by reason of having been cut to pieces by the rod, or twisted out of shape by the gout, or made taller by the rack." [4] My dear Lucilius, you must distinguish between these cases; you will then comprehend that there is something in them that is to be desired. I should prefer to be free from torture; but if the time comes when it must be endured, I shall desire that I may conduct myself therein with bravery, honour, and courage. Of course I prefer that war should not occur; but if war does occur, I shall desire that I may nobly endure the wounds, the starvation, and all that the exigency of war brings. Nor am I so mad as to crave illness; but if I must suffer illness, I shall desire that I may do nothing which shows lack of restraint, and nothing that is unmanly. The conclusion is, not that hardships are desirable, but that virtue is desirable, which enables us patiently to endure hardships.

[5] Certain of our school,[4] think that, of all such qualities, a stout endurance is not desirable,–though not to be deprecated either–because we ought to seek by prayer only the good which is unalloyed, peaceful, and beyond the reach of trouble. Personally, I do not agree with them. And why? First, because it is impossible for anything to be good without being also desirable. Because, again, if virtue is desirable, and if nothing that is good lacks virtue, then everything good is desirable. And, lastly, because a brave endurance even under torture is desirable. [6] At this point I ask you: is not bravery desirable? And yet bravery despises and challenges danger. The most beautiful and most admirable part of bravery is that it does not shrink from the stake, advances to meet wounds, and sometimes does not even avoid the spear, but meets it with opposing breast. If bravery is desirable, so is patient endurance of torture; for this is a part of bravery. Only sift these things, as I have suggested; then there will be nothing which can lead you astray. For it is not mere endurance of torture, but brave endurance, that is desirable. I therefore desire that "brave" endurance; and this is virtue.

[7] "But," you say, "who ever desired such a thing for himself?" Some prayers are open and outspoken, when the requests are offered specifically; other prayers are indirectly expressed, when they include many requests under one title. For example, I desire a life of honour. Now a life of honour includes various kinds of conduct; it may include the chest in which Regulus was confined, or the wound of Cato which was torn open by Cato's own hand, or the exile of Rutilius,[5] or the cup of poison which removed Socrates from gaol to heaven. Accordingly, in praying for a life of honour, I have prayed also for those things without which, on some occasions, life cannot be honourable

> [8] O thrice and four times blest were they
> Who underneath the lofty walls of Troy
> Met happy death before their parents' eyes![6]

What does it matter whether you offer this prayer for some individual, or admit that it was desirable in the past? [9] Decius sacrificed himself for the State; he set spurs to his horse and rushed into the midst of the foe, seeking death. The second Decius, rivalling his father's valour, reproducing the words which had become sacred[7] and already household words, dashed into the thickest of the fight, anxious only that his sacrifice might bring omen of success,[8] and regarding a noble death as a thing to be desired. Do you doubt, then, whether it is best to die glorious and performing some deed of valour? [10] When one endures torture bravely, one is using all the virtues. Endurance may perhaps be the only virtue that is on view and most manifest; but bravery is there too, and endurance and resignation and long-suffering are its branches. There, too, is foresight; for without foresight no plan can be undertaken; it is foresight that advises one to bear as bravely as possible the things one cannot avoid. There also is stead-fastness, which cannot be dislodged from its position, which the wrench of no force can cause to abandon its purpose. There is the whole inseparable company of virtues; every honourable act is the work of one single virtue, but it is in accordance with the judgment of the whole council. And that which is approved by all the virtues, even though it seems to be the work of one alone, is desirable.

[11]What? Do you think that those things only are desirable which come to us amid pleasure and ease, and which we bedeck our doors to welcome?[9] There are certain goods whose features are forbidding. There are certain prayers which are offered by a throng, not of men who rejoice, but of men who bow down reverently and worship. [12]Was it not in this fashion, think you, that Regulus prayed that he might reach Car-thage? Clothe yourself with a hero's courage, and withdraw for a little space from the opinions of the common man. Form a proper conception of the image of virtue, a thing of exceeding beauty and grandeur; this image is not to be worshipped by us with in-cense or garlands, but with sweat and blood. [13]Behold Marcus Cato, laying upon that hallowed breast his unspotted hands, and tearing apart the wounds which had not gone deep enough to kill him! Which, pray, shall you say to him: "I hope all will be as you wish," and "I am grieved," or shall it be "Good fortune in your undertaking!"?

[14]In this connexion I think of our friend Demetrius, who calls an easy existence, untroubled by the attacks of Fortune, a "Dead Sea."[10] If you have nothing to stir you up and rouse you to action, nothing which will test your resolution by its threats and hostilities; if you recline in unshaken comfort, it is not tranquillity; it is merely a flat calm. [15]The Stoic Attalus was wont to say: "I should prefer that Fortune keep me in her camp rather than in the lap of luxury. If I am tortured, but bear it bravely, all is well; if I die, but die bravely, it is also well." Listen to Epicurus; he will tell you that it is actually pleasant.[11] I myself shall never apply an effeminate word to an act so honourable and austere. If I go to the stake, I shall go unbeaten. [16]Why should I not regard this as de-sirable–not because the fire, burns me, but because it does not overcome me? Nothing is more excellent or more beautiful than virtue; whatever we do in obedience to her orders is both good and desirable. Farewell.

Footnotes

1. See Introduction (Vol. I. p. x), and the opening sentences of Epp. lxxvii., lxxxvii., and others.

2. Seneca had a delicate constitution (see Introduction). In the letters he speaks of suf-fering from asthma (liv.), catarrh (lxxviii.), and fever (civ.).

3. Cf. lxxv. 1 *qualis sermo meus esset, si una sederemus aut ambularemus.*

4. i.e., the Stoics.

5. Banished from Rome in 92 B.C. Cf. Ep. xxiv. 4.

6. Vergil, *Aeneid,* i. 94 ff.

7. Cf. Livy, vii. 9. 6 ff. . . . . *legiones auxiliaque hostium mecum deis manibus Tellurique devoveo.*

8. *Ut litaret:* i.e., that by his sacrifice he might secure an omen of success. Cf. Pliny, *N. H.* viii. 45, and Suetonius, *Augustus,* 96: "At the siege of Perusia, when he found the sacrifices were not favourable (*sacrificio non litanti*), Augustus called for more victims."

9. *Donaria* at the doors of temples signified public rejoicing; cf. Tibullus, i. 15 f.

> *Flava Ceres, tibi sit nostro de rure corona*
> *Spicea, quae templi pendeat ante fores.*

Myrtle decorated the bridegroom's house-door; garlands heralded the birth of a child (Juvenal, ix. 85).

10. Cf. Pliny, *N. H.* iv. 13. Besides the Dead Sea of Palestine, the term was applied to any sluggish body of water.

11. Cf. Ep. lxvi. 18.

LXVIII. ON WISDOM AND RETIREMENT

[1]I fall in with your plan; retire and conceal yourself in repose. But at the same time conceal your retirement also. In doing this, you may be sure that you will be following the example of the Stoics, if not their precept. But you will be acting according to their precept also; you will thus satisfy both yourself and any Stoic you please. [2]We Stoics[1] do not urge men to take up public life in every case, or at all times, or without any qualification. Besides, when we have assigned to our wise man that field of public life which is worthy of him,—in other words, the universe,—he is then not apart from public life, even if he withdraws; nay, perhaps he has abandoned only one little corner thereof and has passed over into greater and wider regions; and when he has been set in the heavens, he understands how lowly was the place in which he sat when he mounted the curule chair or the judgment-seat. Lay this to heart, that the wise man is never more active in affairs than when things divine as well as things human have come within his ken.

[3]I now return to the advice which I set out to give you,—that you keep your retirement in the background. There is no need to fasten a placard upon yourself with the words: "Philosopher and Quietist." Give your purpose some other name; call it ill-health and bodily weakness, or mere laziness. To boast of our retirement is but idle self-seeking. [4]Certain animals hide themselves from discovery by confusing the marks of their foot-prints in the neighbourhood of their lairs. You should do the same. Otherwise, there will always be someone dogging your footsteps. Many men pass by that which is visible, and peer after things hidden and concealed; a locked room invites the thief. Things which lie in the open appear cheap; the house-breaker passes by that which is exposed to view. This is the way of the world, and the way of all ignorant men: they crave to burst in upon hidden things. It is therefore best not to vaunt one's retirement. [5]It is, however, a sort of vaunting to make too much of one's concealment and of one's withdrawal from the sight of men. So-and-so[2] has gone into his retreat at Tarentum; that other man has shut himself up at Naples; this third person for many years has not crossed the threshold of his own house. To advertise one's retirement is to collect a crowd. [6]When you withdraw from the world your business is to talk with yourself, not to have men talk about you. But what shall you talk about? Do just what people are fond of doing when they talk about their neighbours,—speak ill of yourself when by yourself; then you will become accustomed both to speak and to hear the truth. Above all, however, ponder that which you come to feel is your greatest weakness. [7]Each man knows best the defects of his own body. And so one relieves his stomach by vomiting, another props it up by frequent eating, another drains and purges his body by periodic fasting. Those whose feet are visited by pain abstain either from wine or from the bath. In general, men who are careless in other respects go out of their way to relieve the disease which frequently afflicts them. So it is with our souls; there are in them certain parts which are, so to speak, on the sick-list,[3] and to these parts the cure must be applied.

[8]What, then, am I myself doing with my leisure? I am trying to cure my own sores. If I were to show you a swollen foot, or an inflamed hand, or some shrivelled sinews in a withered leg, you would permit me to lie quiet in one place and to apply lotions to the diseased member.[4] But my trouble is greater than any of these, and I cannot show it to you. The abscess, or ulcer, is deep within my breast. Pray, pray, do not commend me, do not say: "What a great man! He has learned to despise all things; condemning the madnesses of man's life, he has made his escape!" I have condemned nothing except myself. [9]There is no reason why you should desire to come to me for the sake of making progress. You are mistaken if you think that you will get any assistance from this quarter; it is not a physician that dwells here, but a sick man. I would rather have you say, on leaving my presence: "I used to think him a happy man and a learned one, and I had pricked up my ears to hear him; but I have been defrauded. I have seen nothing, heard nothing which I craved and which I came back to hear." If you feel thus, and speak thus, some progress has been made. I prefer you to pardon rather than

their best to make philosophy seem difficult rather than great.[3]

[7]Socrates, who recalled[4] the whole of philosophy to rules of conduct, and asserted that the highest wisdom consisted in distinguishing between good and evil, said: "Follow these rules, if my words carry weight with you, in order that you may be happy; and let some men think you even a fool. Allow any man who so desires to insult you and work you wrong; but if only virtue dwells with you, you will suffer nothing. If you wish to be happy, if you would be in good faith a good man[5] let one person or another despise you." No man can accomplish this unless he has come to regard all goods as equal, for the reason that no good exists without that which is honourable, and that which is honourable is in every case equal. [8]You may say: "What then? Is there no difference between Cato's being elected praetor and his failure at the polls? Or whether Cato is conquered or conqueror in the battle-line of Pharsalia? And when Cato could not be defeated, though his party met defeat, was not this goodness of his equal to that which would have been his if he had returned victorious to his native land and arranged a peace?" Of course it was; for it is by the same virtue that evil fortune is overcome and good fortune is controlled. Virtue however, cannot be increased or decreased; its stature is uniform. [9]"But," you will object, "Gnaeus Pompey will lose his army; the patricians, those noblest patterns of the State's creation, and the front-rank men of Pompey's party, a senate under arms, will be routed in a single engagement; the ruins of that great oligarchy will be scattered all over the world; one division will fall in Egypt, another in Africa, and another in Spain![6] And the poor State will not be allowed even the privilege of being ruined once for all!" [10]Yes, all this may happen; Juba's familiarity with every position in his own kingdom may be of no avail to him, of no avail the resolute bravery of his people when fighting for their king; even the men of Utica, crushed by their troubles, may waver in their allegiance; and the good fortune which ever attended men of the name of Scipio may desert Scipio in Africa. But long ago destiny "saw to it that Cato should come to no harm."[7]

[11]"He was conquered in spite of it all!" Well, you may include this among Cato's "failures"; Cato will bear with an equally stout heart anything that thwarts him of his victory, as he bore that which thwarted him of his praetorship. The day whereon he failed of election, he spent in play; the night wherein he intended to die, he spent in reading.[8] He regarded in the same light both the loss of his praetorship and the loss of his life; he had convinced himself that he ought to endure anything which might happen. [12]Why should he not suffer, bravely and calmly, a change in the government? For what is free from the risk of change? Neither earth, nor sky, nor the whole fabric of our universe, though it be controlled by the hand of God. It will not always preserve its present order; it will be thrown from its course in days to come.[9] [13]All things move in accord with their appointed times; they are destined to be born, to grow, and to be destroyed. The stars which you see moving above us, and this seemingly immovable earth to which we cling and on which we are set, will be consumed and will cease to exist. There is nothing that does not have its old age; the intervals are merely unequal at which Nature sends forth all these things towards the same goal. Whatever is will cease to be, and yet it will not perish, but will be resolved into its elements. [14]To our minds, this process means perishing, for we behold only that which is nearest; our sluggish mind, under allegiance to the body, does not penetrate to bournes beyond. Were it not so, the mind would endure with greater courage its own ending and that of its possessions, if only it could hope that life and death, like the whole universe about us, go by turns, that whatever has been put together is broken up again, that whatever has been broken up is put together again, and that the eternal craftsmanship of God, who controls all things is working at this task.

[15]Therefore the wise man will say just what a Marcus Cato would say, after reviewing his past life: "The whole race of man, both that which is and that which is to be, is condemned to die. Of all the cities that at any time have held sway over the world, and of all that have been the splendid ornaments of empires not their own, men shall some day ask where they were, and they shall be swept away by destructions of various kinds; some shall be ruined by wars, others shall be wasted away by inactivity and by

the kind of peace which ends in sloth, or by that vice which is fraught with destruction even for mighty dynasties,–luxury. All these fertile plains shall be buried out of sight by a sudden overflowing of the sea, or a slipping of the soil, as it settles to lower levels, shall draw them suddenly into a yawning chasm. Why then should I be angry or feel sorrow, if I precede the general destruction by a tiny interval of time?" [16]Let great souls comply with God's wishes, and suffer unhesitatingly whatever fate the law of the universe ordains; for the soul at death is either sent forth into a better life, destined to dwell with deity amid greater radiance and calm, or else, at least, without suffering any harm to itself, it will be mingled with nature again, and will return to the universe.[10]

Therefore Cato's honourable death was no less a good than his honourable life, since virtue admits of no stretching.[11] Socrates used to say that verity[12] and virtue were the same. Just as truth does not grow, so neither does virtue grow; for it has its due proportions and is complete. [17]You need not, therefore, wonder that goods are equal,[13] both those which are to be deliberately chosen, and those which circumstances have imposed. For if you once adopt the view that they are unequal, deeming, for instance, a brave endurance of torture as among the lesser goods, you will be including it among the evils also; you will pronounce Socrates unhappy in his prison, Cato unhappy when he reopens his wounds with more courage than he allowed in inflicting them, and Regulus the most ill-starred of all when he pays the penalty for keeping his word even with his enemies. And yet no man, even the most effeminate person in the world, has ever dared to maintain such an opinion. For though such persons deny that a man like Regulus is happy, yet for all that they also deny that he is wretched. [18]The earlier Academics[14] do indeed admit that a man is happy even amid such tortures, but do not admit that he is completely or fully happy. With this view we cannot in any wise agree; for unless a man is happy, he has not attained the Supreme Good; and the good which is supreme admits of no higher degree, if only virtue exists within this man, and if adversity does not impair his virtue, and if, though the body be injured, the virtue abides unharmed. And it does abide. For I understand virtue to be high-spirited and exalted, so that it is aroused by anything that molests it. [19]This spirit, which young men of noble breeding often assume, when they are so deeply stirred by the beauty of some honourable object that they despise all the gifts of chance, is assuredly infused in us and communicated to us by wisdom. Wisdom will bring the conviction that there is but one good–that which is honourable; that this can neither be shortened nor extended, any more than a carpenter's rule, with which straight lines are tested, can be bent. Any change in the rule means spoiling the straight line. [20]Applying, therefore, this same figure to virtue, we shall say: virtue also is straight, and admits of no bending. What can be made more tense than a thing which is already rigid? Such is virtue, which passes judgment on everything, but nothing passes judgment on virtue. And if this rule, virtue, cannot itself be made more straight, neither can the things created by virtue be in one case straighter and in another less straight. For they must necessarily correspond to virtue; hence they are equal.

[21]"What," you say, "do you call reclining at a banquet and submitting to torture equally good?" Does this seem surprising to you? You may be still more surprised at the following,–that reclining at a banquet is an evil, while reclining on the rack is a good, if the former act is done in a shameful, and the latter in an honourable manner. It is not the material that makes these actions good or bad; it is the virtue. All acts in which virtue has disclosed itself are of the same measure and value. [22]At this moment the man who measures the souls of all men by his own is shaking his fist in my face because I hold that there is a parity between the goods involved in the case of one who passes sentence honourably, and of one who suffers sentence honourably; or because I hold that there is a parity between the goods of one who celebrates a triumph, and of one who, unconquered in spirit, is carried before the victor's chariot. For such critics think that whatever they themselves cannot do, is not done; they pass judgment on virtue in the light of their own weaknesses. [23]Why do you marvel if it helps a man, and on occasion even pleases him, to be burned, wounded, slain, or bound in prison?

To a luxurious man, a simple life is a penalty; to a lazy man, work is punishment; the dandy pities the diligent man; to the slothful, studies are torture. Similarly, we regard those things with respect to which we are all infirm of disposition, as hard and beyond endurance, forgetting what a torment it is to many men to abstain from wine or to be routed from their beds at break of day. These actions are not essentially difficult; it is we ourselves that are soft and flabby. [24]We must pass judgment concerning great matters with greatness of soul; otherwise, that which is really our fault will seem to be their fault. So it is that certain objects which are perfectly straight, when sunk in water appear to the onlooker as bent or broken off.[15] It matters not only what you see, but with what eyes you see it; our souls are too dull of vision to perceive the truth. [25]But give me an unspoiled and sturdy-minded young man; he will pronounce more fortunate one who sustains on unbending shoulders the whole weight of adversity, who stands out superior to Fortune. It is not a cause for wonder that one is not tossed about when the weather is calm; reserve your wonderment for cases where a man is lifted up when all others sink, and keeps his footing when all others are prostrate.

[26]What element of evil is there in torture and in the other things which we call hardships? It seems to me that there is this evil,–that the mind sags, and bends, and collapses. But none of these things can happen to the sage; he stands erect under any load. Nothing can subdue him; nothing that must be endured annoys him. For he does not complain that he has been struck by that which can strike any man. He knows his own strength; he knows that he was born to carry burdens. [27]I do not withdraw the wise man from the category of man, nor do I deny to him the sense of pain as though he were a rock that has no feelings at all. I remember that he is made up of two parts: the one part is irrational,–it is this that may be bitten, burned, or hurt; the other part is rational,–it is this which holds resolutely to opinions, is courageous, and unconquerable.[16] In the latter is situated man's Supreme Good. Before this is completely attained, the mind wavers in uncertainty; only when it is fully achieved is the mind fixed and steady. [28]And so when one has just begun, or is on one's way to the heights and is cultivating virtue, or even if one is drawing near the perfect good but has not yet put the finishing touch upon it, one will retrograde at times and there will be a certain slackening of mental effort. For such a man has not yet traversed the doubtful ground; he is still standing in slippery places. But the happy man, whose virtue is complete, loves himself most of all when his bravery has been submitted to the severest test, and when he not only, endures but welcomes that which all other men regard with fear, if it is the price which he must pay for the performance of a duty which honour imposes, and he greatly prefers to have men say of him: "how much more noble!" rather than "how much more lucky!"[17]

[29]And now I have reached the point to which your patient waiting summons me. You must not think that our human virtue transcends nature; the wise man will tremble, will feel pain, will turn pale,[18] For all these are sensations of the body. Where, then, is the abode of utter distress, of that which is truly an evil? In the other part of us, no doubt, if it is the mind that these trials drag down, force to a confession of its servitude, and cause to regret its existence. [30]The wise man, indeed, overcomes Fortune by his virtue, but many who profess wisdom are sometimes frightened by the most unsubstantial threats. And at this stage it is a mistake on our part to make the same demands upon the wise man and upon the learner.[19] I still exhort myself to do that which I recommend; but my exhortations are not yet followed. And even if this were the case, I should not have these principles so ready for practice, or so well trained, that they would rush to my assistance in every crisis. [31]Just as wool takes up certain colours at once,[20] while there are others which it will not absorb unless it is soaked and steeped in them many times; so other systems of doctrine can be immediately applied by men's minds after once being accepted, but this system of which I speak, unless it has gone deep and has sunk in for a long time, and has not merely coloured but thoroughly permeated the soul, does not fulfil any of its promises. [32]The matter can be imparted quickly and in very few words: "Virtue is the only good; at any rate there is no good without virtue; and virtue itself is situated in our nobler part, that is, the rational part."

And what will this virtue be? A true and never-swerving judgment. For therefrom will spring all mental impulses, and by its agency every external appearance that stirs our impulses will be clarified. [33] It will be in keeping with this judgment to judge all things that have been coloured by virtue as goods, and as equal goods.

Bodily goods are, to be sure, good for the body; but they are not absolutely good. There will indeed be some value in them; but they will possess no genuine merit, for they will differ greatly; some will be less, others greater. [34] And we are constrained to acknowledge that there are great differences among the very followers of wisdom. One man has already made so much progress that he dares to raise his eyes and look Fortune in the face, but not persistently, for his eyes soon drop, dazzled by her overwhelming splendour; another has made so much progress that he is able to match glances with her,—that is, unless he has already reached the summit and is full of confidence.[21] [35] That which is short of perfection must necessarily be unsteady, at one time progressing, at another slipping or growing faint; and it will surely slip back unless it keeps struggling ahead; for if a man slackens at all in zeal and faithful application, he must retrograde. No one can resume his progress at the point where he left off. [36] Therefore let us press on and persevere. There remains much more of the road than we have put behind us; but the greater part of progress is the desire to progress.

I fully understand what this task is. It is a thing which I desire, and I desire it with all my heart. I see that you also have been aroused and are hastening with great zeal towards infinite beauty. Let us, then, hasten; only on these terms will life be a boon to us; otherwise, there is delay, and indeed disgraceful delay, while we busy ourselves with revolting things. Let us see to it that all time belongs to us. This, however, cannot be unless first of all our own selves begin to belong to us. [37] And when will it be our privilege to despise both kinds of fortune? When will it be our privilege, after all the passions have been subdued and brought under our own control, to utter the words "I have conquered!"? Do you ask me whom I have conquered? Neither the Persians, nor the far-off Medes, nor any warlike race that lies beyond the Dahae;[22] not these, but greed, ambition, and the fear of death that has conquered the conquerors of the world. Farewell.

Footnotes

1. A similar argument is found in Ep. lxv. §§ 5 ff., containing the same figure of thought.

2. For a definition of *honestum* see Cicero, *De Fin.* ii. 45 ff., and Rackham's note, explaining it as "τὸ καλόν, the morally beautiful or good."

3. See, for example, the syllogistic display which is ridiculed in Ep. xlviii. 6.

4. i.e., from being mere word-play.

5. Hense suggests that Seneca may be rendering the phrase of Simonides–ἀνὴρ ἀληθῶς ἀγαθός.

6. Egypt–47 B.C.; Africa (Thapsus)–46 B.C.; Spain (Munda)–45 B.C.

7. A sort of serious parody of the *senatus consultum ultimum*. For a discussion of the history and meaning of the phrase see W. Warde Fowler's *Cicero*, pp. 151-158.

8. Plato's *Phaedo*. Cato slew himself at Utica, 46 B.C., after Scipio's defeat at Thapsus.

9. Cf. Ep. ix. 16 f. *resoluto mundo*, etc.

10. For a clear and full discussion regarding Stoic views of the immortality of the soul, and Seneca's own opinion thereon, see E. V. Arnold, *Roman Stoicism*, pp. 262 ff.

11. Cf. § 20 of this letter: *rigida re quid amplius intendi potest?*

12. i.e., knowledge of facts, as Seneca so often says. Cf. Plato, *Meno*, 87 C ἐπιστήμη τις ἡ ἀρετή, and Aristotle, *Eth.* vi. 13 Σωκράτης . . . λόγους τὰς ἀρετὰς ᾤετο εἶναι, ἐπιστήμας γὰρ εἶναι πάσας.

13. This is the accepted Stoic doctrine; see Ep. lxvi. 5. Goods are equal, absolute, and independent of circumstances; although, as Seneca here maintains, circumstances may bring one or another of them into fuller play.

14. e.g., Xenocrates and Speusippus; cf. Ep. lxxxv. 18. For another answer to the objection that the good depends upon outward circumstances cf. Ep. xcii. 14 f.

15. "An oar, though quite whole, presents the appearance of being broken when seen in clear shallow water."–Seneca, *N. Q.* 1. 3 (Clarke and Geikie).

16. This dualism of soul and body goes back to earlier religions, and especially to the Persian. The rational part (τὸ λογιστικόν), though held by most Stoics to be corporeal, or part of the world-stuff, is closely related to the ἡγεμονικόν, or "principate."

17. i.e., because he has endured and conquered misfortune rather than escaped it.

18. For a similar thought, cf. Ep. xi. 6.

19. Three stages of progress (προκοπή) were defined by Chrysippus. Cf. also Sen. Epp. lxxii. 6 and lxxv. 8 f.

20. Ovid, *Metam.* vi. 9, speaks of *bibula lana,* and Horace, *Ep.* i. 10. 27, of *vellera potantia fucum.*

21. In which case, he would be completely superior to her.

22. A nomad Scythian tribe east of the Caspian Sea.

LXXII. ON BUSINESS AS THE ENEMY OF PHILOSOPHY

[1]The subject[1] concerning which you question me was once clear to my mind, and required no thought, so thoroughly had I mastered it. But I have not tested my memory of it for some time, and therefore it does not readily come back to me. I feel that I have suffered the fate of a book whose rolls have stuck together by disuse; my mind needs to be unrolled, and whatever has been stored away there ought to be examined from time to time, so that it may be ready for use when occasion demands. Let us therefore put this subject off for the present; for it demands much labour and much care. As soon as I can hope to stay for any length of time in the same place, I shall then take your question in hand. [2]For there are certain subjects about which you can write even while travelling in a gig, and there are also subjects which need a study-chair, and quiet, and seclusion. Nevertheless I ought to accomplish something even on days like these,–days which are fully employed, and indeed from morning till night. For there is never a moment when fresh employments will not come along; we sow them, and for this reason several spring up from one. Then, too, we keep adjourning our own cases[2] by saying: "As soon as I am done with this, I shall settle down to hard work," or: "If I ever set this troublesome matter in order, I shall devote myself to study."

[3]But the study of philosophy is not to be postponed until you have leisure;[3] everything else is to be neglected in order that we may attend to philosophy, for no amount of time is long enough for it, even though our lives be prolonged from boyhood to the uttermost bounds of time allotted to man. It makes little difference whether you leave philosophy out altogether or study it intermittently; for it does not stay as it was when you dropped it, but, because its continuity has been broken, it goes back to the position in which it was at the beginning, like things which fly apart when they are stretched taut. We must resist the affairs which occupy our time; they must not be untangled, but rather put out of the way. Indeed, there is no time that is unsuitable for helpful studies; and yet many a man fails to study amid the very circumstances which make study necessary. [4]He says: "Something will happen to hinder me." No, not in the case of the man whose spirit, no matter what his business may be, is happy and alert. It is those who are still short of perfection whose happiness can be broken off; the joy of a wise man, on the other hand, is a woven fabric, rent by no chance happening and by no change of fortune; at all times and in all places he is at peace. For his joy depends on nothing external and looks for no boon from man or fortune. His happiness is something within himself; it would depart from his soul if it entered in from the outside; it is born there. [5]Sometimes an external happening reminds him of his mortality, but it is a light blow, and merely grazes the surface of his skin.[4] Some trouble, I repeat, may touch him like a breath of wind, but that Supreme Good of his is unshaken. This is what I mean: there are external disadvantages, like pimples and boils that break out upon a body which

is normally strong and sound; but there is no deep-seated malady. [6]The difference, I say, between a man of perfect wisdom and another who is progressing in wisdom is the same as the difference between a healthy man and one who is convalescing from a severe and lingering illness, for whom "health" means only a lighter attack of his disease. If the latter does not take heed, there is an immediate relapse and a return to the same old trouble; but the wise man cannot slip back, or slip into any more illness at all. For health of body is a temporary matter which the physician cannot guarantee, even though he has restored it; nay, he is often roused from his bed to visit the same patient who summoned him before. The mind, however, once healed, is healed for good and all.

[7]I shall tell you what I mean by health: if the mind is content with its own self; if it has confidence in itself; if it understands that all those things for which men pray, all the benefits which are bestowed and sought for, are of no importance in relation to a life of happiness; under such conditions it is sound. For anything that can be added to is imperfect; anything that can suffer loss is not lasting; but let the man whose happiness is to be lasting, rejoice in what is truly his own. Now all that which the crowd gapes after, ebbs and flows. Fortune gives us nothing which we can really own.[5] But even these gifts of Fortune please us when reason has tempered and blended them to our taste; for it is reason which makes acceptable to us even external goods that are disagreeable to use if we absorb them too greedily. [8]Attalus used to employ the following simile: "Did you ever see a dog snapping with wide-open jaws at bits of bread or meat which his master tosses to him? Whatever he catches, he straightway swallows whole, and always opens his jaws in the hope of something more. So it is with ourselves; we stand expectant, and whatever Fortune has thrown to us we forthwith bolt, without any real pleasure, and then stand alert and frantic for something else to snatch." But it is not so with the wise man; he is satisfied. Even if something falls to him, he merely accepts it carelessly and lays it aside. [9]The happiness that he enjoys is supremely great, is lasting, is his own. Assume that a man has good intentions, and has made progress, but is still far from the heights; the result is a series of ups and downs; he is now raised to heaven, now brought down to earth. For those who lack experience and training, there is no limit to the downhill course; such a one falls into the Chaos[6] of Epicurus,–empty and boundless. [10]There is still a third class of men,–those who toy with wisdom,–they have not indeed touched it, but yet are in sight of it, and have it, so to speak, within striking distance. They are not dashed about, nor do they drift back either; they are not on dry land, but are already in port.

[11]Therefore, considering the great difference between those on the heights and those in the depths, and seeing that even those in the middle are pursued by an ebb and flow peculiar to their state and pursued also by an enormous risk of returning to their degenerate ways, we should not give ourselves up to matters which occupy our time. They should be shut out; if they once gain an entrance, they will bring in still others to take their places. Let us resist them in their early stages. It is better that they shall never begin than that they shall be made to cease. Farewell.

Footnotes

1. The context furnishes no clue as to what the subject was.

2. Seneca is fond of legal figures; cf. Ep. lxv. 15. For the *dilatio* see Pliny, *Ep.* i. 18. 1 *rogas ut dilationem petam.*

3. Cf. Ep. liii. 9 *(philosophia) non est res subsiciva* ("a matter for spare time"), *ordinaria est; domina est, adesse iubet.*

4. Cf. Ep. xlv. 9 *intrepidus, quem aliqua vis movet, nulla perturbat, quem fortuna . . . pungit, non vulnerat, et hoc raro.*

5. Cf. Lucretius, iii. 971 *vita mancipio nulli datur, omnibus usu.* Our lives are merely loaned to us; Nature retains the *dominium.* Cf. also Seneca's frequent figure of life as an inn, contrasted with a house over which one has ownership.

6. The void *(inane)*, or infinite space, as contrasted with the atoms which form new worlds in continuous succession.

quod tenes, quod tuum dicis, publicum est et quidem generis humani.

5. During certain festivals, either cooked or raw meat was distributed among the people.

6. Vergil, *Eclogue*, i. 6 f. Vergil owes a debt to the Emperor, and regards him as a "god" because of the bestowal of earthly happiness; how much greater is the debt of the philosopher, who has the opportunity to study heavenly things!

7. Vergil, *Eclogue*, i. 9 f.

8. In the Christian religion, God is everything; among the Stoics, the wise man is equal to the gods. Cf., for example, Ep. xli. 4.

9. Vergil, *Aeneid*, ix. 641.

10. Cf. Ep. xli. §§ 1 f. *prope est a te deus, tecum est, intus est.*

LXXIV. ON VIRTUE AS A REFUGE FROM WORLDLY DISTRACTIONS

[1]Your letter has given me pleasure, and has roused me from sluggishness. It has also prompted my memory, which has been for some time slack and nerveless.

You are right, of course, my dear Lucilius, in deeming the chief means of attaining the happy life to consist in the belief that the only good lies in that which is honourable.[1] For anyone who deems other things to be good, puts himself in the power of Fortune, and goes under the control of another; but he who has in every case defined the good by the honourable, is happy with an inward happiness.

[2]One man is saddened when his children die; another is anxious when they become ill; a third is embittered when they do something disgraceful, or suffer a taint in their reputation. One man, you will observe, is tortured by passion for his neighbour's wife, another by passion for his own. You will find men who are completely upset by failure to win an election, and others who are actually plagued by the offices which they have won. [3]But the largest throng of unhappy men among the host of mortals are those whom the expectation of death, which threatens them on every hand, drives to despair. For there is no quarter from which death may not approach. Hence, like soldiers scouting in the enemy's country, they must look about in all directions, and turn their heads at every sound; unless the breast be rid of this fear, one lives with a palpitating heart. [4]You will readily recall those who have been driven into exile and dispossessed of their property. You will also recall (and this is the most serious kind of destitution) those who are poor in the midst of their riches.[2] You will recall men who have suffered shipwreck, or those whose sufferings resemble shipwreck; for they were untroubled and at ease, when the anger or perhaps the envy of the populace,–a missile most deadly to those in high places,[3]–dismantled them like a storm which is wont to rise when one is most confident of continued calm, or like a sudden stroke of lightning which even causes the region round about it to tremble. For just as anyone who stands near the bolt is stunned and resembles one who is struck so in these sudden and violent mishaps, although but one person is overwhelmed by the disaster, the rest are overwhelmed by fear, and the possibility that they may suffer makes them as downcast as the actual sufferer.

[5]Every man is troubled in spirit by evils that come suddenly upon his neighbour. Like birds, who cower even at the whirr of an empty sling, we are distracted by mere sounds as well as by blows. No man therefore can be happy if he yields himself up to such foolish fancies. For nothing brings happiness unless it also brings calm; it is a bad sort of existence that is spent in apprehension. [6]Whoever has largely surrendered himself to the power of Fortune has made for himself a huge web of disquietude, from which he cannot get free; if one would win a way to safety, there is but one road,–to despise externals and to be contented with that which is honourable. For those who regard anything as better than virtue, or believe that there is any good except virtue, are spreading their arms to gather in that which Fortune tosses abroad, and are anx-

iously awaiting her favours. [7]Picture now to yourself that Fortune is holding a festival, and is showering down honours, riches, and influence upon this mob of mortals; some of these gifts have already been torn to pieces in the hands of those who try to snatch them, others have been divided up by treacherous partnerships, and still others have been seized to the great detriment of those into whose possession they have come. Certain of these favours have fallen to men while they were absent-minded;[4] others have been lost to their seekers because they were snatching too eagerly for them, and, just because they are greedily seized upon, have been knocked from their hands. There is not a man among them all, however,–even he who has been lucky in the booty which has fallen to him,–whose joy in his spoil has lasted until the morrow.

The most sensible man, therefore, as soon as he sees the dole being brought in,[5] runs from the theatre; for he knows that one pays a high price for small favours. No one will grapple with him on the way out, or strike him as he departs; the quarrelling takes place where the prizes are. [8]Similarly with the gifts which Fortune tosses down to us; wretches that we are, we become excited, we are torn asunder, we wish that we had many hands, we look back now in this direction and now in that. All too slowly, as it seems, are the gifts thrown in our direction; they merely excite our cravings, since they can reach but few and are awaited by all. [9]We are keen to intercept them as they fall down. We rejoice if we have laid hold of anything; and some have been mocked by the idle hope of laying hold; we have either paid a high price for worthless plunder with some disadvantage to ourselves, or else have been defrauded and are left in the lurch. Let us therefore withdraw from a game like this, and give way to the greedy rabble; let them gaze after such "goods," which hang suspended above them, and be themselves still more in suspense.[6]

[10]Whoever makes up his mind to be happy should conclude that the good consists only in that which is honourable. For if he regards anything else as good, he is, in the first place, passing an unfavourable judgment upon Providence because of the fact that upright men often suffer misfortunes,[7] and that the time which is allotted to us is but short and scanty, if you compare it with the eternity which is allotted to the universe.

[11]It is a result of complaints like these that we are unappreciative in our comments upon the gifts of heaven; we complain because they are not always granted to us, because they are few and unsure and fleeting. Hence we have not the will either to live or to die; we are possessed by hatred of life, by fear of death. Our plans are all at sea, and no amount of prosperity can satisfy us. And the reason for all this is that we have not yet attained to that good which is immeasurable and unsurpassable, in which all wishing on our part must cease, because there is no place beyond the highest. [12]Do you ask why virtue needs nothing? Because it is pleased with what it has, and does not lust after that which it has not. Whatever is enough is abundant in the eyes of virtue.

Dissent from this judgment, and duty and loyalty will not abide. For one who desires to exhibit these two qualities must endure much that the world calls evil; we must sacrifice many things to which we are addicted, thinking them to be goods. [13]Gone is courage, which should be continually testing itself; gone is greatness of soul, which cannot stand out clearly unless it has learned to scorn as trivial everything that the crowd covets as supremely important; and gone is kindness and the repaying of kindness, if we fear toil, if we have acknowledged anything to be more precious than loyalty, if our eyes are fixed upon anything except the best.

[14]But to pass these questions by: either these so-called goods are not goods, or else man is more fortunate than God, because God has no enjoyment of the things which are given to us.[8] For lust pertains not to God, nor do elegant banquets, nor wealth, nor any of the things that allure mankind and lead him on through the influence of degrading pleasure. Therefore, it is, either not incredible that there are goods which God does not possess, or else the very fact that God does not possess them is in itself a proof that these things are not goods. [15]Besides, many things which are wont to be regarded as goods are granted to animals in fuller measure than to men. Animals eat their food with better appetite, are not in the same degree weakened by sexual indulgence, and have a greater and more uniform constancy in their strength. Consequently, they are

when there is any call for activity. For that which is honourable is free from care and untrammelled, is unafraid, and stands girt for action. [31] "What," you ask, "will the wise man experience no emotion like disturbance of spirit? Will not his features change colour,[15] his countenance be agitated, and his limbs grow cold? And there are other things which we do, not under the influence of the will, but unconsciously and as the result of a sort of natural impulse." I admit that this is true; but the sage will retain the firm belief that none of these things is evil, or important enough to make a healthy mind break down. [32] Whatever shall remain to be done virtue can do with courage and readiness. For anyone would admit that it is a mark of folly to do in a slothful and rebellious spirit whatever one has to do, or to direct the body in one direction and the mind in another, and thus to be torn between utterly conflicting emotions. For folly is despised precisely because of the things for which she vaunts and admires herself, and she does not do gladly even those things in which she prides herself. But if folly fears some evil, she is burdened by it in the very moment of awaiting it, just as if it had actually come,–already suffering in apprehension whatever she fears she may suffer. [33] Just as in the body symptoms of latent ill-health precede the disease–there is, for example, a certain weak sluggishness,[16] a lassitude which is not the result of any work, a trembling, and a shivering that pervades the limbs,–so the feeble spirit is shaken by its ills a long time before it is overcome by them. It anticipates them, and totters before its time.

But what is greater madness than to be tortured by the future and not to save your strength for the actual suffering, but to invite and bring on wretchedness? If you cannot be rid of it, you ought at least to postpone it. [34] Will you not understand that no man should be tormented by the future? The man who has been told that he will have to endure torture fifty years from now is not disturbed thereby, unless he has leaped over the intervening years, and has projected himself into the trouble that is destined to arrive a generation later. In the same way, souls that enjoy being sick and that seize upon excuses for sorrow are saddened by events long past and effaced from the records. Past and future are both absent; we feel neither of them. But there can be no pain except as the result of what you feel. Farewell.

Footnotes

1. A doctrine often expressed in the letters; cf., for example, lxxi. 4.

2. Cf. Horace, *Carm.* iii. 16. 28 *magnas inter opes inops.*

3. For the same thought cf. Ep. iv. 7 *Neminem eo fortuna provexit, ut non tantum illi minaretur, quantum permiserat. Noli huic tranquillitati confidere; momento mare evertitur. Eodem die ubi luserunt navigia, sorbentur.*

4. i.e., engaged upon something else. Cf. Ep. i. 1.

5. A distribution of coins, etc., at the public games. Food was also doled out to the populace on similar occasions.

6. This figure of the dole as applied to Fortune is sustained to an extent which is unusual in Seneca.

7. This phrase recalls the title of one of Seneca's philosophical essays: *De Providentia*, or *Quare Bonis Viris Mala Accidant cum sit Providentia.*

8. Cf. Ep. lxxiii. § 14 *Iuppiter uti illis non potest.*

9. *Producta* is a translation of the Stoic term προηγμένα. For a clear exposition of this topic see Cicero, *De Fin.* iii. 52 ff.

10. See Ep. lxvi. 6. The Stoics, unlike the Academics and the Peripatetics, maintained that the good must have "an unconditional value" (Zeller).

11. Cf. *Itane in geometriae pulvere haerebo?*, Ep. lxxxviii. 39 and note.

12. See the argument in Ep. xii. 6 f., and often elsewhere.

13. See § 23.

14. Called by the early Stoics ὁμολογία; the idea of "conformity with nature" is a fundamental doctrine of the school. See Rackham on Cicero, *De Fin.* iii. 21.

15. Cf. Epp. xi. 6 and lxxi. 29.

16. Perhaps a sort of malaria.

LXXV. ON THE DISEASES OF THE SOUL

[1]You have been complaining that my letters to you are rather carelessly written. Now who talks carefully unless he also desires to talk affectedly?[1] I prefer that my letters should be just what my conversation[2] would be if you and I were sitting in one another's company or taking walks together, spontaneous and easy; for my letters have nothing strained or artificial about them. [2]If it were possible, I should prefer to show, rather than speak, my feelings. Even if I were arguing a point, I should not stamp my foot, or toss my arms about, or raise my voice; but I should leave that sort of thing to the orator, and should be content to have conveyed my feelings to you without having either embellished them or lowered their dignity. [3]I should like to convince you entirely of this one fact,—that I feel whatever I say, that I not only feel it, but am wedded to it. It is one sort of kiss which a man gives his mistress and another which he gives his children; yet in the father's embrace also, holy and restrained as it is, plenty of affection is disclosed.

I prefer, however, that our conversation on matters so important should not be meagre and dry; for even philosophy does not renounce the company of cleverness. One should not, however, bestow very much attention upon mere words. [4]Let this be the kernel of my idea: let us say what we feel, and feel what we say; let speech harmonize with life.[3] That man has fulfilled his promise who is the same person both when you see him and when you hear him. [5]We shall not fail to see what sort of man he is and how large a man he is, if only he is one and the same. Our words should aim not to please, but to help. If, however, you can attain eloquence without painstaking, and if you either are naturally gifted or can gain eloquence at slight cost, make the most of it and apply it to the noblest uses. But let it be of such a kind that it displays facts rather than itself. It and the other arts are wholly concerned with cleverness;[4] but our business here is the soul.

[6]A sick man does not call in a physician who is eloquent; but if it so happens that the physician who can cure him likewise discourses elegantly about the treatment which is to be followed, the patient will take it in good part. For all that, he will not find any reason to congratulate himself on having discovered a physician who is eloquent. For the case is no different from that of a skilled pilot who is also handsome. [7]Why do you tickle my ears? Why do you entertain me? There is other business at hand; I am to be cauterized, operated upon, or put on a diet. That is why you were summoned to treat me!

You are required to cure a disease that is chronic and serious,—one which affects the general weal. You have as serious a business on hand as a physician has during a plague. Are you concerned about words? Rejoice this instant if you can cope with *things*. When shall you learn all that there is to learn? When shall you so plant in your mind that which you have learned, that it cannot escape? When shall you put it all into practice? For it is not sufficient merely to commit these things to memory, like other matters; they must be practically tested. He is not happy who only knows them, but he who does them. [8]You reply: "What? Are there no degrees of happiness below your 'happy' man? Is there a sheer descent immediately below wisdom?" I think not. For though he who makes progress is still numbered with the fools, yet he is separated from them by a long interval. Among the very persons who are making progress there are also great spaces intervening. They fall into three classes,[5] as certain philosophers believe. [9]First come those who have not yet attained wisdom but have already gained a place near by. Yet even that which is not far away is still outside. These, if you ask me, are men who have already laid aside all passions and vices, who have learned what things are to be embraced; but their assurance is not yet tested. They have not yet put their good into practice, yet from now on they cannot slip back into the faults which they have escaped. They have already arrived at a point from which there is no while when one is about to win all goods at a single stroke. [7]For there is but a single good,–namely, that which is honourable; in all those other things of which the general opinion approves, you will find no truth or certainty. Why it is, however, that there is but one good, namely, that which is honourable, I shall now tell you, inasmuch as you judge that in my earlier letter[3] I did not carry the discussion far enough, and think that this theory was commended to you rather than proved. I shall also compress the remarks of other authors into narrow compass.

[8]Everything is estimated by the standard of its own good. The vine is valued for its productiveness and the flavour of its wine, the stag for his speed. We ask, with regard to beasts of burden, how sturdy of back they are; for their only use is to bear burdens. If a dog is to find the trail of a wild beast, keenness of scent is of first importance; if to catch his quarry, swiftness of foot; if to attack and harry it, courage. In each thing that quality should be best for which the thing is brought into being and by which it is judged. [9]And what quality is best in man? It is reason; by virtue of reason he surpasses the animals, and is surpassed only by the gods. Perfect reason is therefore the good peculiar to man; all other qualities he shares in some degree with animals and plants. Man is strong; so is the lion. Man is comely; so is the peacock. Man is swift; so is the horse. I do not say that man is surpassed in all these qualities. I am not seeking to find that which is greatest in him, but that which is peculiarly his own. Man has body; so also have trees. Man has the power to act and to move at will; so have beasts and worms. Man has a voice; but how much louder is the voice of the dog, how much shriller that of the eagle, how much deeper that of the bull, how much sweeter and more melodious that of the nightingale! [10]What then is peculiar to man? Reason. When this is right and has reached perfection, man's felicity is complete. Hence, if everything is praiseworthy and has arrived at the end intended by its nature, when it has brought its peculiar good to perfection, and if man's peculiar good is reason; then, if a man has brought his reason to perfection, he is praiseworthy and has readied the end suited to his nature. This perfect reason is called virtue, and is likewise that which is honourable.

[11]Hence that in man is alone a good which alone belongs to man. For we are not now seeking to discover what is a good, but what good is man's. And if there is no other attribute which belongs peculiarly to man except reason, then reason will be his one peculiar good, but a good that is worth all the rest put together. If any man is bad, he will, I suppose, be regarded with disapproval; if good, I suppose he will be regarded with approval. Therefore, that attribute of man whereby he is approved or disapproved is his chief and only good. [12]You do not doubt whether this is a good; you merely doubt whether it is the sole good. If a man possess all other things, such as health, riches, pedigree,[4] a crowded reception-hall, but is confessedly bad, you will disapprove of him. Likewise, if a man possess none of the things which I have mentioned, and lacks money, or an escort of clients, or rank and a line of grandfathers and great-grandfathers, but is confessedly good, you will approve of him. Hence, this is man's one peculiar good, and the possessor of it is to be praised even if he lacks other things; but he who does not possess it, though he possess everything else in abundance is condemned and rejected. [13]The same thing holds good regarding men as regarding things. A ship is said to be good not when it is decorated with costly colours, nor when its prow is covered with silver or gold or its figure-head[5] embossed in ivory, nor when it is laden with the imperial revenues [6] or with the wealth of kings, but when it is steady and staunch and taut, with seams that keep out the water, stout enough to endure the buffeting of the waves' obedient to its helm, swift and caring naught for the winds. [14]You will speak of a sword as good, not when its sword-belt is of gold, or its scabbard studded with gems, but when its edge is fine for cutting and its point will pierce any armour. Take the carpenter's rule: we do not ask how beautiful it is, but how straight it is. Each thing is praised in regard to that attribute which is taken as its standard, in regard to that which is its peculiar quality.

[15]Therefore in the case of man also, it is not pertinent to the question to know how many acres he ploughs, how much money he has out at interest, how many callers

attend his receptions, how costly is the couch on which he lies, how transparent are the cups from which he drinks, but how good he is. He is good, however, if his reason is well-ordered and right and adapted to that which his nature has willed. [16]It is this that is called virtue; this is what we mean by "honourable";[7] it is man's unique good. For since reason alone brings man to perfection, reason alone, when perfected, makes man happy. This, moreover, is man's only good, the only means by which he is made happy. We do indeed say that those things also[8] are goods which are furthered and brought together by virtue,—that is, all the works of virtue; but virtue itself is for this reason the only good, because there is no good without virtue. [17]If every good is in the soul, then whatever strengthens, uplifts, and enlarges the soul, is a good; virtue, however, does make the soul stronger, loftier, and larger. For all other things, which arouse our desires, depress the soul and weaken it, and when we think that they are uplifting the soul, they are merely puffing it up and cheating it with much emptiness. Therefore, that alone is good which will make the soul better.

[18]All the actions of life, taken as a whole, are controlled by the consideration of what is honourable or base; it is with reference to these two things that our reason is governed in doing or not doing a particular thing. I shall explain what I mean: A good man will do what he thinks it will be honourable for him to do, even if it involves toil; he will do it even if it involves harm to him; he will do it even if it involves peril; again, he will not do that which will be base, even if it brings him money, or pleasure, or power. Nothing will deter him from that which is honourable, and nothing will tempt him into baseness. [19]Therefore, if he is determined invariably to follow that which is honourable, invariably to avoid baseness, and in every act of his life to have regard for these two things, deeming nothing else good except that which is honourable, and nothing else bad except that which is base; if virtue alone is unperverted in him and by itself keeps its even course, then virtue is that man's only good, and nothing can thenceforth happen to it which may make it anything else than good. It has escaped all risk of change; folly may creep upwards towards wisdom, but wisdom never slips back into folly.

[20]You may perhaps remember my saying[9] that the things which have been generally desired and feared have been trampled down by many a man in moments of sudden passion. There have been found men who would place their hands in the flames, men whose smiles could not be stopped by the torturer, men who would shed not a tear at the funeral of their children, men who would meet death unflinchingly. It is love, for example, anger, lust, which have challenged dangers. If a momentary stubbornness can accomplish all this when roused by some goad that pricks the spirit, how much more can be accomplished by virtue, which does not act impulsively or suddenly, but uniformly and with a strength that is lasting! [21]It follows that the things which are often scorned by the men who are moved with a sudden passion, and are always scorned by the wise, are neither goods nor evils. Virtue itself is therefore the only good; she marches proudly between the two extremes of fortune, with great scorn for both.

[22]If, however, you accept the view that there is anything good besides that which is honourable, all the virtues will suffer. For it will never be possible for any virtue to be won and held, if there is anything outside itself which virtue must take into consideration. If there is any such thing, then it is at variance with reason, from which the virtues spring, and with truth also, which cannot exist without reason. Any opinion, however, which is at variance with truth, is wrong. [23]A good man, you will admit, must have the highest sense of duty toward the gods. Hence he will endure with an unruffled spirit whatever happens to him; for he will know that it has happened as a result of the divine law, by which the whole creation moves. This being so, there will be for him one good, and only one, namely, that which is honourable; for one of its dictates is that we shall obey the gods and not blaze forth in anger at sudden misfortunes or deplore our lot, but rather patiently accept fate and obey its commands. [24]If anything except the honourable is good, we shall be hounded by greed for life, and by greed for the things which provide life with its furnishings,—an intolerable state, subject to no limits, unstable. The only good, therefore, is that which is honourable, that which is

subject to bounds.

²⁵I have declared[10] that man's life would be more blest than that of the gods, if those things which the gods do not enjoy are goods,–such as money and offices of dignity. There is this further consideration: if only it is true that our souls, when released from the body, still abide, a happier condition is in store for them than is theirs while they dwell in the body. And yet, if those things are goods which we make use of for our bodies' sake, our souls will be worse off when set free; and that is contrary to our belief, to say that the soul is happier when it is cabined and confined than when it is free and has betaken itself to the universe. ²⁶I also said[11] that if those things which dumb animals possess equally with man are goods, then dumb animals also will lead a happy life; which is of course impossible. One must endure all things in defence of that which is honourable; but this would not be necessary if there existed any other good besides that which is honourable.

Although this question was discussed by me pretty extensively in a previous letter,[12] I have discussed it summarily and briefly run through the argument. ²⁷But an opinion of this kind will never seem true to you unless you exalt your mind and ask yourself whether, at the call of duty, you would be willing to die for your country, and buy the safety of all your fellow-citizens at the price of your own; whether you would offer your neck not only with patience, but also with gladness. If you would do this, there is no other good in your eyes. For you are giving up everything in order to acquire this good. Consider how great is the power of that which is honourable: you will die for your country, even at a moment's notice, when you know that you ought to do so. ²⁸Sometimes, as a result of noble conduct, one wins great joy even in a very short and fleeting space of time; and though none of the fruits of a deed that has been done will accrue to the doer after he is dead and removed from the sphere of human affairs, yet the mere contemplation of a deed that is to be done is a delight, and the brave and upright man, picturing to himself the guerdons of his death,–guerdons such as the freedom of his country and the deliverance of all those for whom he is paying out his life,–partakes of the greatest pleasure and enjoys the fruit of his own peril. ²⁹But that man also who is deprived of this joy, the joy which is afforded by the contemplation of some last noble effort, will leap to his death without a moment's hesitation, content to act rightly and dutifully. Moreover, you may confront him with many discouragements; you may say: "Your deed will speedily be forgotten," or "Your fellow-citizens will offer you scant thanks." He will answer: "All these matters lie outside my task. My thoughts are on the deed itself. I know that this is honourable. Therefore, whithersoever I am led and summoned by honour, I will go."

³⁰This, therefore, is the only good, and not only is every soul that has reached perfection aware of it, but also every soul that is by nature noble and of right instincts; all other goods are trivial and mutable. For this reason we are harassed if we possess them. Even though, by the kindness of Fortune, they have been heaped together, they weigh heavily upon their owners, always pressing them down and sometimes crushing them. ³¹None of those whom you behold clad in purple is happy, any more than one of these actors[13] upon whom the play bestows a sceptre and a cloak while on the stage; they strut their hour before a crowded house, with swelling port and buskined foot; but when once they make their exit the foot-gear is removed and they return to their proper stature. None of those who have been raised to a loftier height by riches and honours is really great. Why then does he seem great to you? It is because you are measuring the pedestal along with the man. A dwarf is not tall, though he stand upon a mountain-top; a colossal statue will still be tall, though you place it in a well. ³²This is the error under which we labour; this is the reason why we are imposed upon: we value no man at what he is, but add to the man himself the trappings in which he is clothed. But when you wish to inquire into a man's true worth, and to know what manner of man he is, look at him when he is naked; make him lay aside his inherited estate, his titles, and the other deceptions of fortune; let him even strip off his body. Consider his soul, its quality and its stature, and thus learn whether its greatness is borrowed, or its own.

[33] If a man can behold with unflinching eyes the flash of a sword, if he knows that it makes no difference to him whether his soul takes flight through his mouth or through a wound in his throat,[14] you may call him happy; you may also call him happy if, when he is threatened with bodily torture, whether it be the result of accident or of the might of the stronger, he can without concern hear talk of chains, or of exile, or of all the idle fears that stir men's minds, and can say:

> "O maiden, no new sudden form of toil
> Springs up before my eyes; within my soul
> I have forestalled and surveyed everything.[15]

To-day it is you who threaten me with these terrors; but I have always threatened myself with them, and have prepared myself as a man to meet man's destiny." [34] If an evil has been pondered beforehand, the blow is gentle when it comes. To the fool, however, and to him who trusts in fortune, each event as it arrives "comes in a new and sudden form," and a large part of evil, to the inexperienced, consists in its novelty. This is proved by the fact that men endure with greater courage, when they have once become accustomed to them, the things which they had at first regarded as hardships. [35] Hence, the wise man accustoms himself to coming trouble, lightening by long reflection the evils which others lighten by long endurance. We sometimes hear the inexperienced say: "I knew that this was in store for me." But the wise man knows that all things are in store for him. Whatever happens, he says: "I knew it." Farewell.

Footnotes

1. A mock-heroic nickname for the knights, derived from the town of Trossulum in Etruria, which they captured by a sensational charge. See Persius, i. 82, and Seneca, Ep. lxxxvii. 9.

2. See also Ep. xciii.

3. Ep. lxxiv.

4. Literally "many masks" of his ancestors. These were placed in the *atrium*.

5. Literally "the guardian deity"; cf. Horace, *Od.* i. 14. 10. These were images of the gods, carried and invoked by the ancients, in the same manner as St. Nicholas to-day.

6. The *fiscus* was the private treasury of the Roman Emperor, as contrasted with the *aerarium*, which theoretically was controlled by the Senate.

7. i.e., "moral worth."

8. i.e., peace, the welfare of one's country, dutiful children, etc.

9. Cf. Ep. lxxiv. 21.

10. Cf. Ep. lxxiv. 14 *aut ista bona non sunt, quae vocantur, aut homo felicior deo est, quoniam quidem quae parata nobis sunt, non habet in usu deus.*

11. eg., Ep. lxxiv. 16 *summum bonum . . . obsolescit, si ab optima nostri parte ad pessimam transit et transfertur ad sensus, qui agiliores sunt animalibus mutis.*

12. Ep. lxxiv., esp § 14.

13. Compare the argument in Ep. lxxx. § 7, "This farce of living, in which we act our parts so ill"; § 8, the loudmouthed impersonator of heroes, who sleeps on rags; and § 9 *hominem involutum aestimas?*

14. As the world-soul is spread through the universe, so the human soul (as fire, or breath) is diffused through the body, and may take its departure in various ways.

15. Vergil, *Aeneid*, vi. 103 ff. (The answer of Aeneas to the Sibyl's prophecy.)

LXXVII. ON TAKING ONE'S OWN LIFE

[1] Suddenly there came into our view to-day the "Alexandrian" ships,—I mean those which are usually sent ahead to announce the coming of the fleet; they are called "mail-boats." The Campanians are glad to see them; all the rabble of Puteoli[1] stand on the docks, and can recognize the "Alexandrian" boats, no matter how great the crowd

of vessels, by the very trim of their sails. For they alone may keep spread their topsails, which all ships use when out at sea, [2]because nothing sends a ship along so well as its upper canvas; that is where most of the speed is obtained. So when the breeze has stiffened and becomes stronger than is comfortable, they set their yards lower; for the wind has less force near the surface of the water. Accordingly, when they have made Capreae and the headland whence

Tall Pallas watches on the stormy peak,[2]

all other vessels are bidden to be content with the mainsail, and the topsail stands out conspicuously on the "Alexandrian" mail-boats.

[3]While everybody was bustling about and hurrying to the water-front, I felt great pleasure in my laziness, because, although I was soon to receive letters from my friends, I was in no hurry to know how my affairs were progressing abroad, or what news the letters were bringing; for some time now I have had no losses, nor gains either. Even if I were not an old man, I could not have helped feeling pleasure at this; but as it is, my pleasure was far greater. For, however small my possessions might be, I should still have left over more travelling-money than journey to travel, especially since this journey upon which we have set out is one which need not be followed to the end. [4]An expedition will be incomplete if one stops half-way, or anywhere on this side of one's destination; but life is not incomplete if it is honourable. At whatever point you leave off living, provided you leave off nobly, your life is a whole.[3] Often, however, one must leave off bravely, and our reasons therefore need not be momentous; for neither are the reasons momentous which hold us here.

[5]Tullius Marcellinus,[4] a man whom you knew very well, who in youth was a quiet soul and became old prematurely, fell ill of a disease which was by no means hopeless; but it was protracted and troublesome, and it demanded much attention; hence he began to think about dying. He called many of his friends together. Each one of them gave Marcellinus advice,–the timid friend urging him to do what he had made up his mind to do; the flattering and wheedling friend giving counsel which he supposed would be more pleasing to Marcellinus when he came to think the matter over; [6]but our Stoic friend, a rare man, and, to praise him in language which he deserves, a man of courage and vigour[5] admonished him best of all, as it seems to me. For he began as follows: "Do not torment yourself, my dear Marcellinus, as if the question which you are weighing were a matter of importance. It is not an important matter to live; all your slaves live, and so do all animals; but it is important to die honourably, sensibly, bravely. Reflect how long you have been doing the same thing: food, sleep, lust,–this is one's daily round. The desire to die may be felt, not only by the sensible man or the brave or unhappy man, but even by the man who is merely surfeited."

[7]Marcellinus did not need someone to urge him, but rather someone to help him; his slaves refused to do his bidding. The Stoic therefore removed their fears, showing them that there was no risk involved for the household except when it was uncertain whether the master's death was self-sought or not; besides, it was as bad a practice to kill one's master as it was to prevent him forcibly from killing himself. [8]Then he suggested to Marcellinus himself that it would be a kindly act to distribute gifts to those who had attended him throughout his whole life, when that life was finished, just as, when a banquet is finished,[6] the remaining portion is divided among the attendants who stand about the table. Marcellinus was of a compliant and generous disposition, even when it was a question of his own property; so he distributed little sums among his sorrowing slaves, and comforted them besides. [9]No need had he of sword or of bloodshed; for three days he fasted and had a tent put up in his very bedroom.[7] Then a tub was brought in; he lay in it for a long time, and, as the hot water was continually poured over him, he gradually passed away, not without a feeling of pleasure, as he himself remarked,–such a feeling as a slow dissolution is wont to give. Those of us who have ever fainted know from experience what this feeling is.

[10]This little anecdote into which I have digressed will not be displeasing to you. For you will see that your friend departed neither with difficulty nor with suffering. Though he committed suicide, yet he withdrew most gently, gliding out of life. The

anecdote may also be of some use; for often a crisis demands just such examples. There are times when we ought to die and are unwilling; sometimes we die and are unwilling. [11]No one is so ignorant as not to know that we must at some time die; nevertheless, when one draws near death, one turns to flight, trembles, and laments. Would you not think him an utter fool who wept because he was not alive a thousand years ago? And is he not just as much of a fool who weeps because he will not be alive a thousand years from now? It is all the same; you will not be, and you were not. Neither of these periods of time belongs to you. [12]You have been cast upon this point of time;[8] if you would make it longer, how much longer shall you make it? Why weep? Why pray? You are taking pains to no purpose.

> Give over thinking that your prayers can bend
> Divine decrees from their predestined end.[9]

These decrees are unalterable and fixed; they are governed by a mighty and everlasting compulsion. Your goal will be the goal of all things. What is there strange in this to you? You were born to be subject to this law; this fate befell your father, your mother, your ancestors, all who came before you; and it will befall all who shall come after you. A sequence which cannot be broken or altered by any power binds all things together and draws all things in its course. [13]Think of the multitudes of men doomed to death who will come after you, of the multitudes who will go with you! You would die more bravely, I suppose, in the company of many thousands; and yet there are many thousands, both of men and of animals, who at this very moment, while you are irresolute about death, are breathing their last, in their several ways. But you,–did you believe that you would not some day reach the goal towards which you have always been travelling? No journey but has its end.

[14]You think, I suppose, that it is now in order for me to cite some examples of great men. No, I shall cite rather the case of a boy. The story of the Spartan lad has been preserved: taken captive while still a stripling, he kept crying in his Doric dialect, "I will not be a slave!" and he made good his word; for the very first time he was ordered to perform a menial and degrading service,–and the command was to fetch a chamber-pot,–he dashed out his brains against the wall.[10] [15]So near at hand is freedom, and is anyone still a slave? Would you not rather have your own son die thus than reach old age by weakly yielding? Why therefore are you distressed, when even a boy can die so bravely? Suppose that you refuse to follow him; you will be led. Take into your own control that which is now under the control of another. Will you not borrow that boy's courage, and say: "I am no slave!"? Unhappy fellow, you are a slave to men, you are a slave to your business, you are a slave to life. For life, if courage to die be lacking, is slavery.

[16]Have you anything worth waiting for? Your very pleasures, which cause you to tarry and hold you back, have already been exhausted by you. None of them is a novelty to you, and there is none that has not already become hateful because you are cloyed with it. You know the taste of wine and cordials. It makes no difference whether a hundred or a thousand measures[11] pass through your bladder; you are nothing but a wine-strainer.[12] You are a connoisseur in the flavour of the oyster and of the mullet;[13] your luxury has not left you anything untasted for the years that are to come; and yet these are the things from which you are torn away unwillingly. [17]What else is there which you would regret to have taken from you? Friends? But who can be a friend to you? Country? What? Do you think enough of your country to be late to dinner? The light of the sun? You would extinguish it, if you could; for what have you ever done that was fit to be seen in the light? Confess the truth; it is not because you long for the senate chamber or the forum, or even for the world of nature, that you would fain put off dying; it is because you are loth to leave the fish-market, though you have exhausted its stores.[14]

[18]You are afraid of death; but how can you scorn it in the midst of a mushroom supper?[15] You wish to live; well, do you know how to live? You are afraid to die. But come now: is this life of yours anything but death? Gaius Caesar was passing along the Via Latina, when a man stepped out from the ranks of the prisoners, his grey beard

more violent than usual, it turns to delirium and stupor. [10]This is, accordingly, a conso-lation for excessive pain,–that you cannot help ceasing to feel it if you feel it to excess. The reason, however, why the inexperienced are impatient when their bodies suffer is, that they have not accustomed themselves to be contented in spirit. They have been closely associated with the body. Therefore a high-minded and sensible man divorces soul from body, and dwells much with the better or divine part, and only as far as he must with this complaining and frail portion.

[11]"But it is a hardship," men say, "to do without our customary pleasures,–to fast, to feel thirst and hunger." These are indeed serious when one first abstains from them. Later the desire dies down, because the appetites themselves which lead to desire are wearied and forsake us; then the stomach becomes petulant, then the food which we craved before becomes hateful. Our very wants die away. But there is no bitterness in doing without that which you have ceased to desire. [12]Moreover, every pain sometimes stops, or at any rate slackens; moreover, one may take precautions against its return, and, when it threatens, may check it by means of remedies. Every variety of pain has its premonitory symptoms; this is true, at any rate, of pain that is habitual and recur-rent. One can endure the suffering which disease entails, if one has come to regard its results with scorn. [13]But do not of your own accord make your troubles heavier to bear and burden yourself with complaining. Pain is slight if opinion has added nothing to it; but if, on the other hand, you begin to encourage yourself and say, "It is nothing,–a trifling matter at most; keep a stout heart and it will soon cease"; then in thinking it slight, you will make it slight. Everything depends on opinion; ambition, luxury, greed, hark back to opinion. It is according to opinion that we suffer. [14]A man is as wretched as he has convinced himself that he is. I hold that we should do away with complaint about past sufferings and with all language like this: "None has ever been worse off than I. What sufferings, what evils have I endured! No one has thought that I shall recover. How often have my family bewailed me, and the physicians giv-en me over! Men who are placed on the rack are not torn asunder with such agony!" However, even if all this is true, it is over and gone. What benefit is there in reviewing past sufferings, and in being unhappy, just because once you were unhappy? Besides, every one adds much to his own ills, and tells lies to himself. And that which was bitter to bear is pleasant to have borne; it is natural to rejoice at the ending of one's ills.

Two elements must therefore be rooted out once for all,–the fear of future suffer-ing, and the recollection of past suffering; since the latter no longer concerns me, and the former concerns me not yet. [15]But when set in the very midst of troubles one should say:

> Perchance some day the memory of this sorrow
> Will even bring delight.[7]

Let such a man fight against them with all his might: if he once gives way, he will be vanquished; but if he strives against his sufferings, he will conquer. As it is, howev-er, what most men do is to drag down upon their own heads a falling ruin which they ought to try to support. If you begin to withdraw your support from that which thrusts toward you and totters and is ready to plunge, it will follow you and lean more heavily upon you; but if you hold your ground and make up your mind to push against it, it will be forced back. [16]What blows do athletes receive on their faces and all over their bodies! Nevertheless, through their desire for fame they endure every torture, and they undergo these things not only because they are fighting but in order to be able to fight. Their very training means torture. So let us also win the way to victory in all our struggles,–for the reward is not a garland or a palm or a trumpeter who calls for silence at the proclamation of our names, but rather virtue, steadfastness of soul, and a peace that is won for all time, if fortune has once been utterly vanquished in any combat. You say, "I feel severe pain." [17]What then; are you relieved from feeling it, if you endure it like a woman? Just as an enemy is more dangerous to a retreating army, so every trouble that fortune brings attacks us all the harder if we yield and turn our backs. "But the trouble is serious." What? Is it for this purpose that we are strong,–that we may have light burdens to bear? Would you have your illness long-drawn-out, or would you have it quick and short? If it is long, it means a respite, allows you a period for resting yourself, bestows upon you the boon of time in plenty; as it arises, so it must also subside. A short and rapid illness will do one of two things: it will quench or be quenched. And what difference does it make whether it is not or I am not? In either case there is an end of pain.

[18]This, too, will help—to turn the mind aside to thoughts of other things and thus to depart from pain. Call to mind what honourable or brave deeds you have done; consider the good side of your own life.[8] Run over in your memory those things which you have particularly admired. Then think of all the brave men who have conquered pain: of him who continued to read his book as he allowed the cutting out of varicose veins; of him who did not cease to smile, though that very smile so enraged his torturers that they tried upon him every instrument of their cruelty. If pain can be conquered by a smile, will it not be conquered by reason? [19]You may tell me now of whatever you like—of colds, bad coughing-spells that bring up parts of our entrails, fever that parches our very vitals, thirst, limbs so twisted that the joints protrude in different directions; yet worse than these are the stake, the rack, the red-hot plates, the instrument that reopens wounds while the wounds themselves are still swollen and that drives their imprint still deeper.[9] Nevertheless there have been men who have not uttered a moan amid these tortures. "More yet!" says the torturer; but the victim has not begged for release. "More yet!" he says again; but no answer has come. "More yet!" the victim has smiled, and heartily, too. Can you not bring yourself, after an example like this, to make a mock at pain?

[20]"But," you object, "my illness does not allow me to be doing anything; it has withdrawn me from all my duties." It is your body that is hampered by ill-health, and not your soul as well. It is for this reason that it clogs the feet of the runner and will hinder the handiwork of the cobbler or the artisan; but if your soul be habitually in practice, you will plead and teach, listen and learn, investigate and meditate. What more is necessary? Do you think that you are doing nothing if you possess self-control in your illness? You will be showing that a disease can be overcome, or at any rate endured. [21]There is, I assure you, a place for virtue even upon a bed of sickness. It is not only the sword and the battle-line that prove the soul alert and unconquered by fear; a man can display bravery even when wrapped in his bed-clothes. You have something to do: wrestle bravely with disease. If it shall compel you to nothing, beguile you to nothing, it is a notable example that you display. O what ample matter were there for renown, if we could have spectators of our sickness! Be your own spectator; seek your own applause.

[22]Again, there are two kinds of pleasures. Disease checks the pleasures of the body, but does not do away with them. Nay, if the truth is to be considered, it serves to excite them; for the thirstier a man is, the more he enjoys a drink; the hungrier he is, the more pleasure he takes in food. Whatever falls to one's lot after a period of abstinence is welcomed with greater zest. The other kind, however, the pleasures of the mind, which are higher and less uncertain, no physician can refuse to the sick man. Whoever seeks these and knows well what they are, scorns all the blandishments of the senses. [23]Men say, "Poor sick fellow!" But why? Is it because he does not mix snow with his wine, or because he does not revive the chill of his drink—mixed as it is in a good-sized bowl—by chipping ice into it? Or because he does not have Lucrine[10] oysters opened fresh at his table? Or because there is no din of cooks about his dining-hall, as they bring in their very cooking apparatus along with their viands? For luxury has already devised this fashion—of having the kitchen accompany the dinner, so that the food may not grow luke-warm, or fail to be hot enough for a palate which has already become hardened. [24]"Poor sick fellow!"—he will eat as much as he can digest. There will be no boar lying before his eyes,[11] banished from the table as if it were a common meat; and on his sideboard there will be heaped together no breast-meat of birds, because it sickens him to see birds served whole. But what evil has been done to you? You will dine like a sick man, nay, sometimes like a sound man.[12]

[25]All these things, however, can be easily endured—gruel, warm water, and any-

by flames or by ruins. Hers is the only greatness that knows no lowering; there can be for her no further rising or sinking. Her stature, like that of the stars in the heavens, is fixed. Let us therefore strive to raise ourselves to this altitude.

[11] Already much of the task is accomplished; nay, rather, if I can bring myself to confess the truth, not much. For goodness does not mean merely being better than the lowest. Who that could catch but a mere glimpse of the daylight would boast his powers of vision? One who sees the sun shining through a mist may be contented meanwhile that he has escaped darkness, but he does not yet enjoy the blessing of light. [12] Our souls will not have reason to rejoice in their lot until, freed from this darkness in which they grope, they have not merely glimpsed the brightness with feeble vision, but have absorbed the full light of day and have been restored to their place in the sky,–until, indeed, they have regained the place which they held at the allotment of their birth. The soul is summoned upward by its very origin. And it will reach that goal even before it is released from its prison below, as soon as it has cast off sin and, in purity and lightness, has leaped up into celestial realms of thought.

[13] I am glad, beloved Lucilius, that we are occupied with this ideal, that we pursue it with all our might, even though few know it, or none. Fame is the shadow of virtue; it will attend virtue even against her will. But, as the shadow sometimes precedes and sometimes follows or even lags behind, so fame sometimes goes before us and shows herself in plain sight, and sometimes is in the rear, and is all the greater in proportion as she is late in coming, when once envy has beaten a retreat. [14] How long did men believe Democritus[10] to be mad! Glory barely came to Socrates. And how long did our state remain in ignorance of Cato! They rejected him, and did not know his worth until they had lost him. If Rutilius[11] had not resigned himself to wrong, his innocence and virtue would have escaped notice; the hour of his suffering was the hour of his triumph. Did he not give thanks for his lot, and welcome his exile with open arms? I have mentioned thus far those to whom Fortune has brought renown at the very moment of persecution; but how many there are whose progress toward virtue has come to light only after their death! And how many have been ruined, not rescued, by their reputation? [15] There is Epicurus, for example; mark how greatly he is admired, not only by the more cultured, but also by this ignorant rabble. This man, however, was unknown to Athens itself, near which he had hidden himself away. And so, when he had already survived by many years his friend Metrodorus, he added in a letter these last words, proclaiming with thankful appreciation the friendship that had existed between them: "So greatly blest were Metrodorus and I that it has been no harm to us to be unknown, and almost unheard of, in this well-known land of Greece."[12] [16] Is it not true, therefore, that men did not discover him until after he had ceased to be? Has not his renown shone forth, for all that? Metrodorus also admits this fact in one of his letters:[13] that Epicurus and he were not well known to the public; but he declares that after the lifetime of Epicurus and himself any man who might wish to follow in their footsteps would win great and ready-made renown.

[17] Virtue is never lost to view; and yet to have been lost to view is no loss. There will come a day which will reveal her, though hidden away or suppressed by the spite of her contemporaries. That man is born merely for a few, who thinks only of the people of his own generation. Many thousands of years and many thousands of peoples will come after you; it is to these that you should have regard. Malice may have imposed silence upon the mouths of all who were alive in your day; but there will come men who will judge you without prejudice and without favour. If there is any reward that virtue receives at the hands of fame, not even this can pass away. We ourselves, indeed, shall not be affected by the talk of posterity; nevertheless, posterity will cherish and celebrate us even though we are not conscious thereof. [18] Virtue has never failed to reward a man, both during his life and after his death, provided he has followed her loyally, provided he has not decked himself out or painted himself up, but has been always the same, whether he appeared before men's eyes after being announced, or suddenly and without preparation. Pretence accomplishes nothing. Few are deceived by a mask that is easily drawn over the face. Truth is the same in every part. Things

which deceive us have no real substance. Lies are thin stuff; they are transparent, if you examine them with care. Farewell.

Footnotes

1. Ellis suggests that the poem *Aetna*, of uncertain authorship, may have been written by Lucilius in response to this letter. His view is plausible, but not universally accepted.

2. See Ep. xiv. § 8 and note (Vol. I.).

3. The modern Taormina.

4. Another description of this region is given by Pliny, *N. H.* ii. 106, who says that the stones in the rivers were red-hot! The phenomenon is usually explained by supposing springs of burning naphtha.

5. i.e., merely as an episode, instead of devoting a whole poem to the subject.

6. *Metam.* xv. 340 ff.

7. *Aeneid*, iii. 570 ff.

8. The usual meaning of *paria esse*, or *paria facere* (a favourite phrase with Seneca–see for example Ep. ci. 7), is "to square the account," "balance even."

9. "Qualities desirable in themselves, but not essential for the possession of wisdom, the προηγμένα of the Stoics," (Summers).

10. There is an unauthenticated story that the men of Abdera called in Hippocrates to treat his malady.

11. Cf. Ep. xxiv. 4 *exilium . . . tulit Rutilius etiam libenter.*

12. Frag. 188 Usener.

13. Frag. 43 Körte.

LXXX. ON WORLDLY DECEPTIONS

[1]To-day I have some free time, thanks not so much to myself as to the games, which have attracted all the bores to the boxing-match.[1] No one will interrupt me or disturb the train of my thoughts, which go ahead more boldly as the result of my very confidence. My door has not been continually creaking on its hinges nor will my curtain be pulled aside;[2] my thoughts may march safely on,–and that is all the more necessary for one who goes independently and follows out his own path. Do I then follow no predecessors? Yes, but I allow myself to discover something new, to alter, to reject. I am not a slave to them, although I give them my approval.

[2]And yet that was a very bold word which I spoke when I assured myself that I should have some quiet, and some uninterrupted retirement. For lo, a great cheer comes from the stadium, and while it does not drive me distracted, yet it shifts my thought to a contrast suggested by this very noise. How many men, I say to myself, train their bodies, and how few train their minds![3] What crowds flock to the games, spurious as they are and arranged merely for pastime,–and what a solitude reigns where the good arts are taught! How feather-brained are the athletes whose muscles and shoulders we admire! [3]The question which I ponder most of all is this; if the body can be trained to such a degree of endurance that it will stand the blows and kicks of several opponents at once and to such a degree that a man can last out the day and resist the scorching sun in the midst of the burning dust, drenched all the while with his own blood,–if this can be done, how much more easily might the mind be toughened so that it could receive the blows of Fortune and not be conquered, so that it might struggle to its feet again after it has been laid low, after it has been trampled under foot?

For although the body needs many things in order to be strong, yet the mind grows from within, giving to itself nourishment and exercise. Yonder athletes must have copious food, copious drink, copious quantities of oil, and long training besides; but you can acquire virtue without equipment and without expense. All that goes to make you a good man lies within yourself. [4]And what do you need in order to become good? To wish it. But what better thing could you wish for than to break away from this slavery, a slavery that oppresses us all, a slavery which even chattels of the lowest estate, born amid such degradation, strive in every possible way to strip off? In exchange for freedom they pay out the savings which they have scraped together by cheating their own bellies; shall *you* not be eager to attain liberty at any price, seeing that you claim it as your birthright? [5]Why cast glances toward your strong-box? Liberty cannot be bought. It is therefore useless to enter in your ledger[4] the item of "Freedom," for freedom is possessed neither by those who have bought it, nor by those who have sold it. You must give this good to yourself, and seek it from yourself.

First of all, free yourself from the fear of death, for death puts the yoke about our necks; then free yourself from the fear of poverty. [6]If you would know how little evil there is in poverty, compare the faces of the poor with those of the rich; the poor man smiles more often and more genuinely; his troubles do not go deep down; even if any anxiety comes upon him, it passes like a fitful cloud. But the merriment of those whom men call happy is feigned, while their sadness is heavy and festering, and all the heavier because they may not meanwhile display their grief, but must act the part of happiness in the midst of sorrows that eat out their very hearts. [7]I often feel called upon to use the following illustration, and it seems to me that none expresses more effectively this drama of human life, wherein we are assigned the parts which we are to play so badly. Yonder is the man who stalks upon the stage with swelling port and head thrown back, and says:

> Lo, I am he whom Argos hails as lord,
> Whom Pelops left the heir of lands that spread
> From Hellespont and from th' Ionian sea
> E'en to the Isthmian straits.[5]

And who is this fellow? He is but a slave; his wage is five measures of grain and five denarii. [8]Yon other who, proud and wayward and puffed up by confidence in his power, declaims:

> Peace, Menelaus, or this hand shall slay thee![5]

receives a daily pittance and sleeps on rags. You may speak in the same way about all these dandies whom you see riding in litters above the heads of men and above the crowd; in every case their happiness is put on like the actor's mask. Tear it off, and you will scorn them.

[9]When you buy a horse, you order its blanket to be removed; you pull off the garments from slaves that are advertised for sale, so that no bodily flaws may escape your notice; if you judge a man, do you judge him when he is wrapped in a disguise? Slave dealers hide under some sort of finery any defect which may give offence,[6] and for that reason the very trappings arouse the suspicion of the buyer. If you catch sight of a leg or an arm that is bound up in cloths, you demand that it be stripped and that the body itself be revealed to you. [10]Do you see yonder Scythian or Sarmatian king, his head adorned with the badge of his office? If you wish to see what he amounts to, and to know his full worth, take off his diadem; much evil lurks beneath it. But why do I speak of others? If you wish to set a value on yourself, put away your money, your estates, your honours, and look into your own soul. At present, you are taking the word of others for what you are. Farewell.

Footnotes

1. Probably a contest in which the participants attached leaden weights to their hands in order to increase the force of the blows.

2. Compare Pliny's "den" (Ep. ii. 17. 21): *quae specularibus et velis obductis reductisve modo adicitur cubiculo modo aufertur.*

3. Compare the ideas expressed in Ep. xv. 2 f.

4. For this figure see the *"lucellum," "diurna mercedula,"* etc., of the opening letters of the correspondence (Vol. I.).

5. Authors unknown; Ribbeck, *Frag. Trag.* pp. 289 and 276. The first passage (with one

change) is also quoted by Quintilian, ix. 4. 140. See, however, Tyrrell, *Latin Poetry*, p.39, who calls this passage the beginning of Attius's *Atreus*.

6. A favourite trick; cf. Quintil. ii. 15. 25 *mangones, qui colorem fuco et verum robur inani sagina mentiuntur.*

LXXXI. ON BENEFITS[1]

[1]You complain that you have met with an ungrateful person. If this is your first experience of that sort, you should offer thanks either to your good luck or to your caution. In this case, however, caution can effect nothing but to make you ungenerous. For if you wish to avoid such a danger, you will not confer benefits; and so, that benefits may not be lost with another man, they will be lost to yourself.

It is better, however, to get no return than to confer no benefits. Even after a poor crop one should sow again; for often losses due to continued barrenness of an unproductive soil have been made good by one year's fertility. [2]In order to discover one grateful person, it is worth while to make trial of many ungrateful ones. No man has so unerring a hand when he confers benefits that he is not frequently deceived; it is well for the traveller to wander, that he may again cleave to the path. After a shipwreck, sailors try the sea again. The banker is not frightened away from the forum by the swindler. If one were compelled to drop everything that caused trouble, life would soon grow dull amid sluggish idleness; but in your case this very condition may prompt you to become more charitable. For when the outcome of any undertaking is unsure, you must try again and again, in order to succeed ultimately. [3]I have, however, discussed the matter with sufficient fullness in the volumes which I have written, entitled "On Benefits."[2]

What I think should rather be investigated is this,–a question which I feel has not been made sufficiently clear: "Whether he who has helped us has squared the account and has freed us from our debt, if he has done us harm later." You may add this question also, if you like: "when the harm done later has been more than the help rendered previously." [4]If you are seeking for the formal and just decision of a strict judge, you will find that he checks off one act by the other, and declares: "Though the injuries outweigh the benefits, yet we should credit to the benefits anything that stands over even after the injury." The harm done was indeed greater, but the helpful act was done first. Hence the time also should be taken into account. [5]Other cases are so clear that I need not remind you that you should also look into such points as: How gladly was the help offered, and how reluctantly was the harm done,–since benefits, as well as injuries, depend on the spirit. "I did not wish to confer the benefit; but I was won over by my respect for the man, or by the importunity of his request, or by hope." [6]Our feeling about every obligation depends in each case upon the spirit in which the benefit is conferred; we weigh not the bulk of the gift, but the quality of the good-will which prompted it. So now let us do away with guess-work; the former deed was a benefit, and the latter, which transcended the earlier benefit, is an injury. The good man so arranges the two sides of his ledger[3] that he voluntarily cheats himself by adding to the benefit and subtracting from the injury.

The more indulgent magistrate, however (and I should rather be such a one), will order us to forget the injury and remember the accommodation. [7]"But surely," you say, "it is the part of justice to render to each that which is his due,–thanks in return for a benefit, and retribution,[4] or at any rate ill-will, in return for an injury!" This, I say, will be true when it is one man who has inflicted the injury, and a different man who has conferred the benefit; for if it is the same man, the force of the injury is nullified by the benefit conferred. Indeed, a man who ought to be pardoned, even though there were no good deeds credited to him in the past, should receive something more than mere leniency if he commits a wrong when he has a benefit to his credit. [8]I do not set an equal value on benefits and injuries. I reckon a benefit at a higher rate than an injury. Not all grateful persons know what it involves to be in debt for a benefit; even a thoughtless, crude fellow, one of the common herd, may know, especially soon after he has received the gift; but he does not know how deeply he stands in debt therefor. Only the wise man knows exactly what value should be put upon everything; for the fool whom I just mentioned, no matter how good his intentions may be, either pays less than he owes, or pays it at the wrong time or the wrong place. That for which he should make return he wastes and loses. [9]There is a marvellously accurate phraseology applied to certain subjects,[5] a long-established terminology which indicates certain acts by means of symbols that are most efficient and that serve to outline men's duties. We are, as you know, wont to speak thus: "A. has made a return for the favour bestowed by B." Making a return means handing over of your own accord that which you owe. We do not say, "He has paid back the favour"; for "pay back" is used of a man upon whom a demand for payment is made, of those who pay against their will. Of those who pay under any circumstances whatsoever, and of those who pay through a third party. We do not say, "He has 'restored' the benefit," or 'settled' it; we have never been satisfied with a word which applies properly to a debt of money. [10]Making a return means offering something to him from whom you have received something. The phrase implies a voluntary return; he who has made such a return has served the writ upon himself.

The wise man will inquire in his own mind into all the circumstances: how much he has received, from whom, when, where, how. And so we[6] declare that none but the wise man knows how to make return for a favour; moreover, none but the wise man knows how to confer a benefit,—that man, I mean, who enjoys the giving more than the recipient enjoys the receiving. [11]Now some person will reckon this remark as one of the generally surprising statements such as we Stoics are wont to make and such as the Greeks call "paradoxes,"[7] and will say: "Do you maintain, then, that only the wise man knows how to return a favour? Do you maintain that no one else knows how to make restoration to a creditor for a debt? Or, on buying a commodity, to pay full value to the seller?" In order not to bring any odium upon myself, let me tell you that Epicurus says the same thing. At any rate, Metrodorus remarks[8] that only the wise man knows how to return a favour. [12]Again, the objector mentioned above wonders at our saying: "The wise man alone knows how to love, the wise man alone is a real friend." And yet it is a part of love and of friendship to return favours; nay, further, it is an ordinary act, and happens more frequently than real friendship. Again, this same objector wonders at our saying, "There is no loyalty except in the wise man," just as if he himself does not say the same thing! Or do you think that there is any loyalty in him who does not know how to return a favour? [13]These men, accordingly, should cease to discredit us, just as if we were uttering an impossible boast; they should understand that the essence of honour resides in the wise man, while among the crowd we find only the ghost and the semblance of honour. None but the wise man knows how to return a favour. Even a fool can return it in proportion to his knowledge and his power; his fault would be a lack of knowledge rather than a lack of will or desire. To will does not come by teaching.

[14]The wise man will compare all things with one another; for the very same object becomes greater or smaller, according to the time, the place, and the cause. Often the riches that are spent in profusion upon a palace cannot accomplish as much as a thousand *denarii* given at the right time. Now it makes a great deal of difference whether you give outright, or come to a man's assistance, whether your generosity saves him, or sets him up in life. Often the gift is small, but the consequences great. And what a distinction do you imagine there is between taking something which one lacks,—something which was offered,—and receiving a benefit in order to confer one in return?

[15]But we should not slip back into the subject which we have already sufficiently investigated. In this balancing of benefits and injuries, the good man will, to be sure, judge with the highest degree of fairness, but he will incline towards the side of the benefit; he will turn more readily in this direction. [16]Moreover, in affairs of this kind the person concerned is wont to count for a great deal. Men say: "You conferred a benefit upon me in that matter of the slave, but you did me an injury in the case of my father" or, "You saved my son, but robbed me of a father." Similarly, he will follow up all oth-

er matters in which comparisons can be made, and if the difference be very slight, he will pretend not to notice it. Even though the difference be great, yet if the concession can be made without impairment of duty and loyalty, our good man will overlook that is, provided the injury exclusively affects the good man himself. [17]To sum up, the matter stands thus: the good man will be easy-going in striking a balance; he will allow too much to be set against his credit. He will be unwilling to pay a benefit by balancing the injury against it. The side towards which he will lean, the tendency which he will exhibit, is the desire to be under obligations for the favour, and the desire to make return therefor. For anyone who receives a benefit more gladly than he repays it is mistaken. By as much as he who pays is more light-hearted than he who borrows, by so much ought he to be more joyful who unburdens himself of the greatest debt–a benefit received–than he who incurs the greatest obligations. [18]For ungrateful men make mistakes in this respect also: they have to pay their creditors both capital and interest,[9] but they think that benefits are currency which they can use without interest. So the debts grow through postponement, and the later the action is postponed the more remains to be paid. A man is an ingrate if he repays a favour without interest. Therefore, interest also should be allowed for, when you compare your receipts and your expenses. [19]We should try by all means to be as grateful as possible.

For gratitude is a good thing for ourselves, in a sense in which justice, that is commonly supposed to concern other persons, is not; gratitude returns in large measure unto itself. There is not a man who, when he has benefited his neighbour, has not benefited himself,–I do not mean for the reason that he whom you have aided will desire to aid you, or that he whom you have defended will desire to protect you, or that an example of good conduct returns in a circle to benefit the doer, just as examples of bad conduct recoil upon their authors, and as men find no pity if they suffer wrongs which they themselves have demonstrated the possibility of committing; but that the reward for all the virtues lies in the virtues themselves. For they are not practised with a view to recompense; the wages of a good deed is to have done it.[10] [20]I am grateful, not in order that my neighbour, provoked by the earlier act of kindness, may be more ready to benefit me, but simply in order that I may perform a most pleasant and beautiful act; I feel grateful, not because it profits me, but because it pleases me. And, to prove the truth of this to you, I declare that even if I may not be grateful without seeming ungrateful, even if I am able to retain a benefit only by an act which resembles an injury; even so, I shall strive in the utmost calmness of spirit toward the purpose which honour demands, in the very midst of disgrace. No one, I think, rates virtue higher or is more consecrated to virtue than he who has lost his reputation for being a good man in order to keep from losing the approval of his conscience. [21]Thus, as I have said, your being grateful is more conducive to your own good than to your neighbour's good. For while your neighbour has had a common, everyday experience,–namely, receiving back the gift which he had bestowed,–you have had a great experience which is the outcome of an utterly happy condition of soul,–to have felt gratitude. For if wickedness makes men unhappy and virtue makes men blest, and if it is a virtue to be grateful, then the return which you have made is only the customary thing, but the thing to which you have attained is priceless,–the consciousness of gratitude, which comes only to the soul that is divine and blessed. The opposite feeling to this, however, is immediately attended by the greatest unhappiness; no man, if he be ungrateful, will be unhappy in the future. I allow him no day of grace; he is unhappy forthwith.

[22]Let us therefore avoid being ungrateful, not for the sake of others but for our own sakes. When we do wrong, only the least and lightest portion of it flows back upon our neighbour; the worst and, if I may use the term, the densest portion of it stays at home and troubles the owner.[11] My master Attalus used to say: "Evil herself drinks the largest portion of her own poison." The poison which serpents carry for the destruction of others, and secrete without harm to themselves, is not like this poison; for this sort is ruinous to the possessor. [23]The ungrateful man tortures and torments himself; he hates the gifts which he has accepted, because he must make a return for them, and he tries to belittle their value, but he really enlarges and exaggerates the injuries which he has

not better even to lie idle than to whirl round in these eddies of business distraction?"
Both extremes are to be deprecated–both tension and sluggishness. I hold that he who
lies on a perfumed couch is no less dead than he who is dragged along by the executioner's hook.

Leisure without study is death; it is a tomb for the living man. ⁴What then is the advantage of retirement? As if the real causes of our anxieties did not follow us across the
seas! What hiding-place is there, where the fear of death does not enter? What peaceful
haunts are there, so fortified and so far withdrawn that pain does not fill them with
fear? Wherever you hide yourself, human ills will make an uproar all around. There
are many external things which compass us about, to deceive us or to weigh upon us;
there are many things within which, even amid solitude, fret and ferment.

⁵Therefore, gird yourself about with philosophy, an impregnable wall. Though
it be assaulted by many engines, Fortune can find no passage into it. The soul stands
on unassailable ground, if it has abandoned external things; it is independent in its
own fortress; and every weapon that is hurled falls short of the mark. Fortune has not
the long reach with which we credit her; she can seize none except him that clings to
her. ⁶Let us then recoil from her as far as we are able. This will be possible for us only
through knowledge of self and of the world⁴ of Nature. The soul should know whither
it is going and whence it came, what is good for it and what is evil, what it seeks and
what it avoids, and what is that Reason which distinguishes between the desirable and
the undesirable, and thereby tames the madness of our desires and calms the violence
of our fears.

⁷Some men flatter themselves that they have checked these evils by themselves
even without the aid of philosophy; but when some accident catches them off their
guard, a tardy confession of error is wrung from them. Their boastful words perish
from their lips when the torturer commands them to stretch forth their hands, and
when death draws nearer! You might say to such a man: "It was easy for you to challenge evils that were not near-by; but here comes pain, which you declared you could
endure; here comes death, against which you uttered many a courageous boast! The
whip cracks, the sword flashes:

> Ah now, Aeneas, thou must needs be stout
> And strong of heart!"⁵

⁸This strength of heart, however, will come from constant study, provided that you
practise, not with the tongue but with the soul, and provided that you prepare yourself to meet death. To enable yourself to meet death, you may expect no encouragement or cheer from those who try to make you believe, by means of their hair-splitting
logic, that death is no evil. For I take pleasure, excellent Lucilius, in poking fun at the
absurdities of the Greeks, of which, to my continual surprise, I have not yet succeeded
in ridding myself. ⁹Our master Zeno⁶ uses a syllogism like this: "No evil is glorious;
but death is glorious; therefore death is no evil." A cure, Zeno! I have been freed from
fear; henceforth I shall not hesitate to bare my neck on the scaffold. Will you not utter
sterner words instead of rousing a dying man to laughter? Indeed, Lucilius, I could
not easily tell you whether he who thought that he was quenching the fear of death by
setting up this syllogism was the more foolish, or he who attempted to refute it, just
as if it had anything to do with the matter! ¹⁰For the refuter himself proposed a count-
er-syllogism, based upon the proposition that we regard death as "indifferent,"–one
of the things which the Greeks call ἀδιάφορα.⁷ "Nothing," he says, "that is indifferent
can be glorious; death is glorious; therefore death is not indifferent." You comprehend
the tricky fallacy which is contained in this syllogism.–mere death is, in fact, not glorious; but a brave death is glorious. And when you say, "Nothing that is indifferent is
glorious," I grant you this much, and declare that nothing is glorious except as it deals
with indifferent things. I classify as "indifferent,"–that is, neither good nor evil–sickness, pain, poverty, exile, death. ¹¹None of these things is intrinsically glorious; but
nothing can be glorious apart from them. For it is not poverty that we praise, it is the
man whom poverty cannot humble or bend. Nor is it exile that we praise, it is the man
who withdraws into exile in the spirit in which he would have sent another into exile.

It is not pain that we praise, it is the man whom pain has not coerced. One praises not death, but the man whose soul death takes away before it can confound it. [12]All these things are in themselves neither honourable nor glorious; but any one of them that virtue has visited and touched is made honourable and glorious by virtue; they merely lie in between,[8] and the decisive question is only whether wickedness or virtue has laid hold upon them. For instance, the death which in Cato's case is glorious, is in the case of Brutus[9] forthwith base and disgraceful. For this Brutus, condemned to death, was trying to obtain postponement; he withdrew a moment in order to ease himself; when summoned to die and ordered to bare his throat, he exclaimed: "I will bare my throat, if only I may live!" What madness it is to run away, when it is impossible to turn back! "I will bare my throat, if only I may live!" He came very near saying also: "even under Antony!" This fellow deserved indeed to be consigned to *life*!

[13]But, as I was going on to remark, you see that death in itself is neither an evil nor a good; Cato experienced death most honourably, Brutus most basely. Everything, if you add virtue, assumes a glory which it did not possess before. We speak of a sunny room, even though the same room is pitch-dark at night. [14]It is the day which fills it with light, and the night which steals the light away; thus it is with the things which we call indifferent and "middle,"[10] like riches, strength, beauty, titles, kingship, and their opposites,—death, exile, ill-health, pain, and all such evils, the fear of which upsets us to a greater or less extent; it is the wickedness or the virtue that bestows the name of good or evil. An object is not by its own essence either hot or cold; it is heated when thrown into a furnace, and chilled when dropped into water. Death is honourable when related to that which is honourable; by this I mean virtue and a soul that despises the worst hardships.

[15]Furthermore, there are vast distinctions among these qualities which we call "middle." For example, death is not so indifferent as the question whether your hair should be worn evenly or unevenly. Death belongs among those things which are not indeed evils, but still have in them a semblance of evil; for there are implanted in us love of self, a desire for existence and self-preservation, and also an abhorrence of dissolution, because death seems to rob us of many goods and to withdraw us from the abundance to which we have become accustomed. And there is another element which estranges us from death, we are already familiar with the present, but are ignorant of the future into which we shall transfer ourselves, and we shrink from the unknown. Moreover, it is natural to fear the world of shades, whither death is supposed to lead. [16]Therefore, although death is something indifferent, it is nevertheless not a thing which we can easily ignore. The soul must be hardened by long practice, so that it may learn to endure the sight and the approach of death.

Death ought to be despised more than it is wont to be despised. For we believe too many of the stories about death. Many thinkers have striven hard to increase its ill repute; they have portrayed the prison in the world below and the land overwhelmed by everlasting night, where

> Within his blood-stained cave Hell's warder huge
> Doth sprawl his ugly length on half-crunched bones,
> And terrifies the disembodied ghosts
> With never-ceasing bark.[11]

Even if you can win your point and prove that these are mere stories and that nothing is left for the dead to fear, another fear steals upon you. For the fear of going to the underworld is equalled by the fear of going nowhere.

[17]In the face of these notions, which long-standing opinion has dinned in our ears, how can brave endurance of death be anything else than glorious, and fit to rank among the greatest accomplishments of the human mind? For the mind will never rise to virtue if it believes that death is an evil; but it will so rise if it holds that death is a matter of indifference. It is not in the order of nature that a man shall proceed with a great heart to a destiny which he believes to be evil; he will go sluggishly and with reluctance. But nothing glorious can result from unwillingness and cowardice; virtue does nothing under compulsion. [18]Besides, no deed that a man does is honourable

is what makes us wicked: that no one of us looks back over his own life. Our thoughts are devoted only to what we are about to do. And yet our plans for the future always depend on the past.

³To-day has been unbroken; no one has filched the slightest part of it from me. The whole time has been divided between rest and reading. A brief space has been given over to bodily exercise, and on this ground I can thank old age–my exercise costs very little effort; as soon as I stir, I am tired. And weariness is the aim and end of exercise, no matter how strong one is. ⁴Do you ask who are my pacemakers? One is enough for me,–the slave Pharius, a pleasant fellow, as you know; but I shall exchange him for another. At my time of life I need one who is of still more tender years. Pharius, at any rate, says that he and I are at the same period of life; for we are both losing our teeth.³ Yet even now I can scarcely follow his pace as he runs, and within a very short time I shall not be able to follow him at all; so you see what profit we get from daily exercise. Very soon does a wide interval open between two persons who travel different ways. My slave is climbing up at the very moment when I am coming down, and you surely know how much quicker the latter is. Nay, I was wrong; for now my life is not coming down; it is falling outright. ⁵Do you ask, for all that, how our race resulted to-day? We raced to a tie,⁴–something which rarely happens in a running contest. After tiring myself out in this way (for I cannot call it exercise), I took a cold bath; this, at my house, means just short of hot. I, the former cold-water enthusiast, who used to celebrate the new year by taking a plunge into the canal, who, just as naturally as I would set out to do some reading or writing, or to compose a speech, used to inaugurate the first of the year with a plunge into the Virgo aqueduct,⁵ have changed my allegiance, first to the Tiber, and then to my favourite tank, which is warmed only by the sun, at times when I am most robust and when there is not a flaw in my bodily processes. I have very little energy left for bathing. ⁶After the bath, some stale bread and breakfast without a table; no need to wash the hands after such a meal. Then comes a very short nap. You know my habit; I avail myself of a scanty bit of sleep,–unharnessing, as it were.⁶ For I am satisfied if I can just stop staying awake. Sometimes I know that I have slept; at other times, I have a mere suspicion.

⁷Lo, now the din of the Races sounds about me! My ears are smitten with sudden and general cheering. But this does not upset my thoughts or even break their continuity. I can endure an uproar with complete resignation. The medley of voices blended in one note sounds to me like the dashing of waves,⁷ or like the wind that lashes the tree-tops, or like any other sound which conveys no meaning.

⁸What is it, then, you ask, to which I have been giving my attention? I will tell you, a thought sticks in my mind, left over from yesterday,–namely, what men of the greatest sagacity have meant when they have offered the most trifling and intricate proofs for problems of the greatest importance,–proofs which may be true, but none the less resemble fallacies. ⁹Zeno, that greatest of men, the revered founder of our brave and holy school of philosophy, wishes to discourage us from drunkenness. Listen, then, to his arguments proving that the good man will not get drunk: "No one entrusts a secret to a drunken man; but one will entrust a secret to a good man; therefore, the good man will not get drunk."⁸ Mark how ridiculous Zeno is made when we set up a similar syllogism in contrast with his. There are many, but one will be enough: "No one entrusts a secret to a man when he is asleep; but one entrusts a secret to a good man; therefore, the good man does not go to sleep."⁹ ¹⁰Posidonius pleads the cause of our master Zeno in the only possible way; but it cannot, I hold, be pleaded even in this way. For Posidonius maintains that the word "drunken" is used in two ways,–in the one case of a man who is loaded with wine and has no control over himself; in the other, of a man who is accustomed to get drunk, and is a slave to the habit. Zeno, he says, meant the latter,– the man who is accustomed to get drunk, not the man who is drunk; and no one would entrust to this person any secret, for it might be blabbed out when the man was in his cups. ¹¹This is a fallacy. For the first syllogism refers to him who is actually drunk and not to him who is about to get drunk. You will surely admit that there is a great difference between a man who is drunk and a drunkard. He who is actually drunk may be in

this state for the first time and may not have the habit, while the drunkard is often free from drunkenness. I therefore interpret the word in its usual meaning, especially since the syllogism is set up by a man who makes a business of the careful use of words, and who weighs his language. Moreover, if this is what Zeno meant, and what he wished it to mean to us, he was trying to avail himself of an equivocal word in order to work in a fallacy; and no man ought to do this when truth is the object of inquiry.

[12]But let us admit, indeed, that he meant what Posidonius says; even so, the conclusion is false, that secrets are not entrusted to an habitual drunkard. Think how many soldiers who are not always sober have been entrusted by a general or a captain or a centurion with messages which might not be divulged! With regard to the notorious plot to murder Gaius Caesar,–I mean the Caesar who conquered Pompey and got control of the state,–Tillius Cimber was trusted with it no less than Gaius Cassius. Now Cassius throughout his life drank water; while Tillius Cimber was a sot as well as a brawler. Cimber himself alluded to this fact, saying: "*I carry a master? I cannot carry my liquor!*" [13]So let each one call to mind those who, to his knowledge, can be ill trusted with wine, but well trusted with the spoken word; and yet one case occurs to my mind, which I shall relate, lest it fall into oblivion. For life should be provided with conspicuous illustrations. Let us not always be harking back to the dim past.

[14]Lucius Piso, the director of Public Safety at Rome, was drunk from the very time of his appointment. He used to spend the greater part of the night at banquets, and would sleep until noon. That was the way he spent his morning hours. Nevertheless, he applied himself most diligently to his official duties, which included the guardianship of the city. Even the sainted Augustus trusted him with secret orders when he placed him in command of Thrace.[10] Piso conquered that country. Tiberius, too, trusted him when he took his holiday in Campania, leaving behind him in the city many a critical matter that aroused both suspicion and hatred. [15]I fancy that it was because Piso's drunkenness turned out well for the Emperor that he appointed to the office of city prefect Cossus, a man of authority and balance, but so soaked and steeped in drink that once, at a meeting of the Senate, whither he had come after banqueting, he was overcome by a slumber from which he could not be roused, and had to be carried home. It was to this man that Tiberius sent many orders, written in his own hand,– orders which he believed he ought not to trust even to the officials of his household. Cossus never let a single secret slip out, whether personal or public.

[16]So let us abolish all such harangues as this: "No man in the bonds of drunkenness has power over his soul. As the very vats are burst by new wine, and as the dregs at the bottom are raised to the surface by the strength of the fermentation; so, when the wine effervesces, whatever lies hidden below is brought up and made visible. As a man overcome by liquor cannot keep down his food when he has over-indulged in wine, so he cannot keep back a secret either. He pours forth impartially both his own secrets and those of other persons." [17]This, of course, is what commonly happens, but so does this,–that we take counsel on serious subjects with those whom we know to be in the habit of drinking freely. Therefore this proposition, which is laid down in the guise of a defence of Zeno's syllogism, is false,–that secrets are not entrusted to the habitual drunkard.

How much better it is to arraign drunkenness frankly and to expose its vices! For even the middling good man avoids them, not to mention the perfect sage, who is satisfied with slaking his thirst; the sage, even if now and then he is led on by good cheer which, for a friend's sake, is carried somewhat too far, yet always stops short of drunkenness. [18]We shall investigate later the question whether the mind of the sage is upset by too much wine and commits follies like those of the toper; but meanwhile, if you wish to prove that a good man ought not to get drunk, why work it out by logic? Show how base it is to pour down more liquor than one can carry, and not to know the capacity of one's own stomach; show how often the drunkard does things which make him blush when he is sober; state that drunkenness[11] is nothing but a condition of insanity purposely assumed. Prolong the drunkard's condition to several days; will you have any doubt about his madness? Even as it is, the madness is no less; it merely lasts a shorter time. [19]Think of Alexander of Macedon,[12] who stabbed Clitus, his dearest and most loyal friend, at a banquet; after Alexander understood what he had done, he wished to die, and assuredly he ought to have died.

Drunkenness kindles and discloses every kind of vice, and removes the sense of shame that veils our evil undertakings.[13] For more men abstain from forbidden actions because they are ashamed of sinning than because their inclinations are good. [20]When the strength of wine has become too great and has gained control over the mind, every lurking evil comes forth from its hiding-place. Drunkenness does not create vice, it merely brings it into view; at such times the lustful man does not wait even for the privacy of a bedroom, but without postponement gives free play to the demands of his passions; at such times the unchaste man proclaims and publishes his malady; at such times your cross-grained fellow does not restrain his tongue or his hand. The haughty man increases his arrogance, the ruthless man his cruelty, the slanderer his spitefulness. Every vice is given free play and comes to the front. [21]Besides, we forget who we are, we utter words that are halting and poorly enunciated, the glance is unsteady, the step falters, the head is dizzy, the very ceiling moves about as if a cyclone were whirling the whole house, and the stomach suffers torture when the wine generates gas and causes our very bowels to swell. However, at the time, these troubles can be endured, so long as the man retains his natural strength; but what can he do when sleep impairs his powers, and when that which was drunkenness becomes indigestion?

[22]Think of the calamities caused by drunkenness in a nation! This evil has betrayed to their enemies the most spirited and warlike races; this evil has made breaches in walls defended by the stubborn warfare of many years; this evil has forced under alien sway peoples who were utterly unyielding and defiant of the yoke; this evil has conquered by the wine-cup those who in the field were invincible. [23]Alexander, whom I have just mentioned, passed through his many marches, his many battles, his many winter campaigns (through which he worked his way by overcoming disadvantages of time or place), the many rivers which flowed from unknown sources, and the many seas, all in safety; it was intemperance in drinking that laid him low, and the famous death-dealing bowl of Hercules.[14]

[24]What glory is there in carrying much liquor? When you have won the prize, and the other banqueters, sprawling asleep or vomiting, have declined your challenge to still other toasts; when you are the last survivor of the revels; when you have vanquished every one by your magnificent show of prowess and there is no man who has proved himself of so great capacity as you, you are vanquished by the cask. [25]Mark Antony was a great man, a man of distinguished ability; but what ruined him and drove him into foreign habits and un-Roman vices, if it was not drunkenness and–no less potent than wine–love of Cleopatra? This it was that made him an enemy of the state; this it was that rendered him no match for his enemies; this it was that made him cruel, when as he sat at table the heads of the leaders of the state were brought in; when amid the most elaborate feasts and royal luxury he would identify the faces and hands of men whom he had proscribed;[15] when, though heavy with wine, he yet thirsted for blood. It was intolerable that he was getting drunk while he did such things; how much more intolerable that he did these things while actually drunk! [26]Cruelty usually follows wine-bibbing; for a man's soundness of mind is corrupted and made savage. Just as a lingering illness makes men querulous and irritable and drives them wild at the least crossing of their desires, so continued bouts of drunkenness bestialize the soul. For when people are often beside themselves, the habit of madness lasts on, and the vices which liquor generated retain their power even when the liquor is gone.

[27]Therefore you should state why the wise man ought not to get drunk. Explain by facts, and not by mere words, the hideousness of the thing, and its haunting evils. Do that which is easiest of all–namely, demonstrate that what men call pleasures are punishments as soon as they have exceeded due bounds. For if you try to prove that the wise man can souse himself with much wine and yet keep his course straight, even though he be in his cups, you may go on to infer by syllogisms that he will not die if he swallows poison, that he will not sleep if he takes a sleeping-potion, that he will not

vomit and reject the matter which clogs his stomach when you give him hellebore.[16] But, when a man's feet totter and his tongue is unsteady, what reason have you for believing that he is half sober and half drunk? Farewell.

Footnotes

1. Cf. Ep. xli. 2 *sacer intra nos spiritus, . . . malorum bonorumque nostrorum observator et custos.*

2. Cf. Ep. i. 4 *ratio constat inpensae* (referring to his attempt to employ his time profitably).

3. See Ep. xii. 3 for a similar witticism.

4. *Hieran (coronam)*, as Lipsius thinks, when the result was doubtful, the garland was offered to the gods. From the Greek ἱερός, sacred.

5. Constructed by Marcus Agrippa; now the fountain of Trevi.

6. The same word is used by Seneca in *De Tranq. An.* xvii. 7 *quidam medio die interiunxerunt et in postmeridianas horas aliquid levioris operae distulerunt.*

7. Cf. Ep. lvi. 3 *istum fremitum non magis curo quam fluctum aut deiectum aquae.*

8. Zeno, Frag. 229 von Arnim,—quoting also Philo's εἰ τῷ μεθύοντι οὐκ ἄν τις εὐλόγως λόγον ἀπόρρητον παρακατάθοιτο . . . οὐκ ἄρα μεθύει ὁ ἀστεῖος.

9. Cf. Ep. xlix. 8 *quod non perdidisti, habes; cornua autem non perdidisti; cornua ergo habes,—* and the syllogisms given in Ep. xlviii.

10. In 11 B.C., when the Thracians were attacking Macedonia. The campaign lasted for three years, and Piso was rewarded with a triumph at its close.

11. Like anger, which was interpreted by the ancients as "short-lived madness."

12. For a dramatic account of the murder see Plutarch's *Alexander*, ch. 51.

13. This is the firm conviction of Seneca, himself a most temperate man. §§ 14 and 15 admit that natural genius may triumph over drunkenness; § 17 may allow (with Chrysippus) a certain amount of hilarity; but the general conclusion is obvious.

14. Lipsius quotes Athenaeus as saying that Boeotian silver cups of large size were so called because the Boeotian Hercules drank from them; Servius, however, on Verg. *Aen.* viii. 278, declared that the name was derived from the large wooden bowl brought by Hercules to Italy and used for sacrificial purposes.

15. "Antony gave orders to those that were to kill Cicero, to cut off his head and right hand . . . ; and, when they were brought before him, he regarded them joyfully, actually bursting out more than once into laughter, and when he had satiated himself with the sight of them, ordered them to be hung up . . . in the forum" (Clough's translation of Plutarch's *Antony*, p. 172).

16. A plant which possessed cathartic properties and was widely used by the ancients. It was also applied in cases of mental derangement. The native Latin term is *veratrum*.

LXXXIV. ON GATHERING IDEAS[1]

[1]The journeys to which you refer—journeys that shake the laziness out of my system—I hold to be profitable both for my health and for my studies. You see why they benefit my health: since my passion for literature makes me lazy and careless about my body, I can take exercise by deputy; as for my studies, I shall show you why my journeys help them, for I have not stopped my reading in the slightest degree. And reading, I hold, is indispensable—primarily, to keep me from being satisfied with myself alone, and besides, after I have learned what others have found out by their studies, to enable me to pass judgment on their discoveries and reflect upon discoveries that remain to be made. Reading nourishes the mind and refreshes it when it is wearied with study; nevertheless, this refreshment is not obtained without study. [2]We ought not to confine ourselves either to writing or to reading; the one, continuous writing, will cast a gloom over our strength, and exhaust it; the other will make our strength flabby and watery. It is better to have recourse to them alternately, and to blend one with the other, so that the fruits of one's reading may be reduced to concrete form by the pen.

[3]We should follow, men say, the example of the bees, who flit about and cull the

flowers that are suitable for producing honey, and then arrange and assort in their cells all that they have brought in; these bees, as our Vergil says,

> Pack close the flowing honey,
> And swell their cells with nectar sweet.[2]

'It is not certain whether the juice which they obtain from the flowers forms at once into honey, or whether they change that which they have gathered into this delicious object by blending something therewith and by a certain property of their breath. For some authorities believe that bees do not possess the art of making honey, but only of gathering it; and they say that in India honey has been found on the leaves of certain reeds, produced by a dew peculiar to that climate, or by the juice of the reed itself, which has an unusual sweetness, and richness.[3] And in our own grasses too, they say, the same quality exists, although less clear and less evident; and a creature born to fulfil such a function could hunt it out and collect it. Certain others maintain that the materials which the bees have culled from the most delicate of blooming and flowering plants is transformed into this peculiar substance by a process of preserving and careful storing away, aided by what might be called fermentation,–whereby separate elements are united into one substance.

[5]But I must not be led astray into another subject than that which we are discussing. We also, I say, ought to copy these bees, and sift whatever we have gathered from a varied course of reading, for such things are better preserved if they are kept separate; then, by applying the supervising care with which our nature has endowed us,–in other words, our natural gifts,–we should so blend those several flavours into one delicious compound that, even though it betrays its origin, yet it nevertheless is clearly a different thing from that whence it came. This is what we see nature doing in our own bodies without any labour on our part; [6]the food we have eaten, as long as it retains its original quality and floats, in our stomachs as an undiluted mass, is a burden;[4] but it passes into tissue and blood only when it has been changed from its original form. So it is with the food which nourishes our higher nature,–we should see to it that whatever we have absorbed should not be allowed to remain unchanged, or it will be no part of us. [7]We must digest it; otherwise it will merely enter the memory and not the reasoning power. Let us loyally welcome such foods and make them our own, so that something that is one may be formed out of many elements, just as one number is formed of several elements whenever, by our reckoning, lesser sums, each different from the others, are brought together. This is what our mind should do: it should hide away all the materials by which it has been aided, and bring to light only what it has made of them. [8]Even if there shall appear in you a likeness to him who, by reason of your admiration, has left a deep impress upon you, I would have you resemble him as a child resembles his father, and not as a picture resembles its original; for a picture is a lifeless thing.

"What," you say, "will it not be seen whose style you are imitating, whose method of reasoning, whose pungent sayings?" I think that sometimes it is impossible for it to be seen who is being imitated, if the copy is a true one; for a true copy stamps its own form upon all the features which it has drawn from what we may call the original, in such a way that they are combined into a unity. [9]Do you not see how many voices there are in a chorus? Yet out of the many only one voice results. In that chorus one voice takes the tenor another the bass, another the baritone. There are women, too, as well as men, and the flute is mingled with them. In that chorus the voices of the individual singers are hidden; what we hear is the voices of all together. [10]To be sure, I am referring to the chorus which the old-time philosophers knew; in our present-day exhibitions[5] we have a larger number of singers than there used to be spectators in the theatres of old. All the aisles are filled with rows of singers; brass instruments surround the auditorium; the stage resounds with flutes and instruments of every description; and yet from the discordant sounds a harmony is produced.

I would have my mind of such a quality as this; it should be equipped with many arts, many precepts, and patterns of conduct taken from many epochs of history; but all should blend harmoniously into one. [11]"How," you ask, "can this be accomplished?"

By constant effort, and by doing nothing without the approval of reason. And if you are willing to hear her voice, she will say to you: "Abandon those pursuits which heretofore have caused you to run hither and thither. Abandon riches, which are either a danger or a burden to the possessor. Abandon the pleasures of the body and of the mind; they only soften and weaken you. Abandon your quest for office; it is a swollen, idle, and empty thing, a thing that has no goal, as anxious to see no one outstrip it as to see no one at its heels. It is afflicted with envy, and in truth with a twofold envy; and you see how wretched a man's plight is if he who is the object of envy feels envy also."

[12]Do you behold yonder homes of the great, yonder thresholds uproarious with the brawling of those who would pay their respects? They have many an insult[6] for you as you enter the door, and still more after you have entered. Pass by the steps that mount to rich men's houses, and the porches rendered hazardous by the huge throng; for there you will be standing, not merely on the edge of a precipice but also on slippery ground. Instead of this, direct your course hither to wisdom, and seek her ways, which are ways of surpassing peace and plenty. [13]Whatever seems conspicuous in the affairs of men—however petty it may really be and prominent only by contrast with the lowest objects—is nevertheless approached by a difficult and toilsome pathway. It is a rough road that leads to the heights of greatness; but if you desire to scale this peak, which lies far above the range of Fortune, you will indeed look down from above upon all that men regard as most lofty, but none the less you can proceed to the top over level ground. Farewell.

Footnotes

1. A considerable part of this letter is found in the preface to the *Saturnalia* of Macrobius, without any acknowledgement of indebtedness.

2. *Aeneid*, i. 432 f.

3. Cf. *mel in harundinibus collectum* (from India) in Pliny, *N. H.* xii. 32 (Summers).

4. The same figure is used in reference to reading, in Ep. ii. 2 f., *non prodest cibus nec corpori accedit, qui statim sumptus emittitur*, etc.

5. *Commissio* means an entertainment, or a concert; cf. Pliny, *Panegyric* 54, *ludis et commissionibus*.

6. For such treatment cf. Juvenal iii. 152 f.–

> *Nil habet infelix paupertas durius in se*
> *Quam quod ridiculos homines facit*, etc.

LXXXV. ON SOME VAIN SYLLOGISMS

[1]I had been inclined to spare you, and had omitted any knotty problems that still remained undiscussed; I was satisfied to give you a sort of taste of the views held by the men of our school, who desire to prove that virtue is of itself sufficiently capable of rounding out the happy life. But now you bid me include the entire bulk either of our own syllogisms or of those which have been devised[1] by other schools for the purpose of belittling us. If I shall be willing to do this, the result will be a book, instead of a letter. And I declare again and again that I take no pleasure in such proofs. I am ashamed to enter the arena and undertake battle on behalf of gods and men armed only with an awl.[2]

[2]"He that possesses prudence is also self-restrained; he that possesses self-restraint is also unwavering; he that is unwavering is unperturbed; he that is unperturbed is free from sadness; he that is free from sadness is happy. Therefore, the prudent man is happy, and prudence is sufficient to constitute the happy life."

[3]Certain of the Peripatetics[3] reply to this syllogism by interpreting "unperturbed," "unwavering," and "free from sadness" in such a way as to make "unperturbed" mean one who is rarely perturbed and only to a moderate degree, and not one who is never perturbed. Likewise, they say that a person is called "free from sadness" who is not subject to sadness, one who falls into this objectionable state not often nor in too

great a degree. It is not, they say, the way of human nature that a man's spirit should be exempt from sadness, or that the wise man is not overcome by grief but is merely touched by it, and other arguments of this sort, all in accordance with the teachings of their school. ⁴They do not abolish the passions in this way; they only moderate them. But how petty is the superiority which we attribute to the wise man, if he is merely braver than the most craven, happier than the most dejected, more self-controlled than the most unbridled, and greater than the lowliest! Would Ladas boast his swiftness in running by comparing himself with the halt and the weak?

> For she could skim the topmost blades of corn
> And touch them not, nor bruise the tender ears;
> Or travel over seas, well-poised above
> The swollen floods, nor dip her flying feet
> In ocean's waters.⁴

This is speed estimated by its own standard, not the kind which wins praise by comparison with that which is slowest. Would you call a man well who has a light case of fever? No, for good health does not mean moderate illness. ⁵They say, "The wise man is called unperturbed in the sense in which pomegranates are called mellow–not that there is no hardness at all in their seeds, but that the hardness is less than it was before." That view is wrong; for I am not referring to the gradual weeding out of evils in a good man, but to the complete absence of evils; there should be in him no evils at all, not even any small ones. For if there are any, they will grow, and as they grow will hamper him. Just as a large and complete cataract⁵ wholly blinds the eyes, so a medium-sized cataract dulls their vision.

⁶If by your definition the wise man has any passions whatever, his reason will be no match for them and will be carried swiftly along, as it were, on a rushing stream,– particularly if you assign to him, not one passion with which he must wrestle, but all the passions. And a throng of such, even though they be moderate, can affect him more than the violence of one powerful passion. ⁷He has a craving for money, although in a moderate degree. He has ambition, but it is not yet fully aroused. He has a hot temper, but it can be appeased. He has inconstancy, but not the kind that is very capricious or easily set in motion. He has lust, but not the violent kind. We could deal better with a person who possessed one full-fledged vice, than with one who possessed all the vices, but none of them in extreme form. ⁸Again, it makes no difference how great the passion is; no matter what its size may be, it knows no obedience, and does not welcome advice.⁶ Just as no animal, whether wild or tamed and gentle, obeys reason, since nature made it deaf to advice; so the passions do not follow or listen, however slight they are. Tigers and lions never put off their wildness; they sometimes moderate it, and then, when you are least prepared, their softened fierceness is roused to madness. Vices are never genuinely tamed. ⁹Again, if reason prevails, the passions will not even get a start; but if they get under way against the will of reason, they will maintain themselves against the will of reason. For it is easier to stop them in the beginning than to control them when they gather force. This half-way ground is accordingly misleading and useless; it is to be regarded just as the declaration that we ought to be "moderately" insane, or "moderately" ill. ¹⁰Virtue alone possesses moderation; the evils that afflict the mind do not admit of moderation. You can more easily remove than control them. Can one doubt that the vices of the human mind, when they have become chronic and callous ("diseases" we call them), are beyond control, as, for example, greed, cruelty, and wantonness? Therefore the passions also are beyond control; for it is from the passions that we pass over to the vices. ¹¹Again, if you grant any privileges to sadness, fear, desire, and all the other wrong impulses, they will cease to lie within our jurisdiction. And why? Simply because the means of arousing them lie outside our own power. They will accordingly increase in proportion as the causes by which they are stirred up are greater or less. Fear will grow to greater proportions, if that which causes the terror is seen to be of greater magnitude or in closer proximity; and desire will grow keener in proportion as the hope of a greater gain has summoned it to action. ¹²If the existence of the passions is not in our own control, neither is the

extent of their power; for if you once permit them to get a start, they will increase along with their causes, and they will be of whatever extent they shall grow to be. Moreover, no matter how small these vices are, they grow greater. That which is harmful never keeps within bounds. No matter how trifling diseases are at the beginning, they creep on apace; and sometimes the slightest augmentation of disease lays low the enfeebled body!

[13]But what folly it is, when the beginnings of certain things are situated outside our control, to believe that their endings are within our control! How have I the power to bring something to a close, when I have not had the power to check it at the beginning? For it is easier to keep a thing out than to keep it under after you have let it in. [14]Some men have made a distinction as follows, saying: "If a man has self-control and wisdom, he is indeed at peace as regards the attitude and habit of his mind, but not as regards the outcome. For, as far as his habit of mind is concerned, he is not perturbed, or saddened, or afraid; but there are many extraneous causes which strike him and bring perturbation upon him." [15]What they mean to say is this: "So-and-so is indeed not a man of an angry disposition, but still he sometimes gives way to anger," and "He is not, indeed, inclined to fear, but still he sometimes experiences fear"; in other words, he is free from the fault, but is not free from the passion of fear. If, however, fear is once given an entrance, it will by frequent use pass over into a vice;[7] and anger, once admitted into the mind, will alter the earlier habit of a mind that was formerly free from anger. [16]Besides, if the wise man, instead of despising all causes that come from without, ever fears anything, when the time arrives for him to go bravely to meet the spear, or the flames, on behalf of his country, his laws, and his liberty, he will go forth reluctantly and with flagging spirit. Such inconsistency of mind, however, does not suit the character of a wise man.

[17]Then, again, we should see to it that two principles which ought to be tested separately should not be confused. For the conclusion is reached independently that that alone is good which is honourable, and again independently the conclusion that virtue is sufficient for the happy life. If that alone is good which is honourable, everyone agrees that virtue is sufficient for the purpose of living happily; but, on the contrary, if virtue alone makes men happy, it will not be conceded that that alone is good which is honourable. [18]Xenocrates[8] and Speusippus[8] hold that a man can become happy even by virtue alone, not, however, that that which is honourable is the only good. Epicurus also decides[9] that one who possesses virtue is happy, but that virtue of itself is not sufficient for the happy life, because the pleasure that results from virtue, and not virtue itself, makes one happy. This is a futile distinction. For the same philosopher declares that virtue never exists without pleasure; and therefore, if virtue is always connected with pleasure and always inseparable therefrom, virtue is of itself sufficient. For virtue keeps pleasure in its company, and does not exist without it, even when alone. [19]But it is absurd to say that a man will be happy by virtue alone, and yet not absolutely happy. I cannot discover how that may be, since the happy life contains in itself a good that is perfect and cannot be excelled, If a man has this good, life is completely happy.

Now if the life of the gods contains nothing greater or better, and the happy life is divine, then there is no further height to which a man can be raised. [20]Also, if the happy life is in want of nothing, then every happy life is perfect; it is happy and at the same time most happy. Have you any doubt that the happy life is the Supreme Good? Accordingly, if it possesses the Supreme Good, it is supremely happy. Just as the Supreme Good does not admit of increase (for what will be superior to that which is supreme?), exactly so the happy life cannot be increased either; for it is not without the Supreme Good. If then you bring in one man who is "happier" than another, you will also bring in one who is "much happier"; you will then be making countless distinctions in the Supreme Good; although I understand the Supreme Good to be that good which admits of no degree above itself. [21]If one person is less happy than another, it follows that he eagerly desires the life of that other and happier man in preference to his own. But the happy man prefers no other man's life to his own. Either of these two things is incredible: that there should be anything left for a happy man to wish for in preference to what is, or that he should not prefer the thing which is better than what he already has. For certainly, the more prudent he is, the more he will strive after the best, and he will desire to attain it by every possible means. But how can one be happy who is still able, or rather who is still bound, to crave something else? [22]I will tell you what is the source of this error: men do not understand that the happy life is a unit; for it is its essence, and not its extent, that establishes such a life on the noblest Plane. Hence there is complete equality between the life that is long and the life that is short, between that which is spread out and that which is confined, between that whose influence is felt in many places and in many directions, and that which is restricted to one interest. Those who reckon life by number, or by measure, or by parts, rob it of its distinctive quality. Now, in the happy life, what is the distinctive quality? It is its fulness.[10] [23]Satiety, I think, is the limit to our eating or drinking. A eats more and B eats less; what difference does it make? Each is now sated. Or A drinks more and B drinks less; what difference does it make? Each is no longer thirsty, Again, A lives for many years and B for fewer; no matter, if only A's many years have brought as much happiness as B's few years. He whom you maintain to be "less happy" is not happy; the word admits of no diminution.

[24]"He who is brave is fearless; he who is fearless is free from sadness; he who is free from sadness is happy." It is our own school which has framed this syllogism; they attempt to refute it by this answer, namely, that we Stoics are assuming as admitted a premiss which is false and distinctly controverted,–that the brave man is fearless. "What!" they say, "will the brave man have no fear of evils that threaten him? That would be the condition of a madman, a lunatic, rather than of a brave man. The brave man will, it is true, feel fear in only a very slight degree; but he is not absolutely free from fear." [25]Now those who assert this are doubling back to their old argument, in that they regard vices of less degree as equivalent to virtues.[11] For indeed the man who does feel fear, though he feels it rather seldom and to a slight degree, is not free from wickedness, but is merely troubled by it in a milder form. "Not so," is the reply, "for I hold that a man is mad if he does not fear evils which hang over his head." What you say is perfectly true, if the things which threaten are really evils; but if he knows that they are not evils and believes that the only evil is baseness, he will be bound to face dangers without anxiety and to despise things which other men cannot help fearing. Or, if it is the characteristic of a fool and a madman not to fear evils, then the wiser a man is the more he will fear such things! [26]"It is the doctrine of you Stoics, then," they reply, "that a brave man will expose himself to dangers." By no means; he will merely not fear them, though he will avoid them. It is proper for him to be careful, but not to be fearful.[12] "What then? Is he not to fear death, imprisonment, burning, and all the other missiles of Fortune?" Not at all; for he knows that they are not evils, but only seem to be. He reckons all these things as the bugbears of man's existence. [27]Paint him a picture of slavery, lashes, chains, want, mutilation by disease or by torture,–or anything else you may care to mention; he will count all such things as terrors caused by the derangement of the mind. These things are only to be feared by those who are fearful. Or do you regard as an evil that to which some day we may be compelled to resort of our own free will?

[28]What then, you ask, is an evil? It is the yielding to those things which are called evils; it is the surrendering of one's liberty into their control, when really we ought to suffer all things in order to preserve this liberty. Liberty is lost unless we despise those things which put the yoke upon our necks. If men knew what bravery was, they would have no doubts as to what a brave man's conduct should be. For bravery is not thoughtless rashness, or love of danger, or the courting of fear-inspiring objects; it is the knowledge which enables us to distinguish between that which is evil and that which is not.[13] Bravery takes the greatest care of itself, and likewise endures with the greatest patience all things which have a false appearance of being evil. [29]"What then?" is the query; "if the sword is brandished over your brave man's neck, if he is pierced in this place and in that continually, if he sees his entrails in his lap, if he is tortured again after being kept waiting in order that he may thus feel the torture more keenly, and if

the blood flows afresh out of bowels where it has but lately ceased to flow, has he no fear? Shall you say that he has felt no pain either?" Yes, he has felt pain; for no human virtue can rid itself of feelings. But he has no fear; unconquered he looks down from a lofty height upon his sufferings. Do you ask me what spirit animates him in these circumstances? It is the spirit of one who is comforting a sick friend.

[30.]"That which is evil does harm; that which does harm makes a man worse. But pain and poverty do not make a man worse; therefore they are not evils." "Your proposition," says the objector, "is wrong; for what harms one does not necessarily make one worse. The storm and the squall work harm to the pilot, but they do not make a worse pilot of him for all that." [31]Certain of the Stoic school reply to this argument as follows: "The pilot becomes a worse pilot because of storms or squalls, inasmuch as he cannot carry out his purpose and hold to his course; as far as his art is concerned, he becomes no worse a pilot, but in his work he does become worse." To this the Peripatetics retort: "Therefore, poverty will make even the wise man worse, and so will pain, and so will anything else of that sort. For although those things will not rob him of his virtue, yet they will hinder the work of virtue." [32]This would be a correct statement, were it not for the fact that the pilot and the wise man are two different kinds of person. The wise man's purpose in conducting his life is not to accomplish at all hazards what he tries, but to do all things rightly; the pilot's purpose, however, is to bring his ship into port at all hazards. The arts are handmaids;[14] they must accomplish what they promise to do. But wisdom is mistress and ruler. The arts render a slave's service to life; wisdom issues the commands.

[33]For myself, I maintain that a different answer should be given: that the pilot's art is never made worse by the storm, nor the application of his art either. The pilot has promised you, not a prosperous voyage, but a serviceable performance of his task–that is, an expert knowledge of steering a ship. And the more he is hampered by the stress of fortune, so much the more does his knowledge become apparent. He who has been able to say, "Neptune, you shall never sink this ship except on an even keel,"[15] has fulfilled the requirements of his art; the storm does not interfere with the pilot's work, but only with his success. [34]"What then," you say, "is not a pilot harmed by any circumstance which does not permit him to make port, frustrates all his efforts, and either carries him out to sea, or holds the ship in irons, or strips her masts?" No, it does not harm him as a pilot, but only as a voyager; otherwise, he is no pilot. It is indeed so far from hindering the pilot's art that it even exhibits the art; for anyone, in the words of the proverb, is a pilot on a calm sea. These mishaps obstruct the voyage but not the steersman *qua* steersman. [35]A pilot has a double rôle: one he shares with all his fellow-passengers, for he also is a passenger; the other is peculiar to him, for he is the pilot. The storm harms him as a passenger, but not as a pilot. [36]Again, the pilot's art is another's good–it concerns his passengers just as a physician's art concerns his patients. But the wise man's good is a common good–it belongs both to those in whose company he lives, and to himself also. Hence our pilot may perhaps be harmed, since his services, which have been promised to others, are hindered by the storm; [37]but the wise man is not harmed by poverty, or by pain, or by any other of life's storms. For all his functions are not checked, but only those which pertain to others; he himself is always in action, and is greatest in performance at the very time when fortune has blocked his way. For then he is actually engaged in the business of wisdom; and this wisdom I have declared already to be, both the good of others, and also his own. [38]Besides, he is not prevented from helping others, even at the time when constraining circumstances press him down. Because of his poverty he is prevented from showing how the State should be handled; but he teaches, none the less, how poverty should be handled. His work goes on throughout his whole life.

Thus no fortune, no external circumstance, can shut off the wise man from action. For the very thing which engages his attention prevents him from attending to other things. He is ready for either outcome: if it brings goods, he controls them; if evils, he conquers them. [39]So thoroughly, I mean, has he schooled himself that he makes manifest his virtue in prosperity as well as in adversity, and keeps his eyes on virtue of the Cornelia, has warmed the water with his own hands! For this also used to be the duty of the noblest aediles–to enter these places to which the populace resorted, and to demand that they be cleaned and warmed to a heat required by considerations of use and health, not the heat that men have recently made fashionable, as great as a conflagration–so much so, indeed, that a slave condemned for some criminal offence now ought to be *bathed* alive! It seems to me that nowadays there is no difference between "the bath is on fire," and "the bath is warm."

[11] How some persons nowadays condemn Scipio as a boor because he did not let daylight into his perspiring-room through wide windows, or because he did not roast in the strong sunlight and dawdle about until he could stew in the hot water! "Poor fool," they say, "he did not know how to live! He did not bathe in filtered water; it was often turbid, and after heavy rains almost muddy!" But it did not matter much to Scipio if he had to bathe in that way; he went there to wash off sweat, not ointment. [12] And how do you suppose certain persons will answer me? They will say: "I don't envy Scipio; that was truly an exile's life–to put up with baths like those!" Friend, if you were wiser, you would know that Scipio did not bathe every day. It is stated by those[10] who have reported to us the old-time ways of Rome that the Romans washed only their arms and legs daily–because those were the members which gathered dirt in their daily toil–and bathed all over only once a week. Here someone will retort: "Yes; pretty dirty fellows they evidently were! How they must have smelled!" But they smelled of the camp, the farm, and heroism. Now that spick-and-span bathing establishments have been devised, men are really fouler than of yore. [13] What says Horatius Flaccus, when he wishes to describe a scoundrel, one who is notorious for his extreme luxury? He says. "Buccillus[11] smells of perfume." Show me a Buccillus in these days; his smell would be the veritable goat-smell–he would take the place of the Gargonius with whom Horace in the same passage contrasted him. It is nowadays not enough to use ointment, unless you put on a fresh coat two or three times a day, to keep it from evaporating on the body. But why should a man boast of this perfume as if it were his own?

[14] If what I am saying shall seem to you too pessimistic, charge it up against Scipio's country-house, where I have learned a lesson from Aegialus, a most careful householder and now the owner of this estate; he taught me that a tree can be transplanted, no matter how far gone in years. We old men must learn this precept; for there is none of us who is not planting an olive-yard for his successor. I have seen them bearing fruit in due season after three or four years of unproductiveness.[12] [15] And you too shall be shaded by the tree which

> Is slow to grow, but bringeth shade to cheer
> Your grandsons in the far-off years,[13]

as our poet Vergil says. Vergil sought, however, not what was nearest to the truth, but what was most appropriate, and aimed, not to teach the farmer, but to please the reader. [16] For example, omitting all other errors of his, I will quote the passage in which it was incumbent upon me to-day to detect a fault:

> In spring sow beans then, too, O clover plant,
> Thou'rt welcomed by the crumbling furrows; and
> The millet calls for yearly care.[14]

You may judge by the following incident whether those plants should be set out at the same time, or whether both should be sowed in the spring. It is June at the present writing, and we are well on towards July; and I have seen on this very day farmers harvesting beans and sowing millet.

[17] But to return to our olive-yard again. I saw it planted in two ways. If the trees were large, Aegialus took their trunks and cut off the branches to the length of one foot each; he then transplanted along with the ball, after cutting off the roots, leaving only the thick part from which the roots hang. He smeared this with manure, and inserted it in the hole, not only heaping up the earth about it, but stamping and pressing it down. [18] There is nothing, he says, more effective than this packing process;[15] in other words,

it keeps out the cold and the wind. Besides, the trunk is not shaken so much, and for this reason the packing makes it possible for the young roots to come out and get a hold in the soil. These are of necessity still soft; they have but a slight hold, and a very little shaking uproots them. This ball, moreover, Aegialus lops clean before he covers it up. For he maintains that new roots spring from all the parts which have been shorn. Moreover, the trunk itself should not stand more than three or four feet out of the ground. For there will thus be at once a thick growth from the bottom, nor will there be a large stump, all dry and withered, as is the case with old olive-yards. [19]The second way of setting them out was the following: he set out in similar fashion branches that were strong and of soft bark, as those of young saplings are wont to be. These grow a little more slowly, but, since they spring from what is practically a cutting, there is no roughness or ugliness in them.

[20]This too I have seen recently–an aged vine transplanted from its own plantation. In this case, the fibres also should be gathered together, if possible, and then you should cover up the vine-stem more generously, so that roots may spring up even from the stock. I have seen such plantings made not only in February, but at the very end of March; the plants take hold of and embrace alien elms. [21]But all trees, he declares, which are, so to speak, "thick-stemmed,"[16] should be assisted with tank-water; if we have this help, we are our own rain-makers.

I do not intend to tell you any more of these precepts, lest, as Aegialus did with me, I may be training you up to be my competitor. Farewell.

Footnotes

1. See Ep. li. 11.

2. Cf. Livy xxxvii. 53 *morientem rure eo ipso loco sepeliri se iussisse ferunt monumentumque ibi aedificari.*

3. Herodotus iii. 25 ἐμμανής τε ἐὰν καὶ οὐ φρενήρης.

4. Livy's account (see above) dwells more on the unwillingness of Scipio and his friends to permit the great conqueror to suffer the indignities of a trial.

5. A phrase frequent in Roman literature; see Lucretius iii. 1034 *Scipiadas, belli fulmen, Carthaginis horror.*

6. Porphyry, basalt, etc.

7. i.e., the so-called *giallo antico*, with red and yellow tints predominating.

8. A white variety, from Thasos, an island off the Thracian coast.

9. Cf. Pliny, *Ep.* ii. 17. 12 *piscina, ex qua natantes mare aspiciunt.*

10. e.g., Varro, in the *Catus: balneum non cotidianum.*

11. Horace calls him Rufillus (*Sat.* i. 2. 27): *pastillos Rufillus olet, Gargonius hircum.*

12. This seems to be the general meaning of the passage.

13. *Georgics*, ii. 58.

14. *Georgics*, i. 215 f.

15. In Vitruvius vii. 1 G reads *pinsatione*, referring to the pounding of stones for flooring.

16. An agricultural term not elsewhere found.

LXXXVII. SOME ARGUMENTS IN FAVOUR OF THE SIMPLE LIFE

[1]"I was shipwrecked before I got aboard."[1] I shall not add how that happened, lest you may reckon this also as another of the Stoic paradoxes;[2] and yet I shall, whenever you are willing to listen, nay, even though you be unwilling, prove to you that these words are by no means untrue, nor so surprising as one at first sight would think. Meantime, the journey showed me this: how much we possess that is superfluous; and how easily we can make up our minds to do away with things whose loss, whenever it is neces-

sary to part with them, we do not feel.

[2]My friend Maximus and I have been spending a most happy period of two days, taking with us very few slaves–one carriage-load–and no paraphernalia except what we wore on our persons. The mattress lies on the ground, and I upon the mattress. There are two rugs–one to spread beneath us and one to cover us. [3]Nothing could have been subtracted from our luncheon; it took not more than an hour to prepare, and we were nowhere without dried figs, never without writing tablets.[3] If I have bread, I use figs as a relish; if not, I regard figs as a substitute for bread. Hence they bring me a New Year feast every day,[4] and I make the New Year happy and prosperous by good thoughts and greatness of soul; for the soul is never greater than when it has laid aside all extraneous things, and has secured peace for itself by fearing nothing, and riches by craving no riches. [4]The vehicle in which I have taken my seat is a farmer's cart. Only by walking do the mules show that they are alive. The driver is barefoot, and not because it is summer either. I can scarcely force myself to wish that others shall think this cart mine. My false embarrassment about the truth still holds out, you see; and whenever we meet a more sumptuous party I blush in spite of myself–proof that this conduct which I approve and applaud has not yet gained a firm and steadfast dwelling-place within me. He who blushes at riding in a rattle-trap will boast when he rides in style.

[5]So my progress is still insufficient. I have not yet the courage openly to acknowledge my thriftiness. Even yet I am bothered by what other travellers think of me. But instead of this, I should really have uttered an opinion counter to that in which mankind believe, saying, "You are mad, you are misled, your admiration devotes itself to superfluous things! You estimate no man at his real worth. When property is concerned, you reckon up in this way with most scrupulous calculation those to whom you shall lend either money or benefits; for by now you enter benefits also as payments in your ledger. [6]You say. 'His estates are wide, but his debts are large.' 'He has a fine house, but he has built it on borrowed capital.' 'No man will display a more brilliant retinue on short notice, but he cannot meet his debts.'[5] 'If he pays off his creditors, he will have nothing left.'" So you will feel bound to do in all other cases as well,–to find out by elimination the amount of every man's actual possessions.

[7]I suppose you call a man rich just because his gold plate goes with him even on his travels, because he farms land in all the provinces, because he unrolls a large account-book, because he owns estates near the city so great that men would grudge his holding them in the waste lands of Apulia. But after you have mentioned all these facts, he is poor. And why? He is in debt. "To what extent?" you ask. For all that he has. Or perchance you think it matters whether one has borrowed from another man or from Fortune. [8]What good is there in mules caparisoned in uniform livery? Or in decorated chariots and

> Steeds decked with purple and with tapestry,
> With golden harness hanging from their necks,
> Champing their yellow bits, all clothed in gold?[6]

Neither master nor mule is improved by such trappings.

[9]Marcus Cato the Censor, whose existence helped the state as much as did Scipio's,–for while Scipio fought–against our enemies, Cato fought against our bad morals,–used to ride a donkey, and a donkey, at that, which carried saddle-bags containing the master's necessaries. O how I should love to see him meet today on the road one of our coxcombs,[7] with his outriders and Numidians, and a great cloud of dust before him! Your dandy would no doubt seem refined and well-attended in comparison with Marcus Cato,–your dandy, who, in the midst of all his luxurious paraphernalia, is chiefly concerned whether to turn his hand to the sword or to the hunting-knife.[8]

[10]O what a glory to the times in which he lived, for a general who had celebrated a triumph, a censor, and what is most noteworthy of all, a Cato, to be content with a single nag, and with less than a whole nag at that! For part of the animal was pre-empted by the baggage that hung down on either flank. Would you not therefore prefer Cato's steed, that single steed, saddle-worn by Cato himself, to the coxcomb's whole retinue of plump ponies, Spanish cobs,[9] and trotters?[10] [11]I see that there will be no end in deal-

ing with such a theme unless I make an end myself. So I shall now become silent, at least with reference to superfluous things like these; doubtless the man who first called them "hindrances"[11] had a prophetic inkling that they would be the very sort of thing they now are. At present I should like to deliver to you the syllogisms, as yet very few, belonging to our school and bearing upon the question of virtue, which, in our opinion, is sufficient for the happy life.

[12.] "That which is good makes men good. For example, that which is good in the art of music makes the musician. But chance events do not make a good man; therefore, chance events are not goods." The Peripatetics reply to this by saying that the premiss is false; that men do not in every case become good by means of that which is good; that in music there is something good, like a flute, a harp, or an organ suited to accompany singing; but that none of these instruments makes the musician. [13.] We shall then reply: "You do not understand in what sense we have used the phrase 'that which is good in music.' For we do not mean that which equips the musician, but that which makes the musician; you, however, are referring to the instruments of the art, and not to the art itself.[12] If, however, anything in the art of music is good, that will in every case make the musician." [14.] And I should like to put this idea still more clearly. We define the good in the art of music in two ways: first, that by which the performance of the musician is assisted, and second, that by which his art is assisted. Now the musical instruments have to do with his performance,–such as flutes and organs and harps; but they do not have to do with the musician's art itself. For he is an artist even without them; he may perhaps be lacking in the ability to practise his art. But the good in man is not in the same way twofold; for the good of man and the good of life are the same.

[15.] "That which can fall to the lot of any man, no matter how base or despised he may be, is not a good. But wealth falls to the lot of the pander and the trainer of gladiators; therefore wealth is not a good." "Another wrong premiss," they say, "for we notice that goods fall to the lot of the very lowest sort of men, not only in the scholar's art, but also in the art of healing or in the art of navigating." [16.] These arts, however, make no profession of greatness of soul; they do not rise to any heights nor do they frown upon what fortune may bring.[13] It is virtue that uplifts man and places him superior to what mortals hold dear; virtue neither craves overmuch nor fears to excess that which is called good or that which is called bad. Chelidon, one of Cleopatra's eunuchs, possessed great wealth; and recently Natalis–a man whose tongue was as shameless as it was dirty, a man whose mouth used to perform the vilest offices–was the heir of many, and also made many his heirs. What then? Was it his money that made him unclean, or did he himself besmirch his money? Money tumbles into the hands of certain men as a shilling tumbles down a sewer. [17.] Virtue stands above all such things. It is appraised in coin of its own minting;[14] and it deems none of these random windfalls to be good. But medicine and navigation do not forbid themselves and their followers to marvel at such things. One who is not a good man can nevertheless be a physician, or a pilot or a scholar,–yes just as well as he can be a cook! He to whose lot it falls to possess something which is not of a random sort, cannot be called a random sort of man: a person is of the same sort as that which he possesses. [18.] A strong-box is worth just what it holds; or rather, it is a mere accessory of that which it holds. Who ever sets any price upon a full purse except the price established by the count of the money deposited therein? This also applies to the owners of great estates: they are only accessories and incidentals to their possessions.

Why, then, is the wise man great? Because he has a great soul. Accordingly, it is true that that which falls to the lot even of the most despicable person is not a good. [19.] Thus, I should never regard inactivity as a good; for even the tree-frog and the flea possess this quality.[15] Nor should I regard rest and freedom from trouble as a good; for what is more at leisure than a worm? Do you ask what it is that produces the wise man? That which produces a god.[16] You must grant that the wise man has in an element of godliness, heavenliness, grandeur. The good does not come to every one, nor does it allow any random person to possess it. [20.] Behold:

What fruits each country bears, or will not bear;

Here corn, and there the vine, grow richlier.
And elsewhere still the tender tree and grass
Unbidden clothe themselves in green. Seest thou
How Tmolus ships its saffron perfumes forth,
And ivory comes from Ind; soft Sheba sends
Its incense, and the unclad Chalybes
Their iron.[17]

[21]These products are apportioned to separate countries in order that human beings may be constrained to traffic among themselves, each seeking something from his neighbour in his turn. So the Supreme Good has also its own abode. It does not grow where ivory grows, or iron. Do you ask where the Supreme Good dwells? In the soul. And unless the soul be pure and holy, there is no room in it for God.

[22]"Good does not result from evil. But riches result from greed; therefore, riches are not a good." "It is not true," they say, "that good does not result from evil. For money comes from sacrilege and theft. Accordingly, although sacrilege and theft are evil, yet they are evil only because they work more evil than good. For they bring gain; but the gain is accompanied by fear, anxiety, and torture of mind and body." [23]Whoever says this must perforce admit that sacrilege, though it be an evil because it works much evil, is yet partly good because it accomplishes a certain amount of good. What can be more monstrous than this? We have, to be sure, actually convinced the world that sacrilege, theft, and adultery are to be regarded as among the goods. How many men there are who do not blush at theft, how many who boast of having committed adultery! For petty sacrilege is punished, but sacrilege on a grand scale is honoured by a triumphal procession. [24]Besides, sacrilege, if it is wholly good in some respect, will also be honourable and will be called right conduct; for it is conduct which concerns ourselves. But no human being, on serious consideration, admits this idea.

Therefore, goods cannot spring from evil. For if, as you object, sacrilege is an evil for the single reason that it brings on much evil, if you but absolve sacrilege of its punishment and pledge it immunity, sacrilege will be wholly good. And yet the worst punishment for crime lies in the crime itself. [25]You are mistaken, I maintain, if you propose to reserve your punishments for the hangman or the prison; the crime is punished immediately after it is committed; nay, rather, at the moment when it is committed. Hence, good does not spring from evil, any more than figs grow from olive-trees. Things which grow correspond to their seed; and goods cannot depart from their class. As that which is honourable does not grow from that which is base, so neither does good grow from evil. For the honourable and the good are identical.[18]

[26]Certain of our school oppose this statement as follows: "Let us suppose that money taken from any source whatsoever is a good; even though it is taken by an act of sacrilege, the money does not on that account derive its origin from sacrilege. You may get my meaning through the following illustration: In the same jar there is a piece of gold and there is a serpent. If you take the gold from the jar, it is not just because the serpent is there too, I say, that the jar yields me the gold–because it contains the serpent as well,–but it yields the gold in spite of containing the serpent also. Similarly, gain results from sacrilege, not just because sacrilege is a base and accursed act, but because it contains gain also. As the serpent in the jar is an evil, and not the gold which lies there, beside the serpent; so in an act of sacrilege it is the crime, not the profit, that is evil." [27]But I differ from these men; for the conditions in each case are not at all the same. In the one instance I can take the gold without the serpent, in the other I cannot make the profit without committing the sacrilege. The gain in the latter case does not lie side by side with the crime; it is blended with the crime.

[28]"That which, while we are desiring to attain it, involves us in many evils, is not a good. But while we are desiring to attain riches, we become involved in many evils; therefore, riches are not a good."[19] "Your first premiss," they say, "contains two meanings; one is: we become involved in many evils while we are desiring to attain riches. But we also become involved in many evils while we are desiring to attain virtue. One man, while travelling in order to prosecute his studies, suffers shipwreck, and another

is taken captive. [29]The second meaning is as follows: that through which we become involved in evils is not a good. And it will not logically follow from our proposition that we become involved in evils through riches or through pleasure; otherwise, if it is through riches that we become involved in many evils, riches are not only not a good, but they are positively an evil. You, however, maintain merely that they are not a good. Moreover," the objector says, "you grant that riches are of some use. You reckon them among the advantages; and yet on this basis they cannot even be an advantage, for it is through the pursuit of riches that we suffer much disadvantage." [30]Certain men answer this objection as follows: "You are mistaken if you ascribe disadvantages to riches. Riches injure no one; it is a man's own folly, or his neighbour's wickedness, that harms him in each case, just as a sword by itself does not slay; it is merely the weapon used by the slayer. Riches themselves do not harm you, just because it is on account of riches that you suffer harm."

[31]I think that the reasoning of Posidonius is better: he holds that riches are a cause of evil, not because, of themselves, they do any evil, but because they goad men on so that they are ready to do evil. For the efficient cause, which necessarily produces harm at once, is one thing, and the antecedent cause is another. It is this antecedent cause which inheres in riches; they puff up the spirit and beget pride, they bring on unpopularity and unsettle the mind to such an extent that the mere reputation of having wealth, though it is bound to harm us, nevertheless affords delight. [32]All goods, however, ought properly to be free from blame; they are pure, they do not corrupt the spirit, and they do not tempt us. They do, indeed, uplift and broaden the spirit, but without puffing it up. Those things which are goods produce confidence, but riches produce shamelessness. The things which are goods give us greatness of soul, but riches give us arrogance. And arrogance is nothing else than a false show of greatness.

[33]"According to that argument," the objector says, "riches are not only not a good, but are a positive evil." Now they would be an evil if they did harm of themselves, and if, as I remarked, it were the efficient cause which inheres in them; in fact, however, it is the antecedent cause which inheres in riches, and indeed it is that cause which, so far from merely arousing the spirit, actually drags it along by force. Yes, riches shower upon us a semblance of the good, which is like the reality and wins credence in the eyes of many men. [34]The antecedent cause inheres in virtue also; it is this which brings on envy—for many men become unpopular because of their wisdom, and many men because of their justice. But this cause, though it inheres in virtue, is not the result of virtue itself, nor is it a mere semblance of the reality; nay, on the contrary, far more like the reality is that vision which is flashed by virtue upon the spirits of men, summoning them to love it and marvel thereat.

[35]Posidonius thinks that the syllogism should be framed as follows: "Things which bestow upon the soul no greatness or confidence or freedom from care are not goods. But riches and health and similar conditions do none of these things; therefore, riches and health are not goods." This syllogism he then goes on to extend still farther in the following way: "Things which bestow upon the soul no greatness or confidence or freedom from care, but on the other hand create in it arrogance, vanity, and insolence, are evils. But things which are the gift of Fortune drive us into these evil ways. Therefore these things are not goods." [36]"But," says the objector, "by such reasoning, things which are the gift of Fortune will not even be advantages." No, advantages and goods stand each in a different situation. An advantage is that which contains more of usefulness than of annoyance. But a good ought to be unmixed and with no element in it of harmfulness. A thing is not good if it contains more benefit than injury, but only if it contains nothing but benefit. [37]Besides, advantages may be predicated of animals, of men who are less than perfect, and of fools. Hence the advantageous may have an element of disadvantage mingled with it, but the word "advantageous" is used of the compound because it is judged by its predominant element. The good, however, can be predicated of the wise man alone; it is bound to be without alloy,

[38]Be of good cheer; there is only one knot[20] left for you to untangle, though it is a knot for a Hercules: "Good does not result from evil. But riches result from numerous

cases of poverty; therefore, riches are not a good." This syllogism is not recognized by our school, but the Peripatetics both concoct it and give its solution. Posidonius, however, remarks that this fallacy, which has been bandied about among all the schools of dialectic, is refuted by Antipater[21] as follows: [39] "The word 'poverty' is used to denote, not the possession[22] of something, but the non-possession or, as the ancients have put it, deprivation, (for the Greeks use the phrase 'by deprivation,' meaning 'negatively'). 'Poverty' states, not what a man has, but what he has not. Consequently there can be no fullness resulting from a multitude of voids; many positive things, and not many deficiencies, make up riches. You have," says he, "a wrong notion of the meaning of what poverty is. For poverty does not mean the possession of little, but the non-possession of much; it is used, therefore, not of what a man has, but of what he lacks." [40] I could express my meaning more easily if there were a Latin word which could translate the Greek word which means "not-possessing." Antipater assigns this quality to poverty, but for my part I cannot see what else poverty is than the possession of little. If ever we have plenty of leisure, we shall investigate the question: what is the essence of riches, and what the essence of poverty; but when the time comes, we shall also consider whether it is not better to try to mitigate poverty, and to relieve wealth of its arrogance, than to quibble about the words as if the question of the things were already decided.

[41] Let us suppose that we have been summoned to an assembly; an act dealing with the abolition of riches has been brought before the meeting. Shall we be supporting it, or opposing it, if we use these syllogisms? Will these syllogisms help us to bring it about that the Roman people shall demand poverty and praise it–poverty, the foundation and cause of their empire,–and, on the other hand, shall shrink in fear from their present wealth, reflecting that they have found it among the victims of their conquests, that wealth is the source from which office-seeking and bribery and disorder[23] have burst into a city once characterized by the utmost scrupulousness and sobriety, and that because of wealth an exhibition all too lavish is made of the spoils of conquered nations; reflecting, finally, that whatever one people has snatched away from all the rest may still more easily be snatched by all away from one? Nay, it were better to support this law by our conduct and to subdue our desires by direct assault rather than to circumvent them by logic. If we can, let us speak more boldly; if not, let us speak more frankly.

Footnotes

1. i.e., on my journey I travelled with almost as meagre an equipment as a shipwrecked man.

2. Cf. Ep. lxxxi. 11 and note.

3. As Pliny the Elder (a man of the same inquiring turn of mind) did on his journeys, Pliny, *Ep.* iii. 5. 15.

4. *Caricas* were sent as New Year gifts, implying by their sweetness the good wishes of the sender.

5. *Nomen* in this sense means primarily the name entered in the ledger; secondarily, the item or transaction with which the name is connected.

6. Vergil, *Aeneid,* vii. 277 ff., describing the gifts sent by King Latinus to Aeneas.

7. For *trossuli* cf. Ep. lxxvi. 2, and footnote.

8. i.e., whether to turn gladiator or *bestiarius.*

9. "Amblers" from Asturia in Spain.

10. Horses with rapid steps, compared with *gradarii,* "slow pacers," cf. Ep. xl. 11.

11. The literal meaning of *impedimenta,* "luggage."

12. Cf. Plato, *Phaedo* 86, where Socrates contrasts the material lyre with the "incorporeal, fair, divine" harmony which makes the music.

13. See Ep. lxxxviii., which is devoted to the development of this thought.

14. i.e., at its own worth.

15. Cf. the argument in lxxvi. 9 f.

16. i.e., perfect reason and obedience to Nature.

17. Vergil, *Georg.* i. 53 ff.

18. The good is absolute. The Stoics held that virtue and moral worth were identical, although those who followed the argument to its logical conclusion had to explain away many seeming inconsistencies. Cf. Ep. lxxxv. 17.

19. That riches are not a good, but merely an advantage, was one of the Stoic paradoxes. In another passage (*Dial.* vii. 24. 5) Seneca speaks of them in a kindlier manner: *divitias nego bonum esse; nam si essent, bonos facerent. Ceterum et habendas esse et utiles et magna commoda vitae adferentis fateor.* Cf. § 36 of this letter.

20. The "knot of Hercules" is associated with the *caduceus* (twining serpents) in Macrob. *Sat.* i. 19. 16; and in Pliny, *N. H.* xxviii. 63, it has magic properties in the binding up of wounds.

21. Frag. 54 von Arnim.

22. *Per possessionem* translates the Greek καθ᾽ ἕξιν, as *per orbationem* (or *detractionem*) translates κατὰ στέρησιν.

23. Seneca here bursts into a diatribe on the corruption of Rome, a habit which we find in many other of his writings, especially in the *Naturales Quaestiones*.

LXXXVIII. ON LIBERAL AND VOCATIONAL STUDIES

[1]You have been wishing to know my views with regard to liberal studies.[1] My answer is this: I respect no study, and deem no study good, which results in money-making. Such studies are profit-bringing occupations, useful only in so far as they give the mind a preparation and do not engage it permanently. One should linger upon them only so long as the mind can occupy itself with nothing greater; they are our apprenticeship, not our real work. [2]Hence you see why "liberal studies" are so called; it is because they are studies worthy of a free-born gentleman. But there is only one really liberal study,–that which gives a man his liberty. It is the study of wisdom, and that is lofty, brave, and great-souled. All other studies are puny and puerile. You surely do not believe that there is good in any of the subjects whose teachers are, as you see, men of the most ignoble and base stamp? We ought not to be learning such things; we should have done with learning them.

Certain persons have made up their minds that the point at issue with regard to the liberal studies is whether they make men good; but they do not even profess or aim at a knowledge of this particular subject. [3]The scholar[2] busies himself with investigations into language, and if it be his desire to go farther afield, he works on history, or, if he would extend his range to the farthest limits, on poetry. But which of these paves the way to virtue? Pronouncing syllables, investigating words, memorizing plays, or making rules for the scansion of poetry, what is there in all this that rids one of fear, roots out desire, or bridles the passions? [4]The question is: do such men teach virtue, or not? If they do not teach it, then neither do they transmit it. If they do teach it, they are philosophers. Would you like to know how it happens that they have not taken the chair for the purpose of teaching virtue? See how unlike their subjects are; and yet their subjects would resemble each other if they taught the same thing.[3]

[5]It may be, perhaps, that they make you believe that Homer was a philosopher,[4] although they disprove this by the very arguments through which they seek to prove it. For sometimes they make of him a Stoic, who approves nothing but virtue, avoids pleasures, and refuses to relinquish honour even at the price of immortality; sometimes they make him an Epicurean, praising the condition of a state in repose, which passes its days in feasting and song; sometimes a Peripatetic, classifying goodness in three ways;[5] sometimes an Academic, holding that all things are uncertain. It is clear, however, that no one of these doctrines is to be fathered upon Homer, just because they are all there; for they are irreconcilable with one another. We may admit to these

men, indeed, that Homer was a philosopher; yet surely he became a wise man before
he had any knowledge of poetry. So let us learn the particular things that made Homer
wise.

⁶It is no more to the point, of course, for me to investigate whether Homer or Hesiod was the older poet, than to know why Hecuba, although younger than Helen,⁶
showed her years so lamentably. What, in your opinion, I say, would be the point in
trying to determine the respective ages of Achilles and Patroclus? ⁷Do you raise the
question, "Through what regions did Ulysses stray?" instead of trying to prevent ourselves from going astray at all times? We have no leisure to hear lectures on the question whether he was sea-tost between Italy and Sicily, or outside our known world
(indeed, so long a wandering could not possibly have taken place within its narrow
bounds); we ourselves encounter storms of the spirit, which toss us daily, and our depravity drives us into all the ills which troubled Ulysses. For us there is never lacking
the beauty to tempt our eyes, or the enemy to assail us; on this side are savage mon-
sters that delight in human blood, on that side the treacherous allurements of the ear,
and yonder is shipwreck and all the varied category of misfortunes.⁷ Show me rather,
by the example of Ulysses, how I am to love my country, my wife, my father, and how,
even after suffering shipwreck, I am to sail toward these ends, honourable as they are.
⁸Why try to discover whether Penelope was a pattern of purity,⁸ or whether she had the
laugh on her contemporaries? Or whether she suspected that the man in her presence
was Ulysses, before she knew it was he? Teach me rather what purity is, and how great
a good we have in it, and whether it is situated in the body or in the soul.

⁹Now I will transfer my attention to the musician. You, sir, are teaching me how
the treble and the bass⁹ are in accord with one another, and how, though the strings
produce different notes, the result is a harmony; rather bring my soul into harmony
with itself, and let not my purposes be out of tune. You are showing me what the doleful keys¹⁰ are; show me rather how, in the midst of adversity, I may keep from uttering
a doleful note. ¹⁰The mathematician teaches me how to lay out the dimensions of my
estates; but I should rather be taught how to lay out what is enough for a man to own.
He teaches me to count, and adapts my fingers to avarice; but I should prefer him to
teach me that there is no point in such calculations, and that one is none the happier
for tiring out the book-keepers with his possessions–or rather, how useless property
is to any man who would find it the greatest misfortune if he should be required to
reckon out, by his own wits, the amount of his holdings. ¹¹What good is there for me
in knowing how to parcel out a piece of land, if I know not how to share it with my
brother? What good is there in working out to a nicety the dimensions of an acre, and
in detecting the error if a piece has so much as escaped my measuring-rod, if I am
embittered when an ill-tempered neighbour merely scrapes off a bit of my land? The
mathematician teaches me how I may lose none of my boundaries; I, however, seek
to learn how to lose them all with a light heart. ¹²"But," comes the reply, "I am being
driven from the farm which my father and grandfather owned!" Well? Who owned
the land before your grandfather? Can you explain what people (I will not say what
person) held it originally? You did not enter upon it as a master, but merely as a tenant.
And whose tenant are you? If your claim is successful, you are tenant of the heir. The
lawyers say that public property cannot be acquired privately by possession;¹¹ what
you hold and call your own is public property–indeed, it belongs to mankind at large.
¹³O what marvellous skill! You know how to measure the circle; you find the square of
any shape which is set before you; you compute the distances between the stars; there
is nothing which does not come within the scope of your calculations. But if you are a
real master of your profession, measure me the mind of man! Tell me how great it is,
or how puny! You know what a straight line is; but how does it benefit you if you do
not know what is straight in this life of ours?

¹⁴I come next to the person who boasts his knowledge of the heavenly bodies, who
knows

> Whither the chilling star of Saturn hides,
> And through what orbit Mercury doth stray.¹²

Of what benefit will it be to know this? That I shall be disturbed because Saturn and Mars are in opposition, or when Mercury sets at eventide in plain view of Saturn, rather than learn that those stars, wherever they are, are propitious,[13] and that they are not subject to change? [15]They are driven along by an unending round of destiny, on a course from which they cannot swerve. They return at stated seasons; they either set in motion, or mark the intervals of the whole world's work. But if they are responsible for whatever happens, how will it help you to know the secrets of the immutable? Or if they merely give indications, what good is there in foreseeing what you cannot escape? Whether you know these things or not, they will take place.

> [16]Behold the fleeting sun,
> The stars that follow in his train, and thou
> Shalt never find the morrow play thee false,
> Or be misled by nights without a cloud.[14]

It has, however, been sufficiently and fully ordained that I shall be safe from anything that may mislead me. [17]"What," you say, "does the 'morrow never play me false'? Whatever happens without my knowledge plays me false." I, for my part, do not know what is to be, but I do know what may come to be. I shall have no misgivings in this matter; I await the future in its entirety; and if there is any abatement in its severity, I make the most of it. If the morrow treats me kindly, it is a sort of deception; but it does not deceive me even at that. For just as I know that all things can happen, so I know, too, that they will not happen in every case. I am ready for favourable events in every case, but I am prepared for evil.

[18]In this discussion you must bear with me if I do not follow the regular course. For I do not consent to admit painting into the list of liberal arts, any more than sculpture, marble-working, and other helps toward luxury. I also debar from the liberal studies wrestling and all knowledge that is compounded of oil and mud;[15] otherwise, I should be compelled to admit perfumers also, and cooks, and all others who lend their wits to the service of our pleasures. [19]For what "liberal" element is there in these ravenous takers of emetics, whose bodies are fed to fatness while their minds are thin and dull?[16] Or do we really believe that the training which they give is "liberal" for the young men of Rome, who used to be taught by our ancestors to stand straight and hurl a spear, to wield a pike, to guide a horse, and to handle weapons? Our ancestors used to teach their children nothing that could be learned while lying down. But neither the new system nor the old teaches or nourishes virtue. For what good does it do us to guide a horse and control his speed with the curb, and then find that our own passions, utterly uncurbed, bolt with us? Or to beat many opponents in wrestling or boxing, and then to find that we ourselves are beaten by anger?

[20]"What then," you say, "do the liberal studies contribute nothing to our welfare?" Very much in other respects, but nothing at all as regards virtue. For even these arts of which I have spoken, though admittedly of a low grade—depending as they do upon handiwork—contribute greatly toward the equipment of life, but nevertheless have nothing to do with virtue. And if you inquire, "Why, then, do we educate our children in the liberal studies?"[17] it is not because they can bestow virtue, but because they prepare the soul for the reception of virtue. Just as that "primary course,"[18] as the ancients called it, in grammar, which gave boys their elementary training, does not teach them the liberal arts, but prepares the ground for their early acquisition of these arts, so the liberal arts do not conduct the soul all the way to virtue, but merely set it going in that direction.

[21]Posidonius[19] divides the arts into four classes: first we have those which are common and low, then those which serve for amusement, then those which refer to the education of boys, and, finally, the liberal arts. The common sort belong to workmen and are mere hand-work; they are concerned with equipping life; there is in them no pretence to beauty or honour. [22]The arts of amusement are those which aim to please the eye and the ear. To this class you may assign the stage-machinists, who invent scaffolding that goes aloft of its own accord, or floors that rise silently into the air, and many other surprising devices, as when objects that fit together then fall apart, or ob-

jects which are separate then join together automatically, or objects which stand erect then gradually collapse. The eye of the inexperienced is struck with amazement by these things; for such persons marvel at everything that takes place without warning, because they do not know the causes. [23] The arts which belong to the education of boys, and are somewhat similar to the liberal arts, are those which the Greeks call the "cycle of studies,"[20] but which we Romans call the "liberal." However, those alone are really liberal–or rather, to give them a truer name, "free"–whose concern is virtue.

[24] "But," one will say, "just as there is a part of philosophy which has to do with nature, and a part which has to do with ethics, and a part which has to do with reasoning, so this group of liberal arts also claims for itself a place in philosophy. When one approaches questions that deal with nature, a decision is reached by means of a word from the mathematician. Therefore mathematics is a department of that branch which it aids."[21] [25] But many things aid us and yet are not parts of ourselves. Nay, if they were, they would not aid us. Food is an aid to the body, but is not a part of it. We get some help from the service which mathematics renders; and mathematics is as indispensable to philosophy as the carpenter is to the mathematician. But carpentering is not a part of mathematics, nor is mathematics a part of philosophy. [26] Moreover, each has its own limits; for the wise man investigates and learns the causes of natural phenomena, while the mathematician follows up and computes their numbers and their measurements.[22] The wise man knows the laws by which the heavenly bodies persist, what powers belong to them, and what attributes; the astronomer merely notes their comings and goings, the rules which govern their settings and their risings, and the occasional periods during which they seem to stand still, although as a matter of fact no heavenly body can stand still. [27] The wise man will know what causes the reflection in a mirror; but, the mathematician can merely tell you how far the body should be from the reflection, and what shape of mirror will produce a given reflection.[23] The philosopher will demonstrate that the sun is a large body, while the astronomer will compute just how large, progressing in knowledge by his method of trial and experiment; but in order to progress, he must summon to his aid certain principles. No art, however, is sufficient unto itself, if the foundation upon which it rests depends upon mere favour. [28] Now philosophy asks no favours from any other source; it builds everything on its own soil; but the science of numbers is, so to speak, a structure built on another man's land–it builds on everything on alien soil;[24] It accepts first principles, and by their favour arrives at further conclusions. If it could march unassisted to the truth, if it were able to understand the nature of the universe, I should say that it would offer much assistance to our minds; for the mind grows by contact with things heavenly and draws into itself something from on high. There is but one thing that brings the soul to perfection–the unalterable knowledge of good and evil. But there is no other art[25] which investigates good and evil.

I should like to pass in review the several virtues. [29] Bravery is a scorner of things which inspire fear; it looks down upon, challenges, and crushes the powers of terror and all that would drive our freedom under the yoke. But do "liberal studies"[26] strengthen this virtue? Loyalty is the holiest good in the human heart; it is forced into betrayal by no constraint, and it is bribed by no rewards. Loyalty cries: "Burn me, slay me, kill me! I shall not betray my trust; and the more urgently torture shall seek to find my secret, the deeper in my heart will I bury it!" Can the "liberal arts" produce such a spirit within us? Temperance controls our desires; some it hates and routs, others it regulates and restores to a healthy measure, nor does it ever approach our desires for their own sake. Temperance knows that the best measure of the appetites is not what you want to take, but what you ought to take. [30] Kindliness forbids you to be over-bearing towards your associates, and it forbids you to be grasping. In words and in deeds and in feelings it shows itself gentle and courteous to all men. It counts no evil as another's solely. And the reason why it loves its own good is chiefly because it will some day be the good of another. Do "liberal studies" teach a man such character as this? No; no more than they teach simplicity, moderation and self-restraint, thrift and economy, and that kindliness which spares a neighbour's life as if it were one's own and knows that it is not for man to make wasteful use of his fellow-man.

[31]"But," one says, "since you declare that virtue cannot be attained without the 'liberal studies,' how is it that you deny that they offer any assistance to virtue?"[27] Because you cannot attain virtue without food, either; and yet food has nothing to do with virtue. Wood does not offer assistance to a ship, although a ship cannot be built except of wood. There is no reason, I say, why you should think that anything is made by the assistance of that without which it cannot be made. [32]We might even make the statement that it is possible to attain wisdom without the "liberal studies"; for although virtue is a thing that must be learned, yet it is not learned by means of these studies.

What reason have I, however, for supposing that one who is ignorant of letters will never be a wise man, since wisdom is not to be found in letters? Wisdom communicates facts[28] and not words; and it may be true that the memory is more to be depended upon when it has no support outside itself. [33]Wisdom is a large and spacious thing. It needs plenty of free room. One must learn about things divine and human, the past and the future, the ephemeral and the eternal; and one must learn about Time.[29] See how many questions arise concerning time alone: in the first place, whether it is anything in and by itself; in the second place, whether anything exists prior to time and without time; and again, did time begin along with the universe, or, because there was something even before the universe began, did time also exist then? [34]There are countless questions concerning the soul alone: whence it comes, what is its nature, when it begins to exist, and how long it exists; whether it passes from one place to another and changes its habitation, being transferred successively from one animal shape to another, or whether it is a slave but once, roaming the universe after it is set free; whether it is corporeal or not; what will become of it when it ceases to use us as its medium; how it will employ its freedom when it has escaped from this present prison; whether it will forget all its past, and at that moment begin to know itself when, released from the body, it has withdrawn to the skies.

[35]Thus, whatever phase of things human and divine you have apprehended, you will be wearied by the vast number of things to be answered and things to be learned. And in order that these manifold and mighty subjects may have free entertainment in your soul, you must remove therefrom all superfluous things. Virtue will not surrender herself to these narrow bounds of ours; a great subject needs wide space in which to move. Let all other things be driven out, and let the breast be emptied to receive virtue.

[36]"But it is a pleasure to be acquainted with many arts." Therefore let us keep only as much of them as is essential. Do you regard that man as blameworthy who puts superfluous things on the same footing with useful things, and in his house makes a lavish display of costly objects, but do not deem him blameworthy who has allowed himself to become engrossed with the useless furniture of learning? This desire to know more than is sufficient is a sort of intemperance. [37]Why? Because this unseemly pursuit of the liberal arts makes men troublesome, wordy, tactless, self-satisfied bores, who fail to learn the essentials just because they have learned the non-essentials. Didymus the scholar wrote four thousand books. I should feel pity for him if he had only read the same number of superfluous volumes. In these books he investigates Homer's birthplace,[30] who was really the mother of Aeneas, whether Anacreon was more of a rake or more of a drunkard, whether Sappho was a bad lot,[31] and other problems the answers to which, if found, were forthwith to be forgotten. Come now, do not tell me that life is long! [38]Nay, when you come to consider our own countrymen also, I can show you many works which ought to be cut down with the axe.

It is at the cost of a vast outlay of time and of vast discomfort to the ears of others that we win such praise as this: "What a learned man you are!" Let us be content with this recommendation, less citified though it be: "What a good man you are!" [39]Do I mean this? Well, would you have me unroll the annals of the world's history and try to find out who first wrote poetry? Or, in the absence of written records, shall I make an estimate of the number of years which lie between Orpheus and Homer? Or shall I make a study of the absurd writings of Aristarchus, wherein he branded the text[32] of other men's verses, and wear my life away upon syllables? Shall I then wallow in the geometrician's dust?[33] Have I so far forgotten that useful saw "Save your time"? Must I know these things? And what may I choose not to know?

[40] Apion, the scholar, who drew crowds to his lectures all over Greece in the days of Gaius Caesar and was acclaimed a Homerid[34] by every state, used to maintain that Homer, when he had finished his two poems, the *Iliad* and the *Odyssey*, added a preliminary poem to his work, wherein he embraced the whole Trojan war.[35] The argument which Apion adduced to prove this statement was that Homer had purposely inserted in the opening line two letters which contained a key to the number of his books. [41] A man who wishes to know many things must know such things as these, and must take no thought of all the time which one loses by ill-health, public duties, private duties, daily duties, and sleep. Apply the measure to the years of your life; they have no room for all these things.

[42] I have been speaking so far of liberal studies; but think how much superfluous and unpractical matter the philosophers contain! Of their own accord they also have descended to establishing nice divisions of syllables, to determining the true meaning of conjunctions and prepositions; they have been envious of the scholars, envious of the mathematicians. They have taken over into their own art all the superfluities of these other arts; the result is that they know more about careful speaking than about careful living. [43] Let me tell you what evils are due to over-nice exactness, and what an enemy it is of truth! Protagoras declares that one can take either side on any question and debate it with equal success–even on this very question, whether every subject can be debated from either point of view. Nausiphanes holds that in things which seem to exist, there is no difference between existence and non-existence. [44] Parmenides maintains that nothing exists of all this which seems to exist, except the universe alone.[36] Zeno of Elea removed all the difficulties by removing one; for he declares that nothing exists. The Pyrrhonean, Megarian, Eretrian, and Academic schools are all engaged in practically the same task; they have introduced a new knowledge, non-knowledge. [45] You may sweep all these theories in with the superfluous troops of "liberal" studies; the one class of men give me a knowledge that will be of no use to me, the other class do away with any hope of attaining knowledge. It is better, of course, to know useless things than to know nothing. One set of philosophers offers no light by which I may direct my gaze toward the truth; the other digs out my very eyes and leaves me blind. If I cleave to Protagoras, there is nothing in the scheme of nature that is not doubtful; if I hold with Nausiphanes, I am sure only of this–that everything is unsure; if with Parmenides, there is nothing except the One;[37] if with Zeno, there is not even the One.

[46] What are we, then? What becomes of all these things that surround us, support us, sustain us? The whole universe is then a vain or deceptive shadow. I cannot readily say whether I am more vexed at those who would have it that we know nothing, or with those who would not leave us even this privilege. Farewell.

Footnotes

1. The regular round of education, ἐγκύκλιος παιδεία, including grammar, music, geometry, arithmetic, astrology, and certain phases of rhetoric and dialectic, are in this letter contrasted with liberal studies–those which have for their object the pursuit of virtue. Seneca is thus interpreting *studia liberalia* in a higher sense than his contemporaries would expect. Compare J. R. Lowell's definition of a university, "a place where nothing useful is taught."

2. *Grammaticus* in classical Greek means "one who is familiar with the alphabet"; in the Alexandrain age a "student of literature"; in the Roman age the equivalent of *litteratus*. Seneca means here a "specialist in linguistic science."

3. i.e., philosophy (virtue).

4. This theory was approved by Democritus, Hippias of Elis, and the allegorical interpreters; Xenophanes, Heraclitus, and Plato himself condemned Homer for his supposed unphilosophic fabrications.

5. The *tria genera bonorum* of Cicero's *De Fin* v. 84. Cf. *ib.* 18, where the three proper objects of man's search are given as the desire for pleasure, the avoidance of pain, and

the attainment of such natural goods as health, strength, and soundnesss of mind. The Stoics held that the good was absolute.

6. Summers compares Lucian, *Gall.* 17. Seneca, however, does not take such gossip seriously.

7. This sentence alludes to Calypso, Circe, the Cyclops, and the Sirens.

8. Unfavourable comment by Lycophron, and by Cicero, *De Nat. Deor.* iii. 22 (*Mercurius) ex quo et Penelopa Pana natum ferunt.*

9. With *acutae* and *graves* supply *voces.*

10. Perhaps the equivalent of a "minor."

11. i.e., for a certain term of years; see R. W. Leage, *Roman Private Law,* pp. 133 ff. Compare also Lucretius iii. 971, and Horace, *Ep.* ii. 2. 159.

12. Vergil, *Georg.* i. 336 f.

13. Saturn and Mars were regarded as unlucky stars. Astrology, which dates back beyond 3000 B.C. in Babylonia, was developed by the Greeks of the Alexandrian age and got a foothold in Rome by the second century B.C., flourished greatly under Tiberius. Cf. Horace, *Od.* i. 11. 1 f.; Juv. iii. 42 f., and F. Cumont, *Astrology and Religion among the Greeks and Romans* (trans.), esp. pp. 68 ff. and 84 ff.

14. Vergil, *Georg.* i. 424 ff.

15. An allusion to the sand and oil of the wrestling-ring.

16. Cf. Ep. xv. 3 *copia ciborum subtilitas inpeditur.*

17. In a strict sense; not, as in § 2, as Seneca thinks that the term should really be defined–the "liberal" study, i.e. the pursuit of wisdom.

18. For the πρώτη ἀγωγή see Quintilian, ii. 1. 4.

19. From what work of Posidonius Seneca is here quoting we do not know; it may be from the Προτρεπτικά, or *Exhortations,* indicating the training preliminary to philosophy.

20. See § 1 note.

21. i.e., mathematics is a department of *philosophia naturalis.*

22. This line of argument inversely resembles the criticism by Seneca of Posidonius in Ep. xc.–that the inventions of early science cannot be properly termed a part of philosophy.

23. See *N. Q.* i. 4 ff.

24. According to Roman law, *superficies solo cedit,* "the building goes with the ground."

25. Except philosophy.

26. i.e., in the more commonly accepted sense of the term.

27. This usage is a not infrequent one in Latin; cf. Petronius, *Sat.* 42 *neminem nihil boni facere oportet; id. ib.* 58; Verg. *Ecl.* v. 25, etc. See Draeger, *Hist. Syn.* ii. 75, and Roby, ii. 2246 ff.

28. Cf. Epp. xxxi. 6 and lxxxi. 29 *aestimare res, de quibus . . . cum rerum natura deliberandum est.*

29. The ancient Stoics defined Time as "extension of the world's motion." The seasons were said to be "alive" because they depended on material conditions. But the Stoics really acknowledged Time to be immaterial. The same problem of corporeality was discussed with regard to the "good."

30. Compare the schoolmaster of Juvenal (vii. 234 ff.), who must know

> Nutricem Anchisae, nomen patriamque novercae
> Anchemoli, dicat quot Acestes vixerit annis, etc.,

and Friedländer's note.

31. A tradition, probably begun by the Greek comic-writers, and explained by Professor Smyth (*Greek Melic Poets,* pp. 227 f.) as due to the more independent position of women among the Aeolians. *Transcriber's note: Gummere has euphemistically translated Seneca here. The Latin is "in his an Sappho publica fuerit", and the feminine noun "publica" means "public woman", i.e. a courtesan or prostitute. So Gummere's translation "whether Sappho was a bad lot" is more accurately rendered as "whether Sappho was a prostitute."*

32. Marking supposedly spurious lines by the *obelus*, and using other signs to indicate variations, repetitions, and interpolations. He paid special attention to Homer, Pindar, Hesiod, and the tragedians.

33. The geometricians drew their figures in the dust or sand.

34. Originally, rhapsodists who recited from Homer; in general, "interpreters and admirers–in short, the whole 'spiritual kindred'–of Homer" (D. B. Monro)

35. An ancient explanation of the (now disproved) authorship by Homer of such poems as the *Cypria, Little Iliad, Sack of Troy,* etc.

36. In other words, the unchangeable, perfect Being of the universe is contrasted with the mutable Non-Being of opinion and unreality.

37. i.e., the universe.

LXXXIX. ON THE PARTS OF PHILOSOPHY[1]

[1]It is a useful fact that you wish to know, one which is essential to him who hastens after wisdom–namely, the parts of philosophy and the division of its huge bulk into separate members. For by studying the parts we can be brought more easily to understand the whole. I only wish that philosophy might come before our eyes in all her unity, just as the whole expanse of the firmament is spread out for us to gaze upon! It would be a sight closely resembling that of the firmament. For then surely philosophy would ravish all mortals with love for her;[2] we should abandon all those things which, in our ignorance of what is great, we believe to be great. Inasmuch, however, as this cannot fall to our lot, we must view philosophy just as men gaze upon the secrets of the firmament.

[2]The wise man's mind, to be sure, embraces the whole framework of philosophy, surveying it with no less rapid glance than our mortal eyes survey the heavens; we, however, who must break through the gloom, we whose vision fails even for that which is near at hand, can be shown with greater ease each separate object even though we cannot yet comprehend the universe. I shall therefore comply with your demand, and shall divide philosophy into parts, but not into scraps. For it is useful that philosophy should be divided, but not chopped into bits. Just as it is hard to take in what is indefinitely large, so it is hard to take in what is indefinitely small. [3]The people are divided into tribes, the army into centuries. Whatever has grown to greater size is more easily identified if it is broken up into parts; but the parts, as I have remarked, must not be countless in number and diminutive in size. For over-analysis is faulty in precisely the same way as no analysis at all; whatever you cut so fine that it becomes dust is as good as blended into a mass again.[3]

[4]In the first place, therefore, if you approve, I shall draw the distinction between wisdom and philosophy. Wisdom is the perfect good of the human mind; philosophy is the love of wisdom, and the endeavour to attain it. The latter strives toward the goal which the former has already reached. And it is clear why philosophy was so called. For it acknowledges by its very name the object of its love.[4] [5]Certain persons have defined wisdom as the knowledge of things divine and things human.[5] Still others say: "Wisdom is knowing things divine and things human, and their causes also."[6] This added phrase seems to me to be superfluous, since the causes of things divine and things human are a part of the divine system. Philosophy also has been defined in various ways; some have called it "the study of virtue,"[7] others have referred to it as "a study of the way to amend the mind,"[8] and some have named it "the search for right reason." [6]One thing is practically settled, that there is some difference between philosophy and wisdom. Nor indeed is it possible that that which is sought and that which seeks are identical. As there is a great difference between avarice and wealth, the one being the subject of the craving and the other its object, so between philosophy and wisdom. For the one is a result and a reward of the other. Philosophy does the going, and wisdom is the goal. [7]Wisdom is that which the Greeks call σοφία. The Romans also were wont to use this word in the sense in which they now use "philosophy" also.

This will be proved to your satisfaction by our old national plays, as well as by the epitaph that is carved on the tomb of Dossennus:[9]

Pause, stranger, and read the wisdom of Dossennus.

[8]Certain of our school, however, although philosophy meant to them "the study of virtue," and though virtue was the object sought and philosophy the seeker, have maintained nevertheless that the two cannot be sundered. For philosophy cannot exist without virtue, nor virtue without philosophy. Philosophy is the study of virtue, by means, however, of virtue itself; but neither can virtue exist without the study of itself, nor can the study of virtue exist without virtue itself. For it is not like trying to hit a target at long range, where the shooter and the object to be shot at are in different places. Nor, as roads which lead into a city, are the approaches to virtue situated outside virtue herself; the path by which one reaches virtue leads by way of virtue herself; philosophy and virtue cling closely together.

[9]The greatest authors, and the greatest number of authors, have maintained that there are three divisions of philosophy—moral, natural, and rational.[10] The first keeps the soul in order; the second investigates the universe; the third works out the essential meanings of words, their combinations, and the proofs which keep falsehood from creeping in and displacing truth. But there have also been those who divided philosophy on the one hand into fewer divisions, on the other hand into more. [10]Certain of the Peripatetic school have added a fourth division, "civil philosophy," because it calls for a special sphere of activity and is interested in a different subject matter. Some have added a department for which they use the Greek term "economics,"[11] the science of managing one's own household. Still others have made a distinct heading for the various kinds of life.[12] There is no one of these subdivisions, however, which will not be found under the branch called "moral" philosophy.

[11]The Epicureans[13] held that philosophy was twofold, natural and moral; they did away with the rational branch. Then, when they were compelled by the facts themselves to distinguish between equivocal ideas and to expose fallacies that lay hidden under the cloak of truth they themselves also introduced a heading to which they give the name "forensic and regulative,"[14] which is merely "rational" under another name, although they hold that this section is accessory to the department of "natural" philosophy. [12]The Cyrenaic[15] school abolished the natural as well as the rational department, and were content with the moral side alone; and yet these philosophers also include under another title that which they have rejected. For they divide moral philosophy into five parts: (1) What to avoid and what to seek, (2) The Passions, (3) Actions, (4) Causes, (5) Proofs. Now the causes of things really belong to the "natural" division, the proofs to the "rational." [13]Aristo[16] of Chios remarked that the natural and the rational were not only superfluous, but were also contradictory. He even limited the "moral," which was all that was left to him; for he abolished that heading which embraced advice, maintaining that it was the business of the pedagogue, and not of the philosopher—as if the wise man were anything else than the pedagogue of the human race!

[14]Since, therefore, philosophy is threefold, let us first begin to set in order the moral side. It has been agreed that this should be divided into three parts. First, we have the speculative[17] part, which assigns to each thing its particular function and weighs the worth of each; it is highest in point of utility. For what is so indispensable as giving to everything its proper value? The second has to do with impulse,[18] the third with actions.[19] For the first duty is to determine severally what things are worth; the second, to conceive with regard to them a regulated and ordered impulse; the third, to make your impulse and your actions harmonize, so that under all these conditions you may be consistent with yourself. [15]If any of the three be defective, there is confusion in the rest also. For what benefit is there in having all things appraised, each in its proper relations, if you go to excess in your impulses? What benefit is there in having checked your impulses and in having your desires in your own control, if when you come to action you are unaware of the proper times and seasons, and if you do not know when, where, and how each action should be carried out? It is one thing to understand the merits and the values of facts, another thing to know the precise moment for action,

and still another to curb impulses and to proceed, instead of rushing, toward what is to be done. Hence life is in harmony with itself only when action has not deserted impulse, and when impulse toward an object arises in each case from the worth of the object, being languid or more eager as the case may be, according as the objects which arouse it are worth seeking.

[16]The natural side of philosophy is twofold: bodily and non-bodily.[20] Each is divided into its own grades of importance, so to speak. The topic concerning bodies deals, first, with these two grades: the creative and the created;[21] and the created things are the elements. Now this very topic of the elements, as some writers hold, is integral;[22] as others hold, it is divided into matter, the cause which moves all things, and the elements. [17]It remains for me to divide rational philosophy into its parts. Now all speech is either continuous, or split up between questioner and answerer. It has been agreed upon that the former should be called rhetoric, and the latter dialectic. Rhetoric deals with words, and meanings, and arrangement. Dialectic is divided into two parts: words and their meanings, that is, into things which are said, and the words in which they are said. Then comes a subdivision of each–and it is of vast extent. Therefore I shall stop at this point, and

> But treat the climax of the story;[23]

for if I should take a fancy to give the subdivisions, my letter would become a debater's handbook! [18]I am not trying to discourage you, excellent Lucilius, from reading on this subject, provided only that you promptly relate to conduct all that you have read.

It is your conduct that you must hold in check; you must rouse what is languid in you, bind fast what has become relaxed, conquer what is obstinate, persecute your appetites, and the appetites of mankind, as much as you can; and to those who say: "How long will this unending talk go on?" answer with the words: [19]"I ought to be asking you 'How long will these unending sins of yours go on?'" Do you really desire my remedies to stop before your vices? But I shall speak of my remedies all the more, and just because you offer objections I shall keep on talking. Medicine begins to do good at the time when a touch makes the diseased body tingle with pain. I shall utter words that will help men even against their will. At times you should allow words other than compliments to reach your ears, and because as individuals you are unwilling to hear the truth, hear it collectively. [20]How far will you extend the boundaries of your estates? An estate which held a nation is too narrow for a single lord. How far will you push forward your ploughed fields–you who are not content to confine the measure of your farms even within the amplitude of provinces?[24] You have noble rivers flowing down through your private grounds; you have mighty streams–boundaries of mighty nations–under your dominion from source to outlet. This also is too little for you unless you also surround whole seas with your estates, unless your steward holds sway on the other side of the Adriatic, the Ionian, and the Aegean seas, unless the islands, homes of famous chieftains, are reckoned by you as the most paltry of possessions! Spread them as widely as you will, if only you may have as a "farm" what was once called a kingdom; make whatever you can your own, provided only that it is more than your neighbour's!

[21]And now for a word with you, whose luxury spreads itself out as widely as the greed of those to whom I have just referred. To you I say: "Will this custom continue until there is no lake over which the pinnacles of your country-houses do not tower? Until there is no river whose banks are not bordered by your lordly structures? Wherever hot waters shall gush forth in rills, there you will be causing new resorts of luxury to rise. Wherever the shore shall bend into a bay, there will you straightway be laying foundations, and, not content with any land that has not been made by art, you will bring the sea within your boundaries.[25] On every side let your house-tops flash in the sun, now set on mountain peaks where they command an extensive outlook over sea and land, now lifted from the plain to the height of mountains; build your manifold structures, your huge piles,–you are nevertheless but individuals, and puny ones at that! What profit to you are your many bed-chambers? You sleep in one. No place is yours where you yourselves are not." [22]"Next I pass to you, you whose bottomless

and insatiable maw explores on the one hand the seas, on the other the earth, with enormous toil hunting down your prey, now with hook, now with snare, now with nets of various kinds; no animal has peace except when you are cloyed with it. And how slight a portion of those banquets of yours, prepared for you by so many hands, do you taste with your pleasure-jaded palate! How slight a portion of all that game, whose taking was fraught with danger, does the master's sick and squeamish stomach relish? How slight a portion of all those shell-fish, imported from so far, slips down that insatiable gullet? Poor wretches, do you not know that your appetites are bigger than your bellies?"

[23]Talk in this way to other men,–provided that while you talk you also listen; write in this way,–provided that while you write you read, remembering that everything[26] you hear or read, is to be applied to conduct, and to the alleviation of passion's fury. Study, not in order to add anything to your knowledge, but to make your knowledge better. Farewell.

Footnotes

1. See §§ 9 ff., which give the normal division.

2. See Plato, especially *Symposium* 211 ff.

3. i.e., an infinitely small *divisio* is the same as its opposite–*confusio*.

4. "Love-of-Wisdom."

5. Θείων τε καὶ ἀνθρωπίνων ἐπιστήμη, quoted by Plutarch, *De Plac. Phil.* 874 E.

6. Cicero, *De Off.* ii. 2. 5.

7. The ἄσκησις ἀρετῆς of the earlier Stoics. Seneca (Frag. 17) also calls it *recta vivendi ratio*.

8. i.e., to make a *bona mens* out of a *mala mens*.

9. It is doubtful whether this was the name of a real person, or a mere "Joe Miller" type from the Fabula Atellana. The character in Horace, *Ep.* ii. 1. 173, is certainly the latter; and the testimony of Pliny (*N. H.* xiv. 15), who quotes a line from a play called *Acharistio*, is not reliable.

10. i.e., logic.

11. i.e., "the management of the home."

12. That is, of the various arts which deal with the departments of living, such as generalship, politics, business, etc.

13. Frag. 242 Usener.

14. Seneca by *de iudicio* is translating the Greek adjective δικανικός, "that which has to do with the courts of law," and by *de regula* the word κανονικός, "that which has to do with rules," here the rules of logic. The Epicureans used for logic κανονική, in contrast with Aristotle and his successors, who used λογική. The Latin *rationalis* is a translation of the latter.

15. Led by Aristippus of Cyrene. As the Cynics developed into the Stoics, so the Cyrenaics developed into the Epicureans.

16. Frag. 357 von Arnim.

17. Seneca translates θεωρητική.

18. Ὁρμητική; the ὁρμαί, *impetus*, in the Stoic philosophy, are the natural instincts, which require training and regulation before they can be trusted.

19. Πρακτική.

20. Σωματική and ἀσώματος.

21. Ποιητικά and παθητικά.

22. i.e., has no subdivisions.

23. Vergil, *Aeneid*, i. 342.

24. For the thought compare Petronius, *Sat.* 48 *nunc coniungere agellis Siciliam volo, ut, cum Africam libuerit ire, per meos fines navigem.*

25. i.e., by building embankments, etc. Cf. Horace, *Od.* ii. 18. 22 *parum locuples continente*

ripa.
26. Cf. § 18.

XC. ON THE PART PLAYED BY PHILOSOPHY IN THE PROGRESS OF MAN

[1]Who can doubt, my dear Lucilius, that life is the gift of the immortal gods, but that living well[1] is the gift of philosophy? Hence the idea that our debt to philosophy is greater than our debt to the gods, in proportion as a good life is more of a benefit than mere life, would be regarded as correct, were not philosophy itself a boon which the gods have bestowed upon us. They have given the knowledge thereof to none, but the faculty of acquiring it they have given to all. [2]For if they had made philosophy also a general good, and if we were gifted with understanding at our birth, wisdom would have lost her best attribute—that she is not one of the gifts of fortune. For as it is, the precious and noble characteristic of wisdom is that she does not advance to meet us, that each man is indebted to himself for her, and that we do not seek her at the hands of others.

What would there be in philosophy worthy of your respect, if she were a thing that came by bounty? [3]Her sole function is to discover the truth about things divine and things human. From her side religion never departs, nor duty, nor justice, nor any of the whole company of virtues which cling together in close-united fellowship. Philosophy has taught us to worship that which is divine, to love that which is human;[2] she has told us that with the gods lies dominion, and among men, fellowship. This fellowship remained unspoiled for a long time, until avarice tore the community asunder and became the cause of poverty, even in the case of those whom she herself had most enriched. For men cease to possess all things the moment they desire all things for their own.

[4]But the first men and those who sprang from them, still unspoiled, followed nature, having one man as both their leader and their law, entrusting themselves to the control of one better than themselves. For nature has the habit of subjecting the weaker to the stronger. Even among the dumb animals those which are either biggest or fiercest hold sway. It is no weakling bull that leads the herd; it is one that has beaten the other males by his might and his muscle. In the case of elephants, the tallest goes first; among men, the best is regarded as the highest. That is why it was to the mind that a ruler was assigned; and for that reason the greatest happiness rested with those peoples among whom a man could not be the more powerful unless he were the better. For that man can safely accomplish what he will who thinks he can do nothing except what he ought to do.

[5]Accordingly, in that age which is maintained to be the golden age,[3] Posidonius[4] holds that the government was under the jurisdiction of the wise. They kept their hands under control, and protected the weaker from the stronger. They gave advice, both to do and not to do; they showed what was useful and what was useless. Their forethought provided that their subjects should lack nothing; their bravery warded off dangers; their kindness enriched and adorned their subjects. For them ruling was a service, not an exercise of royalty. No ruler tried his power against those to whom he owed the beginnings of his power; and no one had the inclination, or the excuse, to do wrong, since the ruler ruled well and the subject obeyed well, and the king could utter no greater threat against disobedient subjects than that they should depart from the kingdom.

[6]But when once vice stole in and kingdoms were transformed into tyrannies, a need arose for laws and these very laws were in turn framed by the wise. Solon, who established Athens upon a firm basis by just laws, was one of the seven men renowned for their wisdom.[5] Had Lycurgus lived in the same period, an eighth would have been added to that hallowed number seven. The laws of Zaleucus and Charondas are praised; it was not in the forum or in the offices of skilled counsellors, but in the

silent and holy retreat of Pythagoras, that these two men learned the principles of justice which they were to establish in Sicily (which at that time was prosperous) and throughout Grecian Italy.

[7]Up to this point I agree with Posidonius; but that philosophy discovered the arts of which life makes use in its daily round[6] I refuse to admit. Nor will I ascribe to it an artisan's glory. Posidonius says: "When men were scattered over the earth, protected by eaves or by the dug-out shelter of a cliff or by the trunk of a hollow tree, it was philosophy that taught them to build houses." But I, for my part, do not hold that philosophy devised these shrewdly-contrived dwellings of ours which rise story upon story, where city crowds against city, any more than that she invented the fish-preserves, which are enclosed for the purpose of saving men's gluttony from having to run the risk of storms, and in order that, no matter how wildly the sea is raging, luxury may have its safe harbours in which to fatten fancy breeds of fish. [8]What! Was it philosophy that taught the use of keys and bolts? Nay, what was that except giving a hint to avarice? Was it philosophy that erected all these towering tenements, so dangerous to the persons who dwell in them? Was it not enough for man to provide himself a roof of any chance covering, and to contrive for himself some natural retreat without the help of art and without trouble? Believe me, that was a happy age, before the days of architects, before the days of builders! [9]All this sort of thing was born when luxury was being born,–this matter of cutting timbers square and cleaving a beam with unerring hand as the saw made its way over the marked-out line.

> The primal man with wedges split his wood.[7]

For they were not preparing a roof for a future banquet-ball; for no such use did they carry the pine trees or the firs along the trembling streets[8] with a long row of drays–merely to fasten thereon panelled ceilings heavy with gold. [10]Forked poles erected at either end propped up their houses. With close-packed branches and with leaves heaped up and laid sloping they contrived a drainage for even the heaviest rains. Beneath such dwellings, they lived, but they lived in peace. A thatched roof once covered free men; under marble and gold dwells slavery.

[11]On another point also I differ from Posidonius, when he holds that mechanical tools were the invention of wise men. For on that basis one might maintain that those were wise who taught the arts

> Of setting traps for game, and liming twigs
> For birds, and girdling mighty woods with dogs.[9]

It was man's ingenuity, not his wisdom, that discovered all these devices. [12]And I also differ from him when he says that wise men discovered our mines of iron and copper, "when the earth, scorched by forest fires, melted the veins of ore which lay near the surface and caused the metal to gush forth."[10] Nay, the sort of men who discover such things are the sort of men who are busied with them. [13]Nor do I consider this question so subtle as Posidonius thinks, namely, whether the hammer or the tongs came first into use. They were both invented by some man whose mind was nimble and keen, but not great or exalted; and the same holds true of any other discovery which can only be made by means of a bent body and of a mind whose gaze is upon the ground.

The wise man was easy-going in his way of living. And why not? Even in our own times he would prefer to be as little cumbered as possible. [14]How, I ask, can you consistently admire both Diogenes and Daedalus? Which of these two seems to you a wise man–the one who devised the saw, or the one who, on seeing a boy drink water from the hollow of his hand, forthwith took his cup from his wallet and broke it, upbraiding himself with these words:[11] "Fool that I am, to have been carrying superfluous baggage all this time!" and then curled himself up in his tub and lay down to sleep? [15]In these our own times, which man, pray, do you deem the wiser–the one who invents a process for spraying saffron perfumes to a tremendous height from hidden pipes, who fills or empties canals by a sudden rush of waters, who so cleverly constructs a dining-room with a ceiling of movable panels that it presents one pattern after another, the roof changing as often as the courses,[12]–or the one who proves to others, as well as to himself, that nature has laid upon us no stern and difficult law when she tells us that we can live without the marble-cutter and the engineer, that we can clothe ourselves without traffic in silk fabrics, that we can have everything that is indispensable to our use, provided only that we are content with what the earth has placed on its surface? If mankind were willing to listen to this sage, they would know that the cook is as superfluous to them as the soldier. [16]Those were wise men, or at any rate like the wise, who found the care of the body a problem easy to solve. The things that are indispensable require no elaborate pains for their acquisition; it is only the luxuries that call for labour. Follow nature, and you will need no skilled craftsmen.

Nature did not wish us to be harassed. For whatever she forced upon us, she equipped us. "But cold cannot be endured by the naked body." What then? Are there not the skins of wild beasts and other animals, which can protect us well enough, and more than enough, from the cold? Do not many tribes cover their bodies with the bark of trees? Are not the feathers of birds sewn together to serve for clothing? Even at the present day does not a large portion of the Scythian tribe garb itself in the skins of foxes and mice, soft to the touch and impervious to the winds? [17]"For all that, men must have some thicker protection than the skin, in order to keep off the heat of the sun in summer." What then? Has not antiquity produced many retreats which, hollowed out either by the damage wrought by time or by any other occurrence you will, have opened into caverns? What then? Did not the very first-comers take twigs[13] and weave them by hand into wicker mats, smear them with common mud, and then with stubble and other wild grasses construct a roof, and thus pass their winters secure, the rains carried off by means of the sloping gables? What then? Do not the peoples on the edge of the Syrtes dwell in dug-out houses and indeed all the tribes who, because of the too fierce blaze of the sun, possess no protection sufficient to keep off the heat except the parched soil itself?

[18]Nature was not so hostile to man that, when she gave all the other animals an easy rôle in life, she made it impossible for him alone to live without all these artifices. None of these was imposed upon us by her; none of them had to be painfully sought out that our lives might be prolonged. All things were ready for us at our birth; it is we that have made everything difficult for ourselves, through our disdain for what is easy. Houses, shelter, creature comforts, food, and all that has now become the source of vast trouble, were ready at hand, free to all, and obtainable for trifling pains. For the limit everywhere corresponded to the need; it is we that have made all those things valuable, we that have made them admired, we that have caused them to be sought for by extensive and manifold devices. [19]Nature suffices for what she demands. Luxury has turned her back upon nature; each day she expands herself, in all the ages she has been gathering strength, and by her wit promoting the vices. At first, luxury began to lust for what nature regarded as superfluous, then for that which was contrary to nature; and finally she made the soul a bondsman to the body, and bade it be an utter slave to the body's lusts. All these crafts by which the city is patrolled–or shall I say kept in uproar–are but engaged in the body's business; time was when all things were offered to the body as to a slave, but now they are made ready for it as for a master. Accordingly, hence have come the workshops of the weavers and the carpenters; hence the savoury smells of the professional cooks; hence the wantonness of those who teach wanton postures, and wanton and affected singing. For that moderation which nature prescribes, which limits our desires by resources restricted to our needs, has abandoned the field; it has now come to this–that to want only what is enough is a sign both of boorishness and of utter destitution.

[20]It is hard to believe, my dear Lucilius, how easily the charm of eloquence wins even great men away from the truth. Take, for example, Posidonius–who, in my estimation, is of the number of those who have contributed most to philosophy–when he wishes to describe the art of weaving. He tells how, first, some threads are twisted and some drawn out from the soft, loose mass of wool; next, how the upright warp keeps the threads stretched by means of hanging weights; then, how the inserted thread of

the woof, which softens the hard texture of the web which holds it fast on either side, is forced by the batten to make a compact union with the warp. He maintains that even the weaver's art was discovered by wise men, forgetting that the more complicated art which he describes was invented in later days–the art wherein

> The web is bound to frame; asunder now
> The reed doth part the warp. Between the threads
> Is shot the woof by pointed shuttles borne;
> The broad comb's well-notched teeth then drive it home.[14]

Suppose he had had the opportunity of seeing the weaving of our own day, which produces the clothing that will conceal nothing, the clothing which affords–I will not say no protection to the body, but none even to modesty!

[21]Posidonius then passes on to the farmer. With no less eloquence he describes the ground which is broken up and crossed again by the plough, so that the earth, thus loosened, may allow freer play to the roots; then the seed is sown, and the weeds plucked out by hand, lest any chance growth or wild plant spring up and spoil the crop. This trade also, he declares, is the creation of the wise,–just as if cultivators of the soil were not even at the present day discovering countless new methods of increasing the soil's fertility! [22]Furthermore, not confining his attention to these arts, he even degrades the wise man by sending him to the mill. For he tells us how the sage, by imitating the processes of nature, began to make bread. "The grain,"[15] he says, "once taken into the mouth, is crushed by the flinty teeth, which meet in hostile encounter, and whatever grain slips out the tongue turns back to the selfsame teeth. Then it is blended into a mass, that it may the more easily pass down the slippery throat. When this has readied the stomach, it is digested by the stomach's equable heat; then, and not till then, it is assimilated with the body. [23]Following this pattern," he goes on, "someone placed two rough stones, the one above the other, in imitation of the teeth, one set of which is stationary and awaits the motion of the other set. Then by the rubbing of the one stone against the other, the grain is crushed and brought back again and again, until by frequent rubbing it is reduced to powder. Then this man sprinkled the meal with water, and by continued manipulation subdued the mass and moulded the loaf. This loaf was, at first, baked by hot ashes or by an earthen vessel glowing hot; later on ovens were gradually discovered and the other devices whose heat will render obedience to the sage's will." Posidonius came very near declaring that even the cobbler's trade was the discovery of the wise man.

[24]Reason did indeed devise all these things, but it was not right reason. It was man, but not the wise man, that discovered them; just as they invented ships, in which we cross rivers and seas–ships fitted with sails for the purpose of catching the force of the winds, ships with rudders added at the stern in order to turn the vessel's course in one direction or another. The model followed was the fish, which steers itself by its tail, and by its slightest motion on this side or on that bends its swift course. [25]"But," says Posidonius, "the wise man did indeed discover all these things; they were, however, too petty for him to deal with himself and so he entrusted them to his meaner assistants." Not so; these early inventions were thought out by no other class of men than those who have them in charge to-day. We know that certain devices have come to light only within our own memory–such as the use of windows which admit the clear light through transparent tiles,[16] and such as the vaulted baths, with pipes let into their walls for the purpose of diffusing the heat which maintains an even temperature in their lowest as well as in their highest spaces. Why need I mention the marble with which our temples and our private houses are resplendent? Or the rounded and polished masses of stone by means of which we erect colonnades and buildings roomy enough for nations? Or our signs[17] for whole words, which enable us to take down a speech, however rapidly uttered, matching speed of tongue by speed of hand? All this sort of thing has been devised by the lowest grade of slaves. [26]Wisdom's seat is higher; she trains not the hands, but is mistress of our minds.

Would you know what wisdom has brought forth to light, what she has accomplished? It is not the graceful poses of the body, or the varied notes produced by horn and flute, whereby the breath is received and, as it passes out or through, is transformed into voice. It is not wisdom that contrives arms, or walls, or instruments useful in war; nay, her voice is for peace, and she summons all mankind to concord. [27]It is not she, I maintain, who is the artisan of our indispensable implements of daily use. Why do you assign to her such petty things? You see in her the skilled artisan of life. The other arts, it is true, wisdom has under her control; for he whom life serves is also served by the things which equip life. But wisdom's course is toward the state of happiness; thither she guides us, thither she opens the way for us. [28]She shows us what things are evil and what things are seemingly evil; she strips our minds of vain illusion. She bestows upon us a greatness which is substantial, but she represses the greatness which is inflated, and showy but filled with emptiness; and she does not permit us to be ignorant of the difference between what is great and what is but swollen; nay, she delivers to us the knowledge of the whole of nature and of her own nature. She discloses to us what the gods are and of what sort they are; what are the nether gods, the household deities, and the protecting spirits; what are the souls which have been endowed with lasting life and have been admitted to the second class of divinities,[18] where is their abode and what their activities, powers, and will.

Such are wisdom's rites of initiation, by means of which is unlocked, not a village shrine, but the vast temple of all the gods—the universe itself, whose true apparitions and true aspects she offers to the gaze of our minds. For the vision of our eyes is too dull for sights so great. [29]Then she goes back to the beginnings of things, to the eternal Reason[19] which was imparted to the whole, and to the force which inheres in all the seeds of things, giving them the power to fashion each thing according to its kind. Then wisdom begins to inquire about the soul, whence it comes, where it dwells, how long it abides, into how many divisions it falls. Finally, she has turned her attention from the corporeal to the incorporeal, and has closely examined truth and the marks whereby truth is known, inquiring next how that which is equivocal can be distinguished from the truth, whether in life or in language; for in both are elements of the false mingled with the true.

[30]It is my opinion that the wise man has not withdrawn himself, as Posidonius thinks, from those arts which we were discussing, but that he never took them up at all.[20] For he would have judged that nothing was worth discovering that he would not afterwards judge to be worth using always. He would not take up things which would have to be laid aside.

[31]"But Anacharsis," says Posidonius, "invented the potter's wheel, whose whirling gives shape to vessels."[21] Then because the potter's wheel is mentioned in Homer, people prefer to believe that Homer's verses are false rather than the story of Posidonius! But I maintain that Anacharsis was not the creator of this wheel; and even if he was, although he was a wise man when he invented it, yet he did not invent it *qua* "wise man"–just as there are a great many things which wise men do as men, not as wise men. Suppose, for example, that a wise man is exceedingly fleet of foot; he will outstrip all the runners in the race by virtue of being fleet, not by virtue of his wisdom. I should like to show Posidonius some glass-blower who by his breath moulds the glass into manifold shapes which could scarcely be fashioned by the most skilful hand. Nay, these discoveries have been made since we men have ceased to discover wisdom.

[32]But Posidonius again remarks. "Democritus is said to have discovered the arch,[22] whose effect was that the curving line of stones, which gradually lean toward each other, is bound together by the keystone." I am inclined to pronounce this statement false. For there must have been, before Democritus, bridges and gateways in which the curvature did not begin until about the top. [33]It seems to have quite slipped your memory that this same Democritus discovered how ivory could be softened, how, by boiling, a pebble could be transformed into an emerald,[23]–the same process used even to-day for colouring stones which are found to be amenable to this treatment! It may have been a wise man who discovered all such things, but he did not discover them by virtue of being a wise man; for he does many things which we see done just as well, or even more skilfully and dexterously, by men who are utterly lacking in sagacity.

[34] Do you ask what, then, the wise man has found out and what he has brought to light? First of all there is truth, and nature; and nature he has not followed as the other animals do, with eyes too dull to perceive the divine in it. In the second place, there is the law of life, and life he has made to conform to universal principles; and he has taught us, not merely to know the gods, but to follow them, and to welcome the gifts of chance precisely as if they were divine commands. He has forbidden us to give heed to false opinions, and has weighed the value of each thing by a true standard of appraisement. He has condemned those pleasures with which remorse is intermingled, and has praised those goods which will always satisfy; and he has published the truth abroad that he is most happy who has no need of happiness, and that he is most powerful who has power over himself.

[35] I am not speaking of that philosophy which has placed the citizen outside his country and the gods outside the universe, and which has bestowed virtue upon pleasure,[24] but rather of that philosophy which counts nothing good except what is honourable,—one which cannot be cajoled by the gifts either of man or fortune, one whose value is that it cannot be bought for any value. That this philosophy existed in such a rude age, when the arts and crafts were still unknown and when useful things could only be learned by use,—this I refuse to believe.

[36] Next there came the fortune-favoured period when the bounties of nature lay open to all, for men's indiscriminate use, before avarice and luxury had broken the bonds which held mortals together, and they, abandoning their communal existence, had separated and turned to plunder. The men of the second age were not wise men, even though they did what wise men should do.[25] [37] Indeed, there is no other condition of the human race that anyone would regard more highly; and if God should commission a man to fashion earthly creatures and to bestow institutions upon peoples, this man would approve of no other system than that which obtained among the men of that age, when

> No ploughman tilled the soil, nor was it right
> To portion off or bound one's property.
> Men shared their gains, and earth more freely gave
> Her riches to her sons who sought them not.[26]

[38] What race of men was ever more blest than that race? They enjoyed all nature in partnership. Nature sufficed for them, now the guardian, as before she was the parent, of all; and this her gift consisted of the assured possession by each man of the common resources. Why should I not even call that race the richest among mortals, since you could not find a poor person among them?

But avarice broke in upon a condition so happily ordained, and, by its eagerness to lay something away and to turn it to its own private use, made all things the property of others, and reduced itself from boundless wealth to straitened need. It was avarice that introduced poverty and, by craving much, lost all. [39] And so, although she now tries to make good her loss, although she adds one estate to another, evicting a neighbour either by buying him out or by wronging him, although she extends her country-seats to the size of provinces and defines ownership as meaning extensive travel through one's own property,—in spite of all these efforts of hers no enlargement of our boundaries will bring us back to the condition from which we have departed.

When there is no more that we can do, we shall possess much; but we once possessed the whole world! [40] The very soil was more productive when untilled, and yielded more than enough for peoples who refrained from despoiling one another. Whatever gift nature had produced, men found as much pleasure in revealing it to another as in having discovered it. It was possible for no man either to surpass another or to fall short of him; what there was, was divided among unquarrelling friends. Not yet had the stronger begun to lay hands upon the weaker; not yet had the miser, by hiding away what lay before him, begun to shut off his neighbour from even the necessities of life; each cared as much for his neighbour as for himself. [41] Armour lay unused, and the hand, unstained by human blood, had turned all its hatred against wild beasts. The men of that day, who had found in some dense grove protection against the sun, and security against the severity of winter or of rain in their mean hiding-places, spent their lives under the branches of the trees and passed tranquil nights without a sigh. Care vexes us in our purple, and routs us from our beds with the sharpest of goads; but how soft was the sleep the hard earth bestowed upon the men of that day! [42]No fretted and panelled ceilings hung over them, but as they lay beneath the open sky the stars glided quietly above them, and the firmament, night's noble pageant, marched swiftly by, conducting its mighty task in silence. For them by day, as well as by night, the visions of this most glorious abode were free and open. It was their joy to watch the constellations as they sank from mid-heaven and others, again, as they rose from their hidden abodes. [43]What else but joy could it be to wander among the marvels which dotted the heavens far and wide? But you of the present day shudder at every sound your houses make, and as you sit among your frescoes the slightest creak makes you shrink in terror. *They* had no houses as big as cities. The air, the breezes blowing free through the open spaces, the flitting shade of crag or tree, springs crystal-clear and streams not spoiled by man's work, whether by water-pipe[27] or by any confinement of the channel, but running at will, and meadows beautiful without the use of art,–amid such scenes were their rude homes, adorned with rustic hand. Such a dwelling was in accordance with nature; therein it was a joy to live, fearing neither the dwelling itself nor for its safety. In these days, however, our houses constitute a large portion of our dread.

[44]But no matter how excellent and guileless was the life of the men of that age, they were not wise men; for that title is reserved for the highest achievement. Still, I would not deny that they were men of lofty spirit and–I may use the phrase–fresh from the gods. For there is no doubt that the world produced a better progeny before it was yet worn out. However, not all were endowed with mental faculties of highest perfection, though in all cases their native powers were more sturdy than ours and more fitted for toil. For nature does not bestow virtue; it is an art to become good. [45]They, at least, searched not in the lowest dregs of the earth for gold, nor yet for silver or transparent stones; and they still were merciful even to the dumb animals–so far removed was that epoch from the custom of slaying man by man, not in anger or through fear, but just to make a show! They had as yet no embroidered garments nor did they weave cloth of gold; gold was not yet even mined.

[46]What, then, is the conclusion of the matter? It was by reason of their ignorance of things that the men of those days were innocent; and it makes a great deal of difference whether one wills not to sin or has not the knowledge to sin.[28] Justice was unknown to them, unknown prudence, unknown also self-control and bravery; but their rude life possessed certain qualities akin to all these virtues. Virtue is not vouchsafed to a soul unless that soul has been trained and taught, and by unremitting practice brought to perfection. For the attainment of this boon, but not in the possession of it, were we born; and even in the best of men, before you refine them by instruction, there is but the stuff of virtue, not virtue itself. Farewell.

Footnotes

1. Cf. Plato, *Crito* 48, "not life itself, but a good life, is chiefly to be desired."

2. Compare the "knowledge of things divine and things human" of lxxxix. 5.

3. The "Golden Age" motif was a frequent one in Latin literature. Compare, e.g., Tibullus, i. 3. 35 ff., the passage beginning:

> *Quam bene Saturno vivebant rege, priusquam*
> *Tellus in longas est patefacta vias!*

Cf. § 46, summing up the message of Seneca's letter.

4. While modern philosophy would probably side with Seneca rather than Posidonius, it is interesting to know the opinion of Macaulay, who holds (*Essay on Bacon*) that there is much in common between Posidonius and the English inductive philosopher, and thinks but little of Seneca's ideas on the subject. Cf. W. C. Summers, *Select letters of Seneca*, p. 312.

5. Cleobulus of Rhodes, Periander of Corinth, Pittacus of Mitylene, Bias of Priene,

Thales of Miletus, Chilon of Sparta, and Solon of Athens. For some of these substitutions are made in certain lists.

6. Cf. Ep. lxxxviii. 20 *ad alia multum, ad virtutem nihil.*

7. Vergil, *Georg.* i. 144.

8. Cf. Juvenal, iii. 254 ff.:

> *Longa coruscat*
> *Serraco veniente abies, atque altera pinum*
> *Plaustra vehunt, nutant alte populoque minantur.*

Compare also the "towering tenements" of § 8.

9. Vergil, *Georg.* i. 139 f.

10. Cf. T. Rice Holmes, *Ancient Britain*, pp. 121 f., who concludes that the discovery of ore-smelting was accidental.

11. Cf. Diog. Laert. vi. 37 Θεασάμενός ποτε παιδίον ταῖς χερσὶ ἐξέρδιψε τῆς πήρας τὴν κοτύλην, εἰπών, Παιδίον με νενίκηκεν εὐτελεία.

12. Compare the halls of Nero which Seneca may easily have had in mind: (Suet. *Nero* 31) *cenationes laqueatae tabulis eburneis versatilibus . . . praecipua cenationum rotunda, quae perpetuo diebus ac noctibus vice mundi circumageretur.*

13. Cf. Ovid, *Met.* i. 121 f.:

> *Domus antra fuerunt*
> *Et densi frutices et vinctae cortice virgae.*

Among many accounts by Roman writers of early man, compare this passage of Ovid, and that in the fifth book of Lucretius.

14. Ovid, *Met.* vi. 55 ff.

15. Professor Summers calls attention to the similarity of this passage and Cicero, *De Nat. Deor.* ii. 134 ff. *dentibus manditur . . . a lingua adiuvari videtur . . . in alvo . . . calore . . . in reliquum corpus dividantur.*

16. Besides *lapis specularis* (window-glass) the Romans used alabaster, mica, and shells for this purpose.

17. Suetonius tells us that a certain Ennius, a grammarian of the Augustan age, was the first to develop shorthand on a scientific basis, and that Tiro, Cicero's freedman, had invented the process. He also mentions Seneca as the most scientific and encyclopaedic authority on the subject.

18. Possibly either the *manes* or the *indigitamenta* of the early Roman religion.

19. i.e., λόγος.

20. Seneca, himself one of the keenest scientific observers in history (witness *Nat. Quaest.*, Epp. lvii., lxxix., etc.), is pushing his argument very far in this letter. His message is clear enough; but the modern combination of natural science, psychology, and philosophy shows that Posidonius had some justification for his theories. Cf. also Lucretius, v. 1105-7 ff.

21. This Scythian prince and friend of Solon, who visited Athens in the sixth century B.C., is also said to have invented the bellows and the anchor. Cf., however, *Iliad* xviii. 600 f. ὡς ὅτε τις τροχὸν ἄρμενον ἐν παλάμῃσιν ἑζόμενος κεραμεὺς πειρήσεται, and Leaf's comment: "The potter's wheel was known in pre-Mycenean times, and was a very ancient invention to the oldest Epic poets." Seneca is right.

22. Seneca (see next sentence) is right again. The arch was known in Chaldaea and in Egypt before 3000 B.C. Greek bee-hive tombs, Etruscan gateways, and early Roman remains, testify to its immemorial use.

23. The ancients judged precious stones merely by their colour; their *smaragdus* included also malachite, jade, and several kinds of quartz. Exposure to heat alters the colour of some stones; and the alchemists believed that the "angelic stone" changed common flints into diamonds, rubies, emeralds, etc. See G. F. Kunz, *The Magic of Jewels and Charms*, p. 16. It was also an ancient superstition that emeralds were produced from jasper.

24. i.e., the Epicureans, who withdraw from civil life and regarded the gods as taking no part in the affairs of men.

25. i.e., live according to nature.

26. Verg. *Georg.* i. 125 ff.

27. Cf. Horace, *Ep.* i. 10. 20 f.:

> *Purior in vicis aqua tendit rumpere plumbum*
> *Quam quae per pronum trepidat cum murmure rivum?*

28. Because virtue depends upon reason, and none but voluntary acts should meet with praise or blame.

XCI. ON THE LESSON TO BE DRAWN FROM THE BURNING OF LYONS[1]

[1]Our friend Liberalis[2] is now downcast; for he has just heard of the fire which has wiped out the colony of Lyons. Such a calamity might upset anyone at all, not to speak of a man who dearly loves his country. But this incident has served to make him inquire about the strength of his own character, which he has trained, I suppose, just to meet situations that he thought might cause him fear. I do not wonder, however, that he was free from apprehension touching an evil so unexpected and practically unheard of as this, since it is without precedent. For fire has damaged many a city, but has annihilated none. Even when fire has been hurled against the walls by the hand of a foe, the flame dies out in many places, and although continually renewed, rarely devours so wholly as to leave nothing for the sword. Even an earthquake has scarcely ever been so violent and destructive as to overthrow whole cities. Finally, no conflagration has ever before blazed forth so savagely in any town that nothing was left for a second. [2]So many beautiful buildings, any single one of which would make a single town famous, were wrecked in one night. In time of such deep peace an event has taken place worse than men can possibly fear even in time of war. Who can believe it? When weapons are everywhere at rest and when peace prevails throughout the world, Lyons, the pride of Gaul,[3] is missing!

Fortune has usually allowed all men, when she has assailed them collectively, to have a foreboding of that which they were destined to suffer. Every great creation has had granted to it a period of reprieve before its fall; but in this case, only a single night elapsed between the city at its greatest and the city non-existent. In short, it takes me longer to tell you than it took for the city to perish.

[3]All this has affected our friend Liberalis, bending his will, which is usually so steadfast and erect in the face of his own trials. And not without reason has he been shaken; for it is the unexpected that puts the heaviest load upon us. Strangeness adds to the weight of calamities, and every mortal feels the greater pain as a result of that which also brings surprise.

[4]Therefore, nothing ought to be unexpected by us. Our minds should be sent forward in advance to meet all problems, and we should consider, not what is wont to happen, but what can happen. For what is there in existence that Fortune, when she has so willed, does not drag down from the very height of its prosperity? And what is there that she does not the more violently assail the more brilliantly it shines? What is laborious or difficult for her? [5]She does not always attack in one way or even with her full strength; at one time she summons our own hands against us; at another time, content with her own powers, she makes use of no agent in devising perils for us. No time is exempt; in the midst of our very pleasures there spring up causes of suffering. War arises in the midst of peace, and that which we depended upon for protection is transformed into a cause of fear; friend becomes enemy, ally becomes foeman, The summer calm is stirred into sudden storms, wilder than the storms of winter.[4] With no foe in sight we are victims of such fates as foes inflict, and if other causes of disaster fail, excessive good fortune finds them for itself. The most temperate are assailed by illness, the strongest by wasting disease, the most innocent by chastisement, the most secluded by the noisy mob.

Chance chooses some new weapon by which to bring her strength to bear against

us, thinking we have forgotten her. ⁶Whatever structure has been reared by a long sequence of years, at the cost of great toil and through the great kindness of the gods, is
scattered and dispersed by a single day. Nay, he who has said "a day" has granted too
long a postponement to swift-coming misfortune; an hour, an instant of time, suffices
for the overthrow of empires! It would be some consolation for the feebleness of our
selves and our works, if all things should perish as slowly as they come into being;
but as it is, increases are of sluggish growth, but the way to ruin is rapid. ⁷Nothing,
whether public or private, is stable; the destinies of men, no less than those of cities,
are in a whirl. Amid the greatest calm terror arises, and though no external agencies
stir up commotion, yet evils burst forth from sources whence they were least expected. Thrones which have stood the shock of civil and foreign wars crash to the ground
though no one sets them tottering. How few the states which have carried their good
fortune through to the end!

   We should therefore reflect upon all contingencies, and should fortify our minds
against the evils which may possibly come. ⁸Exile, the torture of disease, wars, shipwreck,–we must think on these.⁵ Chance may tear you from your country or your
country from you, or may banish you to the desert; this very place, where throngs are
stifling, may become a desert. Let us place before our eyes in its entirety the nature of
man's lot, and if we would not be overwhelmed, or even dazed, by those unwonted
evils, as if they were novel, let us summon to our minds beforehand, not as great an
evil as oftentimes happens, but the very greatest evil that possibly can happen. We
must reflect upon fortune fully and completely.

   ⁹How often have cities in Asia, how often in Achaia, been laid low by a single
shock of earthquake! How many towns in Syria, how many in Macedonia, have been
swallowed⁶ up! How often has this kind of devastation laid Cyprus⁶ in ruins! How
often has Paphos collapsed! Not infrequently are tidings brought to us of the utter
destruction of entire cities; yet how small a part of the world are we, to whom such
tidings often come!

   Let us rise, therefore, to confront the operations of Fortune, and whatever happens, let us have the assurance that it is not so great as rumour advertises it to be. ¹⁰A
rich city has been laid in ashes, the jewel of the provinces, counted as one of them and
yet not included with them;⁷ rich though it was, nevertheless it was set upon a single
hill,⁸ and that not very large in extent. But of all those cities, of whose magnificence
and grandeur you hear today, the very traces will be blotted out by time. Do you not
see how, in Achaia, the foundations of the most famous cities have already crumbled
to nothing, so that no trace is left to show that they ever even existed?⁹ ¹¹Not only does
that which has been made with hands totter to the ground, not only is that which has
been set in place by man's art and man's efforts overthrown by the passing days; nay,
the peaks of mountains dissolve, whole tracts have settled, and places which once
stood far from the sight of the sea are now covered by the waves. The mighty power of
fires has eaten away the hills through whose sides they used to glow, and has levelled
to the ground peaks which were once most lofty–the sailor's solace and his beacon.
The works of nature herself are harassed; hence we ought to bear with untroubled
minds the destruction of cities. ¹²They stand but to fall! This doom awaits them, one
and all; it may be that some internal force, and blasts of violence which are tremendous
because their way is blocked, will throw off the weight which holds then down; or that
a whirlpool of raging currents, mightier because they are hidden in the bosom of the
earth, will break through that which resists its power; or that the vehemence of flames
will burst asunder the framework of the earth's crust; or that time, from which nothing
is safe, will reduce them little by little; or that a pestilential climate will drive their inhabitants away and the mould will corrode their deserted walls. It would be tedious to
recount all the ways by which fate may come; but this one thing I know: all the works
of mortal man have been doomed to mortality, and in the midst of things which have
been destined to die, we live!

   ¹³Hence it is thoughts like these, and of this kind, which I am offering as consolation to our friend Liberalis, who burns with a love for his country that is beyond

belief. Perhaps its destruction has been brought about only that it may be raised up again to a better destiny. Oftentimes a reverse has but made room for more prosperous fortune. Many structures have fallen only to rise to a greater height. Timagenes,[10] who had a grudge against Rome and her prosperity, used to say that the only reason he was grieved when conflagrations occurred in Rome was his knowledge that better buildings would arise than those which had gone down in the flames. [14]And probably in this city of Lyons, too, all its citizens will earnestly strive that everything shall be rebuilt better in size and security than what they have lost. May it be built to endure and, under happier auspices, for a longer existence! This is indeed but the hundredth year since this colony was founded–not the limit even of a man's lifetime.[11] Led forth by Plancus, the natural advantages of its site have caused it to wax strong and reach the numbers which it contains to-day; and yet how many calamities of the greatest severity has it endured within the space of an old man's life!

[15]Therefore let the mind be disciplined to understand and to endure its own lot, and let it have the knowledge that there is nothing which fortune does not dare–that she has the same jurisdiction over empires as over emperors, the same power over cities as over the citizens who dwell therein. We must not cry out at any of these calamities. Into such a world have we entered, and under such laws do we live. If you like it, obey; if not, depart whithersoever you wish. Cry out in anger if any unfair measures are taken with reference to you individually; but if this inevitable law is binding upon the highest and the lowest alike, be reconciled to fate, by which all things are dissolved. [16]You should not estimate our worth by our funeral mounds or by these monuments of unequal size which line the road; their ashes level all men! We are unequal at birth, but are equal in death. What I say about cities I say also about their inhabitants. Ardea was captured as well as Rome.[12] The great founder of human law has not made distinctions between us on the basis of high lineage or of illustrious names, except while we live. When, however, we come to the end which awaits mortals, he says: "Depart, ambition! To all creatures that burden the earth let one and the same[13] law apply!" For enduring all things, we are equal; no one is more frail than another, no one more certain of his own life on the morrow.

[17]Alexander, king of Macedon, began to study geometry;[14] unhappy man, because he would thereby learn how puny was that earth of which he had seized but a fraction! Unhappy man, I repeat, because he was bound to understand that he was bearing a false title. For who can be "great" in that which is puny? The lessons which were being taught him were intricate and could be learned only by assiduous application; they were not the kind to be comprehended by a madman, who let his thoughts range beyond the ocean.[15] "Teach me something easy!" he cries; but his teacher answers: "These things are the same for all, as hard for one as for another." [18]Imagine that nature is saying to us: "Those things of which you complain are the same for all. I cannot give anything easier to any man, but whoever wishes will make things easier for himself." In what way? By equanimity. You must suffer pain, and thirst, and hunger, and old age too, if a longer stay among men shall be granted you; you must be sick, and you must suffer loss and death. [19]Nevertheless, you should not believe those whose noisy clamour surrounds you; none of these things is an evil, none is beyond your power to bear, or is burdensome. It is only by common opinion that there is anything formidable in them. Your fearing death is therefore like your fear of gossip. But what is more foolish than a man afraid of words? Our friend Demetrius[16] is wont to put it cleverly when he says: "For me the talk of ignorant men is like the rumblings which issue from the belly. For," he adds, "what difference does it make to me whether such rumblings come from above or from below?" [20]What madness it is to be afraid of disrepute in the judgment of the disreputable! Just as you have had no cause for shrinking in terror from the talk of men, so you have no cause now to shrink from these things, which you would never fear had not their talk forced fear upon you. Does it do any harm to a good man to be besmirched by unjust gossip? [21]Then let not this sort of thing damage death, either, in our estimation; death also is in bad odour. But no one of those who malign death has made trial of it.

Meanwhile it is foolhardy to condemn that of which you are ignorant. This one thing, however, you do know–that death is helpful to many, that it sets many free from tortures, want, ailments, sufferings, and weariness. We are in the power of nothing when once we have death in our own power! Farewell.

Footnotes

1. In spite of the *centesimus annus* of § 14 (q.v.), the most probable date of this letter, based on Tac. *Ann.* xvi. 13 and other general evidence, is July-September 64 A.D. 58 A.D. would be too early for many reasons–among them that "peace all over the world" would not be a true statement until January of 62. (See the monograph of Jonas, O. Binder, Peiper, and Schultess.)

2. Probably Aebutius Liberalis, to whom the treatise De Beneficiis was dedicated.

3. That Lyons, situated at the junction of the Arar and the Rhone, was of especial prominence in Gaul, may be also gathered from the fact that it boasted a government mint and the *Ara Augusti*–a shrine established for the annual worship of all the Gallic states. Moreover, the emperor Claudius delivered his famous address in that city (see Tac. *Ann.* xi. 23 f.).

4. Cf. Ep. iv. 7, esp. the words *noli huic tranquillitati confidere; momento mare evertitur.*

5. The passage bears a striking resemblance to the words of Theseus in an unknown play of Euripides (Nauck. Frag. 964) quoted by Cicero, *Tusc.* iii. 14. 29, and by Plutarch, *Consolation to Apollonius,* 112d.

6. Seneca (*N. Q.* vi. 26) speaks of Paphos (on the island of Cyprus) as having been more than once devastated. We know of two such accidents–one under Augustus and another under Vespasian. See the same passage for other earthquake shocks in various places.

7. Lyons held an exceptional position in relation to the three Gallic provinces; it was a free town, belonging to none and yet their capital, much like the city of Washington in relation to the United States.

8. A fact mentioned merely to suggest Rome with her seven hills.

9. For example, Mycenae and Tiryns.

10. Probably the writer, and intimate friend of Augustus, who began life in Rome as a captive from Egypt. Falling into disfavour with the Emperor, he took refuge with the malcontent Asinius Pollio at Tusculum, and subsequently died in the East. Cf. Seneca, *De Ira,* iii. 23.

11. It was in 43 B.C. that Plancus led out the colonists who were chiefly Roman citizens driven from Vienna. Seneca would have been more accurate had he said "one hundred and eighth (or seventh)." Buecheler and Schultess would (unnecessarily) emend to read *centesimus septimus*. But Seneca was using round numbers.

12. Ardea, the earliest capital of Latium, and Rome, the present capital of the empire. Seneca probably refers to Ardea's capture and destruction by the Samnites in the fourth century; Rome was captured by the Celts in 390 B.C. The former greatness of Ardea was celebrated by Vergil, *Aeneid,* vii. 411 ff.:

> et nunc magnum manet Ardea nomen,
> Sed fortuna fuit.

13. *Siremps* (or *sirempse*–Plaut. *Amph.* 73), an ancient legal term, is derived by Festus from *similis re ipsa*; but Corssen explains it as from *sic rem pse.*

14. i.e., surveying. See Ep. lxxxviii. 10.

15. i.e., Ὠκεανός, the stream which encircles the earth.

16. This plain-living, plain-speaking philosopher appears also in Epp. xx. 9 and lxii. 3. Seneca refers to him as *seminudum, quanto minus quam stramentis incubantem.*

XCII. ON THE HAPPY LIFE[1]

[1]You and I will agree, I think, that outward things are sought for the satisfaction of the body, that the body is cherished out of regard for the soul, and that in the soul there are certain parts which minister to us, enabling us to move and to sustain life,

bestowed upon us just for the sake of the primary part of us.[2] In this primary part there is something irrational, and something rational. The former obeys the latter, while the latter is the only thing that is not referred back to another, but rather refers all things to itself. For the divine reason also is set in supreme command over all things, and is itself subject to none; and even this reason which we possess is the same, because it is derived from the divine reason. [2]Now if we are agreed on this point, it is natural that we shall be agreed on the following also–namely, that the happy life depends upon this and this alone: our attainment of perfect reason. For it is naught but this that keeps the soul from being bowed down, that stands its ground against Fortune; whatever the condition of their affairs may be, it keeps men untroubled. And that alone is a good which is never subject to impairment. That man, I declare, is happy whom nothing makes less strong than he is; he keeps to the heights, leaning upon none but himself; for one who sustains himself by any prop may fall. If the case is otherwise, then things which do not pertain to us will begin to have great influence over us. But who desires Fortune to have the upper hand, or what sensible man prides himself upon that which is not his own?

[3]What is the happy life? It is peace of mind, and lasting tranquillity. This will be yours if you possess greatness of soul; it will be yours if you possess the steadfastness that resolutely clings to a good judgment just reached. How does a man reach this condition? By gaining a complete view of truth, by maintaining, in all that he does, order, measure, fitness, and a will that is inoffensive and kindly, that is intent upon reason and never departs therefrom, that commands at the same time love and admiration. In short, to give you the principle in brief compass, the wise man's soul ought to be such as would be proper for a god. [4]What more can one desire who possesses all honourable things? For if dishonourable things can contribute to the best estate, then there will be the possibility of a happy life under conditions which do not include an honourable life. And what is more base or foolish than to connect the good of a rational soul with things irrational? [5]Yet there are certain philosophers who hold that the Supreme Good admits of increase because it is hardly complete when the gifts of fortune are adverse.[3] Even Antipater,[4] one of the great leaders of this school, admits that he ascribes some influence to externals, though only a very slight influence. You see, however, what absurdity lies in not being content with the daylight unless it is increased by a tiny fire. What importance can a spark have in the midst of this clear sunlight? [6]If you are not contented with only that which is honourable, it must follow that you desire in addition either the kind of quiet which the Greeks call "undisturbedness," or else pleasure. But the former may be attained in any case. For the mind is free from disturbance when it is fully free to contemplate the universe, and nothing distracts it from the contemplation of nature. The second, pleasure, is simply the good of cattle. We are but adding[5] the irrational to the rational, the dishonourable to the honourable. A pleasant physical sensation affects this life of ours; [7]why, therefore, do you hesitate to say that all is well with a man just because all is well with his appetite? And do you rate, I will not say among heroes, but among men, the person whose Supreme Good is a matter of flavours and colours and sounds? Nay, let him withdraw from the ranks of this, the noblest class of living beings, second only to the gods; let him herd with the dumb brutes–an animal whose delight is in fodder!

[8]The irrational part of the soul is twofold:[6] the one part is spirited, ambitious, uncontrolled; its seat is in the passions; the other is lowly, sluggish, and devoted to pleasure. Philosophers have neglected the former, which, though unbridled, is yet better, and is certainly more courageous and more worthy of a man, and have regarded the latter, which is nerveless and ignoble, as indispensable to the happy life. [9]They have ordered reason to serve this latter; they have made the Supreme Good of the noblest living being an abject and mean affair, and a monstrous hybrid, too, composed of various members which harmonize but ill. For as our Vergil, describing Scylla, says[7]

> Above, a human face and maiden's breast,
> A beauteous breast,–below, a monster huge
> Of bulk and shapeless, with a dolphin's tail

Joined to a wolf-like belly.

And yet to this Scylla are tacked on the forms of wild animals, dreadful and swift; but from what monstrous shapes have these wiseacres compounded wisdom! [10]Man's primary art is virtue itself; there is joined to this the useless and fleeting flesh, fitted only for the reception of food, as Posidonius remarks. This divine virtue ends in foulness, and to the higher parts, which are worshipful and heavenly, there is fastened a sluggish and flabby animal. As for the second desideratum,–quiet,–although it would indeed not of itself be of any benefit to the soul, yet it would relieve the soul of hindrances; pleasure, on the contrary, actually destroys the soul and softens all its vigour. What elements so inharmonious as these can be found united? To that which is most vigorous is joined that which is most sluggish, to that which is austere that which is far from serious, to that which is most holy that which is unrestrained even to the point of impurity. [11]"What, then," comes the retort, "if good health, rest, and freedom from pain are not likely to hinder virtue, shall you not seek all these?" Of course I shall seek them, but not because they are goods,–I shall seek them because they are according to nature and because they will be acquired through the exercise of good judgment on my part. What, then, will be good in them? This alone,–that it is a good thing to choose them. For when I don suitable attire, or walk as I should, or dine as I ought to dine, it is not my dinner, or my walk, or my dress that are goods, but the deliberate choice which I show in regard to them, as I observe, in each thing I do, a mean that conforms with reason. [12]Let me also add that the choice of neat clothing is a fitting object of a man's efforts; for man is by nature a neat and well-groomed animal. Hence the choice of neat attire, and not neat attire in itself, is a good; since the good is not in the thing selected, but in the quality of the selection. Our actions are honourable, but not the actual things which we do. [13]And you may assume that what I have said about dress applies also to the body. For nature has surrounded our soul with the body as with a sort of garment; the body is its cloak. But who has ever reckoned the value of clothes by the wardrobe which contained them? The scabbard does not make the sword good or bad. Therefore, with regard to the body I shall return the same answer to you,–that, if I have the choice, I shall choose health and strength, but that the good involved will be my judgment regarding these things, and not the things themselves.

[14]Another retort is: "Granted that the wise man is happy; nevertheless, he does not attain the Supreme Good which we have defined, unless the means also which nature provides for its attainment are at his call. So, while one who possesses virtue cannot be unhappy, yet one cannot be perfectly happy if one lacks such natural gifts as health, or soundness of limb." [15]But in saying this, you grant the alternative which seems the more difficult to believe,–that the man who is in the midst of unremitting and extreme pain is not wretched, nay, is even happy; and you deny that which is much less serious,–that he is completely happy. And yet, if virtue can keep a man from being wretched, it will be an easier task for it to render him completely happy. For the difference between happiness and complete happiness is less than that between wretchedness and happiness. Can it be possible that a thing which is so powerful as to snatch a man from disaster, and place him among the happy, cannot also accomplish what remains, and render him supremely happy? Does its strength fail at the very top of the climb? [16]There are in life things which are advantageous and disadvantageous,– both beyond our control. If a good man, in spite of being weighed down by all kinds of disadvantages, is not wretched, how is he not supremely happy, no matter if he does lack certain advantages? For as he is not weighted down to wretchedness by his burden of disadvantages, so he is not withdrawn from supreme happiness through lack of any advantages; nay, he is just as supremely happy without the advantages as he is free from wretchedness though under the load of his disadvantages. Otherwise, if his good can be impaired, it can be snatched from him altogether.

[17]A short space above,[8] I remarked that a tiny fire does not add to the sun's light. For by reason of the sun's brightness any light that shines apart from the sunlight is blotted out. "But," one may say, "there are certain objects that stand in the way even of the sunlight." The sun, however, is unimpaired even in the midst of obstacles, and,

not as a thing to love, but as a thing to oversee; nor is it subservient to that over which it is set in mastery. For no man is free who is a slave to his body. Indeed, omitting all the other masters which are brought into being by excessive care for the body, the sway which the body itself exercises is captious and fastidious. [34]Forth from this body the soul issues, now with unruffled spirit, now with exultation, and, when once it has gone forth, asks not what shall be the end of the deserted day. No; just as we do not take thought for the clippings of the hair and the beard, even so that divine soul, when it is about to issue forth from the mortal man, regards the destination of its earthly vessel–whether it be consumed by fire, or shut in by a stone, or buried in the earth, or torn by wild beasts–as being of no more concern to itself than is the afterbirth to a child just born. And whether this body shall be cast out and plucked to pieces by birds, or devoured when

> thrown to the sea-dogs as prey,[14]

how does that concern him who is nothing? [35]Nay even when it is among the living, the soul fears nothing that may happen to the body after death; for though such things may have been threats, they were not enough to terrify the soul previous to the moment of death. It says; "I am not frightened by the executioner's hook,[15] nor by the revolting mutilation of the corpse which is exposed to the scorn of those who would witness the spectacle. I ask no man to perform the last rites for me; I entrust my remains to none. Nature has made provision that none shall go unburied. Time will lay away one whom cruelty has cast forth." Those were eloquent words which Maecenas uttered:

> I want no tomb; for Nature doth provide
> For outcast bodies burial.[16]

You would imagine that this was the saying of a man of strict principles. He was indeed a man of noble and robust native gifts, but in prosperity he impaired these gifts by laxness.[17] Farewell.

Footnotes

1. The reader will find this topic treated at greater length in Seneca's *De Vita Beata*.

2. i.e., the soul. See Aristotle, *Eth*. 1. 13: "It is stated that the soul has two parts, one irrational and the other possessing reason." Aristotle further subdivides the irrational part into (1) that which makes for growth and increase, and (2) desire (which will, however, obey reason). In this passage Seneca uses "soul" in its widest sense.

3. Certain of the Peripatetic and Academic school.

4. Probably due to the criticism of the Stoics by Carneades, who said that everything which is according to nature should be classed among the goods.

5. If we call pleasure a good.

6. Cf. § 1 of this letter. Plato gives three divisions–the λογιστικόν, the ἐπιθυμητικόν, and the θυμοειδές which obeys either the first or the second. See his *Republic*, 440.

7. *Aeneid*, iii. 426 ff.

8. § 5.

9. Answering the objection raised in § 14.

10. Cf. Ep. lxxi. 16 *non intenditur virtus*. The Stoic idea of *tension* may be combined here with the raising of a note to a higher pitch.

11. Frag. 138 Usener. Cf. Sen. Ep. lxvi. 47.

12. Vergil, *Aeneid*, v. 363. Vergil MSS. read *pectore*.

13. i.e., to participation in the divine existence.

14. Vergil, *Aeneid*, ix. 485.

15. Cf. Juvenal, x. 65 *Seianus ducitur unco spectandus*. The bodies of criminals were dragged by the hook through the city to the *Scalae Gemoniae*, down which they were flung.

16. Frag. 6 Lunderstedt.

17. The figure is taken from the Roman dress,–one who was "girt high" (*alte cinctus*),

ready for vigorous walking, being contrasted with the loosely-girdled person (*discinctus*), indolent or effeminate. On the character of Maecenas see Epp. cxiv. 4 ff., xix. 9, cxx. 19.

XCIII. ON THE QUALITY, AS CONTRASTED WITH THE LENGTH, OF LIFE

[1]While reading the letter in which you were lamenting the death of the philosopher Metronax[1] as if he might have, and indeed ought to have, lived longer, I missed the spirit of fairness which abounds in all your discussions concerning men and things, but is lacking when you approach one single subject,—as is indeed the case with us all. In other words, I have noticed many who deal fairly with their fellow-men, but none who deals fairly with the gods. We rail every day at Fate, saying "Why has A. been carried off in the very middle of his career? Why is not B. carried off instead? Why should he prolong his old age, which is a burden to himself as well as to others?"

[2]But tell me, pray, do you consider it fairer that you should obey Nature, or that Nature should obey you? And what difference does it make how soon you depart from a place which you must depart from sooner or later? We should strive, not to live long, but to live rightly;[2] for to achieve long life you have need of Fate only, but for right living you need the soul. A life is really long if it is a full life; but fullness is not attained until the soul has rendered to itself its proper Good,[3] that is, until it has assumed control over itself. [3]What benefit does this older man derive from the eighty years he has spent in idleness? A person like him has not lived; he has merely tarried awhile in life. Nor has he died late in life; he has simply been a long time dying. He has lived eighty years, has he? That depends upon the date from which you reckon his death! Your other friend,[4] however, departed in the bloom of his manhood. [4]But he had fulfilled all the duties of a good citizen, a good friend, a good son; in no respect had he fallen short. His age may have been incomplete, but his life was complete. The other man has lived eighty years, has he? Nay, he has existed eighty years, unless perchance you mean by "he has lived" what we mean when we say that a tree "lives."

Pray, let us see to it, my dear Lucilius, that our lives, like jewels of great price, be noteworthy not because of their width but because of their weight.[5] Let us measure them by their performance, not by their duration. Would you know wherein lies the difference between this hardy man who, despising Fortune, has served through every campaign of life and has attained to life's Supreme Good, and that other person over whose head many years have passed? The former exists even after his death; the latter has died even before he was dead.[6]

[5]We should therefore praise, and number in the company of the blest, that man who has invested well the portion of time, however little, that has been allotted to him; for such a one has seen the true light. He has not been one of the common herd. He has not only lived, but flourished. Sometimes he enjoyed fair skies; sometimes, as often happens, it was only through the clouds that there flashed to him the radiance of the mighty star.[7] Why do you ask: "How long did he live?" He still lives! At one bound he has passed over into posterity and has consigned himself to the guardianship of memory.

[6]And yet I would not on that account decline for myself a few additional years; although, if my life's space be shortened, I shall not say that I have lacked aught that is essential to a happy life. For I have not planned to live up to the very last day that my greedy hopes had promised me; nay, I have looked upon every day as if it were my last. Why ask the date of my birth, or whether I am still enrolled on the register of the younger men?[8] What I have is my own. [7]Just as one of small stature can be a perfect man, so a life of small compass can be a perfect life. Age ranks among the external things.[9] How long I am to exist is not mine to decide, but how long I shall go on existing in my present way is in my own control. This is the only thing you have the right to require of me,—that I shall cease to measure out an inglorious age as it were in

most excellent quality: if prolonged it cannot be severe, and if severe it cannot be prolonged;[5] and that we should bravely accept whatever commands the inevitable laws of
the universe lay upon us.

[8]"When by means of such doctrines you have brought the erring man to a sense of
his own condition, when he has learned that the happy life is not that which conforms
to pleasure, but that which conforms to Nature, when he has fallen deeply in love with
virtue as man's sole good and has avoided baseness as man's sole evil, and when he
knows that all other things–riches, office, health, strength, dominion–fall in between
and are not to be reckoned either among goods or among evils, then he will not need
a monitor for every separate action, to say to him: 'Walk thus and so, eat thus and so.
This is the conduct proper for a man and that for a woman; this for a married man and
that for a bachelor.' [9]Indeed, the persons who take the greatest pains to proffer such
advice are themselves unable to put it into practice. It is thus that the pedagogue advises the boy, and the grandmother her grandson; it is the hottest-tempered schoolmaster
who contends that one should never lose one's temper. Go into an elementary school,
and you will learn that just such pronouncements, emanating from high-browed philosophers, are to be found in the lesson-book for boys!

[10]"Shall you then offer precepts that are clear, or precepts that are doubtful? Those
which are clear need no counsellor, and doubtful precepts gain no credence; so the
giving of precepts is superfluous. Indeed you should study the problem in this way: if
you are counselling someone on a matter which is of doubtful clearness and doubtful
meaning, you must supplement your precepts by proofs; and if you must resort to
proofs, your means of proof are more effective and more satisfactory in themselves.
[11]'It is thus that you must treat your friend, thus your fellow citizen, thus your associate.' And why? 'Because it is just.' Yet I can find all that material included under the
head of Justice. I find there that fair play is desirable in itself, that we are not forced
into it by fear nor hired to that end for pay, and that no man is just who is attracted by
anything in this virtue other than the virtue itself. After convincing myself of this view
and thoroughly absorbing it, what good can I obtain from such precepts, which only
teach one who is already trained? To one who knows, it is superfluous to give precepts; to one who does not know, it is insufficient. For he must be told, not only what
he is being instructed to do, but also why. [12]I repeat, are such precepts useful to him
who has correct ideas about good and evil, or to one who has them not? The latter will
receive no benefit from you; for some idea that clashes with your counsel has already
monopolized his attention. He who has made a careful decision as to what should
be sought and what should be avoided knows what he ought to do, without a single
word from you. Therefore, that whole department of philosophy may be abolished.

[13]"There are two reasons why we go astray: either there is in the soul an evil quality
which has been brought about by wrong opinions, or, even if not possessed by false
ideas, the soul is prone to falsehood and rapidly corrupted by some outward appearance which attracts it in the wrong direction. For this reason it is our duty either to
treat carefully the diseased mind and free it from faults, or to take possession of the
mind when it is still unoccupied and yet inclined to what is evil. Both these results can
be attained by the main doctrines of philosophy; therefore the giving of such precepts
is of no use. [14]Besides, if we give forth precepts to each individual, the task is stupen-
dous. For one class of advice should be given to the financier, another to the farmer,
another to the business man, another to one who cultivates the good graces of royalty,
another to him who will seek the friendship of his equals, another to him who will
court those of lower rank. [15]In the case of marriage, you will advise one person how
he should conduct himself with a wife who before her marriage was a maiden, and
another how he should behave with a woman who had previously been wedded to
another; how the husband of a rich woman should act, or another man with a dower-
less spouse. Or do you not think that there is some difference between a barren woman
and one who bears children, between one advanced in years and a mere girl, between a
mother and a step-mother? We cannot include all the types, and yet each type requires
separate treatment; but the laws of philosophy are concise and are binding in all cases.

[16] Moreover, the precepts of wisdom should be definite and certain: when things cannot be defined, they are outside the sphere of wisdom; for wisdom knows the proper limits of things.

"We should therefore do away with this department of precepts, because it cannot afford to all what it promises only to a few; wisdom, however, embraces all. [17] Between the insanity of people in general and the insanity which is subject to medical treatment there is no difference, except that the latter is suffering from disease and the former from false opinions.[6] In the one case, the symptoms of madness may be traced to ill-health; the other is the ill-health of the mind. If one should offer precepts to a madman—how he ought to speak, how he ought to walk, how he ought to conduct himself in public and private, he would be more of a lunatic than the person whom he was advising. What is really necessary is to treat the black bile[7] and remove the essential cause of the madness. And this is what should also be done in the other case—that of the mind diseased. The madness itself must be shaken off; otherwise, your words of advice will vanish into thin air."

[18] This is what Aristo says; and I shall answer his arguments one by one. First, in opposition to what he says about one's obligation to remove that which blocks the eye and hinders the vision. I admit that such a person does not need precepts in order to see, but that he needs treatment for the curing of his eyesight and the getting rid of the hindrance that handicaps him. For it is Nature that gives us our eyesight; and he who removes obstacles restores to Nature her proper function. But Nature does not teach us our duty in every case. [19] Again, if a man's cataract is cured, he cannot, immediately after his recovery, give back their eyesight to other men also; but when we are freed from evil we can free others also. There is no need of encouragement, or even of counsel, for the eye to be able to distinguish different colours; black and white can be differentiated without prompting from another. The mind, on the other hand, needs many precepts in order to see what it should do in life; although in eye-treatment also the physician not only accomplishes the cure, but gives advice into the bargain. [20] He says: "There is no reason why you should at once expose your weak vision to a dangerous glare; begin with darkness, and then go into half-lights, and finally be more bold, accustoming yourself gradually to the bright light of day. There is no reason why you should study immediately after eating; there is no reason why you should impose hard tasks upon your eyes when they are swollen and inflamed; avoid winds and strong blasts of cold air that blow into your face,"—and other suggestions of the same sort, which are just as valuable as drugs themselves. The physician's art supplements remedies by advice.

[21] "But," comes the reply, "error is the source of sin;[8] precepts do not remove error, nor do they rout our false opinions on the subject of Good and Evil." I admit that precepts alone are not effective in overthrowing the mind's mistaken beliefs; but they do not on that account fail to be of service when they accompany other measures also. In the first place, they refresh the memory; in the second place, when sorted into their proper classes, the matters which showed themselves in a jumbled mass when considered as a whole, can be considered in this with greater care. According to our opponents'[9] theory, you might even say that consolation, and exhortation were superfluous. Yet they are not superfluous; neither, therefore, is counsel.

[22] "But it is folly," they retort, "to prescribe what a sick man ought to do, just as if he were well, when you should really restore his health; for without health precepts are not worth a jot." But have not sick men and sound men something in common, concerning which they need continual advice? For example, not to grasp greedily after food, and to avoid getting over-tired. Poor and rich have certain precepts which fit them both. [23] "Cure their greed, then," people say, "and you will not need to lecture either the poor or the rich, provided that in the case of each of them the craving has subsided." But is it not one thing to be free from lust for money, and another thing to know how to use this money? Misers do not know the proper limits in money matters, but even those who are not misers fail to comprehend its use. Then comes the reply: "Do away with error, and your precepts become unnecessary." That is wrong; for suppose that avarice is slackened, that luxury is confined, that rashness is reined in, and

with good men.[18] For the frequent seeing, the frequent hearing of them little by little sinks into the heart and acquires the force of precepts.

We are indeed uplifted merely by meeting wise men; and one can be helped by a great man even when he is silent. [41]I could not easily tell you how it helps us, though I am certain of the fact that I have received help in that way. Phaedo[19] says: "Certain tiny animals do not leave any pain when they sting us; so subtle is their power, so deceptive for purposes of harm. The bite is disclosed by a swelling, and even in the swelling there is no visible wound." That will also be your experience when dealing with wise men, you will not discover how or when the benefit comes to you, but you will discover that you have received it. [42]"What is the point of this remark?" you ask. It is, that good precepts, often welcomed within you, will benefit you just as much as good examples. Pythagoras declares that our souls experience a change when we enter a temple and behold the images of the gods face to face, and await the utterances of an oracle. [43]Moreover, who can deny that even the most inexperienced are effectively struck by the force of certain precepts? For example, by such brief but weighty saws as: "Nothing in excess," "The greedy mind is satisfied by no gains," "You must expect to be treated by others as you yourself have treated them."[20] We receive a sort if shock when we hear such sayings; no one ever thinks of doubting them or of asking "Why?" So strongly, indeed, does mere truth, unaccompanied by reason, attract us. [44]If reverence reins in the soul and checks vice, why cannot counsel do the same? Also, if rebuke gives one a sense of shame, why has not counsel the same power, even though it does use bare precepts? The counsel which assists suggestion by reason—which adds the motive for doing a given thing and the reward which awaits one who carries out and obeys such precepts is—more effective and settles deeper into the heart. If commands are helpful, so is advice. But one is helped by commands; therefore one is helped also by advice.

[45]Virtue is divided into two parts—into contemplation of truth, and conduct. Training teaches contemplation, and admonition teaches conduct. And right conduct both practises and reveals virtue. But if, when a man is about to act, he is helped by advice, he is also helped by admonition. Therefore, if right conduct is necessary to virtue, and if, moreover, admonition makes clear right conduct, then admonition also is an indispensable thing. [46]There are two strong supports to the soul—trust[21] in the truth and confidence; both are the result of admonition. For men believe it, and when belief is established, the soul receives great inspiration and is filled with confidence. Therefore, admonition is not superfluous.

Marcus Agrippa, a great-souled man, the only person among those whom the civil wars raised to fame and power whose prosperity helped the state, used to say that he was greatly indebted to the proverb "Harmony makes small things grow; lack of harmony makes great things decay."[22] [47]He held that he himself became the best of brothers and the best of friends by virtue of this saying. And if proverbs of such a kind, when welcomed intimately into the soul, can mould this very soul, why cannot the department of philosophy which consists of such proverbs possess equal influence? Virtue depends partly upon training and partly upon practice; you must learn first, and then strengthen your learning by action. If this be true, not only do the doctrines of wisdom help us but the precepts also, which check and banish our emotions by a sort of official decree.

[48]It is said: "Philosophy is divided into knowledge and state of mind. For one who has learned and understood what he should do and avoid,[23] is not a wise man until his mind is metamorphosed into the shape of that which he has learned. This third department—that of precept—is compounded from both the others, from dogmas of philosophy and state of mind. Hence it is superfluous as far as the perfecting of virtue is concerned; the other two parts are enough for the purpose." [49]On that basis, therefore, even consolation would be superfluous, since this also is a combination of the other two, as likewise are exhortation, persuasion, and even proof[24] itself. For proof also originates from a well-ordered and firm mental attitude. But, although these things result from a sound state of mind, yet the sound state of mind also results from them; it is

both creative of them and resultant from them. [50]Furthermore, that which you mention is the mark of an already perfect man, of one who has attained the height of human happiness. But the approach to these qualities is slow, and in the meantime in practical matters, the path should be pointed out for the benefit of one who is still short of perfection, but is making progress. Wisdom by her own agency may perhaps show herself this path without the help of admonition; for she has brought the soul to a stage where it can be impelled only in the right direction. Weaker characters, however, need someone to precede them, to say: "Avoid this," or "Do that." [51]Moreover, if one awaits the time when one can know of oneself what the best line of action is, one will sometimes go astray and by going astray will be hindered from arriving at the point where it is possible to be content with oneself. The soul should accordingly be guided at the very moment when it is becoming able to guide itself.[25] Boys study according to direction. Their fingers are held and guided by others so that they may follow the outlines of the letters; next, they are ordered to imitate a copy and base thereon a style of penmanship. Similarly, the mind is helped if it is taught according to direction. [52]Such facts as these prove that this department of philosophy is not superfluous.

The question next arises whether this part alone is sufficient to make men wise. The problem shall be treated at the proper time; but at present, omitting all arguments, is it not clear that we need someone whom we may call upon as our preceptor in opposition to the precepts of men in general? [53]There is no word which reaches our ears without doing us harm; we are injured both by good wishes and by curses. The angry prayers of our enemies instil false fears in us; and the affection of our friends spoils us through their kindly wishes. For this affection sets us a-groping after goods that are far away, unsure, and wavering, when we really might open the store of happiness at home. [54]We are not allowed, I maintain, to travel a straight road. Our parents and our slaves draw us into wrong. Nobody confines his mistakes to himself; people sprinkle folly among their neighbours, and receive it from them in turn. For this reason, in an individual, you find the vices of nations, because the nation has given them to the individual. Each man, in corrupting others, corrupts himself; he imbibes, and then imparts, badness the result is a vast mass of wickedness, because the worst in every separate person is concentrated in one mass.[26]

[55]We should, therefore, have a guardian, as it were, to pluck us continually by the ear and dispel rumours and protest against popular enthusiasms. For you are mistaken if you suppose that our faults are inborn in us; they have come from without, have been heaped upon us. Hence, by receiving frequent admonitions, we can reject the opinions which din about our ears. [56]Nature does not ally us with any vice; she produced us in health and freedom. She put before our eyes no object which might stir in us the itch of greed. She placed gold and silver beneath our feet, and bade those feet stamp down and crush everything that causes us to be stamped down and crushed. Nature elevated our gaze towards the sky and willed that we should look upward to behold her glorious and wonderful works. She gave us the rising and the setting sun, the whirling course of the on-rushing world which discloses the things of earth by day and the heavenly bodies by night, the movements of the stars, which are slow if you compare them with the universe, but most rapid if you reflect on the size of the orbits which they describe with unslackened speed; she showed us the successive eclipses of sun and moon, and other phenomena, wonderful because they occur regularly or because, through sudden causes they help into view—such as nightly trails of fire, or flashes in the open heavens unaccompanied by stroke or sound of thunder, or columns and beams and the various phenomena of flames.[27] [57]She ordained that all these bodies should proceed above our heads; but gold and silver, with the iron which, because of the gold and silver, never brings peace, she has hidden away, as if they were dangerous things to trust to our keeping. It is we ourselves that have dragged them into the light of day to the end that we might fight over them; it is we ourselves who, tearing away the superincumbent earth, have dug out the causes and tools of our own destruction; it is we ourselves who have attributed our own misdeeds to Fortune, and do not blush to regard as the loftiest objects those which once lay in the depths of earth.

[58]Do you wish to know how false is the gleam[28] that has deceived your eyes? There is really nothing fouler or more involved in darkness than these things of earth, sunk and covered for so long a time in the mud where they belong. Of course they are foul; they have been hauled out through a long and murky mine-shaft. There is nothing uglier than these metals during the process of refinement and separation from the ore. Furthermore, watch the very workmen who must handle and sift the barren grade of dirt, the sort which comes from the bottom; see how soot-besmeared they are! [59]And yet the stuff they handle soils the soul more than the body, and there is more foulness in the owner than in the workman.

It is therefore indispensable that we be admonished, that we have some advocate with upright mind, and, amid all the uproar and jangle of falsehood, hear one voice only. But what voice shall this be? Surely a voice which, amid all the tumult of self-seeking, shall whisper wholesome words into the deafened ear, saying: [60]"You need not be envious of those whom the people call great and fortunate; applause need not disturb your composed attitude and your sanity of mind; you need not become disgusted with your calm spirit because you see a great man, clothed in purple, protected by the well-known symbols of authority;[29] you need not judge the magistrate for whom the road is cleared to be any happier than yourself, whom his officer pushes from the road. If you would wield a command that is profitable to yourself, and injurious to nobody, clear your own faults out of the way. [61]There are many who set fire to cities, who storm garrisons that have remained impregnable for generations and safe for numerous ages, who raise mounds as high as the walls they are besieging, who with battering-rams and engines shatter towers that have been reared to a wondrous height. There are many who can send their columns ahead and press destructively upon the rear of the foe, who can reach the Great Sea[30] dripping with the blood of nations; but even these men, before they could conquer their foe, were conquered by their own greed. No one withstood their attack; but they themselves could not withstand desire for power and the impulse to cruelty; at the time when they seemed to be hounding others, they were themselves being hounded. [62]Alexander was hounded into misfortune and dispatched to unknown countries by a mad desire to lay waste other men's territory. Do you believe that the man was in his senses who could begin by devastating Greece, the land where he received his education? One who snatched away the dearest guerdon of each nation, bidding Spartans be slaves, and Athenians hold their tongues? Not content with the ruin of all the states which Philip had either conquered or bribed into bondage,[31] he overthrew various commonwealths in various places and carried his weapons all over the world; his cruelty was tired, but it never ceased–like a wild beast that tears to pieces more than its hunger demands. [63]Already he has joined many kingdoms into one kingdom; already Greeks and Persians fear the same lord; already nations Darius had left free submit to the yoke:[32] yet he passes beyond the Ocean and the Sun, deeming it shame that he should shift his course of victory from the paths which Hercules and Bacchus had trod;[33] he threatens violence to Nature herself. He does not wish to go; but he cannot stay; he is like a weight that falls headlong, its course ending only when it lies motionless.

[64]It was not virtue or reason which persuaded Gnaeus Pompeius to take part in foreign and civil warfare; it was his mad craving for unreal glory. Now he attacked Spain and the faction of Sertorius;[34] now he fared forth to enchain the pirates and subdue the seas.[35] These were merely excuses and pretexts for extending his power. [65]What drew him into Africa, into the North, against Mithridates, into Armenia and all the corners of Asia?[36] Assuredly it was his boundless desire to grow bigger; for only in his own eyes was he not great enough. And what impelled Gaius Caesar to the combined ruin of himself and of the state? Renown, self-seeking, and the setting no limit to pre-eminence over all other men. He could not allow a single person to outrank him, although the state allowed two men to stand at its head. [66]Do you think that Gaius Marius, who was once consul[37] (he received this office on one occasion, and stole it on all the others) courted all his perils by the inspiration of virtue when he was slaughtering the Teutons and the Cimbri, and pursuing Jugurtha through the wilds of Africa?[38] Marius

commanded armies, ambition Marius.

[67]When such men as these[39] were disturbing the world, they were themselves disturbed–like cyclones that whirl together what they have seized, but which are first whirled themselves and can for this reason rush on with all the greater force, having no control over themselves; hence, after causing such destruction to others, they feel in their own body the ruinous force which has enabled them to cause havoc to many. You need never believe that a man can become happy through the unhappiness of another. [68]We must unravel all such cases[39] as are forced before our eyes and crammed into our ears; we must clear out our hearts, for they are full of evil talk. Virtue must be conducted into the place these have seized,–a kind of virtue which may root out falsehood and doctrines which contravene the truth, or may sunder us from the throng, in which we put too great trust, and may restore us to the possession of sound opinions. For this is wisdom–a return to Nature and a restoration to the condition from which man's errors have driven us. [69]It is a great part of health to have forsaken the counsellors of madness and to have fled far from a companionship that is mutually baneful.

That you may know the truth of my remark, see how different is each individual's life before the public from that of his inner self. A quiet life does not of itself give lessons in upright conduct; the countryside does not of itself teach plain living; no, but when witnesses and onlookers are removed, faults which ripen in publicity and display sink into the background. [70]Who puts on the purple robe for the sake of flaunting it in no man's eyes? Who uses gold plate when he dines alone? Who, as he flings himself down beneath the shadow of some rustic tree, displays in solitude the splendour of his luxury? No one makes himself elegant only for his own beholding, or even for the admiration of a few friends or relatives. Rather does he spread out his well-appointed vices in proportion to the size of the admiring crowd. [71]It is so: claqueurs and witnesses are irritants of all our mad foibles. You can make us cease to crave, if you only make us cease to display. Ambition, luxury, and waywardness need a stage to act upon; you will cure all those ills if you seek retirement.

[72]Therefore, if our dwelling is situated amid the din of a city, there should be an adviser standing near us. When men praise great incomes, he should praise the person who can be rich with a slender estate and measures his wealth by the use he makes of it. In the face of those who glorify influence and power, he should of his own volition recommend a leisure devoted to study, and a soul which has left the external and found itself. [73]He should point out persons, happy in the popular estimation, who totter on their envied heights of power, who are dismayed and hold a far different opinion of themselves from what others hold of them. That which others think elevated, is to them a sheer precipice. Hence they are frightened and in a flutter whenever they look down the abrupt steep of their greatness. For they reflect that there are various ways of falling and that the topmost point is the most slippery. [74]Then they fear that for which they strove, and the good fortune which made them weighty in the eyes of others weighs more heavily upon themselves. Then they praise easy leisure and independence; they hate the glamour and try to escape while their fortunes are still unimpaired. Then at last you may see them studying philosophy amid their fear, and hunting sound advice when their fortunes go awry. For these two things are, as it were, at opposite poles–good fortune and good sense; that is why we are wiser when in the midst of adversity. It is prosperity that takes away righteousness. Farewell.

Footnotes

1. For technical terms in Epp. xciv. and xcv. see Appendix.

2. See Cicero, *De Off.* i. 3. 7 ff. for a full discussion of principles and duties. As one would expect, the Romans were more interested in practical precepts than were the Greeks.

3. Frag. 358 von Arnim.

4. In other words, that it is one of the "external" things, *media, indifferentia.*

5. Compare, among similar passages, Ep. xxiv. 14 *levis es, si ferre possum, brevis es, si ferre non possum.*

6. For the same figure, in the same connexion, see Ep. lxviii. 8 *in pectore ipso collectio et vomica est.*

7. By means of hellebore, Lat. *veratrum*, the favourite cathartic of the ancients.

8. This is in harmony with the idea of Socrates; sin is a lack of knowledge regarding what is true and what is false.

9. i.e., Aristo and others.

10. *monitio* includes *consolatio, dissuasio, obiurgatio, laudatio,* and *hortatio.* Cf. § 39 of this letter

11. Quoted also by Quintilian, vi. 1. 13. Between the years 58 and 54 B.C Calvus, a friend of the poet Catullus, in three famous speeches prosecuted Vatinius, one of the creatures of Caesar who had illegally obtained office.

12. *Catonis Reliq.* p. 79 Iordan.

13. From Publilius Syrus–Frag. 250 Ribbeck.

14. A verse made up from Vergil, *Aen.* x. 284, and an unknown author.

15. i.e. who would abolish precepts.

16. A further answer to the objection in § 17 above, where all madness is held curable by physical treatment.

17. See, for example, the Fifth Book, which opens with the preliminary remarks of the Athenian Stranger (pp. 726-34 St.).

18. A frequent thought in Seneca, cf. Ep. xxv. 6, lii. 8, etc.

19. Presumably Phaedo the friend of Plato and pupil of Socrates, author of dialogues resembling those of Plato.

20. Com. incert., Frag. 81 Ribbeck, and Pub. Syrus, Frag. 2 Ribbeck.

21. i.e., belief.

22. From Sallust, *Jugurtha*, x. 6.

23. Cf. Ep. xciv. 12 *exactum indicium de fugiendis petendisque.*

24. The last stage of knowledge–complete assent–according to the Stoic view, which went beyond the mere sensation-theory of Epicurus.

25. In this whole discussion Seneca is a much sounder Stoic than Aristo and the opposition. The next letter (Ep. xcv.) develops still further the preceptive function of philosophy–through προκοπή (progress) to μεταβολή (conversion).

26. This theme is carefully elaborated in Ep. vii., "On Crowds": "There is no person who does not make some vice attractive to us, or stamp it upon us, or taint us unconsciously therewith" (§ 2).

27. These are fully discussed in Seneca's *Naturales Quaestiones*, a work almost contemporary with the Letters.

28. Both literally and figuratively,–the sheen of the metal and the glitter of the false idea.

29. i.e., the bundle of rods and axes, carried by the attendants of a Roman magistrate.

30. A name usually applied to the eastern end of the Mediterranean.

31. Especially Thebes in 335 B.C, which he sacked. Athens and Sparta were treated with more consideration.

32. i.e., the Hyrcanians, and other tribes attacked during and after 330 B.C

33. Heracles in his various forms hails all the way from Tyre to the Atlantic Ocean; Dionysus from India through Lydia, Thrace, and the Eastern Mediterranean to Greece.

34. 76 B.C

35. 67 B.C

36. Beginning with the passage of the Manilian Law of 66 B.C

37. 107 B.C (also 104, 103, 102, 101, 100, and 86).

38. 102 and 101 B.C at Aquae Sextiae and Vercellae; the Jugurthine war lasted from 109 to 106 B.C

39. i.e., as Pompeius, Caesar, Marius.

XCV. ON THE USEFULNESS OF BASIC PRINCIPLES

¹You keep asking me to explain without postponement¹ a topic which I once remarked should be put off until the proper time, and to inform you by letter whether this department of philosophy which the Greeks call *paraenetic*,² and we Romans call the "preceptorial," is enough to give us perfect wisdom. Now I know that you will take it in good part if I refuse to do so. But I accept your request all the more willingly, and refuse to let the common saying lose its point:

> Don't ask for what you'll wish you hadn't got.

²For sometimes we seek with effort that which we should decline if offered voluntarily. Call that fickleness or call it pettishness,³–we must punish the habit by ready compliance. There are many things that we would have men think that we wish, but that we really do not wish. A lecturer sometimes brings upon the platform a huge work of research, written in the tiniest hand and very closely folded; after reading off a large portion, he says: "I shall stop, if you wish;" and a shout arises: "Read on, read on!" from the lips of those who are anxious for the speaker to hold his peace then and there. We often want one thing and pray for another, not telling the truth even to the gods, while the gods either do not hearken, or else take pity on us. ³But I shall without pity avenge myself and shall load a huge letter upon your shoulders; for your part, if you read it with reluctance, you may say: "I brought this burden upon myself," and may class yourself among those men whose too ambitious wives drive them frantic, or those whom riches harass, earned by extreme sweat of the brow, or those who are tortured with the titles which they have sought by every sort of device and toil, and all others who are responsible for their own misfortunes.

⁴But I must stop this preamble and approach the problem under consideration. Men say: "The happy life consists in upright conduct; precepts guide one to upright conduct; therefore precepts are sufficient for attaining the happy life." But they do not always guide us to upright conduct; this occurs only when the will is receptive; and sometimes they are applied in vain, when wrong opinions obsess the soul. ⁵Furthermore, a man may act rightly without knowing that he is acting rightly. For nobody, except he be trained from the start and equipped with complete reason, can develop to perfect proportions, understanding when he should do certain things, and to what extent, and in whose company, and how, and why. Without such training a man cannot strive with all his heart after that which is honourable, or even with steadiness or gladness, but will ever be looking back and wavering.

⁶It is also said: "If honourable conduct results from precepts, then precepts are amply sufficient for the happy life; but the first of these statements is true; therefore the second is true also." We shall reply to these words that honourable conduct is, to be sure, brought about by precepts, but not by precepts alone. ⁷"Then," comes the reply, "if the other arts are content with precepts, wisdom will also be content therewith; for wisdom itself is an art of living. And yet the pilot is made by precepts which tell him thus and so to turn the tiller, set his sails, make use of a fair wind, tack, make the best of shifting and variable breezes–all in the proper manner. Other craftsmen also are drilled by precepts; hence precepts will be able to accomplish the same result in the case of our craftsman in the art of living." ⁸Now all these arts are concerned with the tools of life, but not with life as a whole.⁴ Hence there is much to clog these arts from without and to complicate them–such as hope, greed, fear. But that art⁵ which professes to teach the art of life cannot be forbidden by any circumstance from exercising its functions; for it shakes off complications and pierces through obstacles. Would you like to know how unlike its status is to the other arts? In the case of the latter, it is more pardonable to err voluntarily rather than by accident; but in the case of wisdom the worst fault is to commit sin wilfully. ⁹I mean something like this: A scholar will blush for shame, not if he makes a grammatical blunder intentionally, but if he makes it unintentionally; if a physician does not recognize that his patient is failing, he is a much

dishes which a man swallows almost burning from the kitchen fire, are quenched in
the digestive system without doing harm? How repulsive, then, and how unhealthy
are their belchings, and how disgusted men are with themselves when they breathe
forth the fumes of yesterday's debauch! You may be sure that their food is not being
digested, but is rotting.
²⁶I remember once hearing gossip about a notorious dish into which everything
over which epicures love to dally had been heaped together by a cookshop that was
fast rushing into bankruptcy; there were two kinds of mussels, and oysters trimmed
round at the line where they are edible, set off at intervals by sea-urchins; the whole
was flanked by mullets cut up and served without the bones. ²⁷In these days we are
ashamed of separate foods; people mix many flavours into one. The dinner table does
work which the stomach ought to do. I look forward next to food being served mas-
ticated! And how little we are from it already when we pick out shells and bones and
the cook performs the office of the teeth!

They say: "It is too much trouble to take our luxuries one by one; let us have everything served at the same time and blended into the same flavour. Why should I
help myself to a single dish? Let us have many coming to the table at once; the dainties
of various courses should be combined and confounded. ²⁸Those who used to declare
that this was done for display and notoriety should understand that it is not done for
show, but that it is an oblation to our sense of duty! Let us have at one time, drenched
in the same sauce, the dishes that are usually served separately. Let there be no difference: let oysters, sea-urchins, shell-fish, and mullets be mixed together and cooked
in the same dish." No vomited food could be jumbled up more helter-skelter. ²⁹And
as the food itself is complicated, so the resulting diseases are complex, unaccountable,
manifold, variegated; medicine has begun to campaign against them in many ways
and by many rules of treatment.

Now I declare to you that the same statement applies to philosophy. It was once
more simple because men's sins were on a smaller scale, and could be cured with
but slight trouble; in the face, however, of all this moral topsy-turvy men must leave
no remedy untried. And would that this pest might so at last be overcome! ³⁰We are
mad, not only individually, but nationally. We check manslaughter and isolated mur-
ders; but what of war and the much-vaunted crime of slaughtering whole peoples?
There are no limits to our greed, none to our cruelty. And as long as such crimes are
committed by stealth and by individuals, they are less harmful and less portentous;
but cruelties are practised in accordance with acts of senate and popular assembly,
and the public is bidden to do that which is forbidden to the individual. ³¹Deeds that
would be punished by loss of life when committed in secret, are praised by us because
uniformed generals have carried them out. Man, naturally the gentlest class of being,
is not ashamed to revel in the blood of others, to wage war, and to entrust the waging
of war to his sons, when even dumb beasts and wild beasts keep the peace with one
another. ³²Against this overmastering and widespread madness philosophy has become a matter of greater effort, and has taken on strength in proportion to the strength
which is gained by the opposition forces.

It used to be easy to scold men who were slaves to drink and who sought out more
luxurious food; it did not require a mighty effort to bring the spirit back to the simplicity from which it had departed only slightly. But now

³³One needs the rapid hand, the master-craft.¹⁶

Men seek pleasure from every source. No vice remains within its limits; luxury
is precipitated into greed. We are overwhelmed with forgetfulness of that which is
honourable. Nothing that has an attractive value, is base. Man, an object of reverence
in the eyes of man, is now slaughtered for jest and sport; and those whom it used to
be unholy to train for the purpose of inflicting and enduring wounds, are thrust forth
exposed and defenceless; and it is a satisfying spectacle to see a man made a corpse.

³⁴Amid this upset condition of morals, something stronger than usual is needed,–
something which will shake off these chronic ills; in order to root out a deep-seated
belief in wrong ideas, conduct must be regulated by doctrines. It is only when we add

precepts, consolation, and encouragement to these, that they can prevail; by themselves they are ineffective. [35] If we would hold men firmly bound and tear them away from the ills which clutch them fast, they must learn what is evil and what is good. They must know that everything except virtue changes its name and becomes now good and now bad. Just as the soldier's primary bond of union is his oath of allegiance and his love for the flag, and a horror of desertion, and just as, after this stage, other duties can easily be demanded of him, and trusts given to him when once the oath[17] has been administered; so it is with those whom you would bring to the happy life: the first foundations must be laid, and virtue worked into these men. Let them be held by a sort of superstitious worship of virtue; let them love her; let them desire to live with her, and refuse to live without her.

[36] "But what, then," people say, "have not certain persons won their way to excellence without complicated training? Have they not made great progress by obeying bare precepts alone?"[18] Very true; but their temperaments were propitious, and they snatched salvation as it were by the way. For just as the immortal gods did not learn virtue having been born with virtue complete, and containing in their nature the essence of goodness—even so certain men are fitted with unusual qualities and reach without a long apprenticeship that which is ordinarily a matter of teaching, welcoming honourable things as soon as they hear them. Hence come the choice minds which seize quickly upon virtue, or else produce it from within themselves. But your dull, sluggish fellow, who is hampered by his evil habits, must have this soul-rust incessantly rubbed off. [37] Now, as the former sort, who are inclined towards the good, can be raised to the heights more quickly: so the weaker spirits will be assisted and freed from their evil opinions if we entrust to them the accepted principles of philosophy; and you may understand how essential these principles are in the following way. Certain things sink into us, rendering us sluggish in some ways, and hasty in others. These two qualities, the one of recklessness and the other of sloth, cannot be respectively checked or roused unless we remove their causes, which are mistaken admiration and mistaken fear. As long as we are obsessed by such feelings, you may say to us: "You owe this duty to your father, this to your children, this to your friends, this to your guests"; but greed will always hold us back, no matter how we try. A man may know that he should fight for his country, but fear will dissuade him. A man may know that he should sweat forth his last drop of energy on behalf of his friends, but luxury will forbid. A man may know that keeping a mistress is the worst kind of insult to his wife, but lust will drive him in the opposite direction. [38] It will therefore be of no avail to give precepts unless you first remove the conditions that are likely to stand in the way of precepts; it will do no more good than to place weapons by your side and bring yourself near the foe without having your hands free to use those weapons. The soul, in order to deal with the precepts which we offer, must first be set free. [39] Suppose that a man is acting as he should; he cannot keep it up continuously or consistently, since he will not know the reason for so acting. Some of his conduct will result rightly because of luck or practice; but there will be in his hand no rule by which he may regulate his acts, and which he may trust to tell him whether that which he has done is right. One who is good through mere chance will not give promise of retaining such a character for ever. [40] Furthermore, precepts will perhaps help you to do what should be done; but they will not help you to do it in the proper way; and if they do not help you to this end, they do not conduct you to virtue. I grant you that, if warned, a man will do what he should; but that is not enough, since the credit lies, not in the actual deed, but in the way it is done. [41] What is more shameful than a costly meal which eats away the income even of a knight? Or what so worthy of the censor's condemnation[19] as to be always indulging oneself and one's "inner man,"[20] if I may speak as the gluttons do? And yet often has an inaugural dinner cost the most careful man a cool million! The very sum that is called disgraceful if spent on the appetite, is beyond reproach if spent for official purposes! For it is not luxury but an expenditure sanctioned by custom.

[42] A mullet of monstrous size was presented to the Emperor Tiberius. They say it weighed four and one half pounds (and why should I not tickle the palates of certain

stand that these doctrines are proved by the very arguments through which they seem to disprove them. For what are these men saying? They are saying that precepts are sufficient to develop life, and that the doctrines of wisdom (in other words, dogmas) are superfluous. And yet this very utterance of theirs is a doctrine just as if I should now remark that one must dispense with precepts on the ground that they are super-fluous, that one must make use of doctrines, and that our studies should be directed solely towards this end; thus, by my very statement that precepts should not be tak-en seriously, I should be uttering a precept. [61] There are certain matters in philosophy which need admonition; there are others which need proof, and a great deal of proof, too, because they are complicated and can scarcely be made clear with the greatest care and the greatest dialectic skill. If proofs are necessary, so are doctrines; for doctrines deduce the truth by reasoning. Some matters are clear, and others are vague: those which the senses and the memory can embrace are clear; those which are outside their scope are vague.

But reason is not satisfied by obvious facts; its higher and nobler function is to deal with hidden things. Hidden things need proof; proof cannot come without doc-trines; therefore, doctrines are necessary. [62] That which leads to a general agreement, and likewise to a perfect one,[27] is an assured belief in certain facts; but if, lacking this assurance, all things are adrift in our minds, then doctrines are indispensable; for they give to our minds the means of unswerving decision. [63] Furthermore, when we advise a man to regard his friends as highly as himself, to reflect that an enemy may become a friend,[28] to stimulate love in the friend, and to check hatred in the enemy, we add: "This is just and honourable." Now the just and honourable element in our doctrines is em-braced by reason; hence reason is necessary; for without it the doctrines cannot exist, either. [64] But let us unite the two. For indeed branches are useless without their roots, and the roots themselves are strengthened by the growths which they have produced. Everyone can understand how useful the hands are; they obviously help us. But the heart, the source of the hands growth and power and motion, is hidden. And I can say the same thing about precepts: they are manifest, while the doctrines of wisdom are concealed. And as only the initiated[29] know the more hallowed portion of the rites, so in philosophy the hidden truths are revealed only to those who are members and have been admitted to the sacred rites. But precepts and other such matters are familiar even to the uninitiated.

[65] Posidonius holds that not only precept-giving (there is nothing to prevent my using this word), but even persuasion, consolation, and encouragement, are necessary. To these he adds the *investigation of causes* (but I fail to see why I should not dare to call it *aetiology*, since the scholars who mount guard over the Latin language thus use the term as having the right to do so). He remarks that it will also be useful to illustrate each particular virtue; this science Posidonius calls *ethology*, while others call it *charac-terization*.[30] It gives the signs and marks which belong to each virtue and vice, so that by them distinction may be drawn between like things. [66] Its function is the same as that of precept. For he who utters precepts says: "If you would have self-control, act thus and so!" He who illustrates, says "The man who acts thus and so, and refrains from certain other things, possesses self-control." If you ask what the difference here is, I say that the one gives the precepts of virtue, the other its embodiment. These illustrations, or, to use a commercial term, these *samples*, have, I confess, a certain utility; just put them up for exhibition well recommended, and you will find men to copy them. [67] Would you, for instance, deem it a useful thing to have evidence given you by which you may recognize a thoroughbred horse, and not be cheated in your purchase or waste your time over a low-bred animal?[31] But how much more useful it is to know the marks of a surpassingly fine soul–marks which one may appropriate from another for oneself!

> [68] Straightway the foal of the high-bred drove, nursed up in the pastures,
> Marches with spirited step, and treads with a delicate motion;
> First on the dangerous pathway and into the threatening river,
> Trusting himself to the unknown bridge, without fear at its creakings,
> Neck thrown high in the air, and clear-cut head, and a belly

Spare, back rounded, and breast abounding in courage and muscle.
He, when the clashing of weapons is heard to resound in the distance,
Leaps from his place, and pricks up his ears, and all in a tremble
Pours forth the pent-up fire that lay close-shut in his nostrils.[32]

[69] Vergil's description, though referring to something else, might perfectly well be the portrayal of a brave man; at any rate, I myself should select no other simile for a hero. If I had to describe Cato, who was unterrified amid the din of civil war, who was first to attack the armies that were already making for the Alps, who plunged face-forward into the civil conflict, this is exactly the sort of expression and attitude which I should give him. [70] Surely none could "march with more spirited step" than one who rose against Caesar and Pompey at the same time and, when some were supporting Caesar's party and others that of Pompey, issued a challenge to both leaders,[33] thus showing that the republic also had some backers. For it is not enough to say of Cato "without fear at its creakings." Of course he is not afraid! He does not quail before real and imminent noises; in the face of ten legions, Gallic auxiliaries, and a motley host of citizens and foreigners, he utters words fraught with freedom, encouraging the Republic not to fail in the struggle for freedom, but to try all hazards; he declares that it is more honourable to fall into servitude than to fall in line with it. [71] What force and energy are his! What confidence he displays amid the general panic! He knows that he is the only one whose standing is not in question, and that men do not ask whether Cato is free, but whether he is still *among* the free. Hence his contempt for danger and the sword. What a pleasure it is to say, in admiration of the unflinching steadiness of a hero who did not totter when the whole state was in ruins:

A breast abounding in courage and muscle!

[72] It will be helpful not only to state what is the usual quality of good men, and to outline their figures and features, but also to relate and set forth what men there have been of this kind. We might picture that last and bravest wound of Cato's, through which Freedom breathed her last; or the wise Laelius and his harmonious life with his friend Scipio; or the noble deeds of the Elder Cato at home and abroad; or the wooden couches of Tubero, spread at a public feast, goatskins instead of tapestry, and vessels of earthenware set out for the banquet before the very shrine of Jupiter! What else was this except consecrating poverty on the Capitol? Though I know no other deed of his for which to rank him with the Catos, is this one not enough? It was a censorship, not a banquet.[34] [73] How lamentably do those who covet glory fail to understand what glory is, or in what way it should be sought! On that day the Roman populace viewed the furniture of many men; it marvelled only at that of one! The gold and silver of all the others has been broken up and melted down times without number; but Tubero's earthenware will endure throughout eternity. Farewell.

Footnotes

1. Literally, to pay money on the spot or perform a task without delay.

2. i.e., the department of "advice by precepts," discussed in the preceding letter from another angle. The Greek term is nearest to the Latin sub-division *hortatio*.

3. i.e., the pertness of a home-bred slave (*verna*).

4. The argument here is similar to Ep. lxxxviii. 20 *hae . . . artes ad instrumenta vitae plurimum conferunt, tamen ad virtutem non pertinent*.

5. i.e., philosophy.

6. Hippocrates belonged to the "Clinical" School; Asclepiades and his pupil Themison to the "Methodical." See Index of Proper Names.

7. "Axioms" and "postulates."

8. i. 54 ff.

9. Whether *elementa* and *membra* mean "letters and clauses" or "matter and forms of matter" is difficult to say.

10. i.e., before the advent of any theoretical philosophy.

jests like these he got off unpunished who before the trial was an adulterer, during the trial a pander, and who escaped conviction more vilely than he deserved it.

[7]Do you believe that anything could be more disgraceful than such moral standards–when lust could not keep its hands either from religious worship or from the courts of law, when, in the very inquiry which was held in special session by order of the Senate, more crime was committed than investigated? The question at issue was whether one could be safe after committing adultery; it was shown that one could not be safe without committing adultery! [8]All this bargaining took place in the presence of Pompey and Caesar, of Cicero and Cato,–yes, that very Cato whose presence, it is said, caused the people to refrain from demanding the usual quips and cranks of naked actresses at the Floralia,[4]–if you can believe that men were stricter in their conduct at a festival than in a court-room! Such things will be done in the future, as they have been done in the past; and the licentiousness of cities will sometimes abate through discipline and fear, never of itself.

[9]Therefore, you need not believe that it is we who have yielded most to lust and least to law. For young men of to-day live far more simple lives than those of an epoch when a defendant would plead not guilty to an adultery charge before his judges, and his judges admit it before the defendant, when debauchery was practised to secure a verdict, and when Clodius, befriended by the very vices of which he was guilty, played the procurer during the actual hearing of the case. Could one believe this? He to whom one adultery brought condemnation was acquitted because of many. [10]All ages will produce men like Clodius, but not all ages men like Cato. We degenerate easily, because we lack neither guides nor associates in our wickedness, and the wickedness goes on of itself, even without guides or associates. The road to vice is not only downhill, but steep; and many men are rendered incorrigible by the fact that, while in all other crafts errors bring shame to good craftsmen and cause vexation to those who go astray, the errors of life are a positive source of pleasure. [11]The pilot is not glad when his ship is thrown on her beam-ends; the physician is not glad when he buries his patient; the orator is not glad when the defendant loses a case through the fault of his advocate; but on the other hand every man enjoys his own crimes. A. delights in an intrigue–for it was the very difficulty which attracted him thereto. B. delights in forgery and theft, and is only displeased with his sin when his sin has failed to hit the mark. And all this is the result of perverted habits.

[12]Conversely, however, in order that you may know that there is an idea of good conduct present subconsciously in souls which have been led even into the most depraved ways, and that men are not ignorant of what evil is but indifferent–I say that all men hide their sins, and, even though the issue be successful, enjoy the results while concealing the sins themselves. A good conscience, however, wishes to come forth and be seen of men; wickedness fears the very shadows. [13]Hence I hold Epicurus's saying[5] to be most apt: "That the guilty may haply remain hidden is possible, that he should be sure of remaining hidden is not possible," or, if you think that the meaning can be made more clear in this way: "The reason that it is no advantage to wrong-doers to remain hidden is that even though they have the good fortune they have not the assurance of remaining so." This is what I mean: crimes can be well guarded; free from anxiety they cannot be.

[14]This view, I maintain, is not at variance with the principles of our school, if it be so explained. And why? Because the first and worst penalty of sin is to have committed sin; and crime, though Fortune deck it out with her favours, though she protect and take it in her charge, can never go unpunished; since the punishment of crime lies in the crime itself. But none the less do these second penalties press close upon the heels of the first–constant fear, constant terror, and distrust in one's own security.

Why, then, should I set wickedness free from such a punishment? Why should I not always leave it trembling in the balance? [15]Let us disagree with Epicurus on the one point, when he declares that there is no natural justice, and that crime should be avoided because one cannot escape the fear which results therefrom; let us agree with him on the other–that bad deeds are lashed by the whip of conscience, and that conscience is tortured to the greatest degree because unending anxiety drives and whips it on, and it cannot rely upon the guarantors of its own peace of mind. For this, Epicurus, is the very proof that we are by nature reluctant to commit crime, because even in circumstances of safety there is no one who does not feel fear. [16]Good luck frees many men from punishment, but no man from fear. And why should this be if it were not that we have engrained in us a loathing for that which Nature has condemned? Hence even men who hide their sins can never count upon remaining hidden; for their conscience convicts them and reveals them to themselves. But it is the property of guilt to be in fear. It had gone ill with us, owing to the many crimes which escape the vengeance of the law and the prescribed punishments, were it not that those grievous offences against nature must pay the penalty in ready money, and that in place of suffering the punishment comes fear. Farewell.

Footnotes

1. For the best account of this scandal see Plutarch, *Caesar*, ix. f.

2. From *stilla* "a drop." The phrase is equivalent to our proverbial "last straw."

3. *Epp. ad Atticum*, i. 16.

4. A plebeian festival, held April 28, in honour of Flora, an Italian divinity connected with Ceres and Venus. For the story of Cato (55 B.C.) see Valer. Max. ii. 10. 8.

5. Epic., Frag. 532 Usener.

XCVIII. ON THE FICKLENESS OF FORTUNE

[1]You need never believe that anyone who depends upon happiness is happy! It is a fragile support–this delight in adventitious things; the joy which entered from without will some day depart. But that joy which springs wholly from oneself is leal and sound; it increases and attends us to the last; while all other things which provoke the admiration of the crowd are but temporary Goods. You may reply: "What do you mean? Cannot such things serve both for utility and for delight?" Of course. But only if they depend on us, and not we on them. [2]All things that Fortune looks upon become productive and pleasant, only if he who possesses them is in possession also of himself, and is not in the power of that which belongs to him.[1] For men make a mistake, my dear Lucilius, if they hold that anything good, or evil either, is bestowed upon us by Fortune; it is simply the raw material of Goods and Ills that she gives to us–the sources of things which, in our keeping, will develop into good or ill. For the soul is more powerful than any sort of Fortune; by its own agency it guides its affairs in either direction, and of its own power it can produce a happy life, or a wretched one.

[3]A bad man makes everything bad–even things which had come with the appearance of what is best; but the upright and honest man corrects the wrongs of Fortune, and softens hardship and bitterness because he knows how to endure them; he likewise accepts prosperity with appreciation and moderation, and stands up against trouble with steadiness and courage. Though a man be prudent, though he conduct all his interests with well-balanced judgment, though he attempt nothing beyond his strength, he will not attain the Good which is unalloyed and beyond the reach of threats, unless he is sure in dealing with that which is unsure. [4]For whether you prefer to observe other men (and it is easier to make up one's mind when judging the affairs of others), or whether you observe yourself, with all prejudice laid aside, you will perceive and acknowledge that there is no utility in all these desirable and beloved things, unless you equip yourself in opposition to the fickleness of chance and its consequences, and unless you repeat to yourself often and uncomplainingly, at every mishap, the words: "Heaven decreed it otherwise!"[2] [5]Nay rather, to adopt a phrase which is braver and nearer the truth–one on which you may more safely prop your spirit–say to yourself, whenever things turn out contrary to your expectation: "Heaven decreed *better*!"

If you are thus poised, nothing will affect you and a man will be thus poised if he reflects on the possible ups and downs in human affairs before he feels their force, and

if he comes to regard children, or wife, or property, with the idea that he will not necessarily possess them always and that he will not be any more wretched just because
he ceases to possess them. [6]It is tragic for the soul to be apprehensive of the future and
wretched in anticipation of wretchedness, consumed with an anxious desire that the
objects which give pleasure may remain in its possession to the very end. For such
a soul will never be at rest; in waiting for the future it will lose the present blessings
which it might enjoy. And there is no difference between grief for something lost and
the fear of losing it.

[7]But I do not for this reason advise you to be indifferent. Rather do you turn aside
from you whatever may cause fear. Be sure to foresee whatever can be foreseen by
planning. Observe and avoid, long before it happens, anything that is likely to do
you harm. To effect this your best assistance will be a spirit of confidence and a mind
strongly resolved to endure all things. He who can bear Fortune, can also beware of
Fortune. At any rate, there is no dashing of billows when the sea is calm. And there is
nothing more wretched or foolish than premature fear. What madness it is to anticipate one's troubles! [8]In fine, to express my thoughts in brief compass and portray to
you those busybodies and self-tormentors–they are as uncontrolled in the midst of
their troubles as they are before them. He suffers more than is necessary, who suffers
before it is necessary; such men do not weigh the amount of their suffering, by reason
of the same failing which prevents them from being ready for it; and with the same
lack of restraint they fondly imagine that their luck will last for ever, and fondly imagine that their gains are bound to increase as well as merely continue. They forget this
spring-board[3] on which mortal things are tossed, and they guarantee for themselves
exclusively a steady continuance of the gifts of chance.

[9]For this very reason I regard as excellent the saying[4] of Metrodorus, in a letter of
consolation to his sister on the loss of her son, a lad of great promise: "All the Good of
mortals is mortal." He is referring to those Goods towards which men rush in shoals.
For the real Good does not perish; it is certain and lasting and it consists of wisdom
and virtue; it is the only immortal thing that falls to mortal lot. [10]But men are so wayward, and so forgetful of their goal and of the point toward which every day jostles
them, that they are surprised at losing anything, although some day they are bound
to lose everything. Anything of which you are entitled the owner is in your possession
but is not your own; for there is no strength in that which is weak, nor anything lasting
and invincible in that which is frail. We must lose our lives as surely as we lose our
property, and this, if we understand the truth, is itself a consolation. Lose it with equanimity; for you must lose your life also.

[11]What resource do we find, then, in the face of these losses? Simply this–to keep
in memory the things we have lost, and not to suffer the enjoyment which we have
derived from them to pass away along with them. To have may be taken from us, to
have had, never. A man is thankless in the highest degree if, after losing something,
he feels no obligation for having received it. Chance robs us of the thing, but leaves us
its use and its enjoyment–and we have lost this if we are so unfair as to regret. [12]Just
say to yourself: "Of all these experiences that seem so frightful, none is insuperable.
Separate trials have been overcome by many: fire by Mucius, crucifixion by Regulus,
poison by Socrates, exile by Rutilius, and a sword-inflicted death by Cato; therefore, let
us also overcome something." [13]Again, those objects which attract the crowd under the
appearance of beauty and happiness, have been scorned by many men and on many
occasions. Fabricius when he was general refused riches,[5] and when he was censor
branded them with disapproval. Tubero deemed poverty worthy both of himself and
of the deity on the Capitol when, by the use of earthenware dishes at a public festival,
he showed that man should be satisfied with that which the gods could still use.[6] The
elder Sextius rejected the honours of office;[7] he was born with an obligation to take part
in public affairs, and yet would not accept the broad stripe even when the deified Ju-
lius offered it to him. For he understood that what can be given can also be taken away.

Let us also, therefore, carry out some courageous act of our own accord; let us be
included among the ideal types of history. [14]Why have we been slack? Why do we lose

heart? That which could be done, can be done, if only we purify our souls and follow Nature; for when one strays away from Nature one is compelled to crave, and fear, and be a slave to the things of chance. We may return to the true path; we may be restored to our proper state; let us therefore be so, in order that we may be able to endure pain, in whatever form it attacks our bodies, and say to Fortune: "You have to deal with a man; seek someone whom you can conquer!"

[15]By these words,[8] and words of a like kind, the malignity of the ulcer is quieted down; and I hope indeed that it can be reduced, and either cured or brought to a stop, and grow old along with the patient himself. I am, however, comfortable in my mind regarding him; what we are now discussing is our own loss–the taking-off of a most excellent old man. For he himself has lived a full life, and anything additional may be craved by him, not for his own sake, but for the sake of those who need his services. [16]In continuing to live, he deals generously. Some other person might have put an end to these sufferings; but our friend considers it no less base to flee from death than to flee towards death. "But," comes the answer, "if circumstances warrant, shall he not take his departure?" Of course, if he can no longer be of service to anyone, if all his business will be to deal with pain. [17]This, my dear Lucilius, is what we mean by studying philosophy while applying it, by practising it on truth–note what courage a prudent man possesses against death, or against pain, when the one approaches and the other weighs heavily. What ought to be done must be learned from one who does it. [18]Up to now we have dealt with arguments–whether any man can resist pain, or whether the approach of death can cast down even great souls. Why discuss it further? Here is an immediate fact for us to tackle–death does not make our friend braver to face pain, nor pain to face death. Rather does he trust himself in the face of both; he does not suffer with resignation because he hopes for death, nor does he die gladly because he is tired of suffering. Pain he endures, death he awaits. Farewell.

Footnotes

1. Compare the ἔχω ἀλλ᾽ οὐκ ἔχομαι of Aristippus, and the (equally Epicurean) *mihi res, non me rebus subiungere* of Horace, *Epp.* i. 1. 19.

2. Vergil, *Aen.* ii. 428.

3. i.e., a sort of platform for mountebanks or acrobats,–figuratively applied to life's Vanity Fair.

4. Frag. 35 Körte

5. i.e., when he declined the bribe of Pyrrhus, 280 B.C.

6. Cf. Ep. xcv. 72 f. *omnibus saeculis Tuberonis fictilio durabunt.*

7. Cf. Ep. lix. 7 and note b (vol. i.).

8. The testimony of an ancient grammarian, and the change of subject in the text, may, as Hense states, indicate that a considerable passage is lost and that another letter begins here. Cf. the *senex egregius* of § 15.

XCIX. ON CONSOLATION TO THE BEREAVED

[1]I enclose a copy of the letter which I wrote to Marullus[1] at the time when he had lost his little son and was reported to be rather womanish in his grief–a letter in which I have not observed the usual form of condolence: for I did not believe that he should be handled gently, since in my opinion he deserved criticism rather than consolation. When a man is stricken and is finding it most difficult to endure a grievous wound, one must humour him for a while; let him satisfy his grief or at any rate work off the first shock; [2]but those who have assumed an indulgence in grief should be rebuked forthwith, and should learn that there are certain follies even in tears.[2]

"Is it solace that you look for? Let me give you a scolding instead! You are like a woman in the way you take your son's death; what would you do if you had lost an intimate friend? A son, a little child of unknown promise, is dead; a fragment of time has been lost. ³We hunt out excuses for grief; we would even utter unfair complaints about Fortune, as if Fortune would never give us just reason for complaining! But I had really thought that you possessed spirit enough to deal with concrete troubles, to say nothing of the shadowy troubles over which men make moan through force of habit. Had you lost a friend (which is the greatest blow of all),³ you would have had to endeavour rather to rejoice because you had possessed him than to mourn because you had lost him.

⁴"But many men fail to count up how manifold their gains have been, how great their rejoicings. Grief like yours has this among other evils: it is not only useless, but thankless. Has it then all been for nothing that you have had such a friend? During so many years, amid such close associations, after such intimate communion of personal interests, has nothing been accomplished? Do you bury friendship along with a friend? And why lament having lost him, if it be of no avail to have possessed him? Believe me, a great part of those we have loved, though chance has removed their persons, still abides with us. The past is ours, and there is nothing more secure for us than that which has been. ⁵We are ungrateful for past gains, because we hope for the future, as if the future–if so be that any future is ours–will not be quickly blended with the past. People set a narrow limit to their enjoyments if they take pleasure only in the present; both the future and the past serve for our delight–the one with anticipation, and the other with memories but the one is contingent and may not come to pass, while the other must have been.

"What madness it is, therefore, to lose our grip on that which is the surest thing of all? Let us rest content with the pleasures we have quaffed in past days, if only, while we quaffed them, the soul was not pierced like a sieve, only to lose again whatever it had received. ⁶There are countless cases of men who have without tears buried sons in the prime of manhood–men who have returned from the funeral pyre to the Senate chamber, or to any other official duties, and have straightway busied themselves with something else. And rightly; for in the first place it is idle to grieve if you get no help from grief. In the second place, it is unfair to complain about what has happened to one man but is in store for all. Again, it is foolish to lament one's loss, when there is such a slight interval between the lost and the loser. Hence we should be more resigned in spirit, because we follow closely those whom we have lost.

⁷"Note the rapidity of Time–that swiftest of things; consider the shortness of the course along which we hasten at top speed; mark this throng of humanity all straining toward the same point with briefest intervals between them–even when they seem longest; he whom you count as passed away has simply posted on ahead.⁴ And what is more irrational than to bewail your predecessor, when you yourself must travel on the same journey? ⁸Does a man bewail an event which he knew would take place? Or, if he did not think of death as man's lot, he has but cheated himself. Does a man bewail an event which he has been admitting to be unavoidable? Whoever complains about the death of anyone, is complaining that he was a man. Everyone is bound by the same terms: he who is privileged to be born, is destined to die. ⁹Periods of time separate us, but death levels us. The period which lies between our first day and our last is shifting and uncertain: if you reckon it by its troubles, it is long even to a lad, if by its speed, it is scanty even to a greybeard. Everything is slippery, treacherous, and more shifting than any weather. All things are tossed about and shift into their opposites at the bidding of Fortune; amid such a turmoil of mortal affairs nothing but death is surely in store for anyone. And yet all men complain about the one thing wherein none of them is deceived. ¹⁰'But he died in boyhood.' I am not yet prepared to say that he who quickly comes to the end of his life has the better of the bargain; let us turn to consider the case of him who has grown to old age. How very little is he superior to the child!⁵ Place before your mind's eye the vast spread of time's abyss, and consider the universe; and then contrast our so-called human life with infinity: you will then see how scant is that for which we pray, and which we seek to lengthen. ¹¹How much of this time is taken up with weeping, how much with worry! How much with prayers for death before death arrives, how much with our health, how much with our fears! How much is occupied

by our years of inexperience or of useless endeavour! And half of all this time is wasted in sleeping. Add, besides, our toils, our griefs, our dangers–and you will comprehend that even in the longest life real living is the least portion thereof. [12] Nevertheless, who will make such an admission as: 'A man is not better off who is allowed to return home quickly, whose journey is accomplished before he is wearied out'? Life is neither a Good nor an Evil; it is simply the place where good and evil exist. Hence this little boy has lost nothing except a hazard where loss was more assured than gain. He might have turned out temperate and prudent; he might, with your fostering care, have been moulded to a better standard; but (and this fear is more reasonable) he might have become just like the many. [13] Note the youths of the noblest lineage whose extravagance has flung them into the arena;[6] note those men who cater to the passions of themselves and others in mutual lust, whose days never pass without drunkenness or some signal act of shame; it will thus be clear to you that there was more to fear than to hope for.

"For this reason you ought not to invite excuses for grief or aggravate slight burdens by getting indignant. [14] I am not exhorting you to make an effort and rise to great heights; for my opinion of you is not so low as to make me think that it is necessary for you to summon every bit of your virtue to face this trouble. Yours is not pain; it is a mere sting–and it is you yourself who are turning it into pain.

"Of a surety philosophy has done you much service if you can bear courageously the loss of a boy who was as yet better known to his nurse than to his father! [15] And what, then? Now, at this time, am I advising you to be hard-hearted, desiring you to keep your countenance unmoved at the very funeral ceremony, and not allowing your soul even to feel the pinch of pain? By no means. That would mean lack of feeling rather than virtue–to behold the burial ceremonies of those near and dear to you with the same expression as you beheld their living forms, and to show no emotion over the first bereavement in your family. But suppose that I forbade you to show emotion; there are certain feelings which claim their own rights. Tears fall, no matter how we try to check them, and by being shed they ease the soul. [16] What, then, shall we do? Let us allow them to fall, but let us not command them do so; let us according as emotion floods our eyes, but not as as mere imitation shall demand. Let us, indeed, add nothing to natural grief, nor augment it by following the example of others. The display of grief makes more demands than grief itself: how few men are sad in their own company! They lament the louder for being heard; persons who are reserved and silent when alone are stirred to new paroxysms of tears when they behold others near them! At such times they lay violent hands upon their own persons,–though they might have done this more easily if no one were present to check them; at such times they pray for death; at such times they toss themselves from their couches. But their grief slackens with the departure of onlookers. [17] In this matter, as in others also, we are obsessed by this fault–conforming to the pattern of the many, and regarding convention rather than duty. We abandon nature and surrender to the mob–who are never good advisers in anything, and in this respect as in all others are most inconsistent. People see a man who bears his grief bravely: they call him undutiful and savage-hearted; they see a man who collapses and clings to his dead: they call him womanish and weak. [18] Everything, therefore, should be referred to reason. But nothing is more foolish than to court a reputation for sadness and to sanction tears; for I hold that with a wise man some tears fall by consent, others by their own force.

"I shall explain the difference as follows: When the first news of some bitter loss has shocked us, when we embrace the form that will soon pass from our arms to the funeral flames–then tears are wrung from us by the necessity of Nature, and the life-force, smitten by the stroke of grief, shakes both the whole body, and the eyes also, from which it presses out and causes to flow the moisture that lies within. [19] Tears like these fall by a forcing-out process, against our will; but different are the tears which we allow to escape when we muse in memory upon those whom we have lost. And there is in them a certain sweet sadness when we remember the sound of a pleasant voice, a genial conversation, and the busy duties of yore; at such a time the eyes are loosened, as it were, with joy. This sort of weeping we indulge; the former sort overcomes us.

maintain, it matters a great deal whether it tumbles forth, or flows along. Moreover, there is a deal of deference in this regard also—as I shall make clear to you: [2]Fabianus seems to me to have not so much an "efflux" as a "flow" of words:[1] so copious is it, without confusion, and yet not without speed. This is indeed what his style declares and announces—that he has not spent a long time in working his matter over and twisting it into shape. But even supposing the facts are as you would have them; the man was building up character rather than words, and was writing those words for the mind rather than for the ear. [3]Besides, had he been speaking them in his own person, you would not have had time to consider the details—the whole work would have so swept you along. For as a rule that which pleases by its swiftness is of less value when taken in hand for reading.

Nevertheless, this very quality, too, of attracting at first sight is a great advantage, no matter whether careful investigation may discover something to criticize. [4]If you ask me, I should say that he who has forced approval is greater than he who has earned it; and yet I know that the latter is safer, I know that he can give more confident guarantees for the future. A meticulous manner of writing does not suit the philosopher; if he is timid as to words, when will he ever be brave and steadfast, when will he ever really show his worth? [5]Fabianus's style was not careless, it was assured. That is why you will find nothing shoddy in his work: his words are well chosen and yet not hunted for; they are not unnaturally inserted and inverted, according to the present-day fashion; but they possess distinction, even though they are taken from ordinary speech. There you have honourable and splendid ideas, not fettered into aphorisms, but spoken with greater freedom. We shall of course notice passages that are not sufficiently pruned, not constructed with sufficient care, and lacking the polish which is in vogue nowadays; but after regarding the whole, you will see that there are no futile subtleties of argument. [6]There may, doubtless, be no variety of marbles, no water-supply[2] which flows from one apartment to another, no "pauper-rooms,"[3] or any other device that luxury adds when ill content with simple charms; but, in the vulgar phrase, it is "a good house to live in."

Furthermore, opinions vary with regard to the style. Some wish it to be polished down from all roughness; and some take so great a pleasure in the abrupt manner that they would intentionally break up any passage which may by chance spread itself out more smoothly, scattering the closing words in such a way that the sentences may result unexpectedly. [7]Read Cicero: his style has unity; it moves with a modulated pace, and is gentle without being degenerate. The style of Asinius Pollio, on the other hand, is "bumpy," jerky, leaving off when you least expect it.[4] And finally, Cicero always stops gradually; while Pollio breaks off, except in the very few cases where he cleaves to a definite rhythm and a single pattern.

[8]In addition to this, you say that everything in Fabianus seems to you commonplace and lacking in elevation; but I myself hold that he is free from such a fault. For that style of his is not commonplace, but simply calm and adjusted to his peaceful and well-ordered mind—not on a low level but on an even plane. There is lacking the verve and spur of the orator (for which you are looking), and a sudden shock of epigrams.[5] But look, please, at the whole work, how well-ordered it is: there is a distinction in it. His style does not possess, but will suggest, dignity.

[9]Mention someone whom you may rank ahead of Fabianus. Cicero, let us say, whose books on philosophy are almost as numerous as those of Fabianus. I will concede this point; but it is no slight thing to be less than the greatest. Or Asinius Pollio, let us say. I will yield again, and content myself by replying: "It is a distinction to be third in so great a field." You may also include Livy; for Livy wrote both dialogues (which should be ranked as history no less than as philosophy), and works which professedly deal with philosophy. I shall yield in the case of Livy also. But consider how many writers Fabianus outranks, if he is surpassed by three only—and those three the greatest masters of eloquence!

[10]But, it may be said, he does not offer everything: though his style is elevated, it is not strong; though it flows forth copiously, it lacks force and sweep; it is not trans-

lucent, but it is lucid. "One would fail," you urge, "to find therein any rugged denunciation of vice, any courageous words in the face of danger, any proud defiance of Fortune, any scornful threats against self-seeking. I wish to see luxury rebuked, lust condemned, waywardness crushed out. Let him show us the keenness of oratory, the loftiness of tragedy, the subtlety of comedy." You wish him to rely on that pettiest of things, phraseology; but he has sworn allegiance to the greatness of his subject and draws eloquence after him as a sort of shadow, but not of set purpose.

[11]Our author will doubtless not investigate every detail, nor subject it to analysis, nor inspect and emphasize each separate word. This I admit. Many phrases will fall short, or will fail to strike home, and at times the style will slip along indolently; but there will be plenty of light throughout the work; there will be long stretches which will not weary the reader. And, finally, he will offer this quality of making it clear to you that he meant what he wrote. You will understand that his aim was to have you know what pleased him, rather than that he should please you. All his work makes for progress and for sanity, without any search for applause.

[12]I do not doubt that his writings are of the kind I have described, although I am harking back to him rather than retaining a sure memory of him, and although the general tone of his writings remains in my mind, not from a careful and recent perusal, but in outline, as is natural after an acquaintance of long ago. But certainly, whenever I heard him lecture, such did his work seem to me–not solid but full, the kind which would inspire young men of promise and rouse their ambition to become like him, without making them hopeless of surpassing him; and this method of encouragement seems to me the most helpful of all. For it is disheartening to inspire in a man the desire, and to take away from him the hope, of emulation. At any rate, his language was fluent, and though one might not approve every detail, the general effect was noble. Farewell.

Footnotes

1. i.e., his style is like a river rather than a torrent.

2. *Concisura*: from *concido,* to "cut into sections," "distribute" (of water-pipes).

3. Cf. Ep. xviii. 7, and Martial iii. 48:

> *Pauperis extruxit cellam, sed vendidit Olus*
> *praedia; nunc cellam pauperis Olus habet.*

Rich men sometimes fitted up in their palaces an imitation "poor man's cabin" by way of contrast to their other rooms or as a gesture towards simple living; Seneca uses the phrase figuratively for certain devices in composition.

4. Quintilian x. 1. 113 says: *multa in Asinio Pollione inventio, summa diligentia, adeo ut quibusdam etiam nimia videatur; et consilii et animi satis; a nitore et iucunditate Ciceronis ita longe abest, ut videri possit saeculo prior.*

5. The wording here resembles strikingly that of the Elder Seneca, *Controv.* ii. pr. 2 *deerat illi* (sc. *Fabiano*) *oratorium robur et ille pugnatorius mucro.*

CI. ON THE FUTILITY OF PLANNING AHEAD

[1]Every day and every hour reveal to us what a nothing we are, and remind us with some fresh evidence that we have forgotten our weakness; then, as we plan for eternity, they compel us to look over our shoulders at Death.

Do you ask me what this preamble means? It refers to Cornelius Senecio, a distinguished and capable Roman knight, whom you knew: from humble beginnings he had advanced himself to fortune, and the rest of the path already lay downhill before him. For it is easier to grow in dignity than to make a start; [2]and money is very slow to come where there is poverty; until it can creep out of that, it goes halting. Senecio was already bordering upon wealth, helped in that direction by two very powerful assets–knowing how to make money and how to keep it also; either one of these gifts might have made him a rich man. [3]Here was a person who lived most simply, careful myself over to such a noble hope; for I was already weary of myself, beginning already to despise the fragments of my shattered existence,[1] and feeling that I was destined to pass over into that infinity of time and the heritage of eternity, when I was suddenly awakened by the receipt of your letter, and lost my lovely dream. But, if I can once dispose of you, I shall reseek and rescue it.

[3]There was a remark, at the beginning of your letter, that I had not explained the whole problem wherein I was endeavouring to prove one of the beliefs of our school, that the renown which falls to one's lot after death is a good; for I had not solved the problem with which we are usually confronted: "No good can consist of things that are distinct and separate; yet renown consists of such things." [4]What you are asking about, my dear Lucilius, belongs to another topic of the same subject, and that is why I had postponed the arguments, not only on this one topic, but on other topics which also covered the same ground. For, as you know, certain logical questions are mingled with ethical ones. Accordingly, I handled the essential part of my subject which has to do with conduct—as to whether it is foolish and useless to be concerned with what lies beyond our last day, or whether our goods die with us and there is nothing left of him who is no more, or whether any profit can be attained or attempted beforehand out of that which, when it comes, we shall not be capable of feeling.

[5]All these things have a view to conduct, and therefore they have been inserted under the proper topic. But the remarks of dialecticians in opposition to this idea had to be sifted out, and were accordingly laid aside. Now that you demand an answer to them all, I shall examine all their statements, and then refute them singly. [6]Unless, however, I make a preliminary remark, it will be impossible to understand my rebuttals. And what is that preliminary remark? Simply this: there are certain continuous bodies, such as a man; there are certain composite bodies,—as ships, houses, and everything which is the result of joining separate parts into one sum total: there are certain others made up of things that are distinct,[2] each member remaining separate—like an army, a populace, or a senate. For the persons who go to make up such bodies are united by virtue of law or function; but by their nature they are distinct and individual. Well, what further prefatory remarks do I still wish to make? [7]Simply this: we believe that nothing is a good, if it be composed of things that are distinct. For a single good should be checked and controlled by a single soul; and the essential quality of each single good should be single. This can be proved of itself whenever you desire; in the meanwhile, however, it had to be laid aside, because our own weapons[3] are being hurled at us.

[8]Opponents speak thus: "You say, do you, that no good can be made up of things that are distinct? Yet this renown, of which you speak, is simply the favourable opinion of good men. For just as reputation does not consist of one person's remarks, and as ill repute does not consist of one person's disapproval, so renown does not mean that we have merely pleased one good person. In order to constitute renown, the agreement of many distinguished and praiseworthy men is necessary. But this results from the decision of a number—in other words, of persons who are distinct. Therefore, it is not a good. [9]You say, again, that renown is the praise rendered to a good man by good men. Praise means speech: now speech is utterance with a particular meaning; and utterance, even from the lips of good men, is not a good in itself. For any act of a good man is not necessarily a good; he shouts his applause and hisses his disapproval, but one does not call the shouting or the hissing good—although his entire conduct may be admired and praised—any more than one would applaud a sneeze or a cough. Therefore, renown is not a good. [10]Finally, tell us whether the good belongs to him who praises, or to him who is praised: if you say that the good belongs to him who is praised, you are on as foolish a quest as if you were to maintain that my neighbour's good health is my own. But to praise worthy men is an honourable action; thus the good is exclusively that of the man who does the praising, of the man who performs the action, and not of us, who are being praised. And yet this was the question under discussion."

[11]I shall now answer the separate objections hurriedly. The first question still is, whether any good can consist of things that are distinct—and there are votes cast on

both sides. Again, does renown need many votes? Renown can be satisfied with the decision of one good man: it is one good man who decides that we are good. [12] Then the retort is: "What! Would you define reputation as the esteem of one individual, and ill-repute as the rancorous chatter of one man? Glory, too, we take to be more widespread, for it demands the agreement of many men." But the position of the "many" is different from that of "the one." And why? Because, if the good man thinks well of me, it practically amounts to my being thought well of by all good men; for they will all think the same, if they know me. Their judgment is alike and identical; the effect of truth on it is equal. They cannot disagree, which means that they would all hold the same view, being unable to hold different views. [13] "One man's opinion," you say, "is not enough to create glory or reputation." In the former case,[4] one judgment is a universal judgment, because all, if they were asked, would hold one opinion; in the other case, however, men of dissimilar character give divergent judgments. You will find perplexing emotions–everything doubtful, inconstant, untrustworthy. And can you suppose that all men are able to hold one opinion? Even an individual does not hold to a single opinion. With the good man it is truth that causes belief, and truth has but one function and one likeness; while among the second class of which I spoke, the ideas with which they agree are unsound. Moreover, those who are false are never steadfast: they are irregular and discordant. [14] "But praise," says the objector, "is nothing but an utterance, and an utterance is not a good." When they[5] say that renown is praise bestowed on the good by the good, what they refer to is not an utterance but a judgment. For a good man may remain silent; but if he decides that a certain person is worthy, of praise, that person is the object of praise. [15] Besides, praise is one thing, and the giving of praise another; the latter demands utterance also. Hence no one speaks of "a funeral praise," but says "praise-giving"–for its function depends upon speech. And when we say that a man is worthy of praise, we assure human kindness to him, not in words, but in judgment. So the good opinion, even of one who in silence feels inward approval of a good man, is praise.

[16] Again, as I have said, praise is a matter of the mind rather than of the speech; for speech brings out the praise that the mind has conceived, and publishes it forth to the attention of the many. To judge a man worthy of praise, is to praise him. And when our tragic poet[6] sings to us that it is wonderful "to be praised by a well-praised hero," he means, "by one who is worthy of praise." Again, when an equally venerable bard says:[7] "Praise nurtureth the arts," he does not mean the giving of praise, for that spoils the arts. Nothing has corrupted oratory and all other studies that depend on hearing so much as popular approval.[8] [17] Reputation necessarily demands words, but renown can be content with men's judgments, and suffice without the spoken word. It is satisfied not only amid silent approval, but even in the face of open protest. There is, in my opinion, this difference between renown and glory–the latter depends upon the judgments of the many; but renown on the judgments of good men. [18] The retort comes: "But whose good is this renown, this praise rendered to a good man by good men? Is it of the one praised, or of the one who praises?" Of both, I say. It is my own good, in that I am praised, because I am naturally born to love all men, and I rejoice in having done good deeds and congratulate myself on having found men who express their ideas of my virtues with gratitude; that they are grateful, is a good to the many, but it is a good to me also. For my spirit is so ordered that I can regard the good of other men as my own–in any case those of whose good I am myself the cause. [19] This good is also the good of those who render the praise, for it is applied by means of virtue; and every act of virtue is a good. My friends could not have found this blessing if I had not been a man of the right stamp. It is therefore a good belonging to both sides–this being praised when one deserves it–just as truly as a good decision is the good of him who makes the decision and also of him in whose favour the decision was given. Do you doubt that justice is a blessing to its possessor, as well as to the man to whom the just due was paid? To praise the deserving is justice; therefore, the good belongs to both sides.

[20] This will be a sufficient answer to such dealers in subtleties. But it should not be

fully it is concealed.

You are wrong to trust the countenances of those you meet. They have the aspect of men, but the souls of brutes; the difference is that only beasts damage you at the first encounter; those whom they have passed by they do not pursue. For nothing ever goads them to do harm except when need compels them: it is hunger or fear that forces them into a fight. But man delights to ruin man.

[3]You must, however, reflect thus what danger you run at the hand of man, in order that you may deduce what is the duty of man. Try, in your dealings with others, to harm not, in order that you be not harmed. You should rejoice with all in their joys and sympathize with them in their troubles, remembering what you should offer and what you should withhold. [4]And what may you attain by living such a life? Not necessarily freedom from harm at their hands, but at least freedom from deceit. In so far, however, as you are able, take refuge with philosophy: she will cherish you in her bosom, and in her sanctuary you shall be safe, or, at any rate, safer than before. People collide only when they are travelling the same path. [5]But this very philosophy must never be vaunted by you; for philosophy when employed with insolence and arrogance has been perilous to many. Let her strip off your faults, rather than assist you to decry the faults of others. Let her not hold aloof from the customs of mankind, nor make it her business to condemn whatever she herself does not do. A man may be wise without parade and without arousing enmity. Farewell.

Footnotes

1. Compare this with the Seventh letter (vol. i.).

CIV. ON CARE OF HEALTH AND PEACE OF MIND

[1]I have run off to my villa at Nomentum, for what purpose, do you suppose? To escape the city? No; to shake off a fever which was surely working its way into my system. It had already got a grip upon me. My physician kept insisting that when the circulation was upset and irregular, disturbing the natural poise, the disease was under way. I therefore ordered my carriage to be made ready at once, and insisted on departing in spite of my wife Paulina's[1] efforts to stop me; for I remembered master Gallio's[2] words, when he began to develop a fever in Achaia and took ship at once, insisting that the disease was not of the body but of the place. [2]That is what I remarked to my dear Paulina, who always urges me to take care of my health. I know that her very life-breath comes and goes with my own, and I am beginning, in my solicitude for her, to be solicitous for myself. And although old age has made me braver to bear many things, I am gradually losing this boon that old age bestows. For it comes into my mind that in this old man there is a youth also, and youth needs tenderness. Therefore, since I cannot prevail upon her to love me any more heroically, she prevails upon me to cherish myself more carefully. [3]For one must indulge genuine emotions; sometimes, even in spite of weighty reasons, the breath of life must be called back and kept at our very lips even at the price of great suffering, for the sake of those whom we hold dear; because the good man should not live as long as it pleases him, but as long as he ought. He who does not value his wife, or his friend, highly enough to linger longer in life–he who obstinately persists in dying is a voluptuary.

The soul should also enforce this command upon itself whenever the needs of one's relatives require; it should pause and humour those near and dear, not only when it desires, but even when it has begun, to die. [4]It gives proof of a great heart to return to life for the sake of others; and noble men have often done this. But this procedure also, I believe, indicates the highest type of kindness: that although the greatest advantage of old age is the opportunity to be more negligent regarding self-preservation and to use life more adventurously, one should watch over one's old age with still greater care if one knows that such action is pleasing, useful, or desirable in the eyes of a person whom one holds dear. ⁵This is also a source of no mean joy and profit; for what is sweeter than to be so valued by one's wife that one becomes more valuable to oneself for this reason? Hence my dear Paulina is able to make me responsible, not only for her fears, but also for my own.

⁶So you are curious to know the outcome of this prescription of travel? As soon as I escaped from the oppressive atmosphere of the city, and from that awful odour of reeking kitchens which, when in use, pour forth a ruinous mess of steam and soot, I perceived at once that my health was mending. And how much stronger do you think I felt when I reached my vineyards! Being, so to speak, let out to pasture, I regularly walked into my meals! So I am my old self again, feeling now no wavering languor in my system, and no sluggishness in my brain. I am beginning to work with all my energy.

⁷But the mere place avails little for this purpose, unless the mind is fully master of itself, and can, at its pleasure, find seclusion even in the midst of business; the man, however, who is always selecting resorts and hunting for leisure, will find something to distract his mind in every place. Socrates is reported to have replied, when a certain person complained of having received no benefit from his travels: "It serves you right! You travelled in your own company!"³ ⁸O what a blessing it would be for some men to wander away from themselves! As it is, they cause themselves vexation, worry, de-moralization, and fear! What profit is there in crossing the sea and in going from one city to another? If you would escape your troubles, you need not another place but another personality. Perhaps you have reached Athens, or perhaps Rhodes; choose any state you fancy, how does it matter what its character may be? You will be bringing to it your own.

⁹Suppose that you hold wealth to be a good: poverty will then distress you, and,– which is most pitiable,–it will be an imaginary poverty. For you may be rich, and nev-ertheless, because your neighbour is richer, you suppose yourself to be poor exactly by the same amount in which you fall short of your neighbour. You may deem official position a good; you will be vexed at another's appointment or re-appointment to the consulship; you will be jealous whenever you see a name several times in the state re-cords. Your ambition will be so frenzied that you will regard yourself last in the race if there is anyone in front of you. ¹⁰Or you may rate death as the worst of evils, although there is really no evil therein except that which precedes death's coming–fear. You will be frightened out of your wits, not only by real, but by fancied dangers, and will be tossed for ever on the sea of illusion. What benefit will it be to

> Have threaded all the towns of Argolis,
> A fugitive through midmost press of foes?⁴

For peace itself will furnish further apprehension. Even in the midst of safety you will have no confidence if your mind has once been given a shock; once it has acquired the habit of blind panic, it is incapable of providing even for its own safety. For it does not avoid danger, but runs away. Yet we are more exposed to danger when we turn our backs.

¹¹You may judge it the most grievous of ills to lose any of those you love; while all the same this would be no less foolish than weeping because the trees which charm your eye and adorn your home lose their foliage. Regard everything that pleases you as if it were a flourishing plant; make the most of it while it is in leaf, for different plants at different seasons must fall and die. But just as the loss of leaves is a light thing, because they are born afresh, so it is with the loss of those whom you love and regard as the delight of your life; for they can be replaced even though they cannot be born afresh. ¹²"New friends, however, will not be the same." No, nor will you yourself remain the same; you change with every day and every hour. But in other men you more readily see what time plunders; in your own case the change is hidden, because it will not take place visibly. Others are snatched from sight; we ourselves are being stealthily filched away from ourselves. You will not think about any of these problems, nor will you apply remedies to these wounds. You will of your own volition be sowing a crop of trouble by alternate hoping and despairing. If you are wise, mingle these two

elements: do not hope without despair, or despair without hope.

[13]What benefit has travel of itself ever been able to give anyone? No restraint upon pleasure, no bridling of desire, no checking of bad temper, no crushing of the wild assaults of passion, no opportunity to rid the soul of evil. Travelling cannot give us judgment, or shake off our errors; it merely holds our attention for a moment by a certain novelty, as children pause to wonder at something unfamiliar. [14]Besides, it irritates us, through the wavering of a mind which is suffering from an acute attack of sickness; the very motion makes it more fitful and nervous. Hence the spots we had sought most eagerly we quit still more eagerly, like birds that flit and are off as soon as they have alighted. [15]What travel will give is familiarity with other nations: it will reveal to you mountains of strange shape, or unfamiliar tracts of plain, or valleys that are watered by everflowing springs, or the characteristics of some river that comes to our attention. We observe how the Nile rises and swells in summer, or how the Tigris disappears, runs underground through hidden spaces, and then appears with unabated sweep; or how the Maeander,[5] that oft-rehearsed theme and plaything of the poets, turns in frequent bendings, and often in winding comes close to its own channel before resuming its course. But this sort of information will not make better or sounder men of us.[6]

[16]We ought rather to spend our time in study, and to cultivate those who are masters of wisdom, learning something which has been investigated, but not settled; by this means the mind can be relieved of a most wretched serfdom, and won over to freedom. Indeed, as long as you are ignorant of what you should avoid or seek, or of what is necessary or superfluous, or of what is right or wrong, you will not be travelling, but merely wandering. [17]There will be no benefit to you in this hurrying to and fro; for you are travelling with your emotions and are followed by your afflictions. Would that they were indeed following you! In that case, they would be farther away; as it is, you are carrying and not leading them. Hence they press about you on all sides, continually chafing and annoying you. It is medicine, not scenery, for which the sick man must go a-searching. [18]Suppose that someone has broken a leg or dislocated a joint: he does not take carriage or ship for other regions, but he calls in the physician to set the fractured limb, or to move it back to its proper place in the socket. What then? When the spirit is broken or wrenched in so many places, do you think that change of place can heal it? The complaint is too deep-seated to be cured by a journey. [19]Travel does not make a physician or an orator; no art is acquired by merely living in a certain place.

Where lies the truth, then? Can wisdom, the greatest of all the arts, be picked up on a journey? I assure you, travel as far as you like, you can never establish yourself beyond the reach of desire, beyond the reach of bad temper, or beyond the reach of fear; had it been so, the human race would long ago have banded together and made a pilgrimage to the spot. Such ills, as long as you carry with you their causes, will load you down and worry you to skin and bone in your wanderings over land and sea. [20]Do you wonder that it is of no use to run away from them? That from which you are running, is within you. Accordingly, reform your own self, get the burden off your own shoulders, and keep within safe limits the cravings which ought to be removed. Wipe out from your soul all trace of sin. If you would enjoy your travels, make healthy the companion of your travels. As long as this companion is avaricious and mean, greed will stick to you; and while you consort with an overbearing man, your puffed-up ways will also stick close. Live with a hangman, and you will never be rid of your cruelty. If an adulterer be your club-mate, he will kindle the baser passions. [21]If you would be stripped of your faults leave far behind you the patterns of the faults. The miser, the swindler, the bully, the cheat, who will do you much harm merely by being near you, are within you.

Change therefore to better associations: live with the Catos, with Laelius, with Tubero. Or, if you enjoy living with Greeks also, spend your time with Socrates and with Zeno: the former will show you how to die if it be necessary; the latter how to die before it is necessary. [22]Live with Chrysippus, with Posidonius:[7] they will make you acquainted with things earthly and things heavenly; they will bid you work hard over something more than neat turns of language and phrases mouthed forth for the entertainment of listeners; they will bid you be stout of heart and rise superior to threats. The only harbour safe from the seething storms of this life is scorn of the future, a firm stand, a readiness to receive Fortune's missiles full in the breast, neither skulking nor turning the back. [23] Nature has brought us forth brave of spirit, and, as she has implanted in certain animals a spirit of ferocity, in others craft, in others terror, so she has gifted us with an aspiring and lofty spirit, which prompts us to seek a life of the greatest honour, and not of the greatest security, that most resembles the soul of the universe, which it follows and imitates as far as our mortal steps permit. This spirit thrusts itself forward, confident of commendation and esteem. [24] It is superior to all, monarch of all it surveys; hence it should be subservient to nothing, finding no task too heavy, and nothing strong enough to weigh down the shoulders of a man.

> Shapes dread to look upon, of toil or death[8]

are not in the least dreadful, if one is able to look upon them with unflinching gaze, and is able to pierce the shadows. Many a sight that is held a terror in the night-time, is turned to ridicule by day. "Shapes dread to look upon, of toil or death": our Vergil has excellently said that these shapes are dread, not in reality, but only "to look upon"—in other words, they seem terrible, but are not. [25] And in these visions what is there, I say, as fear-inspiring as rumour has proclaimed? Why, pray, my dear Lucilius, should a man fear toil, or a mortal death? Countless cases occur to my mind of men who think that what they themselves are unable to do is impossible, who maintain that we utter words which are too big for man's nature to carry out. [26] But how much more highly do I think of these men! They can do these things, but decline to do them. To whom that ever tried have these tasks proved false? To what man did they not seem easier in the doing? Our lack of confidence is not the result of difficulty. The difficulty comes from our lack of confidence.

[27] If, however, you desire a pattern, take Socrates, a long-suffering old man, who was sea-tossed amid every hardship and yet was unconquered both by poverty (which his troubles at home made more burdensome) and by toil, including the drudgery of military service. He was much tried at home, whether we think of his wife, a woman of rough manners and shrewish tongue, or of the children whose intractability showed them to be more like their mother than their father.[9] And if you consider the facts, he lived either in time of war, or under tyrants, or under a democracy, which is more cruel than wars and tyrants. [28] The war lasted for twenty-seven years;[10] then the state became the victim of the Thirty Tyrants, of whom many were his personal enemies. At the last came that climax of condemnation under the gravest of charges: they accused him of disturbing the state religion and corrupting the youth,[11] for they declared that he had influenced the youth to defy the gods, to defy the council, and to defy the state in general. Next came the prison, and the cup of poison.[12] But all these measures changed the soul of Socrates so little that they did not even change his features. What wonderful and rare distinction! He maintained this attitude up to the very end, and no man ever saw Socrates too much elated or too much depressed. Amid all the disturbance of Fortune, he was undisturbed.

[29] Do you desire another case? Take that of the younger Marcus Cato, with whom Fortune dealt in a more hostile and more persistent fashion. But he withstood her, on all occasions, and in his last moments, at the point of death, showed that a brave man can live in spite of Fortune, can die in spite of her. His whole life was passed either in civil warfare, or under a political regime which was soon to breed civil war. And you may say that he, just as much as Socrates, declared allegiance to liberty in the midst of slavery—unless perchance you think that Pompey, Caesar, and Crassus[13] were the allies of liberty! [30] No one ever saw Cato change, no matter how often the state changed: he kept himself the same in all circumstances—in the praetorship,[14] in defeat, under accusation,[15] in his province, on the platform, in the army, in death. Furthermore, when the republic was in a crisis of terror, when Caesar was on one side with ten embattled legions at his call, aided by so many foreign nations. and when Pompey was on the other, satisfied to stand alone against all comers, and when the citizens were leaning towards either Caesar or Pompey, Cato alone established a definite party for the Re-

public. [31]If you would obtain a mental picture of that period, you may imagine on one side the people and the whole proletariat eager for revolution–on the other the senators and knights, the chosen and honoured men of the commonwealth; and there were left between them but these two–the Republic and Cato.

I tell you, you will marvel when you see

Atreus' son, and Priam, and Achilles, wroth at both.[16]

Like Achilles, he scorns and disarms each faction. [32]And this is the vote which he casts concerning them both: "If Caesar wins, I slay myself; if Pompey, I go into exile." What was there for a man to fear who, whether in defeat or in victory, had assigned to himself a doom which might have been assigned to him by his enemies in their utmost rage? So he died by his own decision.

[33]You see that man can endure toil: Cato, on foot, led an army through African deserts. You see that thirst can be endured: he marched over sun-baked hills, dragging the remains of a beaten army and with no train of supplies, undergoing lack of water and wearing a heavy suit of armour; always the last to drink of the few springs which they chanced to find. You see that honour, and dishonour too, can be despised: for they report that on the very day when Cato was defeated at the elections, he played a game of ball. You see also that man can be free from fear of those above him in rank: for Cato attacked Caesar and Pompey simultaneously, at a time when none dared fall foul of the one without endeavouring to oblige the other. You see that death can be scorned as well as exile: Cato inflicted exile upon himself and finally death,[17] and war all the while.

[34]And so, if only we are willing to withdraw our necks from the yoke, we can keep as stout a heart against such terrors as these. But first and foremost, we must reject pleasures; they render us weak and womanish; they make great demands upon us, and, moreover, cause us to make great demands upon Fortune. Second, we must spurn wealth: wealth is the diploma of slavery. Abandon gold and silver, and whatever else is a burden upon our richly-furnished homes; liberty cannot be gained for nothing. If you set a high value on liberty, you must set a low value on everything else. Farewell.

Footnotes

1. Pompeia Paulina, the second wife of Seneca; cf. Tac. *Ann.* xv. 60. Though much younger than her husband, she was a model of devotion, and remained loyal to him through all the Neronian persecution.

2. Elder brother of Seneca, whose name before his adoption by Lucius Iunius Gallio was Annaeus Novatus. He was governor of Achaia from A.D. July 1, 51 to July 1, 52. See *Acts* xviii. 11 ff., and Duff, *Three Dialogues of Seneca*, p. xliii.

3. Cf. Ep. x. 1 *"Mecum loquor."* *"Cave, rogo, et diligenter adtende; cum homine malo loqueris."*

4. Vergil, *Aen.* iii. 282 f.

5. See Index of Proper Names.

6. Although Seneca was deeply interested in such matters, as is proved by Ep. lxxix., the *Naturales Quaestiones*, and an early work on the geography of Egypt.

7. These men are patterns or interpreters of the virtues. The first-named three represent courage, justice, and self-restraint respectively. Socrates is the ideal wise man, Zeno, Chrysippus, and Posidonus are in turn the founder, the classifier, and the modernizer of Stoicism.

8. *Aeneid*, vi. 277.

9. At first a sculptor, then an independent seeker after truth, whose wants were reduced to a minimum. Husband of the shrewish Xanthippe and father of the dull and worthless Lamprocles. Brave soldier at Potidaea, Delium, and Amphipolis.

10. 431-404 B.C. (the Peloponnesian War).

11. See Plato's *Apology*, 23 D. They had previously aimed at him a law forbidding the teaching of dialectic.

12. 399 B.C.

13. Triumvirs in 60 B.C. and rivals in acquiring unconstitutional power.

14. 54 B.C.

15. Perhaps a reference to his mission in Cyprus (58-56 B.C.), and his subsequent arraignment by Clodius.

16. Vergil, *Aen.* i. 458.

17. At Utica, in 46 B.C.

CV. ON FACING THE WORLD WITH CONFIDENCE

[1]I shall now tell you certain things to which you should pay attention in order to live more safely. Do you however,–such is my judgment,–hearken to my precepts just as if I were counselling you to keep safe your health in your country-place at Ardea.

Reflect on the things which goad man into destroying man: you will find that they are hope, envy, hatred, fear, and contempt. [2]Now, of all these, contempt is the least harmful, so much so that many have skulked behind it as a sort of cure. When a man despises you, he works you injury, to be sure, but he passes on; and no one persistently or of set purpose does hurt to a person whom he despises. Even in battle, prostrate soldiers are neglected: men fight with those who stand their ground. [3]And you can avoid the envious hopes of the wicked so long as you have nothing which can stir the evil desires of others, and so long as you possess nothing remarkable. For people crave even little things, if these catch the attention or are of rare occurrence.

You will escape envy if you do not force yourself upon the public view, if you do not boast your possessions, if you understand how to enjoy things privately. Hatred comes either from running foul of others: and this can be avoided by never provoking anyone; or else it is uncalled for: and common-sense[1] will keep you safe from it. Yet it has been dangerous to many; some people have been hated without having had an enemy. [4]As to not being feared, a moderate fortune and an easy disposition will guarantee you that; men should know that you are the sort of person who can be offended without danger; and your reconciliation should be easy and sure. Moreover, it is as troublesome to be feared at home as abroad; it is as bad to be feared by a slave as by a gentleman. For every one has strength enough to do you some harm. Besides, he who is feared, fears also; no one has been able to arouse terror and live in peace of mind.

[5]Contempt remains to be discussed. He who has made this quality an adjunct of his own personality, who is despised because he wishes to be despised and not because he *must* be despised, has the measure of contempt under his control. Any inconveniences in this respect can be dispelled by honourable occupations and by friendships with men who have influence with an influential person; with these men it will profit you to engage but not to entangle yourself, lest the cure may cost you more than the risk. [6]Nothing, however, will help you so much as keeping still–talking very little with others, and as much as may be with yourself. For there is a sort of charm about conversation, something very subtle and coaxing, which, like intoxication or love, draws secrets from us. No man will keep to himself what he hears. No one will tell another only as much as he has heard. And he who tells tales will tell names, too. Everyone has someone to whom he entrusts exactly what has been entrusted to him. Though he checks his own garrulity, and is content with one hearer, he will bring about him a nation, if that which was a secret shortly before becomes common talk.

[7]The most important contribution to peace of mind is never to do wrong. Those who lack self-control lead disturbed and tumultuous lives; their crimes are balanced by their fears, and they are never at ease. For they tremble after the deed, and they are embarrassed; their consciences do not allow them to busy themselves with other matters, and continually compel them to give an answer. Whoever expects punishment, receives it, but whoever deserves it, expects it. [8]Where there is an evil conscience something may bring safety, but nothing can bring ease; for a man imagines that, even if he is not under arrest, he may soon be arrested. His sleep is troubled; when he speaks

fold kinds of missiles which are hurled at us. Some are planted in us, some are being brandished and at this very moment are on the way, some which were destined for other men graze us instead. ⁶We should not manifest surprise at any sort of condition into which we are born, and which should be lamented by no one, simply because it is equally ordained for all. Yes, I say, equally ordained; for a man might have experienced even that which he has escaped. And an equal law consists, not of that which all have experienced, but of that which is laid down for all. Be sure to prescribe for your mind this sense of equity; we should pay without complaint the tax of our mortality.

⁷Winter brings on cold weather; and we must shiver. Summer returns, with its heat; and we must sweat. Unseasonable weather upsets the health; and we must fall ill. In certain places we may meet with wild beasts, or with men who are more destructive than any beasts. Floods, or fires, will cause us loss. And we cannot change this order of things; but what we can do is to acquire stout hearts, worthy of good men, thereby courageously enduring chance and placing ourselves in harmony with Nature. ⁸And Nature moderates this world-kingdom which you see, by her changing seasons: clear weather follows cloudy; after a calm, comes the storm; the winds blow by turns; day succeeds night; some of the heavenly bodies rise, and some set. Eternity consists of opposites.

⁹It is to this law that our souls must adjust themselves, this they should follow, this they should obey. Whatever happens, assume that it was bound to happen, and do not be willing to rail at Nature. That which you cannot reform, it is best to endure, and to attend uncomplainingly upon the God under whose guidance everything progresses; for it is a bad soldier who grumbles when following his commander. ¹⁰For this reason we should welcome our orders with energy and vigour, nor should we cease to follow the natural course of this most beautiful universe, into which all our future sufferings are woven.

Let us address Jupiter, the pilot of this world-mass, as did our great Cleanthes in those most eloquent lines—lines which I shall allow myself to render in Latin, after the example of the eloquent Cicero. If you like them, make the most of them; if they displease you, you will understand that I have simply been following the practise of Cicero:

> ¹¹Lead me, O Master of the lofty heavens,
> My Father, whithersoever thou shalt wish.
> I shall not falter, but obey with speed.
> And though I would not, I shall go, and suffer,
> In sin and sorrow what I might have done
> In noble virtue. Aye, the willing soul
> Fate leads, but the unwilling drags along.²

¹²Let us live thus, and speak thus; let Fate find us ready and alert. Here is your great soul—the man who has given himself over to Fate; on the other hand, that man is a weakling and a degenerate who struggles and maligns the order of the universe and would rather reform the gods than reform himself. Farewell.

Footnotes

1. Vergil, *Aen.* vi. 274 f.

2. Cleanthes, Frag. 527 von Arnim. In Epictetus (*Ench.* 53) these verses are assigned to Cleanthes (omitting the last line); while St. Augustine (*Civ. Dei.* v. 8) quotes them as Seneca's: *Annaei Senecae sunt, nisi fallor, hi versus.* Wilamowitz and others follow the latter view.

CVIII. ON THE APPROACHES TO PHILOSOPHY

¹The topic about which you ask me is one of those where our only concern with knowledge is to have the knowledge. Nevertheless, because it does so far concern us, you are in a hurry; you are not willing to wait for the books which I am at this moment

arranging for you, and which embrace the whole department of moral philosophy.[1] I shall send you the books at once; but I shall, before doing that, write and tell you how this eagerness to learn, with which I see you are aflame, should be regulated, so that it may not get in its own way. [2]Things are not to be gathered at random; nor should they be greedily attacked in the mass; one will arrive at a knowledge of the whole by studying the parts. The burden should be suited to your strength, nor should you tackle more than you can adequately handle. Absorb not all that you wish, but all that you can hold. Only be of a sound mind, and then you will be able to hold all that you wish. For the more the mind receives, the more does it expand.

[3]This was the advice, I remember, which Attalus[2] gave me in the days when I practically laid siege to his class-room, the first to arrive and the last to leave. Even as he paced up and down, I would challenge him to various discussions; for he not only kept himself accessible to his pupils, but met them half-way. His words were: "The same purpose should possess both master and scholar–an ambition in the one case to promote, and in the other to progress." [4]He who studies with a philosopher should take away with him some one good thing every day: he should daily return home a sounder man, or in the way to become sounder. And he will thus return; for it is one of the functions of philosophy to help not only those who study her, but those also who associate with her. He that walks in the sun, though he walk not for that purpose, must needs become sunburned. He who frequents the perfumer's shop and lingers even for a short time, will carry with him the scent of the place. And he who follows a philosopher is bound to derive some benefit therefrom, which will help him even though he be remiss. Mark what I say: "remiss," not "recalcitrant."

[5]"What then?" you say, "do we not know certain men who have sat for many years at the feet of a philosopher and yet have not acquired the slightest tinge of wisdom?" Of course I know such men. There are indeed persevering gentlemen who stick at it; I do not call them pupils of the wise, but merely "squatters."[3] [6]Certain of them come to hear and not to learn, just as we are attracted to the theatre to satisfy the pleasures of the ear, whether by a speech, or by a song, or by a play. This class, as you will see, constitutes a large part of the listeners, who regard the philosopher's lecture-room merely as a sort of lounging-place for their leisure. They do not set about to lay aside any faults there, or to receive a rule of life, by which they may test their characters; they merely wish to enjoy to the full the delights of the ear. And yet some arrive even with notebooks, not to take down the matter, but only the words,[4] that they may presently repeat them to others with as little profit to these as they themselves received when they heard them. [7]A certain number are stirred by high-sounding phrases, and adapt themselves to the emotions of the speaker with lively change of face and mind–just like the emasculated Phrygian priests[5] who are wont to be roused by the sound of the flute and go mad to order. But the true hearer is ravished and stirred by the beauty of the subject matter, not by the jingle of empty words. When a bold word has been uttered in defiance of death, or a saucy fling in defiance of Fortune, we take delight in acting straightway upon that which we have heard. Men are impressed by such words, and become what they are bidden to be, should but the impression abide in the mind, and should the populace, who discourage honourable things, not immediately lie in wait to rob them of this noble impulse; only a few can carry home the mental attitude with which they were inspired. [8]It is easy to rouse a listener so that he will crave righteousness; for Nature has laid the foundations and planted the seeds of virtue in us all. And we are all born to these general privileges; hence, when the stimulus is added, the good spirit is stirred as if it were freed from bonds. Have you not noticed how the theatre re-echoes whenever any words are spoken whose truth we appreciate generally and confirm unanimously.

[9]The poor lack much; the greedy man lacks all.[6]

A greedy man does good to none; he does
Most evil to himself.[7]

At such verses as these, your meanest miser claps applause and rejoices to hear

Fly first; disease and bitter eld succeed,
And toil, till harsh death rudely snatches all.[16]

[25]He who considers these lines in the spirit of a philosopher comments on the words in their proper sense: "Vergil never says, 'Time goes,' but 'Time flies,' because the latter is the quickest kind of movement, and in every case our best days are the first to be snatched away; why, then, do we hesitate to bestir ourselves so that we may be able to keep pace with this swiftest of all swift things?" The good flies past and the bad takes its place. [26]Just as the purest wine flows from the top of the jar and the thickest dregs settle at the bottom; so in our human life, that which is best comes first. Shall we allow other men to quaff the best, and keep the dregs for ourselves? Let this phrase cleave to your soul; you should be satisfied thereby as if it were uttered by an oracle:

Each choicest day of hapless human life
Flies first.

[27]Why "choicest day?" Because what's to come is unsure. Why "choicest day"? Because in our youth we are able to learn; we can bend to nobler purposes minds that are ready and still pliable; because this is the time for work, the time for keeping our minds busied in study and in exercising our bodies with useful effort; for that which remains is more sluggish and lacking in spirit–nearer the end.

Let us therefore strive with all courage, omitting attractions by the way; let us struggle with a single purpose, lest, when we are left behind, we comprehend too late the speed of quick-flying time, whose course we cannot stay. Let every day, as soon as it comes, be welcome as being the choicest, and let it be made our own possession. [28]We must catch that which flees. Now he who scans with a scholar's eye the lines I have just quoted, does not reflect that our first days are the best because disease is approaching and old age weighs upon us and hangs over our heads while we are still thinking about our youth. He thinks rather of Vergil's usual collocation of *disease and eld*; and indeed rightly. For old age is a disease which we cannot cure. [29]"Besides," he says to himself, "think of the epithet that accompanies *eld*; Vergil calls it *bitter*,"–

Disease and bitter eld succeed.

And elsewhere Vergil says:

There dwelleth pale disease and bitter eld.[17]

There is no reason why you should marvel that each man can collect from the same source suitable matter for his own studies; for in the same meadow the cow grazes, the dog hunts the hare, and the stork the lizard. [30]When Cicero's book *On the State* is opened by a philologist, a scholar, or a follower of philosophy, each man pursues his investigation in his own way. The philosopher wonders that so much could have been said therein against justice. The philologist takes up the same book and comments on the text as follows: There were two Roman kings–one without a father and one without a mother. For we cannot settle who was Servius's mother, and Ancus, the grandson of Numa, has no father on record.[18] [31]The philologist also notes that the officer whom we call dictator, and about whom we read in our histories under that title, was named in old times the *magister populi*; such is the name existing to-day in the augural records, proved by the fact that he whom the dictator chose as second in command was called *magister equitum*. He will remark, too, that Romulus met his end during an eclipse; that there was an appeal to the people even from the kings (this is so stated in the pontiffs' register and is the opinion of others, including Fenestella[19]). [32]When the scholar unrolls this same volume, he puts down in his notebook the forms of words, noting that *reapse*, equivalent to *re ipsa*, is used by Cicero, and *sepse*[20] just as frequently, which means *se ipse*. Then he turns his attention to changes in current usage. Cicero, for example, says: "Inasmuch as we are summoned back from the very calx by his interruption." Now the line in the circus which we call the *creta*[21] was called the calx by men of old time. [33]Again, he puts together some verses by Ennius, especially those which referred to Africanus:

A man to whom nor friend nor foe could give

Due meed for all his efforts and his deed.[22]

From this passage the scholar declares that he infers the word *opem* to have meant formerly not merely *assistance*, but *efforts*. For Ennius must mean that neither friend nor foe could pay Scipio a reward worthy of his efforts. [34]Next, he congratulates himself on finding the source of Vergil's words:

> Over whose head the mighty gate of Heaven
> Thunders,[23]

remarking that Ennius stole the idea from Homer, and Vergil from Ennius. For there is a couplet by Ennius, preserved in this same book of Cicero's, *On the State*:[24]

> If it be right for a mortal to scale the regions of Heaven,
> Then the huge gate of the sky opens in glory to *me*.

[35]But that I, too, while engaged upon another task, may not slip into the department of the philologist or the scholar, my advice is this–that all study of philosophy and all reading should be applied to the idea of living the happy life, that we should not hunt out archaic or far-fetched words and eccentric metaphors and figures of speech, but that we should seek precepts which will help us, utterances of courage and spirit which may at once be turned into facts. We should so learn them that words may become deeds. [36]And I hold that no man has treated mankind worse than he who has studied philosophy as if it were some marketable trade, who lives in a different manner from that which he advises. For those who are liable to every fault which they castigate advertise themselves as patterns of useless training. [37]A teacher like that can help me no more than a sea-sick pilot can be efficient in a storm. He must hold the tiller when the waves are tossing him; he must wrestle, as it were, with the sea; he must furl his sails when the storm rages; what good is a frightened and vomiting steersman to *me*? And how much greater, think you, is the storm of life than that which tosses any ship! One must steer, not talk.

All the words that these men utter and juggle before a listening crowd, belong to others. [38]They have been spoken by Plato, spoken by Zeno, spoken by Chrysippus or by Posidonius, and by a whole host of Stoics as numerous as excellent. I shall show you how men can prove their words to be their own: it is by doing what they have been talking about. Since therefore I have given you the message I wished to pass on to you, I shall now satisfy your craving and shall reserve for a new letter a complete answer to your summons; so that you may not approach in a condition of weariness a subject which is thorny and which should be followed with an attentive and painstaking ear. Farewell.

Footnotes

1. Cf. Ep. cvi. 2 *scis enim me moralem philosophiam velle conplecti*, etc.

2. Seneca's first and most convincing teacher of Stoicism, to whom this letter is a tribute. The ablest of contemporary philosophers, he was banished during the reign of Tiberius. See Index of Proper Names.

3. Literally "tenants," "lodgers," of a temporary sort.

4. Cf. the dangers of such *lusoria* (Ep. xlviii. 8) and *a rebus studium transferendum est ad verba* (Ep. xl. 14).

5. i.e., mendicant Galli, worshippers of Cybele, the Magna Mater.

6. *Syri Sententiae*, Frag. 236 Ribbeck.

7. *Ib.*, Frag. 234 R.

8. Frag. 487 von Arnim.

9. Pall. Incert. Fab. 65 and 66 Ribbeck.

10. A characteristic Stoic paradox.

11. An almost proverbial saying; cf. the *recte olet ubi nil olet* of Plautus (*Most.* 273), Cicero, and Martial.

12. Pythagorean philosopher of the Augustine age, and one of Seneca's early teachers.

which I include in my volumes *On Moral Philosophy*.[5] Reflect, as I am often wont to tell you, that there is nothing in such topics for us except mental gymnastics. For I return again and again to the thought: "What good does this do me? Make me more brave now, more just, more restrained! I have not yet the opportunity to make use of my training; for I still need the physician. [18]Why do you ask of me a useless knowledge? You have promised great things; test me, watch me! You assured me that I should be unterrified though swords were flashing round me, though the point of the blade were grazing my throat; you assured me that I should be at ease though fires were blazing round me, or though a sudden whirlwind should snatch up my ship and carry it over all the sea. Now make good for me such a course of treatment that I may despise pleasure and glory. Thereafter you shall teach me to work out complicated problems, to settle doubtful points, to see through that which is not clear; teach me now what it is necessary for me to know!" Farewell.

Footnotes

1. i.e., in possession of a perfect, an encyclopaedic, wisdom.

2. In other words, Wisdom, Justice, Courage, and Self-Restraint, together with the other qualities of simplicity, kindness, etc., being "avatars" of Virtue herself, are interrelated.

3. e.g., certain of the Peripatetic school.

4. Sallust, *Cat.* xx. 4 *idem velle atque idem nolle, ea demum firma amicitia est.* Cf. the Greek "ἴσῳ ζυγῷ," "yoked equally together."

5. Cf. Ep. cviii. 1 and note.

CX. ON TRUE AND FALSE RICHES

[1]From my villa at Nomentum[1] I send you greeting and bid you keep a sound spirit within you–in other words, gain the blessing of all the gods, for he is assured of their grace and favour who has become a blessing to himself. Lay aside for the present the belief of certain persons–that a god is assigned to each one of us as a sort of attendant– not a god of regular rank, but one of a lower grade–one of those whom Ovid calls "plebeian gods."[2] Yet, while laying aside this belief, I would have you remember that our ancestors, who followed such a creed, have become Stoics; for they have assigned a Genius or a Juno to every individual.[3] [2]Later on we shall investigate whether the gods have enough time on their hands to care for the concerns of private individuals; in the meantime, you must know that whether we are allotted to special guardians, or whether we are neglected and consigned to Fortune, you can curse a man with no heavier curse than to pray that he may be at enmity with himself.

There is no reason, however, why you should ask the gods to be hostile to anyone whom you regard as deserving of punishment; they *are* hostile to such a person, I maintain, even though he seems to be advanced by their favour. [3]Apply careful investigation, considering how our affairs actually stand, and not what men say of them; you will then understand that evils are more likely to help us than to harm us. For how often has so-called affliction been the source and the beginning of happiness! How often have privileges which we welcomed with deep thanksgiving built steps for themselves to the top of a precipice, still uplifting men who were already distinguished–just as if they had previously stood in a position whence they could fall in safety! [4]But this very fall has in it nothing evil, if you consider the end,[4] after which nature lays no man lower. The universal limit is near; yes, there is near us the point where the prosperous man is upset, and the point where the unfortunate is set free. It is we ourselves that extend both these limits, lengthening them by our hopes and by our fears.

If, however, you are wise, measure all things according to the state of man; restrict at the same time both your joys and your fears. Moreover, it is worth while not to rejoice at anything for long, so that you may not fear anything for long. [5]But why do I confine the scope of this evil? There is no reason why you should suppose that anything is to be feared. All these things which stir us and keep us a-flutter, are empty things. None of us has sifted out the truth; we have passed fear on to one another; none has dared to approach the object which caused his dread, and to understand the nature of his fear–aye, the good behind it. That is why falsehood and vanity still gain credit–because they are not refuted. ⁶Let us account it worth while to look closely at the matter; then it will be clear how fleeting, how unsure, and how harmless are the things which we fear. The disturbance in our spirits is similar to that which Lucretius detected:

> Like boys who cower frightened in the dark,
> So grown-ups in the light of day feel fear.⁵

What, then? Are we not more foolish than any child, we who "in the light of day feel fear"? ⁷But you were wrong, Lucretius; we are not afraid in the daylight; we have turned everything into a state of darkness. We see neither what injures nor what profits us; all our lives through we blunder along, neither stopping nor treading more carefully on this account. But you see what madness it is to rush ahead in the dark. Indeed, we are bent on getting ourselves called back⁶ from a greater distance; and though we do not know our goal, yet we hasten with wild speed in the direction whither we are straining.

⁸The light, however, may begin to shine, provided we are willing. But such a result can come about only in one way–if we acquire by knowledge this familiarity with things divine and human, if we not only flood ourselves but steep ourselves therein, if a man reviews the same principles even though he understands them and applies them again and again to himself, if he has investigated what is good, what is evil, and what has falsely been so entitled; and, finally, if he has investigated honour and baseness, and Providence. ⁹The range of the human intelligence is not confined within these limits; it may also explore outside the universe–its destination and its source, and the ruin towards which all nature hastens so rapidly. We have withdrawn the soul from this divine contemplation and dragged it into mean and lowly tasks, so that it might be a slave to greed, so that it might forsake the universe and its confines, and, under the command of masters who try all possible schemes, pry beneath the earth and seek what evil it can dig up therefrom–discontented with that which was freely offered to it.

¹⁰Now God, who is the Father of us all, has placed ready to our hands those things which he intended for our own good; he did not wait for any search on our part, and he gave them to us voluntarily. But that which would be injurious, he buried deep in the earth. We can complain of nothing but ourselves; for we have brought to light the materials for our destruction, against the will of Nature, who hid them from us. We have bound over our souls to pleasure, whose service is the source of all evil; we have surrendered ourselves to self-seeking and reputation, and to other aims which are equally idle and useless.

¹¹What, then, do I now encourage you to do? Nothing new–we are not trying to find cures for new evils–but this first of all: namely, to see clearly for yourself what is necessary and what is superfluous. What is necessary will meet you everywhere; what is superfluous has always to be hunted-out–and with great endeavour. ¹²But there is no reason why you should flatter yourself over-much if you despise gilded couches and jewelled furniture. For what virtue lies in despising useless things? The time to admire your own conduct is when you have come to despise the necessities. You are doing no great thing if you can live without royal pomp, if you feel no craving for boars which weigh a thousand pounds, or for flamingo tongues, or for the other absurdities of a luxury that already wearies of game cooked whole, and chooses different bits from separate animals; I shall admire you only when you have learned to scorn even the common sort of bread, when you have made yourself believe that grass grows for the needs of men as well as of cattle, when you have found out that food from the treetop⁷ can fill the belly–into which we cram things of value as if it could keep what it has received. We should satisfy our stomachs without being over-nice. How does it matter what the stomach receives, since it must lose whatever it has received? ¹³You enjoy the carefully arranged dainties which are caught on land and sea; some are more pleasing

merely not on speaking terms. Farewell.

Footnotes

1. Seneca was an extensive and prosperous vine-grower. Compare Ep. civ. 6 f. for his description of his hobby at the country-place near Nomentum. There are many figures which deal with the vine scattered through the Letters.

CXIII. ON THE VITALITY OF THE SOUL AND ITS ATTRIBUTES

[1]You wish me to write to you my opinion concerning this question, which has been mooted by our school—whether justice, courage, foresight, and the other virtues, are living things.[1] By such niceties as this, my beloved Lucilius, we have made people think that we sharpen our wits on useless objects, and waste our leisure time in discussions that will be unprofitable. I shall, however, do as you ask, and shall set forth the subject as viewed by our school. For myself, I confess to another belief: I hold that there are certain things which befit a wearer of white shoes and a Greek mantle.[2] But what the beliefs are that have stirred the ancients, or those which the ancients have stirred up for discussion, I shall explain to you.

[2]The soul, men are agreed, is a living thing, because of itself it can make us living things, and because "living things"[3] have derived their name therefrom. But virtue is nothing else than a soul in a certain condition; therefore it is a living thing. Again, virtue is active, and no action can take place without impulse. And if a thing has impulse, it must be a living thing; for none except a living thing possesses impulse. [3]A reply to this is: "If virtue is a living thing, then virtue itself possesses virtue." Of course it possesses its own self! Just as the wise man does everything by reason of virtue, so virtue accomplishes everything by reason of itself. "In that case," say they, "all the arts also are living things, and all our thoughts and all that the mind comprehends. It therefore follows that many thousands of living things dwell in man's tiny heart, and that each individual among us consists of, or at least contains, many living beings."

Are you gravelled for an answer to this remark? Each of these will be a living thing; but they will not be many separate living things. And why? I shall explain, if you will apply your subtlety and your concentration to my words. [4]Each living thing must have a separate substance; but since all the things mentioned above have a single soul, consequently they can be separate living things but without plurality. I myself am a living thing, and a man; but you cannot say that there are two of me for that reason. And why? Because, if that were so, they would have to be two separate existences. This is what I mean: one would have to be sundered from the other so as to produce two. But whenever you have that which is manifold in one whole, it falls into the category of a single nature, and is therefore single.

[5]My soul is a living thing, and so am I; but we are not two separate persons. And why? Because the soul is part of myself. It will only be reckoned as a definite thing in itself when it shall exist by itself. But as long as it shall be part of another, it cannot be regarded as different. And why? I will tell you: it is because that which is different, must be personal and peculiar to itself, a whole, and complete within itself. [6]I myself have gone on record as being of a different opinion;[4] for if one adopts this belief, not only the virtues will be living things, but so will their contrary vices, and the emotions, like wrath, fear, grief, and suspicion. Nay, the argument will carry us still further—all opinions and all thoughts will be living things. This is by no means admissible; since anything that man does is not necessarily the man himself. [7]"What is Justice?" people say. Justice is a soul that maintains itself in a certain attitude. "Then if the soul is a living being, so is Justice." By no means. For Justice is really a state, a kind of power, of the soul; and this same soul is transformed into various likenesses and does not become a different kind of living thing as often as it acts differently. Nor is the result of soul-action a living thing. [8]If Justice, Bravery, and the other virtues have actual life, do

they cease to be living things and then begin life over again, or are they *always* living things?

But the virtues cannot cease to be. Therefore, there are many, nay countless, living things, sojourning in this one soul. [9]"No," is the answer, "not many, because they are all attached to the one, being parts and members of a single whole." We are then portraying for ourselves an image of the soul like that of a many-headed hydra–each separate head fighting and destroying independently. And yet there is no separate living thing to each head; it is the head of a living thing, and the hydra itself is one single living thing. No one ever believed that the Chimaera contained a living lion or a living serpent;[5] these were merely parts of the whole Chimaera; and parts are not living things. [10]Then how can you infer that Justice is a living thing? "Justice," people reply, "is active and helpful; that which acts and is helpful, possesses impulse; and that which possesses impulse is a living thing." True, if the impulse is its own; (but in the case of justice it is not its own;) the impulse comes from the soul. [11]Every living thing exists as it began, until death; a man, until he dies, is a man, a horse is a horse, a dog a dog. They cannot change into anything else. Now let us grant that Justice–which is defined as "a soul in a certain attitude," is a living thing. Let us suppose this to be so. Then Bravery also is alive, being "a soul in a certain attitude." But which soul? That which was but now defined as Justice? The soul is kept within the first-named being, and cannot cross over into another; it must last out its existence in the medium where it had its origin. [12]Besides, there cannot be one soul to two living things, much less to many living things. And if Justice, Bravery, Restraint, and all the other virtues, are living things, how will they have one soul? They must possess separate souls, or else they are not living things. [13]Several living things cannot have one body; this is admitted by our very opponents. Now what is the "body"[6] of justice? "The soul," they admit. And of bravery? "The soul also." And yet there cannot be one body of two living things. [14]"The same soul, however," they answer, "assumes the guise of Justice, or Bravery, or Restraint." This would be possible if Bravery were absent when Justice was present, and if Restraint were absent when Bravery was present; as the case stands now, all the virtues exist at the same time. Hence, how can the separate virtues be living things, if you grant that there is one single soul,[7] which cannot create more than one single living thing?

[15]Again, no living thing is part of another living thing. But Justice is a part of the soul; therefore Justice is not a living thing. It looks as if I were wasting time over something that is an acknowledged fact; for one ought to decry such a topic rather than debate it. And no two living things are equal. Consider the bodies of all beings: every one has its particular colour, shape, and size. [16]And among the other reasons for marvelling at the genius of the Divine Creator is, I believe, this,–that amid all this abundance there is no repetition; even seemingly similar things are, on comparison, unlike. God has created all the great number of leaves that we behold: each, however, is stamped with its special pattern. All the many animals: none resembles another in size–always some difference! The Creator has set himself the task of making unlike and unequal things that are different; but all the virtues, as your argument states, are equal. Therefore, they are not living things.

[17]Every living thing acts of itself; but virtue does nothing of itself; it must act in conjunction with man. All living things either are gifted with reason, like men and gods, or else are irrational, like beasts and cattle. Virtues, in any case, are rational; and yet they are neither men nor gods; therefore they are not living things. [18]Every living thing possessed of reason is inactive if it is not first stirred by some external impression; then the impulse comes, and finally assent confirms the impulse.[8] Now what *assent* is, I shall explain. Suppose that I ought to take a walk: I *do* walk, but only after uttering the command to myself and approving this opinion of mine. Or suppose that I ought to seat myself; I *do* seat myself, but only after the same process. This assent is not a part of virtue. [19]For let us suppose that it is Prudence; how will Prudence assent to the opinion: "I must take a walk"? Nature does not allow this. For Prudence looks after the interests of its possessor, and not of its own self. Prudence cannot walk or be

¹You have been asking me why, during certain periods, a degenerate style of speech comes to the fore, and how it is that men's wits have gone downhill into certain vices—in such a way that exposition at one time has taken on a kind of puffed-up strength, and at another has become mincing and modulated like the music of a concert piece. You wonder why sometimes bold ideas—bolder than one could believe—have been held in favour, and why at other times one meets with phrases that are disconnected and full of innuendo, into which one must read more meaning than was intended to meet the ear. Or why there have been epochs which maintained the right to a shameless use of metaphor. For answer, here is a phrase which you are wont to notice in the popular speech—one which the Greeks have made into a proverb: "Man's speech is just like his life."[1] ²Exactly as each individual man's actions seem to speak, so people's style of speaking often reproduces the general character of the time, if the morale of the public has relaxed and has given itself over to effeminacy. Wantonness in speech is proof of public luxury, if it is popular and fashionable, and not confined to one or two individual instances. ³A man's ability[2] cannot possibly be of one sort and his soul of another. If his soul be wholesome, well-ordered, serious, and restrained, his ability also is sound and sober. Conversely, when the one degenerates, the other is also contaminated. Do you not see that if a man's soul has become sluggish, his limbs drag and his feet move indolently? If it is womanish, that one can detect the effeminacy by his very gait? That a keen and confident soul quickens the step? That madness in the soul, or anger (which resembles madness), hastens our bodily movements from walking to rushing?

And how much more do you think that this affects one's ability, which is entirely interwoven with the soul,—being moulded thereby, obeying its commands, and deriving therefrom its laws! ⁴How Maecenas lived is too well-known for present comment. We know how he walked, how effeminate he was, and how he desired to display himself; also, how unwilling he was that his vices should escape notice. What, then? Does not the looseness of his speech match his ungirt attire?[3] Are his habits, his attendants, his house, his wife,[4] any less clearly marked than his words? He would have been a man of great powers, had he set himself to his task by a straight path, had he not shrunk from making himself understood, had he not been so loose in his style of speech also. You will therefore see that his eloquence was that of an intoxicated man—twisting, turning, unlimited in its slackness.

⁵What is more unbecoming than the words:[5] "A stream and a bank covered with long-tressed woods"? And see how "men plough the channel with boats and, turning up the shallows, leave gardens behind them." Or, "He curls his lady-locks, and bills and coos, and starts a-sighing, like a forest lord who offers prayers with down-bent neck." Or, "An unregenerate crew, they search out people at feasts, and assail households with the wine-cup, and, by hope, exact death." Or, "A Genius could hardly bear witness to his own festival"; or "threads of tiny tapers and crackling meal"; "mothers or wives clothing the hearth."

⁶Can you not at once imagine, on reading through these words, that this was the man who always paraded through the city with a flowing[6] tunic? For even if he was discharging the absent emperor's duties, he was always in undress when they asked him for the countersign. Or that this was the man who, as judge on the bench, or as an orator, or at any public function, appeared with his cloak wrapped about his head, leaving only the ears exposed, [7] like the millionaire's runaway slaves in the farce? Or that this was the man who, at the very time when the state was embroiled in civil strife, when the city was in difficulties and under martial law, was attended in public by two eunuchs—both of them more men than himself? Or that this was the man who had but one wife, and yet was married countless times?[8] ⁷These words of his, put together so faultily, thrown off so carelessly, and arranged in such marked contrast to the usual practice, declare that the character of their writer was equally unusual, unsound, and eccentric. To be sure, we bestow upon him the highest praise for his humanity; he was sparing with the sword and refrained from bloodshed;[9] and he made a show of his power only in the course of his loose living; but he spoiled, by such preposterous finickiness of style, this genuine praise, which was his due. ⁸For it is evident that he

was not really gentle, but effeminate, as is proved by his misleading word-order, his inverted expressions, and the surprising thoughts which frequently contain something great, but in finding expression have become nerveless. One would say that his head was turned by too great success.

This fault is due sometimes to the man, and sometimes to his epoch. [9]When prosperity has spread luxury far and wide, men begin by paying closer attention to their personal appearance. Then they go crazy over furniture. Next, they devote attention to their houses–how to take up more space with them, as if they were country-houses, how to make the walls glitter with marble that has been imported over seas, how to adorn a roof with gold, so that it may match the brightness of the inlaid floors. After that, they transfer their exquisite taste to the dinner-table, attempting to court approval by novelty and by departures from the customary order of dishes, so that the courses which we are accustomed to serve at the end of the meal may be served first, and so that the departing guests may partake of the kind of food which in former days was set before them on their arrival.

[10]When the mind has acquired the habit of scorning the usual things of life, and regarding as mean that which was once customary, it begins to hunt for novelties in speech also; now it summons and displays obsolete and old-fashioned words; now it coins even unknown words or misshapes them; and now a bold and frequent metaphorical usage is made a special feature of style, according to the fashion which has just become prevalent. [11]Some cut the thoughts short, hoping to make a good impression by leaving the meaning in doubt and causing the hearer to suspect his own lack of wit. Some dwell upon them and lengthen them out. Others, too, approach just short of a fault–for a man must really do this if he hopes to attain an imposing effect–but actually love the fault for its own sake. In short, whenever you notice that a degenerate style pleases the critics, you may be sure that character also has deviated from the right standard.

Just as luxurious banquets and elaborate dress are indications of disease in the state, similarly a lax style, if it be popular, shows that the mind (which is the source of the word) has lost its balance. Indeed you ought not to wonder that corrupt speech is welcomed not merely by the more squalid mob[10] but also by our more cultured throng; for it is only in their dress and not in their judgments that they differ. [12]You may rather wonder that not only the effects of vices, but even vices themselves, meet with approval. For it has ever been thus: no man's ability has ever been approved without something being pardoned. Show me any man, however famous; I can tell you what it was that his age forgave in him, and what it was that his age purposely overlooked. I can show you many men whose vices have caused them no harm, and not a few who have been even helped by these vices. Yes, I will show you persons of the highest reputation, set up as models for our admiration; and yet if you seek to correct their errors, you destroy them; for vices are so intertwined with virtues that they drag the virtues along with them. [13]Moreover, style has no fixed laws; it is changed by the usage of the people, never the same for any length of time. Many orators hark back to earlier epochs for their vocabulary, speaking in the language of the Twelve Tables.[11] Gracchus, Crassus, and Curio, in their eyes, are too refined and too modern; so back to Appius and Coruncanius![12] Conversely, certain men, in their endeavour to maintain nothing but well-worn and common usages, fall into a humdrum style. [14]These two classes, each in its own way, are degenerate; and it is no less degenerate to use no words except those which are conspicuous, high-sounding, and poetical, avoiding what is familiar and in ordinary usage. One is, I believe, as faulty as the other: the one class are unreasonably elaborate, the other are unreasonably negligent; the former depilate the leg, the latter not even the armpit.[13]

[15]Let us now turn to the arrangement of words. In this department, what countless varieties of fault I can show you! Some are all for abruptness and unevenness of style, purposely disarranging anything which seems to have a smooth flow of language. They would have jolts in all their transitions; they regard as strong and manly whatever makes an uneven impression on the ear. With some others it is not so much an "ar-

16. For these Sallust fragments see the edition of Kritz, Nos. 33, *Jug.* 37. 4, and 42; for Arruntius see H. Peter, *Frag. Hist. Rom.* ii. pp. 41 f.

17. Literally, "created," "made."

18. "Brought to pass flight for our men"; "Hiero, king of the Syracusans brought about war"; "The news brought the men of Panormus" (now Palermo, Sicily) "to the point of surrendering to the Romans."

19. "Amid the wintry waters"; "The storm suddenly grew wintry"; "The whole year was like winter"; "Then he dispatched sixty transports of light draught besides the soldiers and the necessary sailors amid a wintry storm."

20. The peculiarity here is the use of the plural instead of the singular form. "Amid civil war he seeks reminders of justice and virtue."

21. Vergil, *Georg.* iv. 212 f.

CXV. ON THE SUPERFICIAL BLESSINGS

[1] I wish, my dear Lucilius, that you would not be too particular with regard to words and their arrangement; I have greater matters than these to commend to your care. You should seek what to write, rather than how to write it–and even that not for the purpose of writing but of feeling it, that you may thus make what you have felt more your own and, as it were, set a seal on it. [2] Whenever you notice a style that is too careful and too polished, you may be sure that the mind also is no less absorbed in petty things. The really great man speaks informally and easily; whatever he says, he speaks with assurance rather than with pains.

You are familiar with the young dandies,[1] natty as to their beards and locks, fresh from the bandbox; you can never expect from them any strength or any soundness. Style is the garb of thought: if it be trimmed, or dyed, or treated, it shows that there are defects and a certain amount of flaws in the mind. Elaborate elegance is not a manly garb. [3] If we had the privilege of looking into a good man's soul, oh what a fair, holy, magnificent, gracious, and shining face should we behold–radiant on the one side with justice and temperance, on another with bravery and wisdom! And, besides these, thriftiness, moderation, endurance, refinement, affability, and–though hard to believe–love of one's fellow-men, that Good which is so rare in man, all these would be shedding their own glory over that soul. There, too, forethought combined with elegance and, resulting from these, a most excellent greatness of soul (the noblest of all these virtues)–indeed what charm, O ye heavens, what authority and dignity would they contribute! What a wonderful combination of sweetness and power! No one could call such a face lovable without also calling it worshipful. [4] If one might behold such a face, more exalted and more radiant than the mortal eye is wont to behold, would not one pause as if struck dumb by a visitation from above, and utter a silent prayer, saying: "May it be lawful to have looked upon it!"? And then, led on by the encouraging kindliness of his expression, should we not bow down and worship? Should we not, after much contemplation of a far superior countenance, surpassing those which we are wont to look upon, mild-eyed and yet flashing with life-giving fire–should we not then, I say, in reverence and awe, give utterance to those famous lines of our poet Vergil:

> [5] O maiden, words are weak! Thy face is more
> Than mortal, and thy voice rings sweeter far
> Than mortal man's; . . . .
> Blest be thou; and, whoe'er thou art, relieve
> Our heavy burdens.[2]

And such a vision will indeed be a present help and relief to us, if we are willing to worship it. But this worship does not consist in slaughtering fattened bulls, or in hanging up offerings of gold or silver, or in pouring coins into a temple treasury; rather does it consist in a will that is reverent and upright.

[6] There is none of us, I declare to you, who would not burn with love for this vision

of virtue, if only he had the privilege of beholding it; for now there are many things that cut off our vision, piercing it with too strong a light, or clogging it with too much darkness. If, however, as certain drugs are wont to be used for sharpening and clearing the eyesight, we are likewise willing to free our mind's eye from hindrances, we shall then be able to perceive virtue, though it be buried in the body–even though poverty stand in the way, and even though lowliness and disgrace block the path. We shall then, I say, behold that true beauty, no matter if it be smothered by unloveliness. [7]Conversely, we shall get a view of evil and the deadening influences of a sorrow-laden soul–in spite of the hindrance that results from the widespread gleam of riches that flash round about, and in spite of the false light–of official position on the one side or great power on the other–which beats pitilessly upon the beholder.

[8]Then it will be in our power to understand how contemptible are the things we admire–like children who regard every toy as a thing of value, who cherish necklaces bought at the price of a mere penny as more dear than their parents or than their brothers. And what, then, as Aristo says,[3] is the difference between ourselves and these children, except that we elders go crazy over paintings and sculpture, and that our folly costs us dearer? Children are pleased by the smooth and variegated pebbles which they pick up on the beach, while we take delight in tall columns of veined marble brought either from Egyptian sands or from African deserts to hold up a colonnade or a dining-hall large enough to contain a city crowd; [9]we admire walls veneered with a thin layer of marble, although we know the while what defects the marble conceals. We cheat our own eyesight, and when we have overlaid our ceilings with gold, what else is it but a lie in which we take such delight? For we know that beneath all this gilding there lurks some ugly wood.

Nor is such superficial decoration spread merely over walls and ceilings; nay, all the famous men whom you see strutting about with head in air, have nothing but a gold-leaf prosperity. Look beneath, and you will know how much evil lies under that thin coating of titles. [10]Note that very commodity which holds the attention of so many magistrates and so many judges, and which creates both magistrates and judges–that money, I say, which ever since it began to be regarded with respect, has caused the ruin of the true honour of things; we become alternately merchants and merchandise, and we ask, not what a thing truly is, but what it costs; we fulfil duties if it pays, or neglect them if it pays, and we follow an honourable course as long as it encourages our expectations, ready to veer across to the opposite course if crooked conduct shall promise more. [11]Our parents have instilled into us a respect for gold and silver; in our early years the craving has been implanted, settling deep within us and growing with our growth. Then too the whole nation, though at odds on every other subject, agrees upon this; this is what they regard, this is what they ask for their children, this is what they dedicate to the gods when they wish to show their gratitude–as if it were the greatest of all man's possessions! And finally, public opinion has come to such a pass that poverty is a hissing and a reproach, despised by the rich and loathed by the poor.

[12]Verses of poets also are added to the account–verses which lend fuel to our passions, verses in which wealth is praised as if it were the only credit and glory of mortal man. People seem to think that the immortal gods cannot give any better gift than wealth–or even possess anything better:

> [13]The Sun-god's palace, set with pillars tall,
> And flashing bright with gold.[4]

Or they describe the chariot of the Sun:[5]

> Gold was the axle, golden eke the pole,
> And gold the tires that bound the circling wheels,
> And silver all the spokes within the wheels.

And finally, when they would praise an epoch as the best, they call it the "Golden Age." [14]Even among the Greek tragic poets there are some who regard pelf as better than purity, soundness, or good report:

> Call me a scoundrel, only call me rich!

All ask how great my riches are, but none
Whether my soul is good.

None asks the means or source of your estate,
But merely how it totals.

All men are worth as much as what they own.

What is most shameful for us to possess?
Nothing!

If riches bless me, I should love to live;
Yet I would rather die, if poor.

A man dies nobly in pursuit of wealth.[6]

Money, that blessing to the race of man,
Cannot be matched by mother's love, or lisp
Of children, or the honour due one's sire.
And if the sweetness of the lover's glance
Be half so charming, Love will rightly stir
The hearts of gods and men to adoration.[7]

[15]When these last-quoted lines were spoken at a performance of one of the tragedies of Euripides, the whole audience rose with one accord to hiss the actor and the
play off the stage. But Euripides jumped to his feet, claimed a hearing, and asked them
to wait for the conclusion and see the destiny that was in store for this man who gaped
after gold. Bellerophon, in that particular drama, was to pay the penalty which is ex-
acted of all men in the drama of life. [16]For one must pay the penalty for all greedy acts;
although the greed is enough of a penalty in itself. What tears and toil does money
wring from us! Greed is wretched in that which it craves and wretched in that which
it wins! Think besides of the daily worry which afflicts every possessor in proportion
to the measure of his gain! The possession of riches means even greater agony of spirit
than the acquisition of riches. And how we sorrow over our losses–losses which fall
heavily upon us, and yet seem still more heavy! And finally, though Fortune may leave
our property intact, whatever we cannot gain in addition, is sheer loss!

[17]"But," you will say to me, "people call yonder man happy and rich; they pray
that some day they may equal him in possessions." Very true. What, then? Do you
think that there is any more pitiable lot in life than to possess misery and hatred also?
Would that those who are bound to crave wealth could compare notes with the rich
man! Would that those who are bound to seek political office could confer with ambitious men who have reached the most sought-after honours! They would then surely
alter their prayers, seeing that these grandees are always gaping after new gain, condemning what is already behind them. For there is no one in the world who is contented with his prosperity, even if it comes to him on the run. Men complain about their
plans and the outcome of their plans; they always prefer what they have failed to win.

[18]So philosophy can settle this problem for you, and afford you, to my mind, the
greatest boon that exists–absence of regret for your own conduct. This is a sure happiness; no storm can ruffle it; but you cannot be steered safely through by any subtly
woven words, or any gently flowing language. Let words proceed as they please, provided only your soul keeps its own sure order,[8] provided your soul is great and holds
unruffled to its ideals, pleased with itself on account of the very things which displease
others, a soul that makes life the test of its progress, and believes that its knowledge
is in exact proportion to its freedom from desire and its freedom from fear. Farewell.

Footnotes

1. Elsewhere (Epp. lxxvi. 2 and lxxxvii. 9) called *trossuli,* "fops."

2. *Aen.* i. 327 ff.

3. Frag. 372 von Arnim.

4. Ovid, *Metam.* ii. 1 f.

5. *Id.* ib. ii. 107 ff.

6. Cf. Nauck, *Trag. Gr. fragg.* adesp. 181. 1 and 461.

7. Cf. id., Eurip. *Danaë,* Frag. 324, and Hense's note (ed. of 1914, p. 559).

8. A play on the *compositio* of rhetoric.

CXVI. ON SELF-CONTROL

[1]The question has often been raised whether it is better to have moderate emotions, or none at all.[1] Philosophers of our school reject the emotions; the Peripatetics keep them in check. I, however, do not understand how any half-way disease can be either wholesome or helpful. Do not fear; I am not robbing you of any privileges which you are unwilling to lose! I shall be kindly and indulgent towards the objects for which you strive–those which you hold to be necessary to our existence, or useful, or pleasant; I shall simply strip away the vice. For after I have issued my prohibitions against the desires, I shall still allow you to wish that you may do the same things fearlessly and with greater accuracy of judgment, and to feel even the pleasures more than before; and how can these pleasures help coming more readily to your call, if you are their lord rather than their slave!

[2]"But," you object, "it is natural for me to suffer when I am bereaved of a friend; grant some privileges to tears which have the right to flow! It is also natural to be affected by men's opinions and to be cast down when they are unfavourable; so why should you not allow me such an honourable aversion to bad opinion?"

There is no vice which lacks some plea; there is no vice that at the start is not modest and easily entreated; but afterwards the trouble spreads more widely. If you allow it to begin, you cannot make sure of its ceasing. [3]Every emotion at the start is weak. Afterwards, it rouses itself and gains strength by progress; it is more easy to forestall it than to forgo it. Who does not admit that all the emotions flow as it were from a certain natural source? We are endowed by Nature with an interest in our own well-being; but this very interest, when overindulged, becomes a vice. Nature has intermingled pleasure with necessary things–not in order that we should seek pleasure, but in order that the addition of pleasure may make the indispensable means of existence attractive to our eyes. Should it claim rights of its own, it is luxury.

Let us therefore resist these faults when they are demanding entrance, because, as I have said, it is easier to deny them admittance than to make them depart. [4]And if you cry: "One should be allowed a certain amount of grieving, and a certain amount of fear." I reply that the "certain amount" can be too long-drawn-out, and that it will refuse to stop short when you so desire. The wise man can safely control himself without becoming over-anxious; he can halt his tears and his pleasures at will; but in our case, because it is not easy to retrace our steps, it is best not to push ahead at all. [5]I think that Panaetius[2] gave a very neat answer to a certain youth who asked him whether the wise man should become a lover: "As to the wise man, we shall see later; but you and I, who are as yet far removed from wisdom, should not trust ourselves to fall into a state that is disordered, uncontrolled, enslaved to another,[3] contemptible to itself. If our love be not spurned, we are excited by its kindness; if it be scorned, we are kindled by our pride. An easily won love hurts us as much as one which is difficult to win; we are captured by that which is compliant, and we struggle with that which is hard. Therefore, knowing our weakness, let us remain quiet. Let us not expose this unstable spirit to the temptations of drink, or beauty, or flattery, or anything that coaxes and allures."

[6]Now that which Panaetius replied to the question about love may be applied, I believe, to all the emotions. In so far as we are able, let us step back from slippery places; even on dry ground it is hard enough to take a sturdy stand. [7]At this point, I know, you will confront me with that common complaint against the Stoics: "Your promises are too great, and your counsels too hard. We are mere manikins, unable to deny ourselves everything. We shall sorrow, but not to any great extent; we shall feel desires, but in moderation; we shall give way to anger, but we shall be appeased." [8]And do you know why we have not the power to attain this Stoic ideal? It is because we refuse

to believe in our power. Nay, of a surety, there is something else which plays a part: it is because we are in love with our vices; we uphold them and prefer to make excuses for them rather than shake them off. We mortals have been endowed with sufficient strength by nature, if only we use this strength, if only we concentrate our powers and rouse them all to help us or at least not to hinder us. The reason is unwillingness, the excuse, inability. Farewell.

Footnotes

1. For a discussion of ἀπάθεια see Epp. ix. 2 ff. and lxxxv. 3 ff.

2. Frag. 56 Fowler.

3. Literally, "out of our possession" (from *mancipium*, "ownership").

CXVII. ON REAL ETHICS AS SUPERIOR TO SYLLOGISTIC SUBTLETIES

[1]You will be fabricating much trouble for me, and you will be unconsciously embroiling me in a great discussion, and in considerable bother, if you put such petty questions as these; for in settling them I cannot disagree with my fellow-Stoics without impairing my standing among them, nor can I subscribe to such ideas without impairing my conscience. Your query is, whether the Stoic belief is true: that wisdom is a Good, but that *being wise* is not a Good.[1] I shall first set forth the Stoic view, and then I shall be bold enough to deliver my own opinion.

[2]We of the Stoic school believe that the Good is corporeal, because the Good is active, and whatever is active is corporeal. That which is good, is helpful. But, in order to be helpful, it must be active; so, if it is active, it is corporeal. They (the Stoics) declare that wisdom is a Good; it therefore follows that one must also call wisdom corporeal. [3]But they do not think that *being wise* can be rated on the same basis. For it is incorporeal and accessory to something else, in other words, wisdom; hence it is in no respect active or helpful.

"What, then?" is the reply; "Why do we not say that *being wise* is a Good?" We do say so; but only by referring it to that on which it depends–in other words, wisdom itself. [4]Let me tell you what answers other philosophers make to these objectors, before I myself begin to form my own creed and to take my place entirely on another side. "Judged in that light," they say, "not even *living happily* is a Good. Willy nilly, such persons ought to reply that the happy life is a Good, but that *living happily* is not a Good." [5]And this objection is also raised against our school: "You wish to be wise. Therefore, *being wise* is a thing to be desired. And if it be a thing to be desired it is a Good." So our philosophers are forced to twist their words and insert another syllable into the word "desired,"–a syllable which our language does not normally allow to be inserted. But, with your permission, I shall add it. "That which is good," they say, "is a thing to be desired; the *desirable*[2] thing is that which falls to our lot after we have attained the Good. For the desirable is not sought as a Good; it is an accessory to the Good after the Good has been attained."

[6]I myself do not hold the same view, and I judge that our philosophers[3] have come down to this argument because they are already bound by the first link in the chain and for that reason may not alter their definition. People are wont to concede much to the things which all men take for granted; in our eyes the fact that all men agree upon something is a proof of its truth. For instance, we infer that the gods exist, for this reason, among others–that there is implanted in everyone an idea concerning deity, and there is no people so far beyond the reach of laws and customs that it does not believe at least in gods of some sort. And when we discuss the immortality of the soul, we are influenced in no small degree by the general opinion of mankind, who either fear or worship the spirits of the lower world. I make the most of this general belief: you can find no one who does not hold that wisdom is a Good, and being wise also. [7]I shall not

appeal to the populace, like a conquered gladiator; let us come to close quarters, using our own weapons.

When something affects a given object, is it outside the object which it affects, or is it inside the object it affects? If it is inside the object it affects, it is as corporeal as the object which it affects. For nothing can affect another object without touching it, and that which touches is corporeal. If it is outside, it withdraws after having affected the object. And withdrawal means motion. And that which possesses motion, is corporeal. [8]You expect me, I suppose, to deny that "race" differs from "running," that "heat" differs from "being hot," that "light" differs from "giving light." I grant that these pairs vary, but hold that they are not in separate classes. If good health is an indifferent[4] quality, then so is *being in good health*; if beauty is an indifferent quality, then so is *being beautiful*. If justice is a Good, then so is *being just*. And if baseness is an evil, then it is an evil to be base–just as much as, if sore eyes are an evil, the state of having sore eyes is also an evil. Neither quality, you may be sure, can exist without the other. He who is wise is a man of wisdom; he who is a man of wisdom is wise. So true it is that we cannot doubt the quality of the one to equal the quality of the other, that they are both regarded by certain persons as one and the same.

[9]Here is a question, however, which I should be glad to put: granted that all things are either good or bad or indifferent–in what class does *being wise* belong? People deny that it is a Good; and, as it obviously is not an evil, it must consequently be one of the "media." But we mean by the "medium," or the "indifferent" quality that which can fall to the lot of the bad no less than to the good–such things as money, beauty, or high social position. But the quality of *being wise* can fall to the lot of the good man alone; therefore *being wise* is not an indifferent quality. Nor is it an evil, either; because it cannot fall to the lot of the bad man; therefore, it is a Good. That which the good man alone can possess, is a Good; now *being wise* is the possession of the good man only; therefore it is a Good. [10]The objector replies: "It is only an accessory of wisdom." Very well, then, I say, this quality which you call *being wise*–does it actively produce wisdom, or is it a passive concomitant of wisdom? It is corporeal in either case. For that which is acted upon and that which acts, are alike corporeal; and, if corporeal, each is a Good. The only quality which could prevent it from being a Good, would be incorporeality.

[11]The Peripatetics believe that there is no distinction between *wisdom* and *being wise*, since either of these implies the other also. Now do you suppose that any man can *be wise* except one who possesses wisdom? Or that anyone who *is wise* does not possess wisdom? [12]The old masters of dialectic, however, distinguish between these two conceptions; and from them the classification has come right down to the Stoics. What sort of a classification this is, I shall explain: A field is one thing, and the possession of the field another thing; of course, because "possessing the field" refers to the possessor rather than to the field itself. Similarly, wisdom is one thing and *being wise* another. You will grant, I suppose, that these two are separate ideas–the possessed and the possessor: wisdom being that which one possesses, and he who *is wise* its possessor. Now wisdom is Mind perfected and developed to the highest and best degree. For it is the art of life. And what is *being wise*? I cannot call it "Mind Perfected," but rather that which falls to the lot of him who possesses a "mind perfected"; thus a good mind is one thing, and the so-called possession of a good mind another.

[13]"There are," it is said, "certain natural classes of bodies; we say: 'This is a man,' 'this is a horse.' Then there attend on the bodily natures certain movements of the mind which declare something about the body. And these have a certain essential quality which is sundered from body; for example: 'I see Cato walking.' The senses indicate this, and the mind believes it. What I see, is *body*, and upon this I concentrate my eyes and my mind. Again, I say: 'Cato walks.' What I say," they continue, "is not body; it is a certain declarative fact concerning body–called variously an 'utterance,' a 'declaration,' a 'statement.' Thus, when we say 'wisdom,' we mean something *pertaining* to body; when we say '*he is wise*,' we are speaking *concerning* body. And it makes considerable difference whether you mention the person directly, or speak concerning

the same person.

[30]Let us rush past all this clever nonsense, and hurry on to that which will bring us real assistance. No man who is anxiously running after a midwife for his daughter in her birth-pangs will stop to read the praetor's edict[7] or the order of events at the games. No one who is speeding to save his burning house will scan a checker-board[8] to speculate how the imprisoned piece can be freed. [31]But good heavens!–In your case all sorts of news are announced on all sides–your house afire, your children in danger, your country in a state of siege, your property plundered. Add to this shipwreck, earthquakes, and all other objects of dread; harassed amid these troubles, are you taking time for matters which serve merely for mental entertainment? Do you ask what difference there is between wisdom and *being wise*? Do you tie and untie knots while such a ruin is hanging over your head? [32]Nature has not given us such a generous and free-handed space of time that we can have the leisure to waste any of it. Mark also how much is lost even when men are very careful: people are robbed of one thing by ill-health and of another thing by illness in the family; at one time private, at another public, business absorbs the attention; and all the while sleep shares our lives with us.

Out of this time, so short and swift, that carries us away in its flight, of what avail is it to spend the greater part on useless things? [33]Besides, our minds are accustomed to entertain rather than to cure themselves, to make an aesthetic pleasure out of philosophy, when philosophy should really be a remedy. What the distinction is between wisdom and *being wise* I do not know; but I do know that it makes no difference to me whether I know such matters or am ignorant of them. Tell me: when I have found out the difference between wisdom and *being wise*, shall I be wise?

Why then do you occupy me with the words rather than with the works of wisdom? Make me braver, make me calmer, make me the equal of Fortune, make me her superior. And I can be her superior, if I apply to this end everything that I learn. Farewell.

Footnotes

1. For this sort of discussion see Ep. cxiii. 1 ff.

2. This adjective *expetibilis* is found in Tacitus, *Ann.* xvi. 21, and in Boethius, *Cons.* ii. 6.

3. i.e., the Stoics as mentioned above (with whom Seneca often disagrees on minor details).

4. i.e., the external things; see Ep. xciii. 7 and note,–defined more specifically in § 9 below.

5. Presumably an allusion to the syllogistic enthusiasts rather than to Lucillius and his like.

6. i.e., wisdom or being wise.

7. Cf. Ep. xlviii. 10 and note.

8. Cf. Ep. cvi. 11 and note.

CXVIII. ON THE VANITY OF PLACE-SEEKING

[1]You have been demanding more frequent letters from me. But if we compare the accounts, you will not be on the credit side.[1] We had indeed made the agreement that your part came first, that you should write the first letters, and that I should answer. However, I shall not be disagreeable; I know that it is safe to trust you, so I shall pay in advance, and yet not do as the eloquent Cicero bids Atticus do:[2] "Even if you have nothing to say, write whatever enters your head." [2]For there will always be something for me to write about, even omitting all the kinds of news with which Cicero fills his correspondence: what candidate is in difficulties, who is striving on borrowed resources and who on his own; who is a candidate for the consulship relying on Caesar, or on Pompey, or on his own strong-box; what a merciless usurer is Caecilius,[3] out of whom his friends cannot screw a penny for less than one per cent each month.

But it is preferable to deal with one's own ills, rather than with another's—to sift oneself and see for how many vain things one is a candidate, and cast a vote for none of them. [3]This, my dear Lucilius, is a noble thing, this brings peace and freedom—to canvass for nothing, and to pass by all the elections of Fortune. How can you call it enjoyable, when the tribes are called together and the candidates are making offerings in their favourite temples—some of them promising money gifts and others doing business by means of an agent, or wearing down their hands with the kisses of those to whom they will refuse the least finger-touch after being elected—when all are excitedly awaiting the announcement of the herald, do you call it enjoyable, I say, to stand idle and look on at this Vanity Fair without either buying or selling? [4]How much greater joy does one feel who looks without concern, not merely upon the election of a praetor or of a consul, but upon that great struggle in which some are seeking yearly honours, and others permanent power, and others the triumph and the prosperous outcome of war, and others riches, or marriage and offspring, or the welfare of themselves and their relatives! What a great-souled action it is to be the only person who is canvassing for nothing, offering prayers to no man, and saying: "Fortune, I have nothing to do with you. I am not at your service. I know that men like Cato are spurned by you, and men like Vatinius made by you.[4] I ask no favours." This is the way to reduce Fortune to the ranks.

[5]These, then, are the things about which we may write in turn, and this is the ever fresh material which we may dig out as we scan the restless multitudes of men, who, in order to attain something ruinous, struggle on through evil to evil, and seek that which they must presently shun or even find surfeiting. [6]For who was ever satisfied, after attainment, with that which loomed up large as he prayed for it? Happiness is not, as men think, a greedy thing; it is a lowly thing; for that reason it never gluts a man's desire. You deem lofty the objects you seek, because you are on a low level and hence far away from them; but they are mean in the sight of him who has reached them. And I am very much mistaken if he does not desire to climb still higher; that which you regard as the top is merely a rung on the ladder. [7]Now all men suffer from ignorance of the truth; deceived by common report, they make for these ends as if they were good, and then, after having won their wish, and suffered much, they find them evil, or empty, or less important than they had expected. Most men admire that which deceives them at a distance, and by the crowd good things are supposed to be big things.

[8]Now, lest this happen also in our own case, let us ask what is the Good. It has been explained in various ways; different men have described it in different ways. Some define it in this way. "That which attracts and calls the spirit to itself is a Good." But the objection at once comes up—what if it does attract, but straight to ruin? You know how seductive many evils are. That which is true differs from that which looks like the truth; hence the Good is connected with the true, for it is not good unless it is also true. But that which attracts and allures, is only *like* the truth; it steals your attention, demands your interest, and draws you to itself. [9]Therefore, some have given this definition: "That is good which inspires desire for itself, or rouses towards itself the impulse of a struggling soul." There is the same objection to this idea; for many things rouse the soul's impulses, and yet the search for them is harmful to the seeker. The following definition is better: "That is good which rouses the soul's impulse towards itself in accordance with nature, and is worth seeking only when it begins to be thoroughly worth seeking." It is by this time an honourable thing; for that is a thing completely worth seeking.

[10]The present topic suggests that I state the difference between the Good and the honourable.[5] Now they have a certain quality which blends with both and is inseparable from either: nothing can be good unless it contains an element of the honourable, and the honourable is necessarily good. What, then, is the difference between these two qualities? The honourable is the perfect Good, and the happy life is fulfilled thereby; through its influence other things also are rendered good. [11]I mean something like this: there are certain things which are neither good nor bad—as military or diplomatic service, or the pronouncing of legal decisions. When such pursuits have been honour-

ably conducted, they begin to be good, and they change over from the "indifferent" class into the Good. The Good results from partnership with the honourable, but the honourable is good in itself. The Good springs from the honourable, but the latter from itself. What is good might have been bad; what is honourable could never have been anything but good.

[12]Some have defined as follows: "That is good which is according to nature." Now attend to my own statement: that which is good is according to nature, but that which is according to nature does not also become immediately good; for many things harmonize with nature, but are so petty that it is not suitable to call them good. For they are unimportant and deserve to be despised. But there is no such thing as a very small and despicable good, for, as long as it is scanty, it is not good, and when it begins to be good, it ceases to be scanty. How, then, can the Good be recognized? Only if it is completely according to nature.

[13]People say: "You admit that that which is good is according to nature; for this is its peculiar quality. You admit, too, that there are other things according to nature, which, however, are not good. How then can the former be good, and the latter not? How can there be an alteration in the peculiar quality of a thing, when each has, in common with the other, the special attribute of being in accord with nature?" [14]Surely because of its magnitude. It is no new idea that certain objects change as they grow. A person, once a child, becomes a youth; his peculiar quality is transformed; for the child could not reason, but the youth possesses reason. Certain things not only grow in size as they develop, but grow into something else. [15]Some reply: "But that which becomes greater does not necessarily become different. It matters not at all whether you pour wine into a flask or into a vat; the wine keeps its peculiar quality in both vessels. Small and large quantities of honey are not distinct in taste." But these are different cases which you mention; for wine and honey have a uniform quality; no matter how much the quantity is enlarged, the quality is the same. [16]For some things endure according to their kind and their peculiar qualities, even when they are enlarged.

There are others, however, which, after many increments, are altered by the last addition; there is stamped upon them a new character, different from that of yore. One stone makes an archway—the stone which wedges the leaning sides and holds the arch together by its position in the middle. And why does the last addition, although very slight, make a great deal of difference? Because it does not increase; it fills up. [17]Some things, through development, put off their former shape and are altered into a new figure.[6] When the mind has for a long time developed some idea, and in the attempt to grasp its magnitude has become weary, that thing begins to be called "infinite." And then this has become something far different from what it was when it seemed great but finite. In the same way we have thought of something as difficult to divide; at the very end, as the task grows more and more hard, the thing is found to be "indivisible." Similarly, from that which could scarcely or with difficulty be moved we have advanced on and on—until we reach the "immovable." By the same reasoning a certain thing was according to nature; its greatness has altered it into some other peculiar quality and has rendered it a Good. Farewell.

Footnotes

1. i.e., *solvendo aeri alieno*, "in a position to pay one's debts."

2. *Ad Att.* i. 12. 4.

3. *Ad Att.* i. 12. 1: "Even his relatives can't screw a penny out of Caecilius at less than 12 per cent" (Winstedt).

4. For the character of Vatinius see Ep. xciv. 25 note; for a similar comparison of V. with Cato see Ep. cxx. 19.

5. Discussed in Ep. lxxi. 4 f., lxxiv. 30, lxxvi. 16 ff., and especially lxxxvii. 25: *nam idem est honestum et bonum*. The Academic school tended to draw more of a distinction than the Stoic, as in Ep. lxxxv. 17 f.

6. This argument (that complete virtue is a sort of transforming climax of life) is not to be confused with the theory of *accessio* (a term used also in Roman law), or "addition";

for virtue does not permit of *accessio,* or the addition of any external advantage. See Ep. lxvi. 9 *quid accedere perfecto potest?*

CXIX. ON NATURE AS OUR BEST PROVIDER

[1]Whenever I have made a discovery, I do not wait for you to cry "Shares!" I say it to myself in your behalf. If you wish to know what it is that I have found, open your pocket; it is clear profit.[1] What I shall teach you is the ability to become rich as speedily as possible. How keen you are to hear the news! And rightly; I shall lead you by a short cut to the greatest riches. It will be necessary, however, for you to find a loan; in order to be able to do business, you must contract a debt, although I do not wish you to arrange the loan through a middle-man, nor do I wish the brokers to be discussing your rating. [2]I shall furnish you with a ready creditor, Cato's famous one, who says:[2] "Borrow from yourself!" No matter how small it is, it will be enough if we can only make up the deficit from our own resources. For, my dear Lucilius, it does not matter whether you crave nothing, or whether you possess something. The important principle in either case is the same–freedom from worry.

But I do not counsel you to deny anything to nature–for nature is insistent and cannot be overcome; she demands her due–but you should know that anything in excess of nature's wants is a mere "extra"[3] and is not necessary. [3]If I am hungry, I must eat. Nature does not care whether the bread is the coarse kind or the finest wheat; she does not desire the stomach to be entertained, but to be filled. And if I am thirsty, Nature does not care whether I drink water from the nearest reservoir, or whether I freeze it artificially by sinking it in large quantities of snow. Nature orders only that the thirst be quenched; and it does not matter whether it be a golden, or crystal, or murrine goblet, or a cup from Tibur,[4] or the hollow hand. [4]Look to the end, in all matters, and then you will cast away superfluous things. Hunger calls me; let me stretch forth my hand to that which is nearest; my very hunger has made attractive in my eyes whatever I can grasp. A starving man despises nothing.

[5]Do you ask, then, what it is that has pleased me? It is this noble saying which I have discovered: "The wise man is the keenest seeker for the riches of nature." "What", you ask, "will you present me with an empty plate? What do you mean? I had already arranged my coffers;[5] I was already looking about to see some stretch of water on which I might embark for purposes of trade, some state revenues that I might handle, and some merchandise that I might acquire. That is deceit–showing me poverty after promising me riches." But, friend, do you regard a man as poor to whom nothing is wanting? "It is, however," you reply, "thanks to himself and his endurance, and not thanks to his fortune." Do you, then, hold that such a man is not rich, just because his wealth can never fail? [6]Would you rather have much, or enough? He who has much desires more–a proof that he has not yet acquired enough; but he who has enough has attained that which never fell to the rich man's lot–a stopping-point. Do you think that this condition to which I refer is not riches, just because no man has ever been proscribed as a result of possessing them? Or because sons and wives have never thrust poison down one's throat for that reason? Or because in war-time these riches are unmolested? Or because they bring leisure in time of peace? Or because it is not dangerous to possess them, or troublesome to invest them?

[7]"But one possesses too little, if one is merely free from cold and hunger and thirst." Jupiter himself however, is no better off. Enough is never too little, and not-enough is never too much. Alexander was poor even after his conquest of Darius and the Indies. Am I wrong? He seeks something which he can really make his own, exploring unknown seas, sending new fleets over the Ocean, and, so to speak, breaking down the very bars of the universe. But that which is enough for nature, is not enough for man. [8]There have been found persons who crave something more after obtaining everything; so blind are their wits and so readily does each man forget his start after he has got under way. He who[6] was but lately the disputed lord of an unknown corner of the world, is dejected when, after reaching the limits of the globe, he must march back

through a world which he has made his own. [9]Money never made a man rich; on the contrary, it always smites men with a greater craving for itself. Do you ask the reason for this? He who possesses more begins to be able to possess still more.

To sum up, you may hale forth for our inspection any of the millionaires whose names are told off when one speaks of Crassus and Licinus. Let him bring along his rating and his present property and his future expectations, and let him add them all together: such a man, according to my belief, is poor; according to yours, he may be poor some day. [10]He, however, who has arranged his affairs according to nature's demands, is free from the fear, as well as from the sensation, of poverty. And in order that you may know how hard it is to narrow one's interests down to the limits of nature—even this very person of whom we speak, and whom you call poor, possesses something actually superfluous. [11]Wealth, however, blinds and attracts the mob, when they see a large bulk of ready money brought out of a man's house, or even his walls crusted with abundance of gold, or a retinue that is chosen for beauty of physique, or for attractiveness of attire. The prosperity of all these men looks to public opinion; but the ideal man, whom we have snatched from the control of the people and of Fortune, is happy inwardly. [12]For as far as those persons are concerned, in whose minds bustling[7] poverty has wrongly stolen the title of riches—these individuals have riches just as we say that we "have a fever," when really the fever has us. Conversely, we are accustomed to say: "A fever grips him." And in the same way we should say: "Riches grip him." There is therefore no advice—and of such advice no one can have too much—which I would rather give you than this: that you should measure all things by the demands of Nature; for these demands can be satisfied either without cost or else very cheaply. Only, do not mix any vices with these demands. [13]Why need you ask how your food should be served, on what sort of table, with what sort of silver, with what well-matched and smooth-faced young servants? Nature demands nothing except mere food.

> Dost seek, when thirst inflames thy throat, a cup of gold?
> Dost scorn all else but peacock's flesh or turbot
> When the hunger comes upon thee?[8]

[14]Hunger is not ambitious; it is quite satisfied to come to an end; nor does it care very much what food brings it to an end. Those things are but the instruments of a luxury which is not "happiness"; a luxury which seeks how it may prolong hunger even after repletion, how to stuff the stomach, not to fill it, and how to rouse a thirst that has been satisfied with the first drink. Horace's words are therefore most excellent when he says that it makes no difference to one's thirst in what costly goblet, or with what elaborate state, the water is served. For if you believe it to be of importance how curly-haired your slave is, or how transparent is the cup which he offers you, you are not thirsty.

[15]Among other things, Nature has bestowed upon us this special boon: she relieves sheer necessity of squeamishness. The superfluous things admit of choice; we say: "That is not suitable "; "this is not well recommended"; "that hurts my eyesight." The Builder of the universe, who laid down for us the laws of life, provided that we should exist in well-being, but not in luxury. Everything conducive to our well-being is prepared and ready to our hands; but what luxury requires can never be got together except with wretchedness and anxiety.

[16]Let us therefore use this boon of Nature by reckoning it among the things of high importance; let us reflect that Nature's best title to our gratitude is that whatever we want because of sheer necessity we accept without squeamishness. Farewell.

Footnotes

1. Seneca here reverts to the money-metaphors of Epp. i.-xxxiii.–*lucellum, munusculum, diurna mercedula,* etc.

2. Frag. p. 79 Iordan.

3. i.e., "something for one's spare time"; cf. Ep. liii. 8 note, *non est quod precario philosopheris.*

4. i.e., of common earthenware.

5. i.e., had got my coffers ready for the promised wealth.

6. Alexander the Great.

7. i.e., a "poverty" which is never satisfied.

8. Horace, *Sat.* i. 2. 114 ff.

CXX. MORE ABOUT VIRTUE

¹Your letter roamed, over several little problems, but finally dwelt upon this alone, asking for explanation: "How do we acquire a knowledge of that which is good and that which is honourable?" In the opinion of other schools,¹ these two qualities are distinct; among our followers, however, they are merely divided. ²This is what I mean: Some believe the Good to be that which is useful; they accordingly bestow this title upon riches, horses, wine, and shoes; so cheaply do they view the Good, and to such base uses do they let it descend. They regard as honourable that which agrees with the principle of right conduct–such as taking dutiful care of an old father, relieving a friend's poverty, showing bravery on a campaign, and uttering prudent and well-balanced opinions. ³We, however, do make the Good and the honourable two things, but we make them out of one: only the honourable can be good; also, the honourable is necessarily good. I hold it superfluous to add the distinction between these two qualities, inasmuch as I have mentioned it so many times.² But I shall say this one thing–that we regard nothing as good which can be put to wrong use by any person. And you see for yourself to what wrong uses many men put their riches, their high position, or their physical powers.

To return to the matter on which you desire information: "How we first acquire the knowledge of that which is good and that which is honourable." ⁴Nature could not teach us this directly; she has given us the seeds of knowledge, but not knowledge itself. Some say that we merely happened upon this knowledge; but it is unbelievable that a vision of virtue could have presented itself to anyone by mere chance. We believe that it is inference due to observation, a comparison of events that have occurred frequently; our school of philosophy hold that the honourable and the good have been comprehended by analogy. Since the word "analogy"³ has been admitted to citizen rank by Latin scholars, I do not think that it ought to be condemned, but I do think it should be brought into the citizenship which it can justly claim. I shall, therefore, make use of the word, not merely as admitted, but as established.

Now what this "analogy" is, I shall explain. ⁵We understood what bodily health was: and from this basis we deduced the existence of a certain mental health also. We knew, too, bodily strength, and from this basis we inferred the existence of mental sturdiness. Kindly deeds, humane deeds, brave deeds, had at times amazed us; so we began to admire them as if they were perfect. Underneath, however, there were many faults, hidden by the appearance and the brilliancy of certain conspicuous acts; to these we shut our eyes. Nature bids us amplify praiseworthy things–everyone exalts renown beyond the truth. And thus from such deeds we deduced the conception of some great good. ⁶Fabricius rejected King Pyrrhus's gold, deeming it greater than a king's crown to be able to scorn a king's money. Fabricius also, when the royal physician promised to give his master poison, warned Pyrrhus to beware of a plot. The selfsame man had the resolution to refuse either to be won over by gold or to win by poison. So we admired the hero, who could not be moved by the promises of the king or against the king, who held fast to a noble ideal, and who–is anything more difficult?–was in war sinless; for he believed that wrongs could be committed even against an enemy, and in that extreme poverty which he had made his glory, shrank from receiving riches as he shrank from using poison. "Live," he cried, "O Pyrrhus, thanks to me, and rejoice, instead of grieving as you have done till now, that Fabricius cannot be bribed!"⁴

⁷Horatius Cocles⁵ blocked the narrow bridge alone, and ordered his retreat to be

tain to the very end of life's drama the character which you assumed at the beginning. See to it that men be able to praise you; if not, let them at least identify you. Indeed, with regard to the man whom you saw but yesterday, the question may properly be asked: "Who is he?" So great a change has there been! Farewell.

Footnotes

1. i.e., the Peripatetic and Academic schools.

2. Cf. Ep. cxviii. 10 and note.

3. Consult Sandys, *Hist. Class. Schol.* i. pp. 148 and 175 f. Alexandrian "analogists" opposed Pergamene "anomalists" with reference to the rules affecting the forms of words. Out of the controversy arose the scientific study of grammar.

4. The two stories refer to the years 280 and 279 B.C., during the campaigns of Pyrrhus in Italy.

5. See Livy, ii. 10.

6. Livy (loc cit.) reports him as saying: "*Tiberine pater, te sancte precor, haec arma et hunc militem propitio flumine accipias!*" Macaulay in his ballad translates Livy's quotation almost literally.

7. A chronic disease of Seneca himself. See the autobiographic fragment in Ep. lxxviii. 1 f.

8. Seneca is here developing the thought sketched in Ep. xii. 6 *unus autem dies gradus vitae est.*

9. For the same contrast cf. Ep. cxviii. 4 (and note). For the following names see Index of Proper Names.

10. Horace, *Sat.* i. 3. 11-17.

CXXI. ON INSTINCT IN ANIMALS

[1]You will bring suit against me, I feel sure, when I set forth for you to-day's little problem, with which we have already fumbled long enough. You will cry out again: "What has this to do with character?" Cry out if you like, but let me first of all match you with other opponents,[1] against whom you may bring suit–such as Posidonius and Archidemus;[2] these men will stand trial. I shall then go on to say that whatever deals with character does not necessarily produce good character. [2]Man needs one thing for his food, another for his exercise, another for his clothing, another for his instruction, and another for his pleasure. Everything, however, has reference to man's needs, although everything does not make him better. Character is affected by different things in different ways: some things serve to correct and regulate character, and others investigate its nature and origin. [3]And when I seek the reason why Nature brought forth man, and why she set him above other animals, do you suppose that I have left character-study in the rear? No; that is wrong. For how are you to know what character is desirable, unless you have discovered what is best suited to man? Or unless you have studied his nature? You can find out what you should do and what you should avoid, only when you have learned what you owe to your own nature.

[4]"I desire," you say, "to learn how I may crave less, and fear less. Rid me of my unreasoning beliefs. Prove to me that so-called felicity is fickle and empty, and that the word easily admits of a syllable's increase."[3] I shall fulfil your want, encouraging your virtues and lashing your vices. People may decide that I am too zealous and reckless in this particular; but I shall never cease to hound wickedness, to check the most unbridled emotions, to soften the force of pleasures which will result in pain, and to cry down men's prayers. Of course I shall do this; for it is the greatest evils that we have prayed for, and from that which has made us give thanks comes all that demands consolation.

[5]Meanwhile, allow me to discuss thoroughly some points which may seem now to be rather remote from the present inquiry. We were once debating whether all animals had any feelings about their "constitution."[4] That this is the case is proved particularly

by their making motions of such fitness and nimbleness that they seem to be trained for the purpose. Every being is clever in its own line. The skilled workman handles his tools with an ease born of experience; the pilot knows how to steer his ship skilfully; the artist can quickly lay on the colours which he has prepared in great variety for the purpose of rendering the likeness, and passes with ready eye and hand from palette to canvas. In the same way an animal is agile in all that pertains to the use of its body. ⁶We are apt to wonder at skilled dancers because their gestures are perfectly adapted to the meaning of the piece and its accompanying emotions, and their movements match the speed of the dialogue. But that which art gives to the craftsman, is given to the animal by nature. No animal handles its limbs with difficulty, no animal is at a loss how to use its body. This function they exercise immediately at birth. They come into the world with this knowledge; they are born full-trained.

⁷But people reply: "The reason why animals are so dexterous in the use of their limbs is that if they move them unnaturally, they will feel pain. They are *compelled* to do thus, according to your school, and it is fear rather than will-power which moves them in the right direction." This idea is wrong. Bodies driven by a compelling force move slowly; but those which move of their own accord possess alertness. The proof that it is not fear of pain which prompts them thus, is, that even when pain checks them they struggle to carry out their natural motions. ⁸Thus the child who is trying to stand and is becoming used to carry his own weight, on beginning to test his strength, falls and rises again and again with tears until through painful effort he has trained himself to the demands of nature. And certain animals with hard shells, when turned on their backs, twist and grope with their feet and make motions side-ways until they are restored to their proper position. The tortoise on his back feels no suffering; but he is restless because he misses his natural condition, and does not cease to shake himself about until he stands once more upon his feet.

⁹So all these animals have a consciousness of their physical constitution, and for that reason can manage their limbs as readily as they do; nor have we any better proof that they come into being equipped with this knowledge than the fact that no animal is unskilled in the use of its body. ¹⁰But some object as follows: "According to your account, one's constitution consists of a ruling power⁵ in the soul which has a certain relation towards the body. But how can a child comprehend this intricate and subtle principle, which I can scarcely explain even to you? All living creatures should be born logicians, so as to understand a definition which is obscure to the majority of Roman citizens!" ¹¹Your objection would be true if I spoke of living creatures as understanding "a definition of constitution," and not "their actual constitution." Nature is easier to understand than to explain; hence, the child of whom we were speaking does not understand what "constitution" is, but understands *its own* constitution. He does not know what "a living creature" is, but he feels that he is an animal. ¹²Moreover, that very constitution of his own he only understands confusedly, cursorily, and darkly. We also know that we possess souls, but we do not know the essence, the place, the quality, or the source, of the soul. Such as is the consciousness of our souls which we possess, ignorant as we are of their nature and position, even so all animals possess a consciousness of their own constitutions. For they must necessarily feel this, because it is the same agency by which they feel other things also; they must necessarily have a feeling of the principle which they obey and by which they are controlled. ¹³Every one of us understands that there is something which stirs his impulses, but he does not know what it is. He knows that he has a sense of striving, although he does not know what it is or its source. Thus even children and animals have a consciousness of their primary element, but it is not very clearly outlined or portrayed.

¹⁴"You maintain, do you," says the objector, "that every living thing is at the start adapted to its constitution, but that man's constitution is a reasoning one, and hence man is adapted to himself not merely as a living, but as a reasoning, being? For man is dear to himself in respect of that wherein he is a man. How, then, can a child, being not yet gifted with reason, adapt himself to a reasoning constitution?" ¹⁵But each age has its own constitution, different in the case of the child, the boy, and the old man; they

are all adapted to the constitution wherein they find themselves. The child is toothless, and he is fitted to this condition. Then his teeth grow, and he is fitted to that condition also. Vegetation also, which will develop into grain and fruits, has a special constitution when young and scarcely peeping over the tops of the furrows, another when it is strengthened and stands upon a stalk which is soft but strong enough to bear its weight, and still another when the colour changes to yellow, prophesies threshing-time, and hardens in the ear–no matter what may be the constitution into which the plant comes, it keeps it, and conforms thereto. [16] The periods of infancy, boyhood, youth, and old age, are different; but I, who have been infant, boy, and youth, am still the same. Thus, although each has at different times a different constitution, the adaptation of each to its constitution is the same. For nature does not consign boyhood or youth, or old age, to me; it consigns me to them. Therefore, the child is adapted to that constitution which is his at the present moment of childhood, not to that which will be his in youth. For even if there is in store for him any higher phase into which he must be changed, the state in which he is born is also according to nature. [17] First of all, the living being is adapted to itself, for there must be a pattern to which all other things may be referred. I seek pleasure; for whom? For myself. I am therefore looking out for myself. I shrink from pain; on behalf of whom? Myself. Therefore, I am looking out for myself. Since I gauge all my actions with reference to my own welfare, I am looking out for myself before all else. This quality exists in all living beings–not engrafted but inborn.

[18] Nature brings up her own offspring and does not cast them away; and because the most assured security is that which is nearest, every man has been entrusted to his own self. Therefore, as I have remarked in the course of my previous correspondence, even young animals, on issuing from the mother's womb or from the egg, know at once of their own accord what is harmful for them, and avoid death-dealing things.[6] They even shrink when they notice the shadow of birds of prey which flit overhead.

No animal, when it enters upon life, is free from the fear of death. [19] People may ask: "How can an animal at birth have an understanding of things wholesome or destructive?" The first question, however, is *whether* it can have such understanding, and not *how* it can understand. And it is clear that they have such understanding from the fact that, even if you add understanding, they will act no more adequately than they did in the first place. Why should the hen show no fear of the peacock or the goose, and yet run from the hawk, which is a so much smaller animal not even familiar to the hen? Why should young chickens fear a cat and not a dog.? These fowls clearly have a presentiment of harm–one not based on actual experiments; for they avoid a thing before they can possibly have experience of it. [20] Furthermore, in order that you may not suppose this to be the result of chance, they do not shrink from certain other things which you would expect them to fear, nor do they ever forget vigilance and care in this regard; they all possess equally the faculty of avoiding what is destructive. Besides, their fear does not grow as their lives lengthen.

Hence indeed it is evident that these animals have not reached such a condition through experience; it is because of an inborn desire for self-preservation. The teachings of experience are slow and irregular; but whatever Nature communicates belongs equally to everyone, and comes immediately. [21] If, however, you require an explanation, shall I tell you how it is that every living thing tries to understand that which is harmful? It feels that it is constructed of flesh; and so it perceives to what an extent flesh may be cut or burned or crushed, and what animals are equipped with the power of doing this damage; it is of animals of this sort that it derives an unfavourable and hostile idea. These tendencies are closely connected; for each animal at the same time consults its own safety, seeking that which helps it, and shrinks from that which will harm it. Impulses towards useful objects, and revulsion from the opposite, are according to nature; without any reflection to prompt the idea, and without any advice, whatever Nature has prescribed, is done.

[22] Do you not see how skillful bees are in building their cells? How completely harmonious in sharing and enduring toil? Do you not see how the spider weaves a web

so subtle that man's hand cannot imitate it; and what a task it is to arrange the threads, some directed straight towards the centre, for the sake of making the web solid, and others running in circles and lessening in thickness–for the purpose of tangling and catching in a sort of net the smaller insects for whose ruin the spider spreads the web? [23]This art is born, not taught; and for this reason no animal is more skilled than any other. You will notice that all spider-webs are equally fine, and that the openings in all honeycomb cells are identical in shape. Whatever art communicates is uncertain and uneven; but Nature's assignments are always uniform. Nature has communicated nothing except the duty of taking care of themselves and the skill to do so; that is why living and learning begin at the same time. [24]No wonder that living things are born with a gift whose absence would make birth useless. This is the first equipment that Nature granted them for the maintenance of their existence–the quality of adaptability and self-love. They could not survive except by desiring to do so. Nor would this desire alone have made them prosper, but without it nothing could have prospered. In no animal can you observe any low esteem, or even any carelessness, of self. Dumb beasts, sluggish in other respects, are clever at living. So you will see that creatures which are useless to others are alert for their own preservation.[7] Farewell.

Footnotes

1. i.e., in addition to myself and confirming my statement.

2. Frag. 17 von Arnim.

3. i.e. *felicitas* becomes in*felicitas*.

4. i.e., their physical make-up, the elements of their physical being.

5. i.e., the "soul of the world," of which each living soul is a part. The Stoics believed that it was situated in the heart. Zeno called it ἡγεμονικόν, "ruling power"; while the Romans used the term *principale* or *principatus*. The principle described above is ὀρμή (impulse) or τόνος (tension).

6. Seneca is both sound and modern in his account of animal "intelligence." It is instinct, due to sensory-motor reactions, and depending largely upon type heredity.

7. A theme developed by Cicero (*De fin.* iii. 16): *placet . . . simul atque natum sit animal . . . , ipsum sibi conciliari et commendari ad se conservandum.*

CXXII. ON DARKNESS AS A VEIL FOR WICKEDNESS

[1]The day has already begun to lessen. It has shrunk considerably, but yet will still allow a goodly space of time if one rises, so to speak, with the day itself. We are more industrious, and we are better men if we anticipate the day and welcome the dawn; but we are base churls if we lie dozing when the sun is high in the heavens, or if we wake up only when noon arrives; and even then to many it seems not yet dawn. [2]Some have reversed the functions of light and darkness; they open eyes sodden with yesterday's debauch only at the approach of night. It is just like the condition of those peoples whom, according to Vergil, Nature has hidden away and placed in an abode directly opposite to our own:

> When in our face the Dawn with panting steeds
> Breathes down, for them the ruddy evening kindles
> Her late-lit fires.[1]

It is not the country of these men, so much as it is their life, that is "directly opposite" to our own. [3]There may be Antipodes dwelling in this same city of ours who, in Cato's words,[2] "have never seen the sun rise or set." Do you think that these men know how to live, if they do not know when to live? Do these men fear death, if they have buried themselves alive? They are as weird as the birds of night.[3] Although they pass their hours of darkness amid wine and perfumes, although they spend the whole extent of their unnatural waking hours in eating dinners–and those too cooked separately to make up many courses–they are not really banqueting; they are conducting their own funeral services. And the dead at least have their banquets by daylight.⁴

But indeed to one who is active no day is long. So let us lengthen our lives; for the duty and the proof of life consist in action. Cut short the night: use some of it for the day's business. ⁴Birds that are being prepared for the banquet, that they may be easily fattened through lack of exercise, are kept in darkness; and similarly, if men vegetate without physical activity, their idle bodies are overwhelmed with flesh, and in their self-satisfied retirement the fat of indolence grows upon them. Moreover, the bodies of those who have sworn allegiance to the hours of darkness have a loathsome appearance. Their complexions are more alarming than those of anaemic invalids; they are lackadaisical and flabby with dropsy; though still alive, they are already carrion. But this, to my thinking, would be among the least of their evils. How much more darkness there is in their souls! Such a man is internally dazed; his vision is darkened; he envies the blind. And what man ever had eyes for the purpose of seeing in the dark?

⁵You ask me how this depravity comes upon the soul–this habit of reversing the daylight and giving over one's whole existence to the night? All vices rebel against Nature; they all abandon the appointed order. It is the motto of luxury to enjoy what is unusual, and not only to depart from that which is right, but to leave it as far behind as possible, and finally even take a stand in opposition thereto. ⁶Do you not believe that men live contrary to Nature who drink fasting, ⁵ who take wine into empty veins, and pass to their food in a state of intoxication? And yet this is one of youth's popular vices–to perfect their strength in order to drink on the very threshold of the bath, amid the unclad bathers; nay even to soak in wine and then immediately to rub off the sweat which they have promoted by many a hot glass of liquor! To them, a glass after lunch or one after dinner is *bourgeois*; it is what the country squires do, who are not connoisseurs in pleasure. This unmixed wine delights them just because there is no food to float in it, because it readily makes its way into their muscles; this boozing pleases them just because the stomach is empty.

⁷Do you not believe that men live contrary to Nature who exchange the fashion of their attire with women?⁶ Do not men live contrary to Nature who endeavour to look fresh and boyish at an age unsuitable for such an attempt? What could be more cruel or more wretched? Cannot time and man's estate ever carry such a person beyond an artificial boyhood?⁷ ⁸Do not men live contrary to Nature who crave roses in winter, or seek to raise a spring flower like the lily by means of hot-water heaters and artificial changes of temperature? Do not men live contrary to Nature who grow fruit-trees on the top of a wall? Or raise waving forests upon the roofs and battlements of their houses–the roots starting at a point to which it would be outlandish for the tree-tops to reach? Do not men live contrary to Nature who lay the foundations of bathrooms in the sea and do not imagine that they can enjoy their swim unless the heated pool is lashed as with the waves of a storm?

⁹When men have begun to desire all things in opposition to the ways of Nature, they end by entirely abandoning the ways of Nature. They cry: "It is daytime–let us go to sleep! It is the time when men rest: now for exercise, now for our drive, now for our lunch! Lo, the dawn approaches: it is dinner-time! We should not do as mankind do. It is low and mean to live in the usual and conventional way. Let us abandon the ordinary sort of day. Let us have a morning that is a special feature of ours, peculiar to ourselves!" ¹⁰Such men are, in my opinion, as good as dead. Are they not all but present at a funeral–and before their time too–when they live amid torches and tapers?⁸ I remember that this sort of life was very fashionable at one time: among such men as Acilius Buta, a person of praetorian rank, who ran through a tremendous estate and on confessing his bankruptcy to Tiberius, received the answer: "You have waked up too late!" ¹¹Julius Montanus was once reading a poem aloud he was a middling good poet, noted for his friendship with Tiberius, as well as his fall from favour. He always used to fill his poems with a generous sprinkling of sunrises and sunsets. Hence, when a certain person was complaining that Montanus had read all day long, and declared that no man should attend any of his readings, Natta Pinarius⁹ remarked: "I couldn't

make a fairer bargain than this: I am ready to listen to him from sunrise to sunset!" [12]Montanus was reading, and had reached the words:[10]

> 'Gins the bright morning to spread forth his flames clear-burning; the red dawn
> Scatters its light; and the sad-eyed swallow[11] returns to her nestlings,
> Bringing the chatterers' food, and with sweet bill sharing and serving.

Then Varus, a Roman knight, the hanger-on of Marcus Vinicius,[12] and a sponger at elegant dinners which he earned by his degenerate wit, shouted: "Bed-time for Buta!" [13]And later, when Montanus declaimed

> Lo, now the shepherds have folded their flocks, and the slow-moving darkness
> 'Gins to spread silence o'er lands that are drowsily lulled into slumber,

this same Varus remarked: "What? Night already? I'll go and pay my morning call on Buta!" You see, nothing was more notorious than Buta's upside-down manner of life. But this life, as I said, was fashionable at one time. [14]And the reason why some men live thus is not because they think that night in itself offers any greater attractions, but because that which is normal gives them no particular pleasure; light being a bitter enemy of the evil conscience, and, when one craves or scorns all things in proportion as they have cost one much or little, illumination for which one does not pay is an object of contempt. Moreover, the luxurious person wishes to be an object of gossip his whole life; if people are silent about him, he thinks that he is wasting his time. Hence he is uncomfortable whenever any of his actions escape notoriety.

Many men eat up their property, and many men keep mistresses. If you would win a reputation among such persons, you must make your programme not only one of luxury but one of notoriety; for in such a busy community wickedness does not discover the ordinary sort of scandal. [15]I heard Pedo Albinovanus, that most attractive story-teller, speaking of his residence above the town-house of Sextus Papinius. Papinius belonged to the tribe of those who shun the light. "About nine o'clock at night I hear the sound of whips. I ask what is going on, and they tell me that Papinius is going over his accounts.[13] About twelve there is a strenuous shouting; I ask what the matter is, and they say he is exercising his voice. About two A.M. I ask the significance of the sound of wheels; they tell me that he is off for a drive. [16]And at dawn there is a tremendous flurry-calling of slaves and butlers, and pandemonium among the cooks. I ask the meaning of this also, and they tell me that he has called for his cordial and his appetizer, after leaving the bath. His dinner," said Pedo, "never went beyond the day,[14] for he lived very sparingly; he was lavish with nothing but the night. Accordingly, if you believe those who call him tight-fisted and mean, you will call him also a 'slave of the lamp.'"[15]

[17]You should not be surprised at finding so many special manifestations of the vices; for vices vary, and there are countless phases of them, nor can all their various kinds be classified. The method of maintaining righteousness is simple; the method of maintaining wickedness is complicated, and has infinite opportunity to swerve. And the same holds true of character; if you follow nature, character is easy to manage, free, and with very slight shades of difference; but the sort of person I have mentioned possesses badly warped character, out of harmony with all things, including himself. [18]The chief cause, however, of this disease seems to me to be a squeamish revolt from the normal existence. Just as such persons mark themselves off from others in their dress, or in the elaborate arrangement of their dinners, or in the elegance of their carriages; even so they desire to make themselves peculiar by their way of dividing up the hours of their day. They are unwilling to be wicked in the conventional way, because notoriety is the reward of their sort of wickedness. Notoriety is what all such men seek–men who are, so to speak, *living backwards*.

[19]For this reason, Lucilius, let us keep to the way which Nature has mapped out for us, and let us not swerve therefrom. If we follow Nature, all is easy and unobstructed; but if we combat Nature, our life differs not a whit from that of men who row against the current. Farewell.

past them until he was lashed to the mast. They are no less potent; they lure men from country, parents, friends, and virtuous ways; and by a hope that, if not base, is ill-starred, they wreck them upon a life of baseness. How much better to follow a straight course and attain a goal where the words "pleasant" and "honourable" have the same meaning![3] [13]This end will be possible for us if we understand that there are two classes of objects which either attract us or repel us. We are attracted by such things as riches, pleasures, beauty, ambition, and other such coaxing and pleasing objects; we are repelled by toil, death, pain, disgrace, or lives of greater frugality. We ought therefore to train ourselves so that we may avoid a fear of the one or a desire for the other. Let us fight in the opposite fashion: let us retreat from the objects that allure, and rouse ourselves to meet the objects that attack.

[14]Do you not see how different is the method of descending a mountain from that employed in climbing upwards? Men coming down a slope bend backwards; men ascending a steep place lean forward. For, my dear Lucilius, to allow yourself to put your body's weight ahead when coming down, or, when climbing up, to throw it backward is to comply with vice. The pleasures take one down hill but one must work upwards toward that which is rough and hard to climb; in the one case let us throw our bodies forward, in the others let us put the check-rein on them.

[15]Do you believe me to be stating now that only those men bring ruin to our ears, who praise pleasure, who inspire us with fear of pain–that element which is in itself provocative of fear? I believe that we are also in injured by those who masquerade under the disguise of the Stoic school and at the same time urge us on into vice. They boast that only the wise man and the learned is a lover.[4] "He alone has wisdom in this art; the wise man too is best skilled in drinking and feasting. Our study ought to be this alone: up to what age the bloom of love can endure!" [16]All this may be regarded as a concession to the ways of Greece; we ourselves should preferably turn our attention to words like these: "No man is good by chance. Virtue is something which must be learned. Pleasure is low, petty, to be deemed worthless, shared even by dumb animals–the tiniest and meanest of whom fly towards pleasure. Glory is an empty and fleeting thing, lighter than air. Poverty is an evil to no man unless he kick against the goads.[5] Death is not an evil; why need you ask? Death alone is the equal privilege of mankind. Superstition is the misguided idea of a lunatic; it fears those whom it ought to love; it is an outrage upon those whom it worships. For what difference is there between denying the gods and dishonouring them?"

[17]You should learn such principles as these, nay rather you should learn them by heart; philosophy ought not to try to explain away vice. For a sick man, when his physician bids him live recklessly, is doomed beyond recall. Farewell.

Footnotes

1. i.e., a dinner given by an official when he entered upon (*adeo*) his office.

2. For *symphonia* see Ep. li. 4 and note. Compare also the *commissiones*, orchestral exhibitions, composed of many voices, flutes, and brass instruments, Ep. lxxxiv. 10.

3. i.e., to live by Stoicism rather than by Epicureanism.

4. Meaning, in line with the Stoic paradoxes, that only the sage knows how to be rightly in love.

5. *Transcriber's note: The Latin is "Paupertas nulli malum est nisi repugnanti," i.e. "Poverty is an evil to noone unless they resist." Gummere's odd phrase "kick against the goads" is actually from the Bible (Acts 26:14)*

CXXIV. ON THE TRUE GOOD AS ATTAINED BY REASON

[1]Full many an ancient precept could I give,
Didst thou not shrink, and feel it shame to learn
Such lowly duties.[1]

But you do not shrink, nor are you deterred by any subtleties of study. For your cultivated mind is not wont to investigate such important subjects in a free-and-easy manner. I approve your method in that you make everything count towards a certain degree of progress, and in that you are disgruntled only when nothing can be accomplished by the greatest degree of subtlety. And I shall take pains to show that this is the case now also. Our question is, whether the Good is grasped by the senses or by the understanding; and the corollary thereto is that it does not exist in dumb animals or little children.

[2]Those who rate pleasure as the supreme ideal hold that the Good is a matter of the senses; but we Stoics maintain that it is a matter of the understanding, and we assign it to the mind. If the senses were to pass judgment on what is good, we should never reject any pleasure; for there is no pleasure that does not attract, no pleasure that does not please. Conversely, we should undergo no pain voluntarily; for there is no pain that does not clash with the senses. [3]Besides, those who are too fond of pleasure and those who fear pain to the greatest degree would in that case not deserve reproof. But we condemn men who are slaves to their appetites and their lusts, and we scorn men who, through fear of pain, will dare no manly deed. But what wrong could such men be committing if they looked merely to the senses as arbiters of good and evil? For it is to the senses that you and yours have entrusted the test of things to be sought and things to be avoided!

[4]Reason, however, is surely the governing element in such a matter as this; as reason has made the decision concerning the happy life, and concerning virtue and honour also, so she has made the decision with regard to good and evil. For with them[2] the vilest part is allowed to give sentence about the better, so that the senses–dense as they are, and dull, and even more sluggish in man than in the other animals,–pass judgment on the Good. [5]Just suppose that one should desire to distinguish tiny objects by the touch rather than by the eyesight! There is no special faculty more subtle and acute than the eye, that would enable us to distinguish between good and evil. You see, therefore, in what ignorance of truth a man spends his days and how abjectly he has overthrown lofty and divine ideals, if he thinks that the sense of touch can pass judgment upon the nature of the Supreme Good and the Supreme Evil! [6]He[3] says: "Just as every science and every art should possess an element that is palpable and capable of being grasped by the senses (their source of origin and growth), even so the happy life derives its foundation and its beginnings from things that are palpable, and from that which falls within the scope of the senses. Surely you admit that the happy life takes its beginnings from things palpable to the senses." [7]But we define as "happy" those things that are in accord with Nature. And that which is in accord with Nature is obvious and can be seen at once–just as easily as that which is complete. That which is according to Nature, that which is given us as a gift immediately at our birth, is, I maintain, not a Good, but the beginning of a Good. You, however, assign the Supreme Good, pleasure, to mere babies, so that the child at its birth begins at the point whither the perfected man arrives. You are placing the tree-top where the root ought to be. [8]If anyone should say that the child, hidden in its mother's womb, of unknown sex too, delicate, unformed, and shapeless–if one should say that this child is already in a state of goodness, he would clearly seem to be astray in his ideas. And yet how little difference is there between one who has just lately received the gift of life, and one who is still a hidden burden in the bowels of the mother! They are equally developed, as far as their understanding of good or evil is concerned; and a child is as yet no more capable of comprehending the Good than is a tree or any dumb beast.

But why is the Good non-existent in a tree or in a dumb beast? Because there is no reason there, either. For the same cause, then, the Good is non-existent in a child, for the child also has no reason; the child will reach the Good only when he reaches reason.[4] [9]There are animals without reason, there are animals not yet endowed with reason, and there are animals who possess reason, but only incompletely;[5] in none of these does the Good exist, for it is reason that brings the Good in its company. What, then, is the distinction between the classes which I have mentioned? In that which does not possess reason, the Good will never exist. In that which is not yet endowed with reason, the Good cannot be existent at the time. And in that which possesses reason but only incompletely, the Good is capable of existing, but does not yet exist. [10]This is what I mean, Lucilius: the Good cannot be discovered in any random person, or at any random age; and it is as far removed from infancy as last is from first, or as that which is complete from that which has just sprung into being. Therefore, it cannot exist in the delicate body, when the little frame has only just begun to knit together. Of course not–no more than in the seed. [11]Granting the truth of this, we understand that there is a certain kind of Good of a tree or in a plant; but this is not true of its first growth, when the plant has just begun to spring forth out of the ground. There is a certain Good of wheat: it is not yet existent, however, in the swelling stalk, nor when the soft ear is pushing itself out of the husk, but only when summer days and its appointed maturity have ripened the wheat. Just as Nature in general does not produce her Good until she is brought to perfection, even so man's Good does not exist in man until both reason and man are perfected. [12]And what is this Good? I shall tell you: it is a free mind, an upright mind, subjecting other things to itself and itself to nothing. So far is infancy from admitting this Good that boyhood has no hope of it, and even young manhood cherishes the hope without justification; even our old age is very fortunate if it has reached this Good after long and concentrated study. If this, then, is the Good, the good is a matter of the understanding.

[13]"But," comes the retort, "you admitted that there is a certain Good of trees and of grass; then surely there can be a certain Good of a child also." But the true Good is not found in trees or in dumb animals the Good which exists in them is called good only by courtesy.[6] "Then what is it?" you say. Simply that which is in accord with the nature of each. The real Good cannot find a place in dumb animals–not by any means; its nature is more blest and is of a higher class. And where there is no place for reason, the Good does not exist. [14]There are four natures which we should mention here: of the tree, animal, man, and God. The last two, having reasoning power, are of the same nature, distinct only by virtue of the immortality of the one and the mortality of the other. Of one of these, then–to wit God–it is Nature that perfects the Good; of the other–to wit man–pains and study do so. All other things are perfect only in their particular nature, and not truly perfect, since they lack reason.

Indeed, to sum up, that alone is perfect which is perfect according to nature as a whole, and nature as a whole is possessed of reason. Other things can be perfect according to their kind. [15]That which cannot contain the happy life cannot contain that which produces the happy life; and the happy life is produced by Goods alone. In dumb animals there is not a trace of the happy life, nor of the means whereby the happy life is produced; in dumb animals the Good does not exist. [16]The dumb animal comprehends the present world about him through his senses alone. He remembers the past only by meeting with something which reminds his senses; a horse, for example, remembers the right road only when he is placed at the starting-point. In his stall, however, he has no memory of the road, no matter how often he may have stepped along it. The third state–the future–does not come within the ken of dumb beasts.

[17]How, then, can we regard as perfect the nature of those who have no experience of time in its perfection? For time is three-fold,–past, present, and future. Animals perceive only the time which is of greatest moment to them within the limits of their coming and going–the present. Rarely do they recollect the past–and that only when they are confronted with present reminders. [18]Therefore the Good of a perfect nature cannot exist in an imperfect nature; for if the latter sort of nature should possess the Good, so also would mere vegetation. I do not indeed deny that dumb animals have strong and swift impulses toward actions which seem according to nature, but such impulses are confused and disordered. The Good however, is never confused or disordered.

[19]"What!" you say, "do dumb animals move in disturbed and ill-ordered fashion?" I should say that they moved in disturbed and ill-ordered fashion, if their nature admitted of order; as it is, they move in accordance with their nature. For that is said to be "disturbed" which can also at some other time be "not disturbed"; so, too, that is

said to be in a state of trouble which can be in a state of peace. No man is vicious except one who has the capacity of virtue; in the case of dumb animals their motion is such as results from their nature. [20]But, not to weary you, a certain sort of good will be found in a dumb animal, and a certain sort of virtue, and a certain sort of perfection—but neither the Good, nor virtue, nor perfection in the absolute sense. For this is the privilege of reasoning beings alone, who are permitted to know the cause, the degree, and the means. Therefore, good can exist only in that which possesses reason.

[21]Do you ask now whither our argument is tending, and of what benefit it will be to your mind? I will tell you: it exercises and sharpens the mind, and ensures, by occupying it honourably, that it will accomplish some sort of good. And even that is beneficial which holds men back when they are hurrying into wickedness. However, I will say this also: I can be of no greater benefit to you than by revealing the Good that is rightly yours, by taking you out of the class of dumb animals, and by placing you on a level with God. [22]Why, pray, do you foster and practise your bodily strength? Nature has granted strength in greater degree to cattle and wild beasts. Why cultivate your beauty? After all your efforts, dumb animals surpass you in comeliness. Why dress your hair with such unending attention? Though you let it down in Parthian fashion, or tie it up in the German style, or, as the Scythians do, let it flow wild—yet you will see a mane of greater thickness tossing upon any horse you choose, and a mane of greater beauty bristling upon the neck of any lion. And even after training yourself for speed, you will be no match for the hare. [23]Are you not willing to abandon all these details—wherein you must acknowledge defeat, striving as you are for something that is not your own and come back to the Good that is really yours?

And what is this Good? It is a clear and flawless mind, which rivals that of God,[7] raised far above mortal concerns, and counting nothing of its own to be outside itself. You are a reasoning animal. What Good, then, lies within you? Perfect reason. Are you willing to develop this to its farthest limits—to its greatest degree of increase? [24]Only consider yourself happy when all your joys are born of reason, and when—having marked all the objects which men clutch at, or pray for, or watch over—you find nothing which you will desire; mind, I do not say *prefer*. Here is a short rule by which to measure yourself, and by the test of which you may feel that you have reached perfection: "You will come to your own when you shall understand that those whom the world calls fortunate are really the most unfortunate of all." Farewell.

Footnotes

1. Vergil, *Georg.* i. 176 f.

2. i.e., the Epicureans.

3. i.e., the advocate of the "touch" theory.

4. According to the Stoics (and other schools also), the "innate notions," or groundwork of knowledge, begin to be subject to reason after the attainment of a child's seventh year.

5. i.e., they are limited to "practical judgment."

6. Just as Academic and Peripatetic philosophers sometimes defined as "goods" what the Stoics called "advantages."

7. One of the most conspicuous Stoic paradoxes maintained that "the wise man is a God."

INDEX OF PROPER NAMES

A

Academic school of Philosophy, its lofty ideals, xxix. 11; a definition of happiness, lxxi. 18; scepticism of, lxxxviii. 44 f.

L. Accius (Roman poet, 2nd century B.C.), lviii. 5

Achaia (province of Greece), earthquakes in, xci. 9 f.

Acheron (the lake), lv. 6

Achilles, age of, compared with that of Patroclus, lxxxviii. 6

Aegialus, a farmer on the old estate of Scipio, lxxxvi. 14 ff.

Aelius Sejanus (prime minister of Tiberius), dangers of acquaintance with, lv. 3

Aetna, celebrated by poets, li. 1; proposed ascent of, by Lucilius, lxxix. 2 ff.

Africa, Pompey in, xciv. 65; Cato's march through the deserts of, civ. 33; crops in, cxiv. 26; marbles from, cxv. 8

Agamemnon, his desire to return home to Mycenae, lxvi. 26

M. Vipsanius Agrippa (counsellor of Augustus) on harmony in government, xciv. 46 f.

Alban villa (Seneca's), visit to, cxxiii. 1 f.

Alexander the Great (356-323 B.C.), sayings of, liii. 10, lix. 12; crimes and tragedy of, due to drink, lxxxiii. 19 ff.; his desire to conquer the globe, xci. 17; his conquests of Greece, Persia, and India, xciv. 62 f.; cxiii. 29 f.; cxix. 7

Alexandria, fast sailing ships from, lxxvii. 1 f.

Anacharsis (Scythian philosopher, fl. 600 B.C.), discussed as the inventor of the potter's wheel xc. 31

Ancus Marcius (Roman king), doubtful parentage of, cviii. 30

Antipater (of Tarsus, Stoic philosopher, 2nd century B.C.), refutation of a Peripatetic syllogism, lxxxvii. 38 ff.; his view regarding non-essentials, xcii. 5

M. Antonius (friend of Caesar and rival of Augustus), ruined by wine and Cleopatra, lxxxiii. 25

M. Gavius Apicius (epicure, age of Tiberius), extravagance of, xcv. 42; gluttony of, cxx. 19

Apion (grammarian, 1st century A.D.), his opinion concerning the authorship of the Homeric cycle, lxxxviii. 40 f.

Appius Claudius Caecus (censor 312 B.C.), source for archaic oratorical style, cxiv. 13

Archedemus (Stoic of Tarsus, second century B.C.), authority of, cxxi. 1

Ardea (ancient city of Latium, capital of the Rutulians), capture of, xci. 16; country-place of Lucilius, cv. 1

Argos (kingdom in the Peloponnesus), a fictitious king of, lxxx. 7

Aristo (of Chios, Stoic philosopher, 3rd century B.C.), saying of, xxxvi. 3; weeds out many departments of philosophy, lxxxix. 13; on the superfluity of precepts, xciv. 1 ff.; on admiration of superfluous things, cxv. 8 f.

Aristo (philosopher, identity unknown), anecdotes of, xxix. 6

Aristotle (384-322 B.C.), debt to Socrates, vi. 6; on *genus* and *species*, lviii. 9; on cause, form, matter, etc., lxv. 4

O

P

Z

APPENDIX

Ep. xciv. deals, on the whole, with the question whether doctrines without precepts are enough for the student and the philosopher; Ep. xcv. whether precepts without doctrines will suffice. Seneca concludes that they are both necessary and are complementary to one another, especially in view of the complicated life which one is called upon to live, with its many duties and choices. The terms discussed, with some of the Greek original definitions, may be summed up as follows:-

(1) The outward expressions of ἐπιστήμη (*scientia*, knowledge) and of the κοιναὶ ἔννοιαι (*notiones communes*, προλήψεις, innate ideas) are found in the form of ἀξιώματα (*pronuntiata*, incontrovertible statements), δόγματα (*placita, decreta, scita*, doctrines, tenets, dogmas, principles). Determined by ὅροι (*definitiones*, definitions), they are tested by their ἀξία (*honestum*, moral value), by the κριτήριον (*norma iudicii*, standard of judgement) or κανών (*lex, regula*, etc.), and by the ὀρθὸς λόγος (*recta ratio*, universal law, etc.). By such means the doctrines of philosophy are contrasted with δόξα (*opinio*) and with a κατάληψις (*cognitio* or *comprehensio*) which falls short of completeness and perfection. Conduct which results from a thorough understanding and performance of such doctrines is κατόρθωμα (τέλειον καθῆκον, *perfectum officium*, "absolute duty".

(2) The *pars praeceptiva* (παραινετική) of philosophy, which deals with "average duty" (καθῆκον, *commune* or *medium officium*), is approved, among others, by Posidonius, Cicero (see the De Officiis), and Seneca. It is related to active living and to the ἀδιάφορα (*media* or *indifferentia*) (see Subject Index) which play so large a rôle in the individual's daily existence. This department of "counsel," "admonition," or "advice" has many forms. For παραίνεσις (*monitio*) are needed: the λόγος προτρεπτικός (*exhortatio*), τόπος ὑποθετικός (*suasio*), ἀποτροπή (*dissuasio*), ἐπιτίμησις (*obiurgatio*), λόγος παραμυθητικός (*consolatio*), αἰτιολογία (*causarum inquisitio*), ἠθολογία (*descriptio*), and all the gamut of precepts which run from blame to praise. These are reinforced by ἀπόδειξις (*probatio, argumentum*, proof) and by such helps as χρεῖαι, ἀπομνημονεύματα (*sententiae*, proverbs, maxims).

By such stages of advancement, προκοπή (*progressio*), and relying upon παραδείγματα (*exempla*), one rises, through practical precepts and the observance of duties, to an appreciation of the virtues, the contemplative mastery of the Universe, and to the Supreme Good, conformity with Nature (ὁμολογουμένως τῇ φύσει ζῆν, *vivere convenienter naturae*).

SUBJECT INDEX

A

Accidens (συμβεβηκός, "contingent upon"), cxvii. 3 ff.

ἀδιάφορα (see *media*, "indifferent" things), lxxxii. 10 ff.

adsensio, cxiii. 18 and note

Analogy, with regard to knowledge of the good, cxx. 4 f. and note

Animals, instinct (ὁρμέ) for self-preservation in, cxxi. *passim*

ἀπάθεια, *impatientia*, ix. 1 ff., xiii. 4, lxxxv. 3 ff., cxvi. *passim*

Arch, invention of the, xc. 32

Archaisms, in style and wording, lviii. 1 ff., cxiv. 17 ff.

Arts, four classes of, lxxxviii. 21 ff.; discovery of the, xc. 7 ff.; in relation to doctrines and precepts, xcv. 7 ff.

B

Baths, distractions of the, lvi. 1 ff.; luxury of, lxxxvi. 5 ff.

Being, the only existing fact, according to Parmenides, lxxxviii. 44

Benefits, lxxxi. *passim*

Body, regard for the, xiv. 1 ff.; cxxi. 5 ff.; in relation to mind, cxvii. 13. etc.

bona ("goods"), of various kinds, lxvi. 5 ff.; equality of, ib. 15 ff., lxxi. 7 ff.; desirability of, lxvii. 3 ff.; falsely so called, lxxiv. 12 ff.; varieties of, lxxxviii. 5

bonum (the "good"), xxiii. 6 ff.; defined, xxxi. 6; regarded by Academic School as variable, lxxi. 17 ff., lxxvi. 11 ff.; certain syllogisms on, lxxxvii. *passim*; corporeality of the, cvi. 3 ff., cxvii. 2 ff.; is it a "living thing"? cxiii. 20 ff. (reduc. ad absurdum); defined in several ways, cxviii. 8 ff.; relation to the *honestum*, cxx. 1 ff.; derived from the senses or from the intellect, cxxiv. 1 ff.; limited to reasoning man, cxxiv. 7 ff.

Books, thoroughness in reading, ii. *passim*; xlv. 1-5; selective reading of, lxxxiv. 1 ff.

C

Calx, cviii. 32

Categories, of Aristotle, lxv. 3 ff. and notes

cause (contrasted with matter), as discussed by the Stoics, Aristotle, and Plato, lxv. 2 ff.

Circles, as indications of time, small and large, xii. 6 ff.

compositio (arrangement of words), cxiv. 15 ff.

Consolation, to the bereaved, lxiii., xcix.

Contempt, as a source of safety, cv. 2 ff.

Country-places, Seneca's, xii. 1-4; Scipio's, lxxxvi. *passim*; civ. 1 ff., cx. 1, cxxiii. 1 ff.

D

Death, scorn of, iv. 3 ff., xxii. 13 ff., xxiv. *passim*, xxvi. 4 ff.; anticipation of xxx. 4 ff., xxxvi. 8 ff., lxi., lxxxii. 16 ff., xciii. *passim*, suddenness of, ci. 1 ff.; resignation of, cii. 26 ff.

decreta (dogmas), see Appendix A, Ep. xciv. 32, etc.; specially defined, xcv. 44; necessity

314

Made in the USA
Coppell, TX
19 June 2021